Asian Soups, Stews, & Curries

Asian Soups, Stews, & Curries

More than 200 recipes from the Far East

Alexandra Greeley

MACMILLAN • USA

To Michael, Susan, Christopher, Kathryn, and Mikayla . . .

May the tastes of Asia linger on . . .

03649230

MACMILLAN
A Simon & Schuster Macmillan Company
1633 Broadway
New York, NY 10019-6785

Macmillan Publishing books may be purchased for business or
sales promotional use. For information please write:
Special Markets Department,
Macmillan Publishing USA,
1633 Broadway,
New York, NY 10019

Library of Congress Cataloging-in-Publication Data
Greeley, Alexandra.
Asian soups, stews, and curries: more than 200 recipes from the Far East/Alexandra Greeley.
   p. cm.
Includes bibliographical references (p.) and index.
ISBN: 0-02-861269-8
   1. Soups—Asia. 2. Stews—Asia. 3. Food habits—Asia. 4.Cookery, Oriental. I. Title
TX757.G74 1998   97-30077
641.8'13'095—dc21   CIP

Manufactured in the United States of America

10 9 8 7 6 5 4 3 2 1

Book design by Nick Anderson

Contents

Foreword

For sure, Alexandra Greeley was an Asian—nay, an Indian—in her last birth. She has an instinctive appreciation of Indian cuisine and it has been a pleasure to introduce her to the nuances of Indian gastronomy. We have tried to interpret the food of the subcontinent for a number of foreign friends. Never before have we found anyone with such a passionate involvement and quick grasp of the intricacies of the culinary traditions of this ancient land. The very first time we met her, we realized that we were with an exceptional cookbook writer.

What makes Alexandra Greeley special? Well, a number of things. Foremost, her innate ability to satisfy the American penchant for ethnic cuisine from Asia. This she does with great sensitivity, being content to let different cuisines speak for themselves rather than impose her imprint on them. Second, her infinite patience to work in the most trying conditions, very often with cooks who do not speak English. And, finally, her infectious enthusiasm, which makes even the most secretive of chefs open up and share their trade secrets.

These traits are what endeared Alexandra Greeley to this team of "foodies." It was a delight to encounter a kindred soul who shared the passion for meticulous research and authenticity of recipes. Her concern for detail—every recipe was repeatedly faxed with queries until she was fully satisfied—is what lends distinction to her work. It was very easy to be led by the nose—literally and otherwise—in her perfectionist quest.

In her *Asian Grills*, Ms. Greeley succeeded in accomplishing what she set out to achieve. The recipes are user-friendly, without deviating from the originals. The book provides food lovers—especially the Americans—with a tasty introduction to the *kebab* of Asia. We see *Asian Soups, Stews, & Curries* as its perfect companion. After perusing this wonderful book, it is our fond hope that one day Alexandra Greeley will collaborate with us on an Indian cookbook.

—J. Inder Singh Kalra and Pushpesh Pant

Preface

Finding satisfaction, comfort, and supreme pleasure at the table doesn't always happen. But when it does, we have discovered nirvana.

I argue that people hooked on Asian foods stand the best chance of finding that state of bliss, for Asian cooking has it all. Everyone must know by now about its freshness, its magical flavors and textures, and its vivid colors, its grills, stir-fries, and steamed delights. But how many Westerners have fully explored the great, traditional Asian tureen? Its glories are underrated and its luxuries understated. It is there in the soups, stews, and curries that the true genius of Asian cooking pours forth.

Those hesitant about eating Asian should shed notions that Oriental ingredients and meals are too unfamiliar. Start with small steps—an artistic serving of temperate corn and chicken soup, or a scoop of mild and beguiling Burmese pork curry with rice. From this humble beginning, take that final plunge into a world of brilliant flavors—often hot, usually complex, and always well conceived.

Rejoice in the sensual beauty of foods that are brushed with contrasting flavors before grilling or stewing; that present a spectrum of crunchy textures offset by the smoothness of cooked rice or the suppleness of rice noodles; that meld both complementary and contrasting colors for eye appeal; and that offer a range of dishes from delicate grilled chicken to rib-sticking soups and stews, all at one meal.

Get comfortable with unusual names—though of course, by now, most non-Asians are familiar with Indian and Thai curries, Japanese miso soups, and Vietnamese *phos* (main-dish soups). But take it from a dedicated Asiaphile, these are only at the very surface of the great Asian tureen.

For example, what a lovely and tranquil way to begin mornings: a bowl of steaming Chinese *congee* (rice soup), embellished with shreds of stir-fried pork and sprinkles of soy sauce. This soupy rice serves as a clean slate for you, the culinary artist, to shape at will. Perhaps, instead, you choose as your brushstrokes slivers of hoisin-roasted duck; quartered hard-boiled eggs tinted with soy sauce; strips of green and red chilies and snippets of fresh coriander and scallions; or splashes of plum sauce and steamed fish.

What could be a more satisfying way to dine than with a Thai version of Burmese Noodles (page 44)? It's more than a bowl of chicken soup with noodles: it's a multi-ingredient labor of love that comes to your table sprinkled with rose petals. This exquisite feast produces its own culinary magic, and spellbound guests will shrug off daily responsibilities to enjoy a leisurely—and regal—meal.

In Asia, food has always meant a celebration of life and its many rituals. Even today, despite modern pressures, mealtime brings together family and friends to enjoy companionship and laughter. And they convene over dishes that are still often gastronomic masterpieces, compositions of the freshest and best ingredients prepared with love and skill.

May everyone experience and share that Asian love of beautiful food.

Acknowledgments

When my family moved to Hong Kong many years ago, landing at Kai Tak Airport as a typhoon slipped offshore, Asian cooking seemed as remote as our new homeland. But in the turn of the clock, it became my virtual reality—as did Asia itself. So writing about Asia and its foods and people seems more a pledge of allegiance than business as usual. Thanks to the generosity and enthusiasm of many, this book came about.

For all those who have always been readily at hand, my gratitude—particularly to Michael, Susan, Christopher, and Kathryn, for keeping your wits about. To my very generous sister, Mary Hager, for spending far too many hours searching for obscure ingredients and then cooking them—and then commenting on text. To my travel agent Bob Alcorn, Globe Travel, Washington, D.C., for plotting the best routes. To my dear friend Kathie Gauld, for tromping along through all those wet markets.

Also, the generosity of the chefs, the cooks, and the others who shared their recipes, knowledge, and time has been remarkable, not to mention inspiring. So special thanks to J. Inder Singh (Jiggs) Kalra; Helene Sze McCarthy; Bounsou Sananikone; Majmin Hashim; Joyce Piotrowski; William Mark; David Quang; Geraldene Lowe Ismail; Diana Semon; Than Than Yi; Nick Srisawat; and Hira Lee.

And so also to Bora Chu; Pinkie Imson; Baasim Zafar; B. Runi Mukherji-Ratnam; Bong S. Lee; Jamak and family; Yoko Auslander; Daw May Khin Maung Than; Yoko Morford; Devyani Hinshaw; Nongkran Daks; Daw Yin Yin Mya; Daw Mya Mya Gyi; Daw Anna Khin-Khin Kyawt; Daw Say Htoo; Phetsaphone Phanthavone; Vashouthep Sananikone; Vanessa Rathsvongsach; Somchit Sylapeth and Lavanh Phouk Phanh; Pang V. Lee; Hien Vat-Ho; Neary Saray; Sokheng N. Kheang, The Cambodian Restaurant, Arlington, Virginia; Shirley Janairo Roth; Nguyen Ly; Hien Ngyuen; Evelyn Manuel; Lucy Chew, Harbour View Dai-Ichi Hotel, Singapore; Shirley Yuen; Joseph Soen, Society of Professional Chefs, Singapore; Aziza Ali, Aziza's, Singapore; Fatima, Fatima's,

Singapore; Felicia Wakwella Sørensen; Parkroyal Hotel, Kuala Lumpur, Malaysia; Norhayati Ibrahim; Jack Katayal, Katmandu Restaurant, Washington, D.C.; Goh Ewe-Swee, The Mandarin Inn, Alexandria, Virginia; Nutchanand Osathanond; Sarnsern Gajaseni, The Thai Cooking School, The Oriental Bangkok, Bangkok, Thailand; Muttika Gladson, Thai Luang Restaurant, Herndon, Virginia; Pierre de Lalande, Once Upon a Time, Chiang Mai, Thailand; Mrs. Hanief Djohan; Joeli Tajibnapis; Akademi Pariwisata Bunda Padang, Padang, Sumatra, Indonesia; Hanny Nabiela Sugianto; Embassy of the Republic of Indonesia, Washington, D.C.; Chef Chow Chung, Hyatt Regency Hong Kong, Hong Kong; Chef C.K. Chan, Sheraton Hong Kong Hotel & Towers, Hong Kong; Devagi Shanmugam, the Thompson Cooking School in Singapore; Bi Bi Kearney; Macau Tourist Information Bureau; Hotel Lisboa, Macau; the late Ranjit Rai of New Delhi, India; Sherina Massoumi; Hung Hei Ying, Mandarin House Peking Restaurant, Hong Kong; Aileen T'sing; Suòng Thomas; Tseten Wangchuk; Kinbo Mizutani and Kimiko Gomyo, Rokudan of Kobe restaurant, Los Angeles, California; Young-Mi Pierce; Tomiko Baylis; Katsuko Inatome; Sachi Yamada; Frank Kuge; Umesh Saraf, Hotel Yak & Yeti, Kathmandu, Nepal; Vikrant Kapoor and The Tiffin Room, The Raffles Hotel, Singapore; and Mr. Singh's culinary team for their television program, *Daawat: An Invitation to Indian Cooking.*

For their valuable help, I thank Kathryn Burns Greeley, ITT Sheraton Corporation, Boston, Massachusetts; Nittaya Maphungphong; Dr. Pushpesh Pant; Jack and Katie McDonald; Robert Halliday; Daw Khin Myo Lwin; the Bahá'í Community of Burma; the Bahá'í Community of Thailand; Henry Grossi; Karisa Lui and Stephen Wong, Hong Kong Tourist Association, Hong Kong; Tom Meyer, Clyde's Restaurant Group, Washington, D.C.; Pat Bonifer-Tiedt; Harry Rolnick; Eleanor Law-Yone; Harris Lokmanhakim; S.S.H. Rehman, ITC-Welcomgroup, New Delhi, India; David Wilson, Hyatt Regency Delhi, New Delhi, India; Raminder Malhotra; Bruce Sherman; Irmansjah Madewa, Hotel Pusako, Bukittinggi, Sumatra; Editiawarman, Pangeran's Beach Hotel, Padang, Sumatra; Dr. Sambhu Banik; Tinn Shwe; Michiko Petersen; Yuri Yajima; Hideno Nakatani; Tjitta Kodirun; Mary Lord; Atsuko Craft; and Yann Ker. And also thanks to B.J. Fletcher for sharing the road, to Martha Beshers for her sense of humor and of language, and to Robert Dirmeyer for his input.

To the stolid testers who just kept stirring, thanks Annie Hager (honorable mention!); Ruth Gutheridge (special thanks!); Pete and Ginger Sparber; Anne Parsons; Diana Semon; Norma Toenjes; Jane Roberts; Carole Kauffman; Harris Lokmanhakim; Nick Srisawat; Zuraidah Hashim; Will and Marcia Lindquist; Steve Sauter; Anne Harrington; Phil and Alice Shabecoff; Marsha Weiner; Ellen Uchimiya; John and Dina McElroy; Joyce Piotrowski; and Mary Hager, Jr.

A special thanks to both Tahmineh Irani Parsons for her support and Cynthia Musillo for her keen eye and sharp pencil.

Of course, none of this would *really* have come to pass without my terrific agent, Linda Hayes, of Columbia Literary Associates, who truly kept the faith. That goes as well for my former Macmillan editor, Jane Sigal. Many, many thanks to Macmillan's Amy Gordon, for her help and support, and to my new editor, Jennifer Griffin, who has seen the book through the final stages. Thanks, too, to Kim Werner.

Introduction:

Soups, Stews, and Curries—Asia's Tureen

Food historians have gathered enough evidence to suggest that the Chinese kitchen was a very busy place 9,000 years ago. It's hard to prove, of course, but the early Chinese cooks might even have stirred up the first pot of soup. At least, they had learned enough by then about the rudiments of cooking to offer more than slabs of raw meat to their family and friends.

Consider the data about cooking vessels. As one of the outstanding authorities on Chinese cooking, Kenneth Lo, wrote in his book *The Encyclopedia of Chinese Cooking,* the Chinese used cooking utensils—tripod-shaped metal pots on legs that rested over cook fires—from the earliest period of Chinese civilization, about 5000 B.C. Some experts, writing about Chinese ancient clay and bamboo cooking and serving vessels, have suggested that the Chinese were a full thousand years ahead of the West in creating cookpots of iron.

As for plotting the course of the cuisine, ingenuous cooks must have decided stews were the logical consequence of making robust and hearty soups, rich with meats, herbs, and vegetables cooking in a rich broth. For at some time during the Shang Dynasty, probably about 1500 B.C., cooks developed a group of dishes called *ts'ai,* usually thought of as "rich stews." And slightly later, during the Chou Dynasty, 1028 B.C. to 480 B.C., a dish called *keng,* "a kind of meat soup or stew," became popular. By that time, Chinese cooks were relying on their cookpots, called the *ting,* the *li,* and the *hu,* for cooking foods in liquid.

It would seem natural that wise and scholarly men should begin to celebrate this burgeoning and exquisite cuisine, as did the author of the third century B.C. poem "The Summons of the Soul." Its lines "Sour and bitter blended in the soup of Wu; Stewed turtle and roast kid, served up with yam sauce . . ." describe dishes with a certain degree of sophistication and surely an appeal to those lucky enough to enjoy them. Indeed, one historian talks about a second century B.C. Chinese script that "contains 9,000 characters" pertaining to food and cooking techniques. This suggests that demanding Chinese palates were already putting local cooks to hard work. And it is surely safe to assume that by then, Chinese cooks were skilled makers of soups and stews.

As people everywhere have long since realized, soups and stews are economical, flavorful, nourishing, and comforting. Perhaps the nineteenth-century Frenchman of letters Jean Anthèlme Brillat-Savarin captured soup's appeal the best. As he wrote in his *The Physiology of Taste* (M.F.K. Fisher's translation), "Soup is a healthy, light, sustaining food which is food for everyone; it soothes the stomach and encourages it to receive and digest more nourishment." He obviously had not encountered some of Asia's more complex soups, however, which few would consider light, though they may be healthful and sustaining.

Brillat-Savarin did not try to define what constitutes a soup or a stew. But some of today's food experts have, and they do not universally agree on terms. To avoid confusion, it's safe to turn to one of the most respected sources—the Culinary Institute of America (CIA) in New York—for its say on the topic.

Its textbook, *The New Professional Chef,* sixth edition, describes these foods very clearly. Soups fall into various categories that encompass all the bisques, broths, chowders, consommés, purees, and bouillons served at Western meals. It would seem that the more visible ingredients and the less liquid soups contain, the closer they become to stews.

About stews, the CIA notes that there are two cooking techniques, stewing (more liquid) and braising (less liquid), that are "combination cooking methods" requiring dry heat—searing of meat to seal in flavors—followed by the application of moist heat, a liquid, to finish the cooking. Both stewing and braising generally require long, slow cooking (braising will take longer than stewing) in a covered cookpot, in the oven or on a burner set to low. Curries fall somewhere in the middle, neither really soup nor stew, but with characteristics of both. Yet some Asians say that curries and stews are synonymous.

Many Westerners worry about what makes up a soup or stew and plot ways to dehydrate a soup or distill a soup base into a tin can. But they should stop long enough to sample some of the bounty from Asia's kitchens. They will certainly find their palates challenged by the drama of layered seasonings, and their ideas of soups and stews and curries will change forever.

On Asian Soups, Stews, and Curries

The Chinese with their soups and stews—and at some point in history, the Indians with their noble curries—must surely have influenced neighboring Asians when early traders, conquerors, adventurers, and immigrants crisscrossed Asian borders. Thus, Chinese and Indian cooking traditions, seasonings, techniques, and preferences have through the centuries filtered into every other Asian kitchen—from Tibet to Sri Lanka, from Lahore to Hong Kong.

Soups and Stews

Although generally Westerners think of soups and stews as foods cooked in a certain amount of liquid, Asians have pushed that idea to the limit. In the West, most soups are based on a stock prepared from bones, meat or fish trimmings, and vegetable pairings. In most parts of Asia, cooks frequently turn to a soup or stew stock made of coconut milk or water.

Of course, some Asian soups don't even fall into that category. Take, for example, the lovely

Cantonese soup cooked in a hollowed-out squash called Winter Melon Pond Soup. The Yunnanese have created a steamed soup using a clay device that distills a pure, clear liquid, or stock, into the final broth. The chef at the then-only Yunnan restaurant in Hong Kong seemed delighted to offer me a sample of his fine cooking and served the soup in this strange-looking vessel. Lacking the usual color or complex seasonings of other Chinese dishes, it offered, nonetheless, an unusual taste treat.

Asians—probably the nomadic Mongols in northern China in the twelfth century A.D.—created another type of soup-making we call hot-pot cooking (*shuan*), which requires diners to cook for themselves at the table. In theory and practice, the hot pot resembles fondue, but it uses broth rather than oil as the cooking medium. For a detailed description of this dish, see Mongolian Hot-Pot Cooking, Asian Feasts, page 280. Obviously, the idea of this convenient and communal way of cooking and eating caught on, since almost every Asian country has its own fire-pot-like version. It's a convenient and sensible way to eat, for such meals customarily offer a substantial selection of meats and vegetables for tabletop cooking. But best of all, after all the meat and vegetables are cooked, everyone drinks the remaining rich and flavorful broth or uses it for moistening rice or cooking noodles for their own noodle soup. See recipes for Vietnamese Vinegar Beef (page 116), Japanese Shabu-Shabu (page 148), and Singaporean Steamboat (page 267).

As with soups, Asian stews often do not fit into any clear-cut Western scheme of things. For example, Asian stews and braised dishes rarely require that meat be seared before being combined with liquid. Further, the CIA describes stews and braises as dishes that are cooked in a covered pot. Yet in an Asian kitchen that may not

happen, since many cooks leave their simmering stews uncovered. And some Asian stews—particularly curries—may be cooked over a heat so high, at least for some of the cooking time, that a Western cook might worry.

Thus, unlike Western stews that may bubble and simmer for hours, an Asian stew or curry may be cooked and ready to serve in 30 minutes. This rule does not apply to the technique of Chinese slow cooking, which calls for stewing meat until it is so tender that even a whole roast comes apart easily with chopsticks. Another Chinese stewing technique, *hung shao'*, or red cooking or red stewing, gets its name from the color that soy sauce imparts to the cooking liquid.

Finally, Southeast Asians serve soups and stews that have no Western counterpart. Such dishes include Malaysian *laksas* (page 183), the famous Lao dish *khao poune* (Lao Rice Noodles with Sauce, page 54), and the Burmese *mohinga* (Burmese Fish and Rice Noodle Soup, page 160). Lacking any other term for them, a Westerner would call such dishes "soup" or "stew," but a Malaysian, Laotian, or Burmese thinks of them as vegetables, meat, or seafood and noodles served with a richly seasoned gravy.

As a final observation, Asians generally stock their pantries with basic ingredients many Westerners won't recognize instantly—such as coconut milk, tamarind, and palm sugar. Indeed, cooking vessels differ as well. Whereas a copious stockpot is standard Western soup-making equipment, Asian often use large woks, a utensil most Westerners associate with hot, fast stir-frying. Surprisingly, however, the wok and its various other Asian counterparts are used constantly for making stews and curries. As one Malaysian woman explained, the large surface area the wok affords allows sauces, or gravies, to reduce quickly and reach the desired consistency. The wok is especially useful, she added, when cooking the Malaysian or Indonesian *rendang*, a dry curry in which the liquid evaporates, leaving intensely flavored—and, presumably, well-preserved—meat that can last for one month without refrigeration, assuming the family does not eat it up right away. The Chinese also use the sand, or clay pot for making both stews and soups. And the Indians even use a coconut shell as a cookpot.

Just remember that in making Asian soups, stews, and curries, the rules may be different, the cooking temperatures higher, and the ingredients more exotic to those first exploring the Asian table. But perhaps the biggest difference between East and West is that in Asia, most soups and stews are not relegated to cold-weather eating. They are year-round mealtime staples. As one Vietnamese woman said to me over a relaxed dinner, "We eat soup every day. We cannot live without it."

About Curries

What, then, are curries? Mention "stew" in Asia, and in many kitchens the cook might well think "curry," for a stew and a curry share similar characteristics, making them almost synonymous. Curries are dishes that consist of few or many ingredients—fish, shellfish, meats, vegetables, fruit—that are cooked and served in a thick or thin sauce, or gravy, and served with rice or noodles. Curries are well and thoughtfully seasoned and may be hot or mild, depending on the cook and the country.

Since curries are unique to Asia, I asked my Malaysian friend Harris Lokmanhakim for a simple curry definition. He answered by comparing curries to an American bowl of chili with its infinite variations. Then he added that a curry is a "melange of spices ground to a powder or a paste and used as a base to produce an often thick 'stew' of vegetables, meats, or seafood . . . . Curry potency can range from weak, thin curries used with pan-fried breads to a thick pasty meat curry called *Rendang* served with rice, with countless variations in between."

In other Asian countries, too, the curry starts with a specially blended seasoning paste that will help determine the overall flavor of the dish. The paste is fried first to get rid of its raw taste before other ingredients and the cooking liquid are combined with it.

Understanding all this should immediately dispel the favorite Western notion that a curry is uniquely Indian and derives from sprinkling a distinctive yellow powder into a sauce. "That concept has done much damage in the West to the image of Indian cooking," said amateur Indian cook Dr. Sambhu Banik, of Washington, D.C., adding that curry powder is for lazy cooks. As Dr. Banik explained, "Curry is a term used by Westerners that I do not believe exists in India. Curry is a generic name for a dish Westerners call 'stew.' Stewlike dishes are called by different names, so why should I call them a curry?" For example, he said, a dish with coconut milk, cumin, pepper, salt, and chili powders may be called an *aviyal* or a *shukto* in West Bengal, says my friend B. Runi Mukherji-Ratnam, and a *vindaloo* in Goa. Indeed, there is no single curry flavor, but instead hundreds of variations on the curry theme.

Since the seasonings dictate the result, Asians stock their basic pantry with some essential curry ingredients, including coconut milk; meat, fish, or chicken stock or water; chilies of many shapes; lemon grass; coriander; turmeric; onions; garlic; ginger; and cumin. And these are just at one corner of the curry-seasoning shelf.

With ingenuity and skill, Asian cooks shape their curries with these and numerous other ingredients, giving each curry its distinctive character. This is particularly true in India, where the seasonings are so complex and multilayered that curries become gastronomic surprises. Consider, for example, the Lamb in Saffron, Apricot, Coconut, and Poppy Seed Curry (page 100). This extraordinary recipe calls for at least 19 different ingredients for seasoning and texturing the meat, plus several cooking steps besides.

Although the Indians can probably take credit for inventing the curry concept, the art of curry making really now belongs to no single Asian country and no one people. The Burmese, Malaysians, Vietnamese, Thais, Indonesians, Sri Lankans, Cambodians, Chinese, and Lao have their own curries, though many flavors and techniques both overlap and differ. Even the Japanese, who have earned their reputation for their artistic and temperate cuisine, have their own adaptation of curry—see Japanese-style Chicken Curry (page 91). Indeed, few Asian meals would seem complete without a bowl of curry or other stewlike dish with its companion bowl of rice. In fact, it seems that curries are primarily a way of flavoring and moistening rice.

Learning to eat curry the traditional way in several countries means eating with one's hand, which in and of itself is a practical way to consume food. During one Burmese family meal, I learned the technique: A curry gravy is mixed with some rice to moisten it, and then is mounded together and picked up with the thumb and the first two fingers.

Later, in India, I listened while Dr. Pushpesh Pant described how his father, an eminent and scholarly man, had so perfected eating with his hand that no fingertip was ever soiled. I appreciate the value in this technique. As one Malaysian woman in particular explained about eating this way, "The fragrance of the food lingers on [on our hand] for many hours, so we get to enjoy our meals over and over again."

After observing Asians and cooking their dishes, it is probably safe to say that a curry takes on certain characteristics depending on its country of origin. And even there, cooks put their own individual interpretation on a curry recipe. There seem to be few absolutes in the curry-making business. I decided this after watching how Raminder Malhotra in India, Than Than Yi of Burma, and Majmin Hashim from Malaysia cooked their particular curries. The dishes were certainly different. But each was excellent, vibrant with aroma, flavor, and texture.

On Asian Ingredients and Recipes

Soup, stew, and curry basics—such as chicken, pork, beef, rice, noodles, onions, and garlic—would not be out of place in any kitchen, Western or Asian. But for Westerners taking the Asian culinary plunge, finding less familiar ingredients may be more challenging. Fortunately, American grocers are responding to the demands of incoming Asians

and to a more cosmopolitan American eating public. Thus, for example, an occasional supermarket in the metropolitan Washington, D.C., area will sell fresh lemon grass, and most carry bunches of fresh coriander and baskets of Asian chilies. Shoppers elsewhere, particularly on the West Coast, where large Asian populations have created a market niche for Asian ingredients, are even more fortunate.

And where Asians live, Asians usually own markets. Take my area, for instance. Not only do I have a neighborhood warehouse-sized Asian market run by a Cambodian (whose wife contributed several recipes to this book), but I can think of nearly two dozen Asian groceries within the vicinity manned by the very people who know their foods best.

Of course, shoppers elsewhere may need to be more resourceful in their search for ingredients. Having Asian friends is a good first step, since many know local sources of ingredients or often grow their own. In my area, there is a Vietnamese farm lady who grows and sells her native produce and a retired Burmese businessman who grows his own native plants. My Lao friend Bounsou Sananikone grows her own lime trees and chilies, and another Asian woman has a small plot of fresh lemon grass in her backyard. And my Vietnamese friend Helene Sze McCarthy one evening cheerfully produced a bagful of fresh, young bamboo stalks that she had cooked for us at a local Chinese restaurant.

As with good cooking anywhere, the trick is finding the freshest ingredients local markets offer. But failing that, frozen, dried, and canned products will do, though most Asians won't be satisfied. A case in point: Dr. Sambhu Banik of Maryland told me about his brother-in-law, who had decided to move to the United States. "He had to leave the country in a few months' time and return to India," said Dr. Banik. "He could not tolerate eating food cooked in the morning and then served in the evening. It had to be freshly prepared at each meal." He could not survive eating "second-hand food" or processed foods.

Westerners interested in Asian cooking would also benefit from familiarizing themselves with some of the more exotic ingredients: pandan leaves, rhizome, rice cakes, seaweed, and tamarind come to mind. Touring the aisles of an Asian market and asking the manager questions will help to demystify Asian cooking, making the whole process much more accessible. But having said that, I still cannot swallow my Western timidity at the prospect of buying—to say nothing of eating—ant eggs from Laos and the extract from the cockroachlike *mangda* from Thailand.

With a few exceptions, such as goat, yak, and water buffalo, most Asians start with generally the same meat, poultry, and seafood basics as Westerners do, except where local customs and perhaps the local economy make some ingredients off limits. For example, Indonesian Muslims will not eat pork, but Indonesian Hindus on the island of Bali do. And, in the past, chickens in Vietnam were costly and so were reserved for special occasions. However, few Asians could prepare or serve a traditional meal without several fundamental ingredients: rice and noodles, coconut milk, chilies, onions, garlic, ginger, and fresh coriander. Of these, indisputably rice rules the kitchen.

Rice Varieties and Cooking Techniques

Often I have heard Asians say they would forego any other of their indigenous daily foods, but they would not let a day pass without their bowl of rice. Of all the commentaries on Asian food I have heard, this is probably the most accurate, because Asians revere rice. So profound is this reverence that some come to know which age and which season's rice they prefer. Some, such as J. Inder Singh Kalra of New Delhi, even know by taste, texture, and aroma in which acreage a particular crop of rice was grown.

Apart from its sustaining nourishment and affordability, rice is a cook's dream. Its inherent blandness is the perfect complement and foil for any number of flavors, textures, and temperatures, to say nothing of the many ways an Asian can shape rice to fit a particular role—as in Indonesia, where it is steamed in hollow bamboo stalks or in woven banana-leaf parcels. Indeed, rice may be molded and shaped into other rice products, such as the rice cakes Koreans use (see Rice Cake Soup, page 141), sweetened for a dessert dish (see Taiwanese Fermented Rice, page 234), or ground into a flour for thickening.

Not only that, but rice itself often becomes the meal in the form of a soup (see Asian Rice Soups, page 236). As an added attraction, rice comes in so many flavorful varieties and splashy colors, from white to red to purple to brown-black, that it becomes a true sensual pleasure.

In particular, at most Asian tables, plain rice is the medium that one serves with a soup, curry, or stew for more flavorful eating. As Kenneth Lo wrote in *A Guide to Chinese Eating*, "Many Chinese are so appreciative of good gravy and rice that they often prefer the mixture to meat itself." That certainly may be said of other Asians as well.

Asian rices come in a seemingly infinite variety, but practically speaking, the most commonly eaten rices are, in India, the basmati—a fragrant, long-grain rice with a distinctive aroma and taste; in Southeast Asia, the Thai jasmine rice—a fragrant, long-grain rice that retains a firm texture after cooking—and other standard long-grain rices; and in Korea and Japan, varieties of short-grain sweet rice that can be boiled or steamed according to the recipe and that, because the grains stick together, are ideal for eating with chopsticks. The "sticky," or glutinous or sweet, rice—a long-grain opaque and very starchy rice—needs to be cooked by soaking and steaming rather than boiling. This rice is eaten daily by the Laotians and enjoyed for its unique clumping characteristic. When steamed, the grains of rice cling together and shape easily into clumps or balls for eating. The Laotians clump the rice together and use it as a utensil to pick up bits of food. The Vietnamese and Thais, and sometimes the Chinese, use this rice in desserts. There is also a long-grain black sticky rice used in the Philippines and Indonesia.

Not surprisingly, cooking rice becomes both important and, after years of Asian practice, a reflex action. As a Westerner in search of the perfect rice-cooking method, I have found that few recipes are identical and much depends on the cook, the country, the variety, and even the age of the rice. Water-to-rice ratios thus can range from two parts water and one part rice to one part water and one part rice. With inborn knowledge and much practice, cooks know that Thai jasmine rice, for example, is much softer than Indian basmati rice and so would keep the water-to-rice ratio at about one-to-one.

Cooking methods vary too, causing confusion for those who find cooking perfect rice a new experience. As I look at the stack of cookbooks at my feet, it seems every Asian cook has a personal preference and style, so no one iron-clad cooking method exists. Indeed, few agree even on whether or not to rinse rice before use and, if so, for how long. For example, some say rinsing wastes time.

Other cooks say that rinsing the rice until the water runs clear assures that the cooked rice looks better and does not stick. Obviously, cooks have found some additional bonuses for rinsing, since many use the first rinse water for starching clothes and the third for use in soups and stews.

Another factor that may cause confusion for Westerners is the seeming interchangeability of the terms "steaming" and "boiling" rice. As Bruce Cost explains in his book *Bruce Cost's Asian Ingredients*, Asians actually call the cooking process of boiling, then covering, rice "steaming."

Long ago, an Asian cook taught me to put the long-grain rice into boiling water and immediately reduce the temperature to low, cover the rice, and let it cook for about 20 minutes—and that has worked perfectly well. But recently, another Asian cook said that the furious-boil "knuckle method" works best, and that is what I now use. Besides, this method needs no measuring: Pour rice into the cookpot and add cold water to the depth of one knuckle length above the top of the rice. (Do not stick your finger through the rice to the bottom of your pot—just rest the tip on the surface of the rice.) Bring the water to a boil and cook the rice over medium heat, uncovered, until it absorbs almost all the water. Joyce Piotrowski describes this as the "dragon's eyes" method, because when the water has almost cooked away, bubbles of starch appear on the surface of the rice, resembling eyes. Then, fluff the rice with chopsticks, reduce the heat to low, cover, and cook for another 10 minutes—without looking or stirring. Remove from the heat and set aside until ready to serve. The rice should be tender, moist but not mushy, and the grains should be separate.

Many Asians now use the simple automated rice-cooker so that warm, "perfect" rice is on hand for hours. But rice cooking without gadgets is uncomplicated—and, to ease the Western mind, speedy.

For steaming the long-grain, opaque "sticky," or glutinous rice favored by the Lao, Thai, and Vietnamese and served as a sweet by other Asians: Rinse 2 to 3 cups rice until the water runs clear. Soak the rice for at least 6 hours or overnight in cold water to cover. (If you are in a rush, you can shorten the soaking time by about 3 hours by starting off with hot rather than cold water.) Drain, scoop the soaked rice into a woven bamboo cone-shaped basket or other steaming basket, and set it in the traditional Lao container over boiling water. (The basket and metal container are readily available at Asian markets.) Using a lid, cover the rice to trap the steam, and bring the water to a boil. The bamboo basket holds the rice above the water, allowing the steam to filter its way through the grains. The steaming takes about 30 to 40 minutes. About 5 minutes before the rice is done, you must flip it over—Thai cooks use a long wooden spoon to stir it—so that the top layer of rice is directly above the steam. Once the grains are tender, spread the rice out on a platter or towel so that it cools evenly; otherwise the grains will be too sticky for proper eating. Then you should put the rice back in the bamboo cone, or into special woven bamboo baskets or any other container with a cover, for storing. Although I have used only the Lao technique, I would imagine that any small-mesh steaming device that fits over boiling water and that can be covered during steaming will work.

If time runs very short, you can boil sticky rice in the ratio of 1 cup water to 1 cup rice by rinsing the rice, putting it into boiling water, stirring it once or twice, and cooking it covered over high heat for several minutes. Then pour off any excess water, replace the lid, and cook over very low heat for 10 to 15 minutes. When it is cooked, the boiled rice will be tender, but gummier than the steamed version.

For cooking the short-grain Japanese and Korean rices: Use $1^1/_4$ parts water to 1 part rice. For example, pour 2 cups rice and $2^1/_2$ cups water into a cookpot, cover with a tight-fitting lid, and bring the water to a rapid boil. When the starchy liquid ceases to steam out from under the lid, reduce the heat to the lowest setting and cook for 20 minutes more without removing the lid. Take the pot off the burner and let it stand, covered, for 10 minutes before serving.

The Vietnamese-Chinese cook Helene Sze McCarthy thinks the best-cooked rice comes from combining short- and long-grain rices, which results in a cooked rice that is neither too dry nor too moist, but instead "chewy and sticky."

These basic, general rules will produce wonderful rice. And after several attempts, you may wish to refine the method by altering the rice-to-water ratio to suit your tastes. Or you may wish to read up on rice-cooking techniques and combine methods that work best for you.

Because rice is the critical part of their diet, Asians are very fussy rice cooks. And Westerners will be too, once they have tasted simple, natural, well-cooked rice. They will undoubtedly toss away their instant, parboiled, brutalized rices as being an unworthy grain. For more information on rice varieties, see page 304.

Noodles

Among other things, the Chinese are credited with creating noodles in a seemingly endless range of varieties and shapes—long, wispy, wide, or thick—out of many ingredients, including rice, wheat, buckwheat, *agar agar*, tofu, eggs, and mung bean starch. They have also created countless noodle dishes and have shared their thoughts with their Asian cousins. Noodle lovers everywhere can now appreciate Malaysian *laksas*; the Burmese *mohinga* and *ohn-no-khauk-swe*; and the Vietnamese *phos*—all of which have noodles as their base. Most Asians rank noodles second behind rice as a favorite starch. For cooking instructions and information on specific types of noodles, see page 302.

Dal

The word *dal* refers not only to popular Indian legume dishes but also to the many types of lentils, peas, and beans—all of which are legumes—used in Indian cooking. Among these, however, is not the gray-brown lentil used in European cooking, which Indians apparently never use. Indians are not the only Asian cooks who use legumes. A wonderful meat substitute and protein source, legumes are also used plentifully throughout China and in parts of Southeast Asia.

All legumes need to be rinsed and picked through to remove any foreign matter (such as twigs and tiny stones) before soaking or cooking, and some require soaking in cold water to cover for 6 to 12 hours before cooking. (My Indian friend B. Runi Mukherji-Ratnam explained an easy tip for determining which legumes need soaking: Red lentils and legumes that are split and hulled require no soaking, although *chana dal* is an exception to this rule; whole unhulled legumes, on the other hand, must be soaked. To avoid confusion, I have specified in each recipe when legumes need to be soaked.) A very general rule of thumb for cooking legumes is to use 3 to $3^1/_2$ parts water to 1 part legumes, but some may require more; you may add more, a little at a time, if the legumes dry out too much during cooking. For information on specific types of *dal*, see page 297.

Tofu

Tofu, also known as bean curd, is a popular, inexpensive, and major protein source throughout most of Asia, except India. Made from soaked, pureed, and boiled soybeans that are then coagulated to form solids, tofu is readily adaptable to a variety of cooking methods and is beloved because it seems to soak up the flavors of sauces and other accompanying ingredients; indeed, clever Asian cooks have contrived tofu recipes for every kind of dish, from soups and salads to desserts. Tofu is readily available in supermarkets in water-packed tubs. It is also sold loose at Asian markets or water-packed in large sealed plastic containers. Because it is perishable, you must change the water daily in its storage container. It will remain fresh for about five days when stored in the refrigerator.

Coconut Milk

Rarely or never used in Chinese, Japanese, or Korean kitchens, coconut milk is an essential ingredient in tropical Asian cuisines, where coconut palms grow abundantly. Coconut milk turns up in unexpected places, from temperate soups to blazing curries, sweetened desserts to plump, gooey confections. Rich and oily, versatile coconut milk can double as cream, sweetener, and thickener; and because of its oil content, coconut milk may be used for pan-frying spices and pastes prior to cooking a curry or a soup.

"Coconut milk" actually refers to both the thick milk, or "cream," produced from the first pressing of coconut shreds and the thinner, more watery liquid—the thin milk—from the second and later pressings. The very thin liquid—coconut water—that sloshes around inside a coconut is an almost-clear water that serves as a very refreshing drink. One Asian woman told me that drinking this water helps prevent aging skin. That may be folklore, but I also heard that rubbing coconut oil in one's hair prevents hair from graying.

Without question, fresh coconut milk is best, and some Asian women who live in the West still grate their own coconuts daily to make fresh milk. Malaysian cook Majmin Hashim remembers that one of her childhood duties was to peel off the hard outer shell and grate the meat inside. "I sat on a little stool with a wooden neck and a metal head [the grater]. As I grated, the shreds fell in a pot," she said. But, she added, times have changed: "Maybe 10 years ago a chef might have argued about the virtues of hand-grated versus machine-grated coconut, but not anymore." As an alternative to using fresh coconut meat, some Asian women use frozen grated coconut instead.

If you wish to make your own coconut milk, soak 2 cups frozen grated coconut, freshly grated coconut, or shredded dried unsweetened coconut in 2 cups hot water for 20 minutes. Squeeze out the liquid by wrapping the shreds in several layers of cheesecloth and wringing them dry—this will give you the "first pressing," or the thick milk. Repeat the process for the second "pressing," or the thin milk. Or you can process the shreds with the water in a blender or food processor and strain off the liquid. The first time produces the thick milk and the second, the thin milk.

Many Asian cooks prefer the convenience of the less desirable frozen or canned milks, which do not have the same fresh quality or taste. If you use a commercial product, choose one that is thick and creamy. One test for thickness, I've been told, is to shake the unopened can; if you hear splashing sounds, the milk may not be thick enough. However, this is not always a reliable test, so experiment with brands until you find one you like.

Some Asian cooks have told me that with canned coconut milk, the thick milk is the white solid portion of the canned contents and the thin milk is the white liquid. If a recipe calls for simply coconut milk—without qualifying thick or thin—use the contents of the can. To follow a recipe that calls for only the thick milk, carefully spoon out what you need of the solidified coconut liquid. If the recipe calls for thin milk only, carefully pour out the thin milk. Other recipes in the book call for both thick and thin coconut milks—the oilier thick milk is usually used for frying, while the thin milk is generally used as a cooking liquid. Unfortunately, not every brand of coconut milk has this thick-and-thin separation in the cans, so, if necessary, just use the milk as it comes from the can. If you have leftovers, remember that canned or fresh coconut milk is extremely perishable and lasts in the refrigerator for only about two days. If you need to store it for longer, freeze it in a covered container for up to one month.

To avoid extra calories and fat, some may choose to forego coconut milk altogether, without realizing that it provides its own cooking alchemy. If you are tempted to substitute whole or skimmed cow's milk, the results will not be the same. On principle, I have not tried the Western fat-reduced coconut milk products, so I do not know whether they are adequate substitutes for the real thing.

Chilies

Except for Japanese and Filipino cooks, most Asians readily toss chilies into the wok or cookpot because they love the heat and flavor. Each chili variety definitely has its own level of fire and its own special taste and even texture. For example, as Malaysian cook Majmin Hashim explains, the Malaysian language contains many words that describe chilies' taste, aroma, and heat. And Laotian Bounsou Sananikone tells me that the reason Thais love their *prig khee nu* (bird's eye chilies) for curries is that these are particularly velvety after pounding.

But many Westerners find chilies an intimidating food, both to handle and to eat. For one, volatile components can burn fingers and any other skin surface they touch. So you would be wise to protect your hands by wearing rubber gloves when working with chilies, particularly if your skin is sensitive. You also should avoid rubbing your face or eyes with your fingers during or after handling chilies and before washing your hands. If chilies do irritate your skin, wash with plenty of water, detergent, and/or vegetable oil. If you eat something that seems too hot, consume milk, yogurt, buttermilk, or something starchy like rice to help ease the sting.

As for eating: Many recipes in this book call for chili amounts that sound daunting. As with any assertive ingredient, you alone must judge what you can tolerate. Sensible cooking would suggest starting with fewer chilies rather than more and working up to your tolerance level. And you should know some ground rules first. Since the heat of the chili really comes from the membranes holding the seeds, chili experts suggest you remove these, plus the seeds, to make chilies less fierce. In some recipes, an Asian cook might recommend removing the seeds, particularly from dried chilies, prior to grinding them to a paste. But remember: In general, most Asians like it hot.

Some of the recipes in this book call for roasting chilies to intensify their flavor and, in some cases, to add a smoky undertone. To roast fresh or dried red chilies, heat them in an ungreased skillet until browned and fragrant, or broil or grill them for several minutes just until they begin to darken or char. This gives them a wonderful smoky flavor.

As for selecting fresh chilies, the various shapes and colors may seem confusing. But unless you have a well-stocked grocery nearby, you may have only a few choices. I have used the generic short red or green chilies—green chilies are generally milder than red chilies—known as "Thai hot" (bird's eye chilies) and the longer Thai green or red chilies known as "finger hot." At times I have found the much longer green chilies from an Indian grocer or even a local supermarket and have used those as well. You may find many other varieties to experiment with. Incidentally, you may use the fresh Mexican jalapeño chili as a fine substitute in Indian dishes if nothing else is available. Also, if you are preparing a paste that calls for red chilies and you cannot find good fresh ones, you may use dried red chilies instead, though you may need to add several more to increase the heat level.

If you want to stock up on chilies, refrigerate them in plastic bags or containers for short-term storage. Fresh chilies freeze well, but they do not retain their shape or texture. Thawed chilies are suitable for grinding into a paste or a sauce as thickeners. But test the heat—you may need to add some fresh chilies to fire it up.

As for using dried chilies, cooks say that you can reduce their heat level by snapping off the stem end and shaking out the seeds. You can take this step prior to roasting them in a hot skillet or to soaking them before grinding with wet seasonings, such as lemon grass, garlic, or ginger. Since not all dried chilies snap apart easily, Bounsou Sananikone taught me how to seed the stubborn dried chili: after soaking, simply cut it in half lengthwise and scoop out the seeds.

Flavor Basics: Onions, Garlic, Ginger, Fresh Coriander, and Lemon Grass

Most Westerners will certainly use onions and garlic often and should recognize ginger, fresh coriander, and lemon grass. In an Asian kitchen, however, most cooks would use these five on a daily basis, for in many ways they form the backbone of Asian cuisine.

Onions, particularly shallots, are smaller in Asia, and using fewer of the Western varieties in these recipes would not cause problems. Shallots are almost uniformly required in many Asian kitchens for their delicate oniony flavor. Indians generally use a reddish onion that is sweet and delicate and that looks like a cross between a shallot and a Western red onion. I have been told that the reddish onions sold at Korean markets are very similar to these Indian red onions. Shallots or small yellow onions also make fine substitutes. Another Korean variety, known as the Korean green onion, or *negi*, resembles a cross between a leek and a scallion. *Negi* are also sold at Korean markets, but if you cannot find them, substitute leeks.

Fresh garlic is commonly used, so keep plenty on hand. You may be tempted to use the commercial prechopped or pressed garlic stored in oil, but this does not produce the same flavor.

Sometimes a recipe calls for roasting onions, shallots, chilies, or garlic. To do this, heat a grill or broiler until very hot. Cook the ingredients until the exterior begins to char and the interior softens. (Be sure to turn the ingredients often to prevent burning.) Alternatively, you may pan-roast them in a dry skillet or fry them until they begin to darken and become fragrant. When they are cool enough to handle, you may rub or peel off their skins. Roasting ingredients sharpens the flavor and adds color to the finished dish.

Fresh ginger—grated, minced, pureed, pounded, juiced, slivered, or diced—is used liberally in almost every Asian dish, and its cool-hot flavor enhances any food it touches. Most Asian cooks measure ginger by the inch—very roughly speaking, a 1-inch slice of ginger equals about 1 tablespoon of grated fresh ginger. But no one ever cares if that inch is wide or narrow, because, it seems, using more rather than less is fine. As with garlic, the commercial oil-packed chopped or minced ginger lacks the character of the fresh. Never substitute dried ginger, the confectioner's ingredient, for fresh. Some recipes call for "smashing" or "mashing" ginger; this process helps to release all the juices prior to mincing it, so don't skip over this step.

Fresh coriander, also known as cilantro or Chinese parsley, has a delicious pungency and musky aroma that enhance numerous dishes. It is available at most supermarkets. The Thais and some Indian cooks appreciate that much of this herb's flavor is concentrated in the roots, so they often chop up or pound the roots and add these to dishes requiring a fully developed coriander flavor.

Stalks of lemon grass with their bulbous ends lend a delicate citrusy flavor and fragrance to many Southeast Asian dishes. Fortunately for Western cooks, lemon grass is sold fresh in most Asian markets and is often available in supermarkets too. But even frozen lemon grass is preferable to the dried or powdered product, known as *laos*. If you find a supply, you can store lemon grass for up to a week in the refrigerator and for several months in the freezer.

MSG

MSG is a subject all its own. I have been told, but cannot verify, that the original MSG, *aji no moto,* is a natural substance derived from seaweed; the MSG that causes so many bad reactions is an artificially compounded chemical. In any case, my Lao friend Bounsou Sananikone gives the best comment on the use of MSG: "If you are not a very good cook, it helps."

Pastes and Sauces

Other essential seasoning ingredients are the numerous varieties of pastes and sauces Asian cooks use to add their element of magic to the finished recipe. For the Western cook, the sight of at least 30 different brands of fish sauce and at least that many different soy sauces on an Asian grocer's shelf may seem daunting. However, these various flavor enhancers seem more approachable with a little basic knowledge.

Fish Pastes

The assortment of fish-based pastes used in Lao and Cambodian cooking—*prahok* and *padek,* respectively—are fermented fish seasonings that add their own distinctive level of flavor to dishes. Many kinds appear very liquidy, with chunks of fish suspended in the liquid, but this salty ingredient is usually a combination of the thick residue from the manufacture of fish sauce and thickening agents.

Shrimp Pastes

Made from dried, salted shrimp crushed with other ingredients, shrimp paste is an acquired taste for some Westerners, but it is an absolutely vital ingredient in most Southeast Asian cuisines. This product comes in two very different forms—the thick dark pastes from Thailand and Malaysia and the spoonable pink-gray sauces from China and Vietnam—so it is important to use the paste from the country of origin of your recipe, or at least a paste that is of similar consistency.

To rid the firm paste of its strong, fishy smell, I have fried or dry-roasted it before use. To fry it, heat no more than 1 tablespoon of oil in a wok or skillet, add the paste, and cook for 1 minute per side. Or use a nonstick wok or skillet and dry-roast the paste for about 1 minute per side. The saucelike Chinese and Vietnamese pastes are even more potent, yet there is little you can do to temper their fishy smell.

Soybean Pastes

Soybean paste is an important seasoning in Singapore, Thailand, Malaysia, and many parts of China. It is made from fermented black or yellow soybeans and adds a strong, salty flavor to dishes. Hot soybean paste, a mixture of chopped dried red chilies and mashed soybeans, is sold at most Asian markets. Shopping for soybean pastes may be mystifying, for they are also labeled soybean sauce, bean paste, bean sauce, and miso, and some actually come packed with whole soybeans in a thick liquid, so be sure to use the type specified in the recipe.

Soy Sauces

Almost every Asian kitchen except the Indian one has its own type of soy sauce, and almost every type can be found in a well-stocked Asian market. To generalize about soy sauces, the Chinese produce a dark, strong-tasting soy, a mushroom-flavored soy, and an oyster-flavored soy; the Japanese, a light, mild soy; and the Indonesians, a thick, sweet soy. A well-stocked soy shelf should contain at least one Chinese, one Japanese, and one Indonesian soy sauce.

Fish Sauces

This fermented fish product shares the limelight with soy sauce when it comes to seasoning basics. Although I have been told by some that you should use the fish sauce from the country whose food you are cooking, several Asian cooks, regardless of their origins, swear by a particular Vietnamese brand of fish sauce, the Three Crabs Brand. For this reason, I have not specified any particular type in the recipes—except that I will add that my personal favorite is that very same Vietnamese brand.

Chili Pastes and Sauces

A universal Asian seasoning, chili paste, which is sometimes labeled sauce, is made from ground or crushed fresh chilies, salt, oil, garlic, and sometimes vinegar, plus other ingredients that vary according to the country and the cuisine. Some pastes and sauces may be used for both cooking and as a table condiment, such as the Indonesian *sambal oelek* and Vietnamese chili sauce, but the thicker pastes really are not meant for table use. Since the terms "paste" and "sauce" are used interchangeably, it is important to check the consistency of the product and not to rely on the label.

Seasonings and Aromatics

Many of the recipes in this book call for a variety of spices used for their flavor and aroma. No one could ever deny that their subtle use can produce unforgettable dishes of sublime character, but their careless use can be fatal to a recipe. Most Westerners not accustomed to using a spectrum of seasonings should approach cinnamon and cardamom, black cumin and asafoetida, and all the others in the Asian spice arsenal with some caution until they understand the various characteristics of each seasoning. More is definitely not better.

Besides seeds, other Asian seasonings and aromatics include everything from tamarind juice to galangal and kaffir lime leaf and its rind. Asians will also use a variety of other ingredients less regularly, such as fresh turmeric root and a Thai root called rhizome, which helps cut fish flavors when preparing certain seafood dishes.

On Roasting Seasonings and Aromatics

In general, dry spices and seeds should be roasted before use to enhance their flavor—that is, cooked without oil in a heavy skillet over medium-low heat, stirring constantly, until fragrant (this is usually only a matter of a minute or two). If recipes call for a number of roasted ingredients, roast each separately unless instructed otherwise. Alternatively, spices and seeds can be toasted in an oven or toaster oven at 200°F until fragrant, about 5 minutes.

Once you become truly adept at using these seasonings, you will know when to roast them—as Indian cook B. Runi Mukherji-Ratnam explained to me, cooks in India know when to roast and when not to, depending on the final effect they want. The recipes in this book instruct when to roast spices, so you don't need to guess.

On Grinding the Seasoning or Curry Paste

Combining ingredients correctly to produce the seasoning or curry paste that characterizes much of Asian cooking is a matter of experience, since most Asian cooks never really measure, but rather add ingredients by eye, by taste, and by instinct. In some traditional Asian kitchens, and even in some modern ones in the West, an Asian cook will still pull out her mortar and pestle and pound a handful of ingredients into a wonderful paste. The pounding apparently does something that chopping in a blender or food processor can't—it releases aromatic juices and flavors trapped in the plant's cell.

But pounding is not necessary when making a paste. If you are using a small quantity of ingredients, try using a spice grinder or coffee grinder—you may not even have to use water or other liquids, such as coconut milk, to help the processing. For larger quantities, I have found that, overall, the blender produces a better result than the food processor and consistently grinds up even the most stubborn chunk of lemon grass. However, do not worry if your blender does not produce a velvety paste—it will smooth out during cooking. Note: Whether you process with a blender or spice grinder, several cooks say you should cook the paste first (without oil) to evaporate the excess moisture that might otherwise dilute the flavor. But not everyone agrees with that theory. You may also use coconut milk to help the processing if you are going on to cook the paste in this liquid.

If you wish to use a mortar and pestle to make the pastes, you will achieve more authentic results. René de Berval, in a passage in his book *Kingdom of Laos, The Land of the Million*

Elephants and of the White Parasol, describes the Lao use of the "little hand-mortar" of rough stone with a wooden pestle "where so many pimentoes [*sic*] are pounded and in which food is reduced to powders so fine they are a challenge even to the best of 'mixers.'"

If you are going to pulverize a spice in a grinder before incorporating it into a seasoning paste or curry paste, let the heated spice cool before grinding, because the trapped heat could "burn" it and affect the flavor. Ideally, each spice or seasoning should be coarsely ground before being combined with other ones for grinding into a seasoning or curry paste, but few cooks in their recipes say to do that.

About the Recipes in This Book

Asians rarely sit down to a one-course, one-plate meal. Instead, they prefer a meal with many small components, balanced for texture, flavor, and color. Typically, meals consist of a soup, curry, or stew, grilled meats, raw and cooked vegetables, and fruit. Occasionally, some sort of sweet comes as dessert. For Asians, soups, stews, and curries are components of a larger whole, each adding their particular taste and texture for a pleasingly balanced meal.

For a Westerner, this concept of many courses suggests overeating and gluttony. But the Asian trick is to serve small portions of everything—mounding food on a plate Western-style would probably seem barbaric. You may find that many recipes in this book marked to serve four to six people might really feed only two at a Western table. But think Asian—and plan meals with numerous courses. And certainly always offer plenty of rice or noodles. Most meals would include one or the other starch.

Most Asian cooks never use cookbooks or a printed recipe, relying instead on taste, smell, and experience—cooking as their mothers and grandmothers once did. And few Asian cooks ever measure anything. They simply toss ingredients into the cookpot until the taste, texture, and aroma are correct. For some of the recipes in this book, this tendency resulted in interesting moments, as I wrote down amounts as quickly as the cook threw in ingredients.

So Westerners could never be more "Asian" than if they were to freely adapt ingredient quantities to suit their particular palate. After all, as a Nyonya acquaintance expostulated, "A recipe is only a guide." In that spirit, I tested these recipes, most of which remain as the cook gave them; but for some, I, too, have been "Asian" and adjusted liquid or oil amounts and adapted a recipe slightly to suit the final appeal. I strongly urge those with delicate taste buds to consider using fewer chilies than what is suggested in the recipes.

The glossary includes descriptions of many basic Asian ingredients and should help cooks when shopping for and preparing these meals.

Cooking times are only approximate, since times depend on so many variables, including the temperature of your stovetop burners, the size of slices of meat and vegetables, the quality of meat and the freshness of vegetables and spices, how much stirring goes on, and the number of interruptions. As one cook noted, "The food is ready when it smells cooked." Curries and curry pastes must be cooked until they lose their "raw" smell and have a rich, developed scent; coconut milk should be cooked until a film of oil rises to the surface of the liquid. Tougher cuts of meat and chicken, of course, should be cooked until tender.

For cooking equipment, use large skillets or saucepans of 4- or 6-quart capacity or a very large wok, unless a recipe calls for a stockpot. In that case, ingredient amounts require a very large cooking vessel. Once again, use common sense when selecting the size of your pots and pans.

As for frying, you can test whether the oil is hot enough to add other ingredients, as cook Joyce Piotrowski teaches, by plunging a bamboo chopstick into at least 1 inch of oil—bamboo contains just enough moisture to cause the chopstick to sizzle when the oil is hot enough for frying.

Finally, these recipes are memorable, and some even startling—and inherently traditional. They have not been "Westernized" nor even particularly simplified. However, I am both a Westerner and—despite the years I lived in Hong Kong and the number of Asian meals I have cooked and eaten—an outsider. So my understanding of the various customs, techniques, and flavors is not native-born. I have probably broken some intrinsic Asian culinary rules with this collection, but the assembled recipes should inspire some lingering Asian dreams.

Recipe Basics

Although Asian cooks usually put their individual stamp on recipes, Westerners may find tackling the Asian kitchen much easier with some standards to follow. This selection of recipes will familiarize you with some of the basic components of Asian dishes, and with this foundation, you can develop your own flavor combinations.

Garlic Oil

This is a basic flavoring oil that Thais and others use to keep strands of cooked noodles separated while adding a spark of flavor. You may also want to use this oil for frying or adding a subtle hint of garlic to cooked rice or other dishes.

2 cups vegetable oil

2 heads garlic, cloves separated, peeled, and chopped

Heat the oil in a large wok or skillet. Add the garlic and stir-fry until golden. Remove from the heat. Drain on paper towels and let cool completely. Store the oil in a tightly sealed container for up to 2 months.

MAKES ABOUT 2 CUPS

Roasted Red Chili Powder

Presumably every Asian cook who uses this powerful seasoning has a personal recipe, but two Asian friends suggested making the red chili powder used extensively in Thai, Malaysian, Burmese, and Singaporean cuisine by the following method.

25 to 30 dried red chilies

Heat a wok or skillet and roast the red chilies until they expand and turn dark red-brown in color, about 1 minute. Then crush them into flakes or put them in a spice grinder or blender and pulverize. If you choose the latter technique, ventilate your kitchen well or you will sneeze for some time to come—the fumes are potent. Store the pulverized chilies in a jar. As my Burmese friend Than Than Yi observes, many Burmese cooks in the West simply use commercially prepared crushed red peppper flakes straight from the jar. Cayenne pepper also is a good substitute.

ABOUT ¹/₃ CUP

Ghee

This yellow butter product is essential to proper Indian cooking and is used for frying or seasoning. It is always available at an Indian market, but you can also make your own.

1 pound unsalted butter

Melt butter over very low heat. When it begins to bubble, let it cook until all the sizzling and crackling sounds stop; this means that the moisture has evaporated. Continue cooking until the milk solids on the bottom of the pan brown. Remove the butter from the heat and when cool, carefully pour off the yellow liquid (the ghee), leaving any brown particles behind. Store the ghee, covered, in the refrigerator for up to 3 months. Some say it can be stored at room temperature, but refrigerating it will prolong its life. Although ghee is easy enough to make, vegetable oil can be substituted; however, the flavor will not be the same.

MAKES ABOUT 1^1/$_2$ CUPS

Fried Shallots

A popular garnish for many Asian dishes, fried shallots are easy to prepare and have a livelier flavor than the commercial product, which is available at Asian markets.

1^1/$_2$ cups vegetable oil
1 pound shallots, peeled and
   thinly sliced

Heat the oil in a large wok or skillet over medium heat. Add the shallots and cook, stirring, until golden brown and crispy, 7 to 10 minutes. Transfer to paper towels to drain. Store in a tightly sealed container for up to 1 month.

MAKES ABOUT 1 CUP

Fried Garlic

Very thin slices of golden-fried garlic are often used to garnish and flavor dishes. This is simple to make, but you may also purchase fried sliced garlic packed in small plastic jars at Asian markets.

2 cups vegetable oil

2 large heads garlic, separated into cloves, peeled and thinly sliced

Heat the oil in a large wok or saucepan. Add the garlic slices and cook over medium heat, stirring constantly, until golden, 2 to 3 minutes. (Do not let the garlic burn, or it will be bitter.) Transfer the garlic to paper towels to drain. Store in a tightly sealed container for up to 1 month.

MAKES ABOUT 1 CUP

Fried Tofu

Tofu, or bean curd, eaten plain, steamed, deep-fried, or stir-fried, as in this recipe, is a nutritious and healthful component of many Asian dishes and meals. Once Westerners learn its ease of preparation and appreciate its subtle flavor, tofu should become a commonplace food. Cooks often suggest using firm tofu for stir-frying to maintain its shape, but even soft tofu, if handled gently, will work well.

1 pound firm or soft tofu

1/3 cup vegetable oil

1. Slice the tofu in half horizontally and press between layers of paper towels. Change the towels and repeat the process until most of the excess water has been removed. Cut the tofu into cubes.

2. Heat the oil in a large wok or skillet. Add the tofu and cook, gently turning, until heated through and turning golden, 10 to 15 minutes. Transfer to paper towels to drain. Store leftovers in a tightly sealed container in the refrigerator for up to 3 days.

MAKES 4 TO 6 SERVINGS

Basic Chicken Stock

No cook should be without a recipe for chicken stock, easily one of the most needed basics for making soups, stews, and curries in any kitchen. This is my recipe, and one which I may alter—adding more or less of one ingredient or another—depending on what's on hand. I would usually add oregano, sage, and thyme for Western dishes. My friend Joyce Piotrowski says that adding chicken feet greatly improves the flavor.

8 cups water

2 pounds chicken pieces, including feet, necks, and backs

2 onions, quartered

$1/2$ bunch fresh parsley

2 stalks celery

1 carrot, peeled and cut into chunks

Salt and freshly ground black pepper to taste

Combine the water and chicken in a stockpot and bring to a boil. Skim the foam; then add the remaining ingredients. Reduce the heat to low and cook, skimming often, for 3 hours or until the liquid has reduced to 6 cups. Strain through a fine-mesh sieve and discard the solids. Use immediately, or let cool to room temperature and store in a tightly sealed container in the refrigerator for up to 4 days or in the freezer for up to 1 month. Skim off the fat before reheating.

MAKES ABOUT 6 CUPS

Basic Beef Stock

This simple recipe is from cook Joyce Piotrowski. Ask your butcher to crack the bones for you.

7 to 8 pounds beef knuckle bones, cracked

2 large unpeeled onions, quartered

4 carrots, peeled and trimmed

1 star anise

4 sprigs fresh coriander

10 to 12 cups water

1. Preheat the oven to 375°F.

2. Place the beef bones, onions, and carrots in a large roasting pan. Roast until browned, $1^1/2$ to 2 hours.

3. Transfer the bones, onions, and carrots to a stockpot. Add the star anise, coriander, and water to cover and bring to a boil. Reduce the heat to low and cook, skimming often, for up to 4 hours. Strain through a fine-mesh sieve and discard the solids. Use immediately, or let cool to room temperature and store in a tightly sealed container in the refrigerator for up to 4 days or in the freezer for up to 1 month.

MAKES ABOUT 8 CUPS

Basic Pork Stock

Cook Joyce Piotrowski uses this pork stock recipe for her Chinese dishes because it captures some beloved flavors, such as ginger and soy sauce.

2 pounds pork trimmings and bones, trimmed of all visible fat

$1/2$ cup sliced scallions

2 thin slices fresh ginger

1 tablespoon Chinese rice wine

2 teaspoons soy sauce

6 cups water

Combine all ingredients in a stockpot and bring to a boil. Reduce the heat to medium-low and cook, skimming often, for $1 1/2$ hours. Strain through a fine-mesh sieve and discard the solids. Use immediately, or let cool to room temperature and store in a tightly sealed container in the refrigerator for up to 4 days or in the freezer for up to 1 month.

MAKES ABOUT 6 CUPS

Basic Lamb Stock

This basic lamb stock from Joyce Piotrowski has a nice, rich flavor.

2 pounds lamb breast, cut into pieces

3 quarts water

2 large unpeeled onions, quartered

2 carrots, peeled and chopped

One 2-inch piece fresh ginger, smashed

4 cloves garlic, unpeeled

1 teaspoon Szechuan peppercorns

1 teaspoon black peppercorns

1 teaspoon cumin seeds

1 teaspoon coriander seeds

1. Preheat the oven to 375°F.

2. Place the lamb in a large roasting pan. Roast until browned, about 1 hour.

3. Drain off the fat and transfer the lamb to a stockpot. Add just enough water to the roasting pan to deglaze the drippings and scrape into the stockpot. Add the onions, carrots, ginger, garlic, peppercorns, cumin, coriander, and the remaining water and bring to a boil. Reduce the heat to medium-low and cook, skimming often, for 2 hours. Strain through a fine-mesh sieve and discard the solids. Use immediately, or let cool to room temperature and store in a tightly sealed container in the refrigerator for up to 4 days or in the freezer for up to 1 month.

MAKES ABOUT 8 CUPS

Basic Fish Stock

This basic fish stock from Joyce Piotrowski calls for using all the bones, including the head and tail, of the fish. By omitting the rice wine, you may use this for non-Asian dishes.

3 pounds fish bones (including head and tails) from non-oily fish

2 cups shrimp shells (optional)

One 1-inch piece ginger, smashed

1 bunch scallions, trimmed and smashed

$1/4$ cup Chinese rice wine

$1/2$ teaspoon Szechuan peppercorns

$1/2$ teaspoon black peppercorns

Salt to taste

8 cups water

Combine ingredients in a stockpot and bring to a boil. Skim off the foam, reduce the heat to low, and cook for 20 minutes. Strain through a fine-mesh sieve and discard the solids. Use immediately, or let cool to room temperature and store in a tightly sealed container in the refrigerator for up to 4 days or in the freezer for up to 1 month.

MAKES ABOUT 6 CUPS

China

Chinese Chicken Stock

Hong Kong gastronome William Mark offers this basic recipe for Chinese chicken stock. It is so light and delicate that you will be tempted to use it often.

One 4- to 5-pound chicken, cleaned
   and cut into pieces, or the equivalent
   in bones, including necks, backs,
   and feet
4 scallions, trimmed and smashed
One 1-inch piece fresh ginger,
   smashed
1 small clove garlic, peeled
$^1/_2$ cup Chinese rice wine, such as
   Shaoshing yellow rice wine
Salt to taste
8 cups water

Combine ingredients in a stockpot and bring to a boil. Reduce the heat to medium-low and cook, skimming often, for 3 hours. Taste, and if the stock seems too weak, continue to cook. When the stock is ready, strain through a fine-mesh sieve and discard the solids. Use immediately, or let cool to room temperature and store in a tightly sealed container in the refrigerator for up to 2 days or in the freezer for up to 3 months.

MAKES ABOUT 6 CUPS

Chinese Superior Stock

William Mark, Hong Kong's superlative chef/gastronome, provided this recipe for Chinese Superior Stock, which, according to Chinese chefs, is vital in the preparation of truly excellent classic soups and sauces. Reading Kenneth Lo's description in his Encyclopedia of Chinese Cooking *of making even a pared-down, simplified version—slow simmering, chilling, and straining several times—of this lengthy traditional stock is cause for panic. Fortunately, Mr. Mark's simplified version makes Superior Stock accessible to harried Western cooks.*

Traditionally, Superior Stock recipes call for a very special Chinese ham, the Yunnan ham, which may be very difficult to find in the West. It imparts an incomparable flavor to the stock, and because of that, cooks use no other seasonings. But a good substitute is the Virginia country ham or even prosciutto.

2 pounds chicken bones, including
  necks, backs, and feet
2 pounds pork spareribs, cut
  into sections
4 quarts water
1 pound Virginia ham, chopped
One 2-inch piece fresh ginger

1. Fill a stockpot with water and bring to a boil. Add the chicken and ribs, and cook until the juices are no longer pink, about 15 minutes. Discard the water.

2. Pour the 4 quarts water into the stockpot with the chicken and ribs, and bring to a boil. Stir in the ham and ginger, and return to a boil. Reduce the heat to low and cook for 4 hours. Strain through a fine-mesh sieve and discard the solids. Use immediately, or let cool to room temperature and store in a tightly sealed container in the refrigerator for up to 4 days or in the freezer for up to 1 month.

MAKES ABOUT 3 QUARTS

Ginger Juice

A useful seasoning in Chinese and some Southeast Asian cooking, ginger juice is easy to obtain. You can make a reasonable facsimile by stirring 1 teaspoon ground (powdered) ginger into 1 cup water.

Fresh ginger

Grate the ginger, wringing out the juice from the shreds and diluting it with water in the ratio of 6 parts water to 2 parts juice. This keeps in the refrigerator for up to 1 week.

Thailand

A variety of curry pastes form the basis of the luscious Thai curries that are a major component of many Thai meals. Depending on the kinds of chilies and ingredients used, many curry pastes are named for their color: red, green, and yellow, for example. An exception is the Mussaman paste, which is very distinctive and includes peanuts in the basic mixture. Although Thai cooks may have their own favorite curry paste recipe, the following basic pastes are a good starting point.

Thai Yellow Curry Paste

3 dried red chilies, soaked in hot water
　for 20 minutes and seeded
10 shallots, peeled and chopped
1 tablespoon chopped garlic
1 tablespoon coriander seeds
2 teaspoons curry powder
1 teaspoon cumin seeds
1 teaspoon chopped fresh ginger
About $^3/_4$ cup coconut milk
2 stalks lemon grass, trimmed and
　thinly sliced
1 teaspoon salt
1 teaspoon Thai or Malaysian
　shrimp paste

1. Roast separately the chilies, shallots, garlic, coriander seeds, curry, cumin seeds, and ginger in a wok or skillet over low heat, stirring constantly, until fragrant.

2. Transfer to a blender, add just enough coconut milk to process, and blend until smooth. Add the lemon grass, salt, and remaining coconut milk to process and blend until smooth. Add the shrimp paste and blend until combined—if necessary, pour off some of the paste and do this procedure in stages. Store in a tightly sealed container in the refrigerator for up to 3 days or in the freezer for up to 1 month.

MAKES ABOUT 1$^1/_2$ CUPS

Thai Red Curry Paste

20 dried red chilies, soaked in hot
water for 20 minutes and seeded

10 shallots, peeled and chopped

4 stalks lemon grass, trimmed and
thinly sliced

10 white peppercorns

2 tablespoons coarsely chopped garlic

1 tablespoon coarsely chopped fresh
coriander root

1 tablespoon minced galangal

1 teaspoon minced kaffir lime leaves

1 teaspoon salt

About 1 cup coconut milk

1 tablespoon Thai or Malaysian
shrimp paste

1 tablespoon coriander seeds

1 teaspoon cumin seeds

Combine the chilies, shallots, lemon grass, peppercorns, garlic, coriander, galangal, lime leaves, and salt in a blender. Add just enough coconut milk to process and blend until coarsely chopped. Add the shrimp paste, coriander, and cumin, and blend until smooth. Store in a tightly sealed container in the refrigerator for up to 3 days or in the freezer for up to 1 month.

MAKES ABOUT 3 CUPS

Thai Green Curry Paste

1 tablespoon coriander seeds, roasted
(see page 11)

1 teaspoon cumin seeds, roasted
(see page 11)

1 tablespoon chopped lemon grass

1 tablespoon minced garlic

1 teaspoon chopped coriander root

1 teaspoon chopped galangal

1 teaspoon salt

5 white peppercorns

$1/2$ teaspoon chopped kaffir lime rind

12 green chilies

6 shallots, peeled and chopped

About $1/2$ cup coconut milk

1 teaspoon Thai or Malaysian
shrimp paste

To make the curry paste, pulverize the coriander seeds and cumin seeds in a spice grinder. Place the lemon grass, garlic, coriander root, galangal, salt, peppercorns, lime rind, chilies, and shallots in a blender. Add just enough coconut milk to process and blend until smooth. Add the shrimp paste and the coriander-and-cumin-seed mixture, and blend until combined.

MAKES ABOUT 2$1/2$ CUPS

Mussaman Curry Paste

This recipe for this very spicy curry paste comes from Nick Srisawat, owner of the Tara Thai restaurants in the Washington, D.C., area. It makes plenty, so store leftovers in the freezer.

3 stalks lemon grass, trimmed and
   thinly sliced

$^1/_2$ cup coarsely chopped garlic

2 tablespoons finely chopped galangal

2 tablespoons cumin seeds

2 teaspoons coriander seeds

1 teaspoon whole cloves

About $^3/_4$ cup coconut milk

2 teaspoons salt

1 teaspoon ground cardamom

1 teaspoon ground cinnamon

1 teaspoon ground mace

1 teaspoon ground nutmeg

1 teaspoon black peppercorns

12 small dried red chilies, or to taste,
   soaked in hot water for 20 minutes
   and seeded

$^1/_2$ cup coarsely chopped shallots

1 tablespoon Thai or Malaysian
   shrimp paste

Roast separately the lemon grass, garlic, galangal, cumin, coriander, and cloves in a wok or skillet over low heat until fragrant. Transfer to a blender, add just enough coconut milk to process, and blend until smooth. Add the salt, cardamom, cinnamon, mace, nutmeg, peppercorns, chilies, shallots, and just enough coconut milk to process, and blend until smooth. Add the shrimp paste and blend until combined. Store in a tightly sealed container in the refrigerator for up to 5 days or in the freezer for up to 1 month.

MAKES ABOUT 2$^1/_2$ CUPS

Chili Jam

Nam Prik Phao

It seems that the Thai often use this "jam" made from roasted and ground chilies to sharpen and intensify the flavors of many different dishes. I've been told that Thai cooks often stir this into the shrimp-and-lemon grass soup classic, tom yam kung. *It's so good that, as Sarnsern Gajaseni says, you can use it as a toast spread in the morning.*

10 shallots, roasted and peeled
  (see page 8)

10 dried or fresh red chilies, roasted
  (see page 7)

10 cloves garlic, roasted (see page 8)

1 teaspoon Thai or Malaysian shrimp
  paste, roasted (see page 10)

2 tablespoons tamarind juice

3 tablespoons vegetable oil

1 cup shrimp powder

2 tablespoons sugar

1 tablespoon fish sauce

1. Combine the shallots, chilies, garlic, and shrimp paste in a blender. Add the tamarind juice and blend until smooth.

2. Heat the oil in a skillet over medium heat. Add the seasoning paste and cook, stirring, until fragrant, 3 to 4 minutes. Stir in the shrimp powder, sugar, and fish sauce, and cook, stirring often, until very dark, about 15 minutes.

MAKES ABOUT 2 CUPS

India

Indian Seasonings

Perhaps no other cuisine relies so heavily on the sublime interplay of seasonings and levels of flavors as does Indian cooking. The following are just four of the perhaps millions of seasoning suggestions in India. J. Inder Singh Kalra has provided the three seasoning paste recipes; I have provided the recipe for the garam masala.

Ginger Paste

1 cup chopped fresh ginger
3 tablespoons water

Combine the ginger and water in a blender and blend until smooth. Refrigerate in a tightly sealed container for up to 3 days.

MAKES ABOUT 1 CUP

Garlic Paste

1 cup chopped garlic
3 tablespoons water

Combine the garlic and water in a blender and blend until smooth. Refrigerate in a tightly sealed container for up to 3 days.

MAKES ABOUT 1 CUP

Fried Onion Paste

1 cup peanut oil, or more if needed
2¹/₃ pounds onions, peeled and sliced
1 cup plain yogurt

1. Heat the oil in a large skillet over medium heat. Add the onions and cook, stirring, until browned, about 15 minutes. (Add more oil if the mixture seems dry.) Transfer the onions to paper towels to drain.

2. When the onions are cool, combine in a blender with the yogurt and process until smooth. Refrigerate in a tightly sealed container for up to 3 days.

MAKES ABOUT 2 CUPS

Garam Masala

1 whole nutmeg

1 teaspoon whole cloves

2 teaspoons green cardamom pods

Two 1-inch pieces cinnamon stick

6 bay leaves

1 tablespoon black peppercorns

4 teaspoons coriander seeds

3 teaspoons cumin seeds

1. Roast each ingredient separately in a wok or skillet over low heat, stirring constantly to avoid burning, until fragrant. Set aside to cool.

2. Combine the roasted spices in a spice grinder or blender and pulverize. Store in a tightly sealed container for up to 1 month.

MAKES ABOUT 3/4 CUP

Sri Lanka

Sri Lankan Fragrant Curry Powder

One of many flavor combinations in Sri Lankan cooking, this recipe from Felicia Wakwella Sørensen contains numerous ingredients but comes together easily.

3 tablespoons coriander seeds

3 tablespoons cumin seeds

1 1/2 tablespoons anise seeds

One 2-inch piece cinnamon stick

10 curry leaves

10 green cardamom pods

10 whole cloves

1/2 teaspoon fenugreek seeds

1/2 teaspoon mustard seeds

1 tablespoon long-grain white rice

1 tablespoon shredded unsweetened
   coconut

1/4 teaspoon freshly grated nutmeg

1. Roast each ingredient separately in a wok or skillet over low heat, stirring constantly to avoid burning, until fragrant. Set aside to cool.

2. Combine the roasted spices in a spice grinder or blender and pulverize. Store in a tightly sealed container for up to 1 month.

MAKES ABOUT 1 1/2 CUPS

Malaysia

Malaysian Curry Powders

The recipes for these Malaysian seasonings come from Majmin Hashim and Chef Gunter Deseke and from a young Malaysian woman named Norliah, all from Kuala Lumpur.

A native Malaysian, Mrs. Hashim has memories of grinding curry powders when she was a child. "We used to grind this [curry powder] fresh when the seeds were soft and wet. No one will do that anymore because you need a special grinding stone. My mother-in-law gave one to me before I was married. I used to make the maid grind it."

Today, for much the same result, heat the seeds until crisp before grinding in a spice grinder or blender.

Malaysian Meat or Chicken Curry Powder

6 dried red chilies, or to taste

$^1/_2$ cup coriander seeds

1 tablespoon cumin seeds

1 teaspoon ground turmeric

$^1/_2$ teaspoon fennel seeds

$^1/_2$ teaspoon freshly ground
   black pepper

1 tablespoon Roasted Red Chili
   Powder (page 16) or cayenne
   pepper, or more to taste

1. Roast each ingredient separately in a wok or skillet over low heat, stirring constantly to avoid burning, until fragrant. Set aside to cool.

2. Combine the roasted chilies and spices in a spice grinder or blender and pulverize. Store in a tightly sealed container for up to 1 month.

MAKES ABOUT $^3/_4$ CUP

Note: Meat or Chicken Curry Powder may be used to flavor fish by grinding 1 stalk lemon grass, trimmed and thinly sliced, one $1^1/_2$-inch piece galangal, chopped, and 1 tablespoon shredded unsweetened coconut with just enough water to process and then mixing it with the curry powder. This seasoning keeps for just 2 weeks in a tightly sealed container in the refrigerator. For another curry seasoning for fish, see below.

Malaysian Fish Curry Powder

1 tablespoon ground cumin

1 tablespoon ground fennel

3½ tablespoons Roasted Red Chili
    Powder (page 16) or
    cayenne pepper

3 tablespoons ground coriander

1½ tablespoons ground turmeric

1. Roast each ingredient separately in a wok or skillet over low heat, stirring constantly to avoid burning, until fragrant. Set aside to cool.

2. Combine the roasted spices in a spice grinder or blender and pulverize. Store in a tightly sealed container for up to 1 month.

MAKES ABOUT ½ CUP

Malaysian Soup Spices

These are the traditional spices used to flavor Malaysian chicken or beef soups.

1 tablespoon ground coriander

1 teaspoon ground cumin

1 teaspoon ground fennel

Freshly ground black pepper (no more
    than 1 teaspoon)

1. Roast each ingredient separately in a wok or skillet over low heat, stirring constantly to avoid burning, until fragrant. Set aside to cool.

2. Combine the roasted spices in a spice grinder or blender and pulverize. Store in a tightly sealed container for up to 1 month.

MAKES ABOUT 2 TABLESPOONS

Ponzu Shoyu Dipping Sauce

¹/₄ cup soy sauce

3 tablespoons *dai dai* (**Japanese citrus**)
   or lemon juice

Pinch of sugar

Stir together the soy sauce, *dai dai* or lemon juice, and sugar. Stir well. Store in the refrigerator in a tightly covered container.

MAKES ABOUT ¹/₂ CUP

Note: Cook Yoko Morford explains that for certain dishes such as shabu-shabu and *mizutaki*, a traditional cook would go one step further in preparing the ponzu sauce by adding 2 scallions, trimmed and finely chopped; ¹/₂ daikon radish, peeled and grated; and 1 tablespoon *shichimi*. Or, if desired, replace the grated daikon and *shichimi* with the following recipe for *momiji oroshi*:

Cut a 2-inch length of daikon from the thick end of the radish. Peel off the skin. Make a hole in the center of the daikon with a chopstick. Fill the whole with 1 dried red chili. Grate the chili-filled daikon into the ponzu sauce and serve.

Japanese Soup Stocks

Cook Yoko Morford explains that the Japanese use several basic ingredients to make their soup stock, including *katsuo-bushi* (bonito shavings), dried *kombu* (seaweed or kelp), and *niboshi* (sun-dried sardines).

The first two are combined to make the fundamental soup stock, *dashi*, the flavor and quality of which determine the success of a stock-based dish. Traditionally, *dashi* was made fresh just prior to use by combining the right proportion of bonito shavings and *kombu*. Today's cooks can turn to instant *dashi* preparations, a stock concentrate available as a powder or liquid and used like instant bouillon—this is called *dashi-no-moto*. But none of the instant products can match the subtleties of the authentic stock.

Making an authentic *dashi* means starting with a high-quality chunk of bonito, a member of the mackerel family, which is boiled, then smoked and dried repeatedly until it turns rock hard. In earlier times, the home cook had to shave bonito flakes off the hardened piece of fish with a special tool. Today, bonito shavings are available in packets, but their flavor deteriorates, so these should be stored in tightly sealed containers and used up quickly.

Kombu is a Pacific kelp that thrives in the coldest sea water and is harvested off the northern Japanese island of Hokkaido. After the leaves are thoroughly sun-dried, they are cut, folded, and wrapped in air-tight packages. You will notice that the surface of the dried *kombu* has whitish areas—these should not be rinsed off, because they add flavor to the stock. You need only wipe off the surface of the kelp with a damp towel. Some cooks soak the seaweed overnight before cooking; some also make slashes on its surface for a more intense flavor.

The Japanese make two different types of *dashi* according to the type of soup they are preparing. The recipes for First Stock and Second Stock were provided by Yoko Morford.

Japanese First Stock

Known as ichiban dashi, *this is a clear stock for cooking vegetables and making clear soups.*

4 cups water
One 4¹/₂-inch-square piece dried
    kombu (Japanese seaweed)
¹/₃ to ¹/₂ ounce bonito shavings

1. In a saucepan, bring the water to a boil. Wipe off the *kombu* and make a few slashes in the seaweed with a sharp knife. Drop the *kombu* into the boiling water. Just before the water returns to a boil, remove the *kombu* and reserve for use in making Second Stock.

2. Reduce the heat to medium-low and drop the bonito shavings into the water. Immediately remove the saucepan from the heat. Strain the stock through a fine-mesh sieve. Reserve the shavings for use in making the Second Stock.

MAKES ABOUT 4 CUPS

Japanese Second Stock

Known as niban dashi, *this stock is used for making thick soups, such as miso, and also for cooking vegetables.*

3¹/₂ cups water
One 4¹/₂-inch-square piece dried
    kombu (Japanese seaweed) (reserved
    from Japanese First Stock)
¹/₃ to ¹/₂ ounce bonito shavings
    (reserved from Japanese First Stock)

Bring the water to a boil. Add the reserved *kombu* and bonito shavings. Just before the water returns to a boil, remove the *kombu*. Reduce the heat to medium-low and cook until reduced by about one-quarter. Strain through a fine-mesh sieve, and discard the *kombu* and bonito shavings.

MAKES ABOUT 3 CUPS

Korean Hot Pepper Seasoning Paste

This is so delicious that I know of people who make up batches of the hot mixture and use it to spike rice and other bland dishes.

3 scallions, trimmed and
   very thinly sliced
2 tablespoons Korean
   red pepper powder
2 teaspoons toasted sesame oil
1 teaspoon sesame seeds, toasted
   until golden
$1/2$ teaspoon garlic powder or
   1 teaspoon grated fresh garlic
Pinch of freshly ground black pepper
$1/4$ cup soy sauce, or more if needed

Combine the ingredients in a bowl. Add more soy sauce, if desired, to thin the paste. Store in a tightly sealed container in the refrigerator up to 1 month.

MAKES ABOUT $3/4$ CUP

Cambodia

Cambodian Curry Pastes

Cambodian cook Bora Chu generously shared many dishes from her native kitchens. The following two recipes are for basic Cambodian curry pastes.

Cambodian Green Curry Paste

In Cambodia, the curry paste would be made with lemon grass leaves, which have a mild citrusy taste. Unless you grow your own, the leaves will be difficult to find in the West, so use lemon grass stalks instead.

2 stalks lemon grass, trimmed and cut into pieces, or lemon grass leaves from 2 stalks

2 to 3 knobs rhizome

3 to 4 cloves garlic

Rind of 1 kaffir lime

$^1/_2$ teaspoon ground turmeric

1 pound firm-fleshed fish fillets, such as trout or catfish, grilled or broiled (see Note), skin and bones removed

About $^1/_2$ cup water

Combine the lemon grass, rhizome, garlic, lime rind, turmeric, and fish in a blender. Add just enough water to process and blend until smooth. Store in a tightly sealed container in the refrigerator for up to 1 week or in the freezer for up to 2 months.

MAKES ABOUT 3 CUPS

Note: Ideally the fish should be cooked over a charcoal or wood fire until the meat is opaque in the center, 2 to 3 minutes each side, depending on the heat of the fire and the thickness of the fish; but you can get good results by broiling the fish 4 to 6 inches from the heat.

Cambodian Red Curry Paste

For a brighter red, double the recipe, but omit the fish in one batch, since they make the color less intense. Then combine the two batches.

2 to 3 stalks lemon grass, trimmed and
    cut into pieces

4 knobs rhizome

3 shallots, peeled and sliced

3 dried red chilies, soaked in hot water
    for 20 minutes, seeded, and sliced

5 cloves garlic, peeled

1 teaspoon Thai or Malaysian shrimp
    paste

1 pound firm-fleshed fish fillets, such
    as trout or catfish, grilled or broiled
    (see Note opposite)

About ¹/₂ cup water

Combine the lemon grass, rhizome, shallots, chilies, garlic, shrimp paste, and fish in a blender. Add just enough water to process and blend until smooth. Store in a tightly sealed container in the refrigerator for up to 1 week or in the freezer for up to 2 months.

MAKES ABOUT 2¹/₂ CUPS

Subcontinental Divide— India, Sri Lanka, and Nepal

Separating Europe from the rest of Asia, the countries of India, Sri Lanka, and tiny, mountainous Nepal may be the true Asian melting pot. Through the centuries, foreign traders, armies, explorers, colonists, and immigrants crisscrossed the Indian Subcontinent in search of their own treasures. In their wake, local cookpots began to simmer with some very new ingredients.

India

Perhaps the best example of this melding comes from the kitchens of Northern India, where in the sixteenth century, nomadic Tartars set about building India's Moghul empire and kitchens. With its Persian roots, the cuisine they created was both elegant and sensuous, fit for the Maharajahs who feasted on it.

But this Moghul food—with its slow-cooked silken curries, complex seasonings, and tandoori-grilled meats and breads—is only one portion of India's culinary tradition, for in every region, state, village, and home, daily foods reflect countless influences: geographical, spiritual, cultural, religious, medical, and agricultural. As a result, there is no single Indian cuisine, and certainly no single national dish. There is just one national reverence for seasonings and textures and one vast Indian buffet that casts a spell on the hungry.

Because New Delhi is the capital, many visitors end up in the North, stopping in Delhi to gaze at history and certainly to sample some sublime cooking. I was one of those visitors, hoping to grasp the essence of this extraordinary cuisine in a crash culinary course. To do that, I spent several days in the inner sanctum—that is, in the several kitchens—of the Maurya Sheraton Hotel & Towers. I also partook in hours of food talk with the Indian food historians J. Inder Singh (Jiggs) Kalra and Dr. Pushpesh Pant.

In the end, I learned that seemingly more than anyone else, Indian cooks have perfected the subtle art of seasoning. And watching the hotel's cooks at work confirmed this: frying yellow dal brightened with splashes of turmeric; tempering curries with ghee, mustard seeds, slivered garlic, and wrinkly dried chilies; beating vats of yogurt enriched with asafoetida, green chilies, and chopped ginger; stretching and twirling blobs of dough for tandoori baking; and accenting potato masala with handfuls of mustard seeds and diced red onions.

Then the gentle and kindly master of the South Indian kitchen, Chef N. Rajan—with his graceful walrus mustache—showed me his distinctive dishes: the *sambar, kabhi, avial, iddli, sadan, wada,* and *saviya kheer* he was preparing for a buffet, all foods with a much more aggressive level of seasonings than their Northern counterparts. Though we did not speak a common language—except food—his gestures told the story.

Later, I watched chef Raminder Malhotra preparing pots of curries in his *dhaba* kitchen on the outskirts of New Delhi, where the ubiquitous cow strolled by. This little stand—a physical, but not a gastronomic, equivalent of an American fast-food place—attracts a large following because of Malhotra's genius. In a site not much larger than a closet and staffed with a surfeit of workers wedged together by the cook fires, this *dhaba* turns out a remarkable number of dishes, including the most dazzling *rogan josh* and butter chicken imaginable.

Such is the magic of New Delhi's food. I can only dream about the rest of India.

Sri Lanka

Poised off the tip of India like a drop of golden water, the island of Sri Lanka—once described by the Chinese as "the land without sorrow"—is a hot, tropical country where the cooking mirrors that of South India, resplendent with curries, coconuts, and chilies. For those who love pungent curries and an abundance of seafood, Sri Lanka could very well be gastronomic paradise.

Of course, other influences come into play as well, for over the years this island has been home to many different nationalities—the Dutch, Portuguese, British, Malays, and Arabs, to name a few—each of which has contributed to the local cuisine. So don't be surprised to find the Muslim-inspired dessert *wattalapan* (page 266) or the famous Dutch-inspired multicourse feast *lampries* (page 258). Western influences also show up, said one Sri Lankan woman now living in the United States, and most modern kitchens in large urban areas have food processors and other labor-saving gadgets. In fact, she noted, freshly ground spices, grated coconuts, and brewed Ceylon teas—all that a slower, simpler lifestyle implies—are giving way to convenience foods. In today's cities, for example, few women use the mortar and pestle for pounding and grinding spices, favoring instead the faster food processor.

It would seem, however, that many Sri Lankan cooks respect and adhere to the traditional ways. This same Sri Lankan woman still shreds her own coconuts and wrings out her own coconut milk, making it fresh on the days she plans to cook with it. "I never use canned coconut milk," she said. That may be a gesture to the old ways, the old flavors, but it also indicates that many Sri Lankan cooks still revere the richness and brilliance of a cuisine based on a kaleidoscope of spices, on the superlative creamy richness of coconut milk, and on the blaze of chili fire.

Nepal

Whenever I think of Nepal, I fantasize about trekking into the Himalayas and finding

Shangri-la. I also think about the Nepalese Gurkhas, the tough Nepalese soldiers enlisted by the British Army as much for their mountain endurance as for their courage. For years the Gurkhas have seemed a part of my Himalayan dream—a romantic image as well as fact. They are not fantasy, of course, though perhaps fantastic, and when we lived in Hong Kong, we saw them often, parading at public festivals and playing their skirling bagpipes.

I even once spent a day among the Gurkhas in their Hong Kong camp, judging their cooking contest at a country location near the Chinese border. Moving from one cook fire to the next, I sampled steaming, chili-laden dishes that, at the time, seemed hopelessly exotic. Today, of course, I understand more about their robust cuisine developed to counter the frigid temperatures of their homeland. It closely resembles North Indian cooking, with an emphasis on savory vegetarian fare, yogurt, and rice.

As elsewhere in Asia, so it is in Nepal: Rice is queen of the kitchen. To accompany this primary starch, the Nepalese often serve rich lentil soups and a variety of meats—goat, sometimes yak, poultry, but never beef in this Hindu country. To complement or substitute for rice, the Nepalese may prepare *tsampa*, a raw grain that is ground and mixed with milk, tea, or water. Chilies seem to play more than a minor role, for the Nepalese food I've tasted has been extremely hot.

Breakfasts may be simple, a snack of corn popped in a clay pot or maybe some leftover rice. But a midmorning meal the size of a Western brunch really fuels the day, as it consists of rice, lentils, pickles, and a curry or two, said my Nepalese acquaintance Jamak. Should hunger strike before evening, the Nepalese may nibble on sliced bread, *chiura* (beaten rice), or boiled eggs. And the day closes with a meal much like breakfast.

Besides rice, the other constant in the Nepalese diet seems to be hot, strong tea: Mugs of this brew, enriched with milk and heavily sweetened, keep the Nepalese company from dawn to dusk.

Partial to Poultry

"I would rather eat four ounces
of the flying species than four pounds
of the animals of the land."

—Ancient Chinese proverb

Burmese Noodles

Khao Soi

A remarkable feast gilded with such luxuries as scented rose petals and saffron, this chicken-and-noodle meal-in-one elevates the whole concept of "chicken noodle soup" to a realm far beyond the mundane. The title belies this outstanding, not to mention unusual, dish—it deserves to be called something like Royal Thai Feast or Rose-Scented Noodles.

Also, despite the name, this is a Thai variation on a traditional Burmese dish. Or at least it's how Nutchanand Osathanond, the Bangkok cook who gave me the recipe, puts together the popular noodle meal. It's hard to imagine the average Thai housewife whipping up anything like it on a regular basis: Preparing all the garnishes makes this dish a labor-intensive one, but don't let this keep you from trying out the recipe. Think of this as a basic Asian chicken-and-noodle curry with some extras. When you plan to prepare it, ask a friend or family member to lend you a hand.

One of the intriguing aspects of this version of Burmese Noodles is the array of crisp-fried garnishes that add texture, flavor, and eye appeal to the finished dish. Of these, the chrysanthemum flowers and rose petals provide the most exotic accent. The cook suggests selecting very fresh petals from unsprayed, scented roses—wilted rose petals are sour, she says, and unscented roses add no flavor. Another recommendation: Use only egg noodles, preferably homemade. The wide rice noodles popular in Thailand are not an alternative. You may be tempted to use a Thai curry paste, but this really calls for an Indian-style curry powder, she says.

Curry Paste

Ten 1-inch pieces fresh ginger

10 cloves garlic, peeled

6 shallots, peeled and chopped

About ¹/₂ cup water

Curry

One 3- to 4-pound chicken, roasted (see Note) and cooled

3 tablespoons vegetable oil

6 cups Basic Chicken Stock (page 19)

12 shallots, peeled and thinly sliced

2 tablespoons curry powder

1 tablespoon ground turmeric

Salt to taste

2 cups coconut milk

1. To make the curry paste, combine the ginger, garlic, and shallots in a blender. Add just enough water to process, and blend until smooth.

2. To make the curry, remove the skin and meat from the chicken and cut the meat in strips across the grain. Discard the skin and bones.

3. Heat the oil in a large saucepan over medium heat, add the curry paste, and cook, stirring, about 5 minutes or until fragrant. Add the chicken and stir in the stock. Reduce the heat to low and cook for 10 minutes. Add the shallots, curry powder, turmeric, salt, and coconut milk, and cook for 30 minutes more. Meanwhile, prepare the batter and cook the noodles for garnish.

4. To make the batter, combine the flour, rice flour, oil or lard, and baking soda. Add just enough water or coconut milk to thin the batter to a pourable consistency.

Batter

1 cup all-purpose flour

$^1/_2$ cup rice flour

2 tablespoons vegetable oil or
  melted lard

Pinch of baking soda

About $^1/_2$ cup water or coconut milk

Garnishes

1 pound wide dried egg noodles or
  2 pounds wide fresh egg noodles,
  cooked (see page 303) and tossed
  with $^1/_4$ cup Garlic Oil (page 16)

Garnishes for Batter Dipping and Frying

3 cups vegetable oil for deep-frying

1 small pumpkin or winter squash,
  thinly sliced

20 long beans, trimmed and cut into
  1-inch lengths

One 15- to 17-ounce can baby corn, or
  kernels from 1 or 2 fresh ears of corn

2 cups tender, young edible leaves (the
  cook recommends young leaves from
  an unsprayed rosebush) or 1-inch
  pieces leafy vegetables, such as
  spinach or Swiss chard

2 cups 1-inch pieces leafy vegetables,
  such as spinach or Swiss chard

2 cups edible chrysanthemum flowers
  (crown daisy)

2 cups large, fragrant rose petals

Garnishes for Frying

12 hard-boiled eggs, shelled

1 cup small dried red chilies, or to taste

1 cup sliced shallots

$^1/_2$ cup sliced garlic

5. To make the garnishes, line a tray with paper towels. Arrange the garnishes in separate piles. Heat the oil in a large wok or saucepan over medium-high heat. Working with the batter-dipped garnishes first, dip one set of ingredients at a time into the batter and plunge them into the hot oil until golden brown. Using a slotted spoon, transfer the garnishes to paper towels to drain. Repeat the process until all the batter-dipped garnishes have been dipped and fried. Working with the fried garnishes next, deep-fry each set separately in the oil until golden brown. Using a slotted spoon, transfer the garnishes to paper towels to drain. Cut the eggs into quarters.

6. To serve, arrange the garnishes in separate serving dishes. Place a portion of noodles in each person's bowl, ladle the curry over the noodles, and let guests help themselves to the garnishes.

MAKES 6 TO 8 SERVINGS

Note: To roast the chicken, preheat the oven to 425°F. Clean the chicken and rinse the cavity; pat dry with paper towels. Rub the skin with vegetable oil and sprinkle lightly with salt. Set the chicken on a rack in a roasting pan, reduce the heat to 375°F, and cook until the skin is crisp and the joints move easily, about 1$^1/_2$ hours.

Sri Lankan Mulligatawny Soup

Translated literally as "pepper water," mulligatawny is really an Indian soup that supposedly was inspired by the South Indian rasam *(page 224)*. This Sri Lankan version is much more substantial than the Indian soup and calls for an entirely different set of ingredients that come together as a complete, filling meal when served with rice. It also offers a different set of tastes that are at once layered and piquant. If you cannot cope with a generous chili flavor, you may cut back on the number of chilies, though the finished dish will lack its customary bite.

The instructions call for cutting the chicken into serving pieces, but you might want to cut it into even smaller pieces—for example, cutting each whole breast into quarters—for easier eating. You may use goat meat in place of the chicken, but chicken makes this such a satisfying dish, and goat is not an easy meat to find in most areas. The recipe calls for curry onions, which I could not find or even identify—neither, for that matter, could my Indian grocer. I used shallots instead. The curry leaves add their own distinctive flavor, but if you cannot find them in an Asian or Indian market (they are most likely to be found in the freezer section), make the dish anyway.

Don't let the long list of ingredients throw you off. The dish is not difficult to assemble, especially if you have everything prepared and ready to go.

Seasoning Mixture

8 dried red chilies, roasted
   (see page 7)
1 tablespoon coriander seeds, roasted
   (see page 11)
1 teaspoon fennel seeds, roasted
   (see page 11)
1/4 teaspoon cumin seeds, roasted
   (see page 11)
1/4 teaspoon black peppercorns,
   roasted (see page 11)
1/3 cup gram flour (besan)
1 1/2 cups thick coconut milk
   (see page 6)

1. To make the seasoning mixture, grind the chilies, coriander, fennel, cumin, and peppercorns in a spice grinder or blender. Mix the seeds with the flour and coconut milk.

2. To make the soup, put the chicken or goat pieces in a stockpot and add the water. Stir in the tomatoes, shallots, garlic, curry leaves, *pandan* leaf if using, lemon grass, cinnamon, ginger, and fennel. Bring to a boil, reduce the heat to medium-low, and cook until the meat is tender, about 30 minutes. Stir in the seasoning mixture, saffron, lime juice, and salt.

3. To make the flavoring, heat the ghee or oil in a large wok or skillet over medium heat. Add the shallots and cook, stirring occasionally, 8 to 10 minutes or until lightly crisp. Add the curry leaves, if using, and fennel and cook, stirring, 2 to 3 minutes more or until fragrant. Stir into the soup and serve immediately.

MAKES 6 TO 8 SERVINGS

Soup

Two 2- to 3-pound chickens, cleaned
    and cut into serving pieces, or
    $2^{1}/_{2}$ pounds goat breast meat, with
    bones, cut into serving pieces
3 quarts water
3 medium tomatoes, quartered
18 shallots, peeled and cubed
8 cloves garlic, peeled and sliced
4 to 5 curry leaves (optional)
One 2-inch piece *pandan* leaf
One 2-inch piece lemon grass stalk
One 2-inch piece cinnamon stick
One $^{1}/_{2}$-inch piece fresh ginger,
    thinly sliced
$^{1}/_{4}$ teaspoon fennel seeds
Pinch of saffron
Fresh lime juice to taste
Salt to taste

Flavoring and Garnishes

$^{1}/_{2}$ cup Ghee (page 17) or
    vegetable oil
6 shallots, peeled and thinly sliced
10 curry leaves (optional)
1 teaspoon fennel seeds, roasted
    (see page 11)

Burmese Coconut Noodles

Ohn-no-khauk-swe

Unlike Burmese Noodles (page 44), the Thai version of a Burmese classic, this noodle dish is pure Burmese. This dish is a resplendent offering—rich, satisfying, and creamy. It is perhaps one of the best known of Burmese dishes and may have as many variations as Burma has cooks.

My first morning in Rangoon, Daw May Khin Maung Than, a renowned local cook and cooking teacher, invited me to breakfast on this classic Burmese meal. She had purchased the thick, freshly made rice noodles just a few hours before we ate, so that their rich taste was still very evident. This kind of noodle is not available in the West, but the Chinese wheat-flour noodles or the thick, round Chinese or Vietnamese rice noodles are acceptable substitutes.

On paper, ohn-no-khauk-swe sounds complicated. But actually it is very easy to assemble. In fact, my Burmese friend Than Than Yi explained that many Burmese women take certain shortcuts, such as not boiling and pureeing the chana dal *used for thickening the soup. Instead, they mix about 1 cup gram flour, or besan, with enough water to make a thick paste and stir that into the coconut milk to act as a thickening agent. Yet there is something very wholesome and filling about using the* dal, *and cooking and pureeing them does not really add much extra work; it only requires some planning, because the* dal *need to soak in cold water for 6 to 12 hours and take some time to cook. Than Than Yi also omits the eggs used for thickening and the evaporated milk, because both make the dish very rich.*

Chicken Stock

One 3- to 4-pound chicken, cleaned and cut into serving pieces
5 stalks lemon grass, trimmed
1/4 cup fish sauce
1 tablespoon salt
10 cups water

Seasoning Paste

6 large onions, peeled and quartered
10 cloves garlic, peeled
One 2-inch piece fresh ginger
1 tablespoon paprika
About 1/2 cup water

1. To make the stock, combine the chicken, lemon grass, fish sauce, salt, and water in a large stockpot and bring to a boil. Cook for about 40 minutes. Remove from the heat. When the chicken is cool enough to handle, transfer to a cutting board, remove the meat from the bones, and chop into bite-sized pieces. Set aside. Reserve the stock for later use.

2. To make the seasoning paste, combine the onions, garlic, ginger, and paprika in a blender. Add just enough water to process and blend to a coarse paste.

3. While the stock is cooking, make the soup. Combine the split peas and water in a large saucepan and bring to a boil. Reduce the heat to medium-low and cook 25 to 30 minutes until soft. Transfer the split peas to a blender or food processor, add just enough of the cooking water to process, and blend until smooth.

Soup

1 pound yellow split peas (*chana dal*), rinsed, picked clean, and soaked in cold water to cover for 6 to 12 hours

10 cups water

$^1/_3$ cup vegetable oil, preferably peanut oil

2 tablespoons Roasted Red Chili Powder (page 16) or cayenne pepper

4 cups coconut milk

1 cup evaporated milk (optional)

3 tablespoons sugar

Salt to taste

Fish sauce to taste

3 large eggs, beaten (optional)

Accompaniments

2 pounds fresh or 1 pound dried Chinese wheat or Thai rice stick noodles, cooked (see page 302)

$^1/_4$ pound rice vermicelli, fried until golden and crumbled

3 large onions, peeled and thinly sliced

1 lemon or lime, cut into 8 wedges

$^1/_2$ cup Roasted Red Chili Powder (page 16) or cayenne pepper

3 or 4 hard-boiled eggs, shelled and quartered

4. Meanwhile, heat the oil in a large wok or saucepan over medium heat. Add the seasoning paste and cook, stirring, about 5 minutes or until fragrant. Add the chili powder or cayenne pepper and stir well. Add the chicken and cook, stirring occasionally, for 20 minutes.

5. While the chicken is cooking, whisk the pureed split peas into the stock and set over medium-high heat. When the stock comes to a boil, stir in the chicken mixture. Stir in the coconut milk, evaporated milk if using, sugar, salt, and fish sauce. Reduce the heat to medium-low and cook until the oil from the coconut milk appears on the surface, about 20 minutes. If you are using the optional eggs, whisk some of the hot liquid into the beaten eggs. Slowly pour the eggs in a thin stream into the soup, stirring constantly to prevent them from forming lumps or strands. Reduce the heat to low, cover, and cook for 15 minutes.

6. Arrange the accompaniments in individual serving bowls. Pour the hot soup into a tureen and serve it at the table: Place a portion of noodles in each soup bowl and ladle the soup over the noodles. Repeat for each person and pass the accompaniments.

MAKES 6 TO 8 SERVINGS

Burmese Chicken and Noodle Curry

Panthay Khauk-swe

My Burmese friend Than Than Yi offered me this poultry version of the popular noodle dish from the Shan States in Burma. Unlike the lamb version (see Burmese Lamb and Noodle Curry, page 104), this recipe does not call for chilies or coconut milk, so the effect is much more subdued. It has the added benefit of being simple and quick, so you can dig into a Burmese noodles meal without much time fussing in the kitchen. Than Than says that because local chickens in Rangoon are lean, cooks do not remove the skin before cooking. But in the West, chickens are fattier, so you may skin the chicken if you wish. After boiling the noodles, you may stir-fry them with some soy sauce, but this extra step is just to add flavor, not to make the noodles crisp.

One 4- to 5-pound chicken, cleaned
    and cut into serving pieces

3 cloves garlic, peeled and finely minced

One 1-inch piece fresh ginger,
    finely minced

1 teaspoon ground turmeric

1 teaspoon salt

1 teaspoon Garam Masala (page 29)

$1/3$ cup vegetable oil

1 large onion, peeled and minced

2 teaspoons paprika

1 teaspoon Roasted Red Chili Powder
    (page 16) or cayenne pepper

1 medium tomato, finely chopped

$1/2$ teaspoon cumin seeds

1 cup water, or more if needed

Accompaniments

1 pound fresh egg noodles, cooked (see
    page 303)

1 large onion, peeled and thinly sliced

$1/2$ head green Western cabbage, cored
    and thinly sliced

Lime wedges

Roasted Red Chili Powder (page 16)
    or cayenne pepper

1. Place the chicken in a large bowl and rub the surfaces with the garlic, ginger, turmeric, salt, and garam masala.

2. Heat the oil in a large wok or saucepan over medium heat. Add the onions and cook, stirring and sprinkling with the paprika and chili powder or cayenne pepper from time to time, until browned, 4 to 5 minutes. Add the tomatoes and cumin, and cook until pastelike, 2 to 3 minutes. (Add a little water if the mixture seems dry.)

3. Add the chicken and 1 cup water. Reduce the heat to low, cover, and cook, about 30 minutes or until chicken is tender. (Add more water if the mixture seems dry.)

4. Arrange a portion of noodles on each plate and serve the chicken over the noodles. Pass around the other accompaniments.

MAKES 4 SERVINGS

Spicy Chicken Curry

The Burmese have numerous chicken curry recipes, and this one from Daw Yin Yin Mya—with its earthiness and subtle chili heat—is particularly delicious. You can vary this dish by adding 5 to 6 boiled, peeled, and halved potatoes to the chicken about 10 minutes before it finishes cooking. You may also use beef or mutton instead of chicken for a very different taste.

Curry Paste

3 medium onions, peeled and chopped

5 cloves garlic, peeled

1 tablespoon Roasted Red Chili
   Powder (page 16) or cayenne pepper

$1\frac{1}{2}$ teaspoons Indian curry powder

About $\frac{1}{2}$ cup water

Curry

One $2\frac{1}{2}$-to 3-pound chicken, cleaned
   and cut into serving pieces

$1\frac{1}{2}$ tablespoons Ginger Juice
   (page 23)

2 teaspoons ground turmeric

1 tablespoon salt

1 teaspoon sugar

$\frac{1}{2}$ cup vegetable oil, or more if needed

5 medium onions, peeled and
   thinly sliced

4 bay leaves, crushed

1. To make the curry paste, combine the onions, garlic, chili powder or cayenne pepper, and $\frac{3}{4}$ teaspoon of the curry powder in a blender. Add just enough water to process and blend until smooth.

2. To make the curry, place the chicken pieces in a large bowl and rub with the ginger juice, turmeric, $1\frac{1}{2}$ teaspoons of the salt, and the sugar.

3. Heat the oil in a large wok or skillet over medium heat. Add the onions and cook, stirring often, about 10 minutes, until crisp. Transfer to paper towels to drain.

4. Reheat the oil over medium heat. Add the bay leaves and cook about 1 minute, until fragrant. Stir in the curry paste and cook about 5 minutes, until fragrant. (Add more oil if the mixture seems dry.) Add the chicken and stir until covered with the paste. Reduce the heat to medium-low, cover, and cook for 15 minutes. Stir in the remaining $1\frac{1}{2}$ teaspoons salt, the fried onions, the remaining $\frac{3}{4}$ teaspoon curry powder, and enough hot water to cover. Cook until the chicken is tender, about 15 minutes more. Serve hot.

MAKES 4 TO 6 SERVINGS

Lemon Grass Chicken Curry

Known in Burma as "young man's chicken," the dish is so simple that even a youngster can fix it, explains Burmese cook Than Than Yi. This curry, with its fresh citrus-ginger undertones, comes together quickly and is ideal for cooks with little available time. To make the preparation even simpler, the curry paste for this recipe needs to be only coarsely chopped before cooking. For a traditional taste, serve this with Burmese Coconut Rice (page 229).

Curry Paste

2 medium onions, peeled and chopped

2 stalks lemon grass, trimmed and thinly sliced

One 1-inch piece fresh ginger, sliced

2 cloves garlic, peeled and chopped

About $1/4$ cup water

Curry

One 3-pound chicken, cleaned and cut into serving pieces

1 teaspoon ground turmeric

Salt to taste

1 large tomato, chopped

1 teaspoon Roasted Red Chili Powder (page 16) or cayenne pepper

1 teaspoon paprika

1 teaspoon salt

$3/4$ cup vegetable oil

$1^1/2$ cups water

1. To make the curry paste, combine the onions, lemon grass, ginger, and garlic in a blender. Add just enough water to process, and blend to a coarse paste.

2. To make the curry, place the chicken in a large bowl and sprinkle with the turmeric and salt. Rub with the curry paste and layer the tomatoes, chili powder or cayenne pepper, paprika, and salt on top.

3. Heat the oil in a large wok or skillet until medium-hot. Add the chicken mixture, cover, and cook, stirring occasionally, for 10 minutes. Stir in the water. Reduce the heat to medium-low, cover, and cook about 10 minutes more, or until the chicken is tender. Serve hot.

MAKES 4 TO 6 SERVINGS

Lao Chicken Soup with Galangal

The Lao and their Asian neighbors borrow and swap culinary ideas back and forth across their mutual borders. So it is not surprising that this soup from Vasouthep Sananikone is very reminiscent of the Thai Chicken and Coconut Milk Soup (page 56). You may prepare it with coconut milk, but if you wish to make this more authentically Laotian, use water as the liquid instead. This soup comes together quickly and makes a nourishing light supper when served with fruit.

6 cups water or coconut milk

2 pounds chicken legs and thighs,
    with bones

8 shallots, grilled, peeled, and pounded
    (see Note)

2 stalks lemon grass, trimmed, grilled,
    and pounded (see Note)

4 cloves garlic, grilled, peeled, and
    pounded (see Note)

One 2-inch piece galangal, grilled and
    pounded (see Note)

1 bunch scallions, trimmed and
    thinly sliced

6 kaffir lime leaves, thinly sliced

$1/2$ cup fresh lime juice

1 tablespoon fish sauce

4 to 6 fresh red or green chilies,
    thinly sliced

Heat the water or coconut milk in a large saucepan over medium heat until it just begins to boil. Using a sharp cleaver, cut the chicken pieces in half. Add to the saucepan and stir in the shallots, lemon grass, garlic, galangal, scallions, lime leaves, lime juice, and fish sauce, and return to a boil. Reduce the heat to medium-low and cook, until the chicken is tender, 15 to 20 minutes. Garnish with the chilies and serve hot.

MAKES 4 TO 6 SERVINGS

Note: You may grill the shallots, lemon grass, garlic, and galangal over a charcoal fire until browned and smoke-scented. Alternatively, you may broil or pan-roast the ingredients until browned and fragrant. After grilling, broiling, or pan-roasting, pound the ingredients to release their flavors, then add them to the recipe. Pounding is easy even without a mortar and pestle: Lay the grilled ingredients on a flat surface and smack them with the flat side of a meat or Chinese cleaver or other broad-bladed knife.

Lao Grilled Chicken Soup

My Lao friend Bounsou Sananikone reminisces often about her native home, and her memories of this popular soup remain very vivid. "Every year, in the shadow of the shrine of That Luang in Vientiane, situated in the heart of Laos, during three days and three nights of the festival in celebration of the shrine, Lao from all over the country come as pilgrims to worship. . . . Lines of women and young girls are selling foods—sweet rice served with grilled chicken and the famous chicken soup with galangal," she said.

Lao Rice Noodles with Sauce

Khao Poune

Noodles, meat, and vegetables are served together with a rich, nourishing broth in this famous Laotian dish. In the classic method, a cook enriches the broth with any number of ingredients, including a pig's head, pig's fat, and pig's blood; freshwater fish, chicken, or beef; and fresh banana blossoms, picked just for this dish. Westerners may have a hard time finding the fresh blossoms unless they live in a tropical setting or near a large Asian population, so that markets might stock this delicacy. But the canned blossoms, or even shredded cabbage, would do fine. If you like fiery foods, you can, as the Laotians do, turn this into a chilied affair by garnishing the broth with a layer of fresh red chilies, sliced in half lengthwise. Recipes for the dish vary widely, but, explains Bounsou Sananikone from Vientiane, Laos, one ingredient remains constant: fresh rice noodles.

As Ms. Sananikone tells it, the Laotians do not think of khao poune *as a soup or stew, but as noodles served with a rich sauce. "I remember long ago in 1946, at a gathering in Vientiane," she recounts, "and they served* khao poune *near the river. The sauce was very good, made with fish from the river and no coconut milk."*

Seasoning Paste
4 cloves garlic, peeled
4 shallots, peeled and sliced
4 to 6 fresh red chilies
One 1-inch piece galangal
About $1/2$ cup water

Soup
6 cups water
1 pound boneless chicken breast,
   boneless beef roast, boneless pork
   roast, or firm-fleshed fish fillets,
   skin removed, cubed
5 stalks lemon grass, trimmed and
   lightly pounded
2 tablespoons fish sauce
1 tablespoon Lao fish paste (*padek*) or
   Thai or Malaysian shrimp paste, or a
   combination
2 cups coconut milk

1. To make the seasoning paste, combine the garlic, shallots, chilies, and galangal in a blender. Add just enough water to process, and blend until smooth.

2. To make the soup, place the water and meat or fish in a large saucepan and bring to a boil. Stir in the lemon grass, fish sauce, and fish paste and/or shrimp paste. Reduce the heat to medium-low, cover, and cook about 20 minutes, or until the meat or fish is very tender.

3. Remove the meat or fish and lemon grass from the stock. Discard the lemon grass. Pound the meat or fish with a mortar and pestle or mash with a large spoon.

4. Heat 1 cup of the coconut milk in a large wok or saucepan over medium heat until it just begins to boil. Add the seasoning paste, stir well, and cook until the mixture is fragrant and a layer of oil appears on the surface, about 5 minutes. Stir in the pounded or mashed meat or fish and cook for 10 minutes. Strain the stock into the saucepan and stir in the remaining 1 cup coconut milk. Discard the solids. Reduce the heat to low and cook for 10 minutes more.

Accompaniments

¹/₂ **pound rice vermicelli, cooked (see page 302)**

¹/₄ **pound bean sprouts**

6 kaffir lime leaves, thinly sliced

1 cup Thai basil leaves

1 cup fresh mint leaves

1 cup sliced banana flowers or shredded western cabbage

1 cup sliced fresh red chilies

5. To serve, arrange portions of the noodles and bean sprouts in individual soup bowls. Ladle in the hot soup and sprinkle with the lime leaves, basil leaves, mint leaves, banana blossoms or cabbage, and chilies. Alternatively, you may pour the soup into a tureen, place the noodles in a large serving bowl, and arrange the accompaniments on a platter. Place a portion of noodles in each individual serving bowl, ladle a portion of the liquid over the noodles, and pass around the accompaniments. Serve hot.

MAKES 5 OR 6 SERVINGS

Khao Poune

One of the traditional dishes of Laos, *khao poune* is served for festivals, such as weddings, family reunions, and community festivities, as well as at family meals. The name of this dish also refers to the type of rice noodles used in it. In Laos, families used to make their own noodles from soaked and pounded sticky (glutinous) rice that is made into a paste and forced through the holes of a colanderlike utensil. These noodles, arranged on bamboo trays, were also sold fresh in the marketplace.

Thai Chicken in Coconut Milk Soup

Tom Kha Gai

This recipe from two Thai cooks—Khun Satit and Rungnapa Routh—is one of the classics of the Thai table, and it is beloved by anyone who tries it. The galangal—known as Thai ginger—is what gives this soup its incredibly delicate flavor. Of course, combining coconut milk with anything makes for wonderful eating. Busy cooks can rejoice at the simplicity of putting this soup together.

2 cups coconut milk

$1/2$ pound boneless, skinless chicken breast, cut into bite-sized pieces

Ten $1/2$-inch-thick slices galangal

5 fresh red or green chilies, finely minced

3 stalks lemon grass, trimmed, cut into 1-inch pieces, and crushed

3 kaffir lime leaves

3 tablespoons fish sauce

Juice of 2 limes

$1/4$ cup chopped fresh coriander

Bring the coconut milk and chicken to a boil in a large saucepan. Add the galangal, chilies, lemon grass, lime leaves, fish sauce, and lime juice, reduce the heat to low, and cook for 10 minutes. Sprinkle with the coriander before serving.

MAKES 2 TO 3 SERVINGS

Portuguese Saucepan Soup

Macau sits at the edge of Southern China, but it has been under Portuguese rule for many centuries. So it should be no surprise that much Macanese food shows strong European influences. This soup is a fine example of that, since bacon, Portuguese sausage, and French bread are certainly not typical Chinese ingredients. You'll find this a hearty soup, ideal for a light winter's meal. The Macau Tourist Information Board received this recipe from Macau resident Maria de Lourdes Modesto.

1 chicken quarter

1 Portuguese sausage, sliced

$^1/_2$ large onion, peeled and chopped

1 strip bacon, diced

6 cups water

1 sprig parsley, chopped

Salt and freshly ground black pepper
   to taste

4 to 6 slices toasted French bread

Sprigs of mint

1. Combine the chicken, sausage, onion, bacon, water, parsley, salt, and pepper in a large saucepan and bring to a boil. Reduce the heat to medium-low and cook about 30 minutes, or until the chicken is tender. Remove the chicken from the water and set aside. When it is cool enough to handle, remove the meat from the bones and cut into bite-sized pieces. Discard the bones.

2. To serve, line serving dishes or a soup tureen with the bread, add the chicken pieces, and ladle in the soup. Garnish with mint sprigs and serve immediately, before the bread becomes soggy.

MAKES 2 SERVINGS

Lao Curried Chicken

Startlingly hot, this fiery coconut milk–based stew can be tempered by omitting some of the fresh chilies, but chili lovers will adore this concoction as is. What's more, the heat quotient seems to intensify in any leftovers.

As she prepared it one day, Lao cook Vanessa Rathsvongsach said this curry requires several hours for its preparation—but you will find it is worth every moment in the kitchen. She used a commercial curry paste, but you can make your own yellow curry paste if you wish. An adaptable dish, this tastes just fine with beef instead of chicken. And you may make this soupier by adding one or two extra cups of water during the cooking. Although the addition of potatoes turns this into a full meal, you may prefer to serve the stew with rice to buffer the chili heat.

4 cups coconut milk

$^1/_4$ cup Yellow Curry Paste (page 24)

2 large onions, peeled and chopped

4 cloves garlic, peeled and minced

One 3- to 4-pound chicken, cleaned, cut into serving pieces, and skinned

Salt to taste

5 to 6 fresh red or green chilies, halved lengthwise, or 10 whole dried red chilies

2 stalks lemon grass, trimmed, halved lengthwise, and diagonally sliced into 2-inch lengths

3 medium potatoes, peeled and cubed

1 pound long beans or green beans, trimmed and diagonally sliced into 2-inch lengths

3 tablespoons fish sauce

1. Heat 1 cup of the coconut milk in a large saucepan over medium heat until it just begins to boil. Stir in the curry paste, reduce the heat to medium-low, and cook until the mixture is fragrant, about 5 minutes. Stir in the onions and garlic, and cook for 5 minutes more.

2. Meanwhile, remove the breast meat from the bones and cube the meat. Using a sharp cleaver, cut the chicken wings and thighs in half and stir into the curry mixture. Add the breast meat and drumsticks, and stir until covered with the curry paste. (Discard the back and bones or reserve for another use.) Cook for 10 minutes.

3. Stir in the salt and remaining 3 cups coconut milk, and reduce the heat to low. Stir in the chilies and lemon grass, cover, and cook for 10 minutes more. Stir in the potatoes, cover, and cook until the potatoes are soft, about 10 minutes more. Stir in the beans and cook, uncovered, until tender, about 10 minutes more. Just before serving, stir in the fish sauce. Serve hot.

MAKES 4 TO 6 SERVINGS

Crispy Roast Duck Sour Soup

While reminiscing about the upheavals in her Cambodian homeland, Neary Saray remembered fondly some of her favorite dishes, and this soup is one of them. It brings together gamey duck, citrusy lemon grass, and salty fish sauce in an unusual and distinctive dish. Some Westerners may find fermented fish paste somewhat pungent, so feel free to omit it. Mrs. Saray chops the duck into bite-sized pieces, bones and all, but I just took the meat off the bones and cubed it.

Seasoning Paste

5 stalks lemon grass, trimmed and
    thinly sliced
5 to 6 dried red chilies, soaked in hot
    water for 20 minutes and seeded
One 2-inch piece galangal,
    thinly sliced
One 1-inch piece turmeric root,
    thinly sliced
About $1/2$ cup water

Soup

2 tablespoons vegetable oil
One 4- to 5-pound duck, roasted
    (see Note) and cooled
7 shallots, roasted and peeled
    (see page 8)
$1/4$ cup Cambodian fish paste (*prahok*)
Sugar to taste
3 tablespoons tamarind juice
Fish sauce to taste
$2^1/2$ cups water

Garnishes

4 kaffir lime leaves, thinly sliced
4 to 5 fresh red chilies, thinly sliced
1 cup fresh coriander leaves

1. To make the seasoning paste, combine the lemon grass, chilies, galangal, and turmeric in a blender. Add just enough water to process, and blend until smooth.

2. To make the soup, heat the oil in a large wok or saucepan over medium heat. Add the seasoning paste and cook, stirring, about 5 minutes, or until fragrant.

3. Meanwhile, remove the cooled meat from the bones and cut into bite-sized pieces. Stir the duck meat, shallots, fish paste, sugar, tamarind juice, and fish sauce into the paste. Add enough water to cover, and bring to a boil. Reduce the heat to medium-low and cook for 20 minutes. Stir in the $2^1/2$ cups water and cook until it comes to a boil. Sprinkle with the garnishes and serve hot.

MAKES 3 TO 4 SERVINGS

Note: To roast the duck, preheat the oven to 350°F. Remove the giblets and extra fat. Prick the skin all over with a fork and sprinkle with salt. Place the duck, breast side up, on a rack in a roasting pan. Cook until the skin is brown and crisp, about 30 minutes per pound.

Cambodian Chicken Curry

In the kitchen of a Cambodian monastery in Maryland, the cook who provided this recipe, Hien Vat-Ho, scurried around putting this hearty dish together. As she worked, she explained that duck is a fine substitute for the chicken, but that it makes a richer, costlier meal. Because she prefers a higher ratio of vegetables to meat, Hien Vat-Ho often uses five pounds of potatoes and two pounds of onions instead of the quantities below, but she also adjusts the amount of liquid she uses to compensate for the extra ingredients. To speed your preparation time along, buy your favorite chicken parts instead of a whole bird. Rice is a typical accompaniment, but you may also serve bread for dunking in the sauce. While there are many types of curry powder on an Asian grocer's shelf, she uses the Vietnamese Golden Bell blend.

^{1}/$_4$ cup vegetable oil

One 5-pound chicken, cleaned and cut
   into serving pieces

3 cups coconut milk

2 to 3 cups Thai Red Curry Paste
   (page 25)

5 tablespoons fish sauce

2 tablespoons sugar

1 tablespoon salt

1 teaspoon Thai or Malaysian
   shrimp paste

Pinch of MSG (optional)

4 stalks lemon grass, trimmed and
   root ends smashed

20 curry leaves

1 tablespoon curry powder

1 cup Basic Chicken Stock (page 19)
   or water, or more if needed

6 medium potatoes, peeled
   and quartered

4 onions, peeled and sliced

1. Heat the oil in a large wok or saucepan over medium heat. Add the chicken and cook 15 to 20 minutes, or until golden on all sides. Remove from the pan and set aside. Increase the heat to medium-high and stir in 1 cup of the coconut milk. Bring to a boil and cook, stirring often, until a layer of oil appears on the surface, 5 to 10 minutes.

2. Stir in the curry paste, fish sauce, sugar, salt, shrimp paste, and MSG if using. Then stir in the lemon grass, curry leaves, and curry powder, and cook for 5 minutes more. Stir in the remaining 2 cups coconut milk and the stock, and cook for 10 minutes. (Add more stock if the curry seems too thick.) Reduce the heat to medium-low and add the chicken, potatoes, and onions. Cook until the vegetables are tender, or for about 15 minutes. Remove the surface oil before serving. Serve hot.

MAKES 4 TO 6 SERVINGS

Vietnamese Lime Duck Soup

A bowl of this rich soup, with its intriguing, sourish flavor, served with rice and vegetables makes a satisfying meal. What gives this dish its distinctive tang is a product known as preserved lime. Such limes, explains my Vietnamese friend David Quang are whole limes that have been pickled in water and salt for six months to one year. The limes are ready for use when the skins have turned brown and the flesh has become very tender. But since these limes are not readily available in the United States, you may use Chinese preserved plums instead.

Depending on the number of people you are serving, you may use a whole or half duck; but since duck is not very meaty, a whole duck makes more sense. Serve the clear broth and pass the duck separately, either on or off the bones. Accompany it with the dunking sauce; for a different taste, offer a chili sauce or soy sauce for dunking.

One 5- to 6-pound duck, cleaned

8 cups water

One 12-ounce jar preserved
(pickled) plums

1/2 cup preserved (pickled) plum liquid

5 tablespoons fish sauce

5 tablespoons white vinegar

2 tablespoons minced fresh ginger

1. Bring a large stockpot of water to a boil. Add the duck and cook until the juices are no longer pink, about 10 minutes. Remove the duck, wash thoroughly under cold running water, and set aside. Discard the water in the stockpot.

2. Bring the 8 cups water to a boil. Add the duck, preserved plums, and plum liquid. Reduce the heat to low and cook until the duck is tender, about 1 hour. Remove the duck from the broth and set aside until it is cool enough to handle.

3. Meanwhile, make the sauce by whisking together the fish sauce, vinegar, and ginger. Cut the duck into serving pieces and serve with the broth and sauce alongside.

MAKES 4 TO 6 SERVINGS

Savory Duck Stew with Sticky Rice

In Vietnam, this stew has been traditionally served for such celebratory occasions as holidays, weddings, and other festive banquets. It also calls for that very special ingredient, sticky (glutinous or sweet) rice, a grain with its own very distinctive sweet-nutty flavor. Do not substitute regular long-grain rice, because the effect will not be the same.

The cook who provided this recipe, Helene Sze McCarthy, offers some useful preparation tips: Use a very large wok or saucepan for frying the whole, and unwieldy, duck. To gain extra time on the day you plan to serve this, you may prepare the duck up to one week in advance, refrigerate it, and reheat it in the oven or a large steamer. Do not add the soy sauce until after the first hour of stewing, or the duck will lose its natural sweet flavor. And as for eating this meal, she warns that the rice stuffing remains so hot long after serving the duck that it can burn your tongue.

4 cups vegetable oil, or more if needed

5 tablespoons ground pork

$^1/_4$ cup chopped onions

2 to 2$^1/_4$ cups sticky (glutinous) rice, cooked (see page 4)

3 mushrooms, rinsed and thinly sliced

3 dried Chinese mushrooms, soaked in hot water for 20 minutes, stems removed, cut into squares

4 scallions, trimmed and thinly sliced, plus 1 bunch scallions, trimmed

6 tablespoons chopped water chestnuts

Salt to taste

Sugar to taste

One 5- to 6-pound duck, cleaned, patted dry, and salted inside and out

1 large onion, unpeeled, charred (see Note on page 66)

2 tablespoons soy sauce, or more to taste

1. Heat $^1/_4$ cup of the oil in a large wok or skillet over medium heat. Add the pork and cook, stirring, until no longer pink, about 2 minutes. Add the onions and cook, stirring, about 3 minutes, or until golden. Transfer to paper towels to drain.

2. Combine the rice, mushrooms, dried mushrooms, sliced scallions, water chestnuts, pork, and fried onions in a large bowl. Stir in the salt and sugar.

3. Hold the duck with the open cavity facing upward and spoon the rice mixture into the cavity. When the cavity is full, use a skewer to close it.

4. Heat the remaining 3$^3/_4$ cups oil in a very large wok or saucepan over medium heat. Add the duck and cook until the skin is browned on all sides, about 20 minutes. (Use large tongs to turn the duck.)

5. Place the bunch of scallions on the bottom of a large roasting pan with high sides and set the duck on top. (The scallions provide a "bed" for the duck to prevent it from burning.) Add enough water to cover. Wrap the charred onion in cheesecloth and place it in the water with the duck. Cook over medium-low heat until at least half the water has evaporated, about 45 minutes. Stir in the soy sauce. Rotate the duck, taking care not to disturb the stuffing; reduce the heat to low; and cook, uncovered, until tender, about 1 hour.

6. Transfer the duck to a serving platter. Alternatively, set the duck aside to cool before wrapping in foil if you plan to reheat and serve it at a later time. Serve hot with the soy stock alongside.

MAKES 4 TO 6 SERVINGS

"Salty" Bean Curd Chicken

Fermented (also known as preserved or "salty") bean curd, or tofu, gives this dish its flavor, and there is nothing else on the market quite like it. Resembling Roquefort cheese in its pungency, fermented bean curd might be potent eaten alone, but here sugar cuts any sourness and the result is pleasing though unusual. For a sweeter flavor, stir up to 3 more tablespoons of sugar into the finished dish. Because it is a popular Chinese and Thai ingredient, fermented bean curd is readily available in Asian markets; select the type without chilies added. Technically, says the Chinese-Vietnamese cook Helene Sze McCarthy, this is really a Chinese recipe, but the dish is served and enjoyed in Vietnam, too. It's easy to prepare and should be served hot over steamed rice.

6 pieces fermented bean curd, each
    about 1-inch square

2 to 8 tablespoons sugar, or to taste

$\frac{1}{2}$ cup vegetable oil

One 4- to 5-pound chicken, cleaned
    and cut into serving pieces

1 head garlic, cloves separated
    and peeled

2 cups water

4 dried Chinese mushrooms or shiitake
    mushrooms, soaked in hot water for
    20 minutes, stems removed, chopped

1 cup bamboo shoots

1 onion, peeled and thinly sliced

1. Combine the bean curd and sugar in a bowl and stir to form a paste.

2. Heat the oil in a large wok or skillet over medium heat. Add the chicken and cook, turning occasionally, about 20 minutes, or until golden. Stir in the garlic just before the chicken is finished cooking so the cloves do not burn. Remove from the heat.

3. Pour the water into a large saucepan and stir in the bean curd–sugar paste. Transfer the chicken pieces and garlic to the pan and stir in the mushrooms, bamboo shoots, and onion. Bring the water to a boil and cook over medium-high heat about 15 minutes, or until the chicken is tender. Serve hot.

MAKES 4 TO 6 SERVINGS

Burmese Chicken Curry, Family-Style

This is a simple family dish, the recipe for which was given to me over dinner in the home of a Bahá'í family in Rangoon, Burma. The wife had prepared a truly typical Burmese meal—and, I am afraid, spent her family's weekly budget to feed my American friend and me. Her husband, Tinn Shwe, sat with us, while the rest of the family scurried back and forth bringing us each successive dish. We ate by candlelight seated on the floor, and because there was a local power outage, the children fanned us energetically to counter the intense heat and humidity. The recipe has my suggested quantities in parentheses, since the wife never measures and couldn't give me any amounts:

"Cut the meat (about 2 pounds chicken parts with bones) to the size you want. Pound together garlic (2 or 3 cloves, peeled), onions (2 whole onions, peeled and cubed), ginger (one 1-inch piece), and red chili powder [Roasted Red Chili Powder (page 16) or cayenne pepper] (about 1 tablespoon). Fry this mixture with oil (about ⅓ cup), and stir in ground turmeric (2 teaspoons). Add the meat. Add a little water, but not too much. As you cook, add more water, and if you want the curry to cook more quickly, add a pinch of sugar."

"The curry will be as beautiful as my daughter," said Tinn Shwe.

Vietnamese Curry Chicken

The Vietnamese have no tradition of curries, says the cook Helene Sze McCarthy, and she thought this dish must have come from the Thais. But the Indians who once lived in South Vietnam may have been the real source for this curry inspiration. The Vietnamese, however, have taken the curry idea one step further by pairing white potatoes (often an Indian curry staple) with sweet potatoes. This combination makes for a very flavorful meal.

This version also calls for roasting whole onions over a direct flame—an outdoor fire or the gas burner of a stove—or under an oven broiler. Helene Sze McCarthy learned both traditional Vietnamese and French cooking techniques as a young girl in Hue, in central Vietnam, and she remembers French nuns teaching this roasting technique. Such cooking brings out the natural sugars in onions and softens their delicate flesh.

The dish is rather soupy, and the Vietnamese enjoy sopping up the extra liquid with chunks of bread. Rather than rice, an ideal accompaniment is rice vermicelli. Serve this curry with several separate condiment dishes—one with a combination of salt and pepper, one with lemon and lime slices, and one with chili sauce.

One 3- to 4-pound chicken, cleaned
   and cut into serving pieces
Sprinkle of sugar
6 tablespoons vegetable oil
6 cloves garlic, peeled and chopped
3 tablespoons Indian curry powder
One 4-inch piece fresh ginger, chopped
3 carrots, peeled and sliced
5 cups water
3 sweet potatoes, peeled and cubed
2 baking potatoes, peeled and cubed
3 large onions, unpeeled, charred
   (see Note)
Salt to taste
Fish sauce to taste

Accompaniments

Salt and freshly ground black pepper
   to taste
8 to 12 lemon and lime slices
1/4 cup Vietnamese chili sauce,
   preferably the chunky Tuong
   Ot Toi Viet-Nam brand

1. Sprinkle the chicken with sugar. Heat the oil in a large saucepan over medium heat. Add the garlic and cook, stirring, about 1 minute, or until golden. Stir in the curry powder and add the chicken, ginger, and carrots. Cook, stirring often, for 5 minutes. Add the water, reduce the heat to medium-low, and cook about 15 minutes, or until the chicken is tender. Stir in the sweet potatoes and potatoes, cover, and cook until the potatoes are tender, 10 to 15 minutes more.

2. Chop the charred onions and stir into the curry along with the salt and fish sauce. Cook for 5 minutes more. Arrange the accompaniments in individual bowls and serve alongside the curry.

MAKES 4 TO 6 SERVINGS

Note: To char the onions, cook them over a direct flame or under a broiler until the skins blacken and the interiors soften. Remove from the heat. When they are cool enough to handle, rinse under cold running water and wash away and discard the charred skins.

Spicy Curry Noodles with Chicken

This Malaysian curry recipe bears both the traditional Chinese and Malaysian traits characteristic of Nyonya-style cooking, a style that the Malaysian wives of Chinese husbands adapted to please the palates of both partners in the marriage. The Nyonya cook, Goh Ewe-Swee, had just returned to the United States from a trip to her Malaysian home in Penang when she prepared this dish for me. For neater presentation, you'll want to use a good firm tofu that will stand up to the long cooking time.

Curry Paste

8 dried red chilies, soaked in hot water
    for 20 minutes and seeded
8 shallots, peeled and sliced
4 cloves garlic, peeled
1 stalk lemon grass, trimmed and
    thinly sliced
One 1-inch piece fresh ginger
One 1-inch piece galangal
$^1/_2$ teaspoon ground turmeric
About $^1/_2$ cup water

Curry

$^1/_2$ cup vegetable oil
One 3- to 4-pound chicken, with
    bones, cleaned and cut into small
    serving pieces
4 cups Basic Chicken Stock (page 19)
$^1/_2$ pound firm tofu, cubed
2 cups coconut milk
1 teaspoon salt
1 teaspoon sugar

Accompaniments

1 pound fresh Chinese egg noodles,
    cooked (see page 303)
$^1/_2$ pound firm tofu, cubed
$^1/_4$ pound bean sprouts, blanched in
    boiling water for 1 minute
$^1/_4$ pound green beans, trimmed and
    blanched in boiling water for 2 minutes
1 cup mint leaves

1. To make the curry paste, combine the chilies, shallots, garlic, lemon grass, ginger, galangal, and turmeric in a blender. Add just enough water to process, and blend until smooth.

2. To make the curry, heat the oil in a large saucepan over medium heat. Add the curry paste and cook, stirring, about 5 minutes, or until fragrant. Add the chicken and cook, stirring, 3 to 5 minutes, or until golden. Stir in the stock and bring to a boil. Stir in the tofu, coconut milk, salt, and sugar. Reduce the heat to low and cook until the chicken is tender, about 30 minutes.

3. To serve, place a portion of noodles into individual bowls and layer each serving with tofu, bean sprouts, green beans, and mint leaves. Ladle a portion of the chicken curry over the noodles. Serve hot.

MAKES 4 TO 6 SERVINGS

Lao Chicken and Vegetable Stew

O or Or

Often when I have visited with my Lao friend Bounsou Sananikone, she has talked about a robust Laotian dish that sounded like "auk" or "au." Apparently this is as much a Lao favorite as chicken noodle soup is in Western homes, although this dish is certainly more exotic to a Westerner. For one thing, it calls for some rather unusual vegetables, including strips of rattan—something the Lao love for its bitterness—and the flowery parts of Chinese bok choy. You may also use Asian pumpkin, young pumpkin leaves, and long beans as substitutes.

Bounsou Sananikone arranged for another Laotian, Phetsaphone Phanthavone, to teach me this dish, using the traditional Lao mortar and pestle for pounding the seasoning ingredients into a paste. Phetsaphone Phanthavone gathered her ingredients, which included the rattan strips, and began the cooking. She had dried rattan strips from Laos, but most Westerners will be able to find only canned rattan— an acceptable substitute. A traditional recipe calls for phak itu lao *leaves, which have a slight citrusy taste and are, it seems, related to the more familiar Thai basil. Since the former are difficult to find in the West, use Thai basil instead. As Phetsaphone Phanthavone seasoned her soup, she kept pouring in the fish sauce to suit her own palate; so if you want a saltier taste than the recipe provides, just add more fish sauce.*

Seasoning Paste

4 to 6 fresh red chilies

4 to 6 shallots, peeled

1 stalk lemon grass, trimmed and thinly sliced

2 cloves garlic, peeled

About ¹/₂ cup water

Soup

3 tablespoons vegetable oil

2 pounds chicken pieces (wings, thighs, and breasts), with bones, cut into small serving pieces

2 kaffir lime leaves

One 1-inch piece galangal, thinly sliced

1 tablespoon Lao fish paste (*padek*)

1 tablepoon fish sauce

¹/₄ cup glutinous rice flour mixed with enough water to make a thin paste

¹/₄ cup water

1. To make the seasoning paste, combine the chilies, shallots, lemon grass, and garlic in a blender. Add just enough water to process, and grind to a coarse paste.

2. To make the soup, heat the oil in a large wok or saucepan over medium heat. Add the seasoning paste and cook, stirring, about 5 minutes, until fragrant. Add the chicken and cook, 4 to 5 minutes, or until just golden. Stir in enough water to cover and add the lime leaves, galangal, fish paste, and fish sauce. Bring to a boil, cover, and cook for 10 minutes.

5 golf-ball-sized Thai eggplants, each
    sliced into 6 pieces

1 cup Thai pea eggplants

$^{1}/_{2}$ cup chopped fresh dill

3 scallions, trimmed and thinly sliced

4 sprigs Thai basil

Salt to taste

1 cup chili leaves (optional)

One 15-ounce can rattan, drained and
    rinsed

Pinch of MSG (optional)

3. Meanwhile, stir 3 tablespoons of the rice flour paste with $^{1}/_{4}$ cup water. Let the rice sediment sink to the bottom and spoon about 2 tablespoons of the rice water into the soup. Discard the remainder. Stir in the eggplants, dill, scallions, basil, and salt. Then stir in the chili leaves, rattan, and MSG if using. Return to a boil and cook, uncovered, until the chicken is tender, about 10 minutes. Serve hot.

MAKES 4 TO 6 SERVINGS

Yellow Curry with Chicken

Gaeng Karee Gai

From southern Thailand, this mild chicken curry recipe from restaurant owner Nick Srisawat, of the Tara Thai restaurants in the Washington, D.C., metropolitan area, goes well with sliced cucumbers, plain or prepared as the popular salad that accompanies the Thai version of grilled satay (see Note).

3 tablespoons vegetable oil

1/2 cup Yellow Curry Paste (page 24)

3 1/2 cups coconut milk

4 large boneless chicken breast halves, sliced across the grain into 1/2 -inch-thick strips

1/2 pound small boiling potatoes, peeled and halved

1/2 cup pearl onions, peeled

3 tablespoons fish sauce

1 tablespoon palm sugar or dark brown sugar, or more to taste

1. Heat the oil in a large wok or skillet over medium heat. Add the curry paste, reduce the heat to medium-low, and cook until fragrant, about 5 minutes. Add 3/4 cup of the coconut milk and stir until well blended.

2. Add the chicken, increase the heat to medium, and cook, stirring, until the chicken is fully coated with the curry paste. Stir in the potatoes, onions, and remaining 2 3/4 cups coconut milk. Cook, stirring occasionally, 20 to 25 minutes, or until the potatoes and onions are tender. Stir in the fish sauce and sugar, and serve hot.

MAKES 4 TO 6 SERVINGS

Note: My Thai friend Nittaya Maphungphong gave me the following cucmber salad recipe. To make this simple salad, peel, quarter, and thinly slice 3 cucumbers. Place them in a bowl and add 4 thinly sliced fresh red chilies and 3 thinly sliced shallots. In a small saucepan over medium heat, cook 3/4 cup white vinegar and 3/4 cup sugar until the sugar is dissolved. Stir in a pinch of salt and remove from the heat. When cool, pour over the cucumbers and serve. The salad may be refrigerated for up to 3 days.

Singaporean-Malay Chicken Curry

Energetic Aziza Ali broke all the local rules about women becoming restaurant chefs, and she now owns and runs one of Singapore's most successful eateries, Aziza's. Because she is Malaysian herself, Aziza Ali specializes in the zesty and often fiery foods of Malaysia. And she proves with this dish—here smoothed with coconut milk and sweetened with toasted coconut shreds—that there can be infinite variations on the chicken-curry theme. You can intensify the chili sting by adding as many green chilies as you can tolerate and by increasing the amount of chili paste. Serve with Singaporean Dal Rice (page 228) for a satisfying meal.

Curry Paste

¹/₂ cup shredded unsweetened coconut, toasted until golden

2 large onions, peeled and cut into large pieces

6 cloves garlic, peeled

One ¹/₂-inch piece fresh ginger

About ¹/₂ cup water

Curry

3 tablespoons vegetable oil

3 tablespoons Malaysian Meat or Chicken Curry Powder (page 31)

One 1-inch piece cinnamon stick

2 star anise

5 green cardamom pods

1 to 2 teaspoons Indonesian chili paste (*sambal oelek*), or more to taste

2 cups coconut milk

¹/₂ cup tamarind juice

One 4- to 5-pound chicken, cleaned and cut into serving pieces

3 green chilies, halved lengthwise, or more to taste

5 okra, halved lengthwise

3 large tomatoes, halved

Salt to taste

Sugar to taste

1 cup mint leaves

1. To make the curry paste, place the toasted coconut in a blender and grind until it is very fine and the oil begins to separate from the coconut shreds, 1 to 2 minutes. Add the onions, garlic, ginger, and just enough water to process, and blend until smooth.

2. To make the curry, heat the oil in a large wok or skillet over medium heat. Add the curry paste and cook, stirring, about 5 minutes, until fragrant. Stir in the curry powder, cinnamon, star anise, cardamom, and chili paste, and cook, stirring, 2 to 3 minutes, until fragrant. Stir in the coconut milk, tamarind juice, and chicken. Reduce the heat to medium-low and cook for 20 minutes. Stir in the chilies, okra, tomatoes, salt, and sugar, and cook until the chicken and vegetables are tender, about 15 minutes more. Stir in the mint leaves and cook for another 5 minutes. Remove and discard the star anise. Serve hot or at room temperature.

MAKES 4 TO 6 SERVINGS

Malaysian Chicken Soup

From the recipe files of the Parkroyal Hotel in Malaysia's capital city, Kuala Lumpur, this Malaysian chicken soup offers a medley of spices in a subtle and refreshing combination that's just as restoring as a bowl of chicken soup with rice. This is a good way to use up leftover roasted chicken. Of course, your chicken stock can be made ahead, frozen, and then thawed for easy preparation.

3 tablespoons vegetable oil

3 shallots, peeled and sliced

$^1/_2$ cup sliced fresh ginger

$^1/_4$ cup sliced garlic

3 star anise

3 cinnamon sticks

2 tablespoons Malaysian Soup Spices
   (page 32)

3 quarts Basic Chicken Stock
   (page 19)

$1^1/_2$ pounds boneless chicken breasts,
   cubed

Salt and freshly ground black pepper
   to taste

Pinch of MSG (optional)

Garnishes

1 cup chopped scallions

1 cup Fried Shallots (page 17)

1. Heat the oil in a large stockpot over medium heat. Add the shallots, ginger, garlic, star anise, cinnamon, and soup spices, and cook, stirring, about 5 minutes, or until fragrant.

2. Stir in the stock and chicken, and bring to a boil. Reduce the heat to medium-low and cook until the chicken is cooked through, about 15 minutes. Stir in the salt, pepper, and MSG if using. Ladle into individual soup bowls, and garnish each serving with a sprinkle of scallions and fried shallots.

MAKES 4 TO 6 SERVINGS

Stewed Chicken in Coconut Milk and Fresh Turmeric

Pungent and fiery, yet sweetened by the coconut milk, this Malaysian chicken dish is delicious served with rice and leafy greens. Its dramatic golden color comes from the use of fresh turmeric, called for by the Parkroyal Hotel chefs in Kuala Lumpur. Fresh turmeric is a rare commodity in the United States, but fortunately many Asian markets now stock whole turmeric in their freezer case. Should you not find it, substitute the ground turmeric as directed. To add the chili heat, you may use the Indonesian sambal oelek, *a jarred chili paste available in most Asian markets.*

Seasoning Paste

4 stalks lemon grass, trimmed
    and sliced
5 shallots, peeled
6 to 8 cloves garlic, peeled
One 3-inch piece fresh ginger, sliced
One 4-inch piece galangal,
    thinly sliced
1/3 cup macadamia nuts or candlenuts
1/3 cup chopped fresh or frozen
    turmeric root or 1 tablespoon
    ground turmeric
About 1/2 cup water

Stew

1/2 cup vegetable oil
1/4 cup Indonesian chili paste
    (*sambal oelek*)
2 cups coconut milk
1/2 cup tamarind juice
2 1/2 tablespoons sugar
1 teaspoon ground cumin
1 teaspoon fennel seeds
Salt to taste
Pinch of MSG (optional)
One 4- to 5-pound chicken, cleaned
    and cut into serving pieces
2 turmeric leaves, sliced (optional)

1. To make the seasoning paste, combine the lemon grass, shallots, garlic, ginger, galangal, nuts, and turmeric in a blender. Add just enough water to process, and blend until smooth.

2. To make the stew, heat the oil in a large wok or saucepan over medium heat. Add the seasoning paste and cook, stirring, about 5 minutes, or until fragrant. Add the chili paste and cook, stirring, until well blended, about 3 minutes. Stir in the coconut milk, tamarind juice, sugar, cumin, fennel seeds, salt, and MSG if using. Add the chicken, reduce the heat to medium-low, and cook, uncovered, until the chicken is tender, 30 to 40 minutes. Just a few minutes before the chicken is fully cooked, stir in the sliced turmeric leaves if using. Serve hot.

MAKES 4 TO 6 SERVINGS

Crispy Duck and Noodle Soup

This Thai soup means real comfort, combining a rich broth, crisped duck, slippery, fresh rice noodles (the wide, flat type), crunchy veggies—and as many pickled green chilies as one can tolerate (see Note). The cook who provided this recipe, Muttika Gladson, suggests a time-saving step: Poach the duck a day in advance, wrap it in foil, and refrigerate it until you are ready to crisp-fry the meat.

1½ cups fresh coriander leaves and
    roots, rinsed

1 stalk celery

2 tablespoons black peppercorns

2 tablespoons soy sauce

2 tablespoons fish sauce

Pinch of sugar

6 cups water

One 4- to 5-pound duck, cleaned

1 cup tapioca flour

3 cups vegetable oil

½ pound fresh wide rice noodles,
    rinsed, or ¼ pound dried rice stick
    noodles, soaked in hot water for
    15 minutes

1 bunch scallions, trimmed and
    thinly sliced

½ pound bean sprouts, blanched in
    boiling water for 1 minute

1 cup fresh coriander leaves

2 tablespoons Garlic Oil (page 16)

1. Combine the coriander, celery, peppercorns, soy sauce, fish sauce, and sugar in a large stockpot. Stir in the water and bring to a boil. Add the duck, gizzards and all. Reduce the heat to medium-low, cover, and cook until the duck is tender, 2 to 3 hours. Transfer the duck to a colander to drain and cool.

2. Meanwhile, strain the broth and discard the gizzards. Return the broth to the stockpot. When it is cool, split the duck and remove the breast meat from the bones. Slice the duck breast across the grain into 1-inch-wide strips. Moisten the meat by dipping it in the broth and dredge with the tapioca flour.

3. Heat the oil in a large wok or saucepan over medium-high heat. Add the duck meat and deep-fry until crisp, about 3 minutes, or until crispy. Transfer to paper towels to drain.

4. Meanwhile, heat the broth until it comes to a simmer. Hold the noodles with tongs and dip in the hot liquid for 45 to 60 seconds. Transfer to a plate.

5. Fill individual soup bowls or a large tureen with the hot broth. Add the scallions, bean sprouts, and coriander. Place the noodles on top and arrange the meat on the noodles. Sprinkle the soup with garlic oil and serve immediately.

MAKES 4 TO 6 SERVINGS

Note: To make pickled green chilies, slice as many green chilies as you wish, cover them with white vinegar, and stir in a pinch of salt. Serve immediately or, for a more developed flavor, let marinate overnight.

Red Curry with Roast Duck

Gaeng Ped Yang

This luscious duck dish seems to be a classic at the Thai table, for it is immensely popular and a sensational combination of flavors and heat. For duck lovers, this dish is a must. For convenience's sake, Nick Srisawat, owner of the Tara Thai restaurants in the Washington, D.C., metropolitan area, suggests buying a pre-roasted duck from a Chinese market or contacting a local Chinese restaurant for an already roasted duck.

$1/2$ cup Thai Red Curry Paste
  (page 25)

2 cups coconut milk

One 5- to 6-pound roast duck
  (see Note on page 59), boned
  and cut across the grain into
  1-inch-wide strips

10 cherry tomatoes

$1/2$ cup cubed fresh pineapple

$1/2$ cup Thai basil leaves

$1/4$ cup seedless green grapes

4 kaffir lime leaves, shredded

$1/2$ teaspoon salt

1 teaspoon palm sugar or dark
  brown sugar

$1/4$ cup fish sauce

Heat a large wok or saucepan over medium heat. Reduce the heat to medium-low, add $1/2$ cup of the curry paste, and cook, stirring, until fragrant, about 5 minutes. Stir in $3/4$ cup of the coconut milk until well blended. Stir in the duck, the remaining $1\,1/4$ cups coconut milk, and the tomatoes, pineapple, basil, grapes, lime leaves, salt, sugar, and fish sauce. Cook until the duck is heated through and the curry thickens slightly, about 15 minutes more. Serve hot.

MAKES 4 TO 6 SERVINGS

Fiery Green Curry with Roast Duck

Gaeng Khiew Waan Ped Yang

One of the staples of the Thai curry kitchen is a green curry based on green chilies. Although roasted duck is classically served with a red curry paste, this dramatic dish—possibly an invention of Sarnsern Gajaseni of The Thai Cooking School at The Oriental, Bangkok—pairs duck with green curry for breathtaking results. Sarnsern Gajaseni recommends using 25 Thai prig khee nu *(bird's eye) chilies, a quantity that many Westerners will find too hot, so feel free to use fewer chilies. Tiny bird's eye chilies are available at most Asian markets, but you may substitute other hot green chilies if you wish. He also calls for another chili variety called* prig chee far *(Thai finger hot) for garnish. Dark brown sugar may be substituted for the palm sugar. See page 11 to roast seeds and page 6 for information about coconut milk.*

Curry Paste
25 green chilies

5 shallots, peeled

1 stalk lemon grass, trimmed and sliced

3 cloves garlic, peeled

7 very thin slices galangal

1 teaspoon chopped kaffir lime rind

1 teaspoon chopped coriander root

1 teaspoon Thai or Malaysian
   shrimp paste

1/2 teaspoon coriander seeds, roasted

1/2 teaspoon cumin seeds, roasted

About 1/2 cup coconut milk

Curry
1 cup thick coconut milk

1 teaspoon palm sugar

2 cups sliced roasted duck breast (with
   skin, sliced across the grain), see Note

2 1/2 cups thin coconut milk

3 to 4 tablespoons fish sauce

3 tablespoons green peppercorns,
   preferably fresh (optional)

Garnishes
5 to 7 kaffir lime leaves, shredded

10 fresh red chilies, thinly sliced

1 cup Thai basil leaves

1. To make the curry paste, combine the chilies, shallots, lemon grass, garlic, galangal, lime rind, coriander root, shrimp paste, coriander seeds, and cumin seeds in a blender. Add enough coconut milk to process and blend until smooth.

2. To make the curry, heat the thick coconut milk over medium heat and bring it to a boil. Stir in the curry paste and cook, stirring occasionally, about 15 minutes, or until thickened and fragrant. Stir in the sugar. Add the duck and, stirring constantly, gradually add the thin coconut milk, fish sauce, and peppercorns. Reduce the heat to medium-low and cook, stirring occasionally, for 10 minutes more. Either stir in the garnishes or sprinkle them on top before serving. Serve hot.

MAKES 4 TO 6 SERVINGS

Note: For the duck breast meat, place one whole boneless duck breast (with skin) on a baking sheet on the middle rack under a preheated broiler. Cook until the skin is crisp and the juices are no longer pink, 7 to 10 minutes per side.

Potato Pancakes

Perkadel

As Indonesian food expert Sri Owen wrote in her book about Indonesian cooking, these potato pancakes may have originated with the Dutch who settled in Indonesia many years ago, but their flavor is reminiscent of American corned beef hash. They are now a common accompaniment to many Indonesian meals, enjoyed either as a garnish for soups, as in Indonesian Chicken Soup (page 78), or with various rice dishes. They are equally good hot or cold. For this version, Mrs. Hanief Djohan fried the potato quarters before mashing them, but you could probably boil the potatoes instead.

3 cups vegetable oil

6 large potatoes, peeled and quartered

1 cup minced corned beef

2 large eggs, lightly beaten

3 tablespoons minced scallions

1 tablespoon Fried Shallots (page 17)

Salt and ground white pepper to taste

1. Heat the oil in a large wok or saucepan over medium heat. Add the potatoes and cook, turning often, about 20 minutes, or until light golden and soft. Transfer to paper towels to drain and cool. Reserve the oil.

2. When cool enough to handle, mash the potatoes in a large bowl. Stir in the corned beef, eggs, scallions, shallots, salt, and pepper until thoroughly mixed.

3. Reheat the oil. Using your hands or two large spoons, shape the mixture into 3-inch-long oval pancakes. Add the pancakes and cook, 5 to 6 minutes per slide, until golden and crisp on both sides. Transfer to paper towels to drain.

MAKES ABOUT 40 PANCAKES; 4 TO 6 SERVINGS

Indonesian Chicken Soup

Soto Ayam

Most Indonesians would agree that a bowl of Indonesian soto ayam, *or chicken soup, makes a satisfying meal, since this is one of their national favorites. It's a versatile dish that serves well as a solo first course or, as in this version, the entire meal. When the Hanief Djohan family from Jakarta prepared this one winter's day in Washington, D.C., its warmth cheered everyone at the table. Yet Indonesia is hardly a cold country, and* soto ayam *is just as welcome in the tropics.*

The soup is customarily served with a type of potato pancake called perkadel *(see Potato Pancakes, page 77), fortified with a variety of vegetable accompaniments, and garnished with the ubiquitous puffy, crisp Indonesian shrimp crackers.*

Seasoning Paste

4 large shallots, peeled and quartered
3 cloves garlic, peeled
4 macadamia nuts or candlenuts
One 1-inch piece fresh ginger
One 1/2-inch piece galangal
About 1/2 cup coconut milk

Soup

One 3- to 4-pound chicken, cleaned
  and cut into serving pieces, or
  2 whole chicken breasts, with bones
3 quarts water
3 tablespoons plus 3 cups vegetable oil
1/2 teaspoon ground turmeric
1 stalk lemon grass, trimmed and stem
  end crushed
3 Indonesian or Western bay leaves
2 teaspoons salt, or to taste
1 teaspoon freshly ground
  white pepper
1/2 cup coconut milk

1. To make the seasoning paste, combine the shallots, garlic, nuts, ginger, and galangal in a blender. Add just enough coconut milk to process, and blend until smooth.

2. To make the soup, place the chicken and water in a stockpot and bring to a boil. Reduce the heat to medium-low and cook until the chicken is tender, about 30 minutes. Remove the chicken from the broth and set aside to cool.

3. While the soup is cooking, heat 3 tablespoons of the oil in a large skillet over medium heat. Add the seasoning paste and cook, stirring, about 5 minutes, or until fragrant. Stir in the turmeric, lemon grass, bay leaves, salt, and pepper, and cook, stirring, for 5 minutes more. Stir in the coconut milk and cook, stirring often, until the mixture comes to a boil. Cover and cook for 10 minutes. Reduce the heat to medium-low and cook, uncovered, for 10 minutes more.

4. Meanwhile, heat the remaining 3 cups oil in a large wok or saucepan and fry the chicken pieces until golden on all sides. Transfer to paper towels to drain. When cool enough to handle, remove the skin from the chicken and take the meat off the bones. Cut the meat into small cubes.

Accompaniments

3 ounces rice stick noodles, soaked in
   hot water for 15 minutes and cut
   into 6- or 7-inch lengths

About 40 Potato Pancakes (page 77)

4 large potatoes, boiled until tender,
   peeled, and quartered

6 hard-boiled eggs, shelled
   and quartered

$1/2$ pound bean sprouts, blanched in
   boiling water for 1 minute

5 stalks celery, trimmed and sliced

2 scallions, trimmed and thinly sliced

$1/2$ cup chopped fresh coriander

$1/4$ cup sweet soy sauce

$1/4$ cup white vinegar or fresh
   lemon juice

$1/2$ cup Fried Shallots (page 17)

20 Indonesian shrimp crackers, fried
   (see Note)

5. To serve, arrange the noodles, potato pancakes, quartered potatoes, eggs, cubed chicken, bean sprouts, celery, scallions, and coriander leaves on a platter. Pour the soy sauce and vinegar or lemon juice into separate serving bowls for passing around. Arrange the fried shallots and shrimp crackers in separate bowls for passing around. Pour the soup into a large tureen and transfer to the table. Ladle the hot soup into individual serving bowls and pass the accompaniments.

MAKES 4 TO 6 SERVINGS

Note: The shrimp crackers are easy to prepare. Either follow the package directions or heat 3 cups oil in a large wok or skillet and cook several crackers at a time until puffed—they will cook in just seconds—and transfer to paper towels to drain.

Suribayan Chicken and Noodle Soup

Soto Suribaya

Mrs. Joeli Tajibnapis from Suribaya, Indonesia, who now lives in Virginia, describes this as a versatile dish served often in her hometown. As with many Indonesian dishes, chilies play a key seasoning role, but here they are added almost as an afterthought as a garnish and with the chili paste seasoning. Indeed, the chicken broth relies on galangal, garlic, and ginger for the main flavor accents.

You have several serving choices here, for you can offer the chicken pieces separately or remove the meat from the bones, cube it, and return the cubes to the broth. Either way, you may find using assorted chicken parts easier than cutting a whole roaster into serving pieces. Hot, buttery French bread and a side salad make fine accompaniments to this flavorful soup.

Seasoning Mixture

2 tablespoons vegetable oil

4 to 6 cloves garlic, peeled and sliced

Two 2-inch pieces fresh ginger, chopped

One 2-inch piece galangal, chopped

2 kaffir lime leaves, shredded

1 teaspoon freshly ground black pepper

1/2 teaspoon ground turmeric

Salt to taste

Soup

One 3- to 4-pound chicken, cleaned and quartered

5 cups water, or more if needed

Chili Paste

6 to 10 small fresh red chilies, or to taste

1 teaspoon ground macadamia nuts or candlenuts

1 teaspoon minced garlic

Salt to taste

Sugar to taste

About 2 tablespoons water

1. To make the seasoning mixture, heat the oil in a large saucepan over medium-high heat. Stir in the garlic, ginger, galangal, lime leaves, pepper, turmeric, and salt, and cook, stirring, 2 to 3 minutes, until fragrant.

2. To make the soup, add the chicken to the seasoning mixture and stir to coat. Pour in the water and bring to a boil. Reduce the temperature to medium-low and cook, uncovered, 35 to 40 minutes, or until the chicken is tender. If you are planning to serve the meat off the bones, remove the cooked chicken from the broth and set aside to cool. When it is cool enough to handle, remove the meat from the bones, cube it, and return it to the broth. Discard the bones and reheat the broth before serving.

3. Meanwhile, make the chili paste by combining the chilies, nuts, garlic, salt, and sugar in a blender. Add just enough water to process, and blend until smooth.

Accompaniments

$^1/_2$ pound rice vermicelli, cooked
  (see page 302), or 1 cup rice, cooked
  (see page 4)

4 hard-boiled eggs, shelled and quartered

Juice of 1 lime

2 tablespoons Fried Garlic (page 18)

4 scallions, trimmed and thinly sliced

4 fresh red chilies, thinly sliced (optional)

4. To serve, place a portion of noodles or rice in each individual serving bowl and add a portion of the chicken and broth. Distribute half of the hard-boiled eggs among the bowls. Garnish each serving with the lime juice, garlic, scallions, chilies, and the remaining hard-boiled eggs. Pass around the chili paste with the soup. Serve hot.

MAKES 4 TO 6 SERVINGS

Creamy Coconut Duck Curry

From Suribaya, Indonesia, this temperate curry has no chili, but it is nonetheless a very pleasing, rich dish that goes well with rice and a watercress salad. The cook, Joeli Tajibnapis, suggests chicken as a low-calorie substitute for the duck. If you follow this suggestion, add 1 teaspoon Thai or Malaysian shrimp paste to the curry paste and use 4 to 6 hard-boiled eggs for garnish.

Curry Paste

8 shallots, peeled and chopped

4 cloves garlic, peeled

About $^1/_4$ cup water

Curry

$^1/_3$ cup vegetable oil, or more if needed

1 stalk lemon grass, trimmed and
   thinly sliced

3 kaffir lime leaves, shredded

One 1-inch piece fresh ginger,
   chopped

2 Indonesian bay leaves, crumbled

1 teaspoon minced galangal

1 teaspoon ground coriander

1 teaspoon freshly ground black pepper

$^1/_2$ teaspoon ground cumin

$^1/_4$ teaspoon ground turmeric

Salt to taste

Sugar to taste

One 4- to 5-pound duck, cleaned and
   cut into serving pieces

4 cups coconut milk

1 to 2 cups water, if needed

Garnish

1 cup Fried Shallots (page 17) or
   Fried Garlic (page 18)

1. To make the curry paste, combine the shallots and garlic in a blender. Add just enough water to process, and blend until smooth.

2. Heat the oil in a large saucepan over medium-high heat. Add the curry paste and cook, stirring, 2 to 3 minutes, or until fragrant. Stir in the lemon grass, lime leaves, ginger, bay leaves, galangal, coriander, pepper, cumin, turmeric, salt, and sugar. Cook, stirring, until fragrant, about 5 minutes. (Add more oil if the mixture seems dry.)

3. Add the duck pieces and coat them well in the seasoning mixture. Add the coconut milk and reduce the heat to low. Cook, uncovered, stirring occasionally, until the duck is tender, $1^1/_2$ to 2 hours. Add the water, as needed, if the mixture gets too thick. Garnish with the fried shallots or fried garlic and serve hot.

MAKES 4 TO 6 SERVINGS

Three-Spice Suribayan Chicken Curry

One taste of this mild curry and you'll understand why Indonesia was nicknamed the "Spice Islands," since the flavors come from smatterings of some favorites, including cinnamon, nutmeg, cumin, and coriander. What's missing is the chili heat, but you'll enjoy the creamy subtleties of the dish. Best of all, Indonesian cook Joeli Tajibnapis's curry comes together quickly. Serve this with noodles or rice and a tossed salad.

Curry Paste

8 shallots, peeled and sliced

3 cloves garlic, peeled

3 macadamia nuts or candlenuts

About $1/4$ cup water

Curry

$1/3$ cup vegetable oil, or more if needed

1 stalk lemon grass, trimmed and
    thinly sliced

One 4-inch piece cinnamon stick

One 2-inch piece galangal,
    thinly sliced

2 Indonesian bay leaves, crumbled

4 whole cloves

2 teaspoons ground coriander

1 teaspoon ground cumin

$1/2$ teaspoon ground turmeric

$1/2$ teaspoon ground nutmeg

One 4- to 5-pound chicken, cleaned
    and cut into serving pieces

2 cups coconut milk

Salt to taste

Garnish

1 cup Fried Shallots (page 17)

1. To make the curry paste, combine the shallots, garlic, and nuts in a blender. Add just enough water to process, and blend until smooth.

2. To make the curry, heat the oil in a large wok or saucepan over medium heat. Add the curry paste, lemon grass, cinnamon, galangal, bay leaves, cloves, coriander, cumin, turmeric, and nutmeg, and cook, stirring, about 5 minutes, or until fragrant. (Add more oil if the mixture seems dry.) Add the chicken pieces and coat them with the seasoning mixture. Stir in the coconut milk and salt. Reduce the heat to medium-low and cook the chicken, uncovered, 30 to 45 minutes, or until tender. Garnish with the shallots and serve hot.

MAKES 3 TO 4 SERVINGS

Chilied Chicken Curry

An accomplished cook and a leading spokeswoman for local culinary traditions, Hanny Nabiela Sugianto lives in the city of Medan on the island of Sumatra in Indonesia. After a sweltering morning trip to several local markets, we returned to her kitchen, where she assembled a multicourse repast, which I ate alone: The Muslim festival of Ramadan had just begun and the family was fasting. But there was plenty left over for the family's after-sundown meal, and this curry was just one of the dishes they would later enjoy.

Like some other curry pastes, this needs only coarse chopping by hand, or in a blender if you prefer, before you start to cook. The chilies are left in large pieces, yet they add just a trace of heat to the overall dish and can be removed before serving if you want to avoid fiery mouthfuls. Hanny served this with plenty of rice and some cooling jasmine tea.

$1/4$ cup vegetable oil, or more if needed

6 shallots, peeled and chopped

2 tablespoons minced fresh ginger

2 teaspoons ground turmeric

6 green chilies, stems removed,
   halved lengthwise

$1/2$ cup water

1 stalk lemon grass, trimmed and
   thinly sliced

6 kaffir lime leaves, very thinly sliced

6 Indonesian bay leaves

2 turmeric leaves

1 tablespoon minced galangal

One 3- to 4-pound chicken, cleaned
   and cut into serving pieces

2 sprigs curry leaves

3 cups coconut milk

Heat the oil in a large wok or saucepan over medium heat. Add the shallots, ginger, and turmeric and cook, stirring, about 5 minutes, or until fragrant. (Add more oil if the mixture seems dry.) Stir in the chilies and water. Stir in the lemon grass, lime leaves, bay leaves, turmeric leaves, and galangal. Reduce the heat to low and cook for 5 minutes more. Stir in the chicken, curry leaves, and $1^{1}/_{2}$ cups of the coconut milk. Cook, uncovered, 45 minutes to 1 hour, or until the chicken is tender. Stir in the remaining $1^{1}/_{2}$ cups coconut milk and cook until slightly thickened, about 10 minutes more.

MAKES 4 TO 6 SERVINGS

Cantonese Duck Stew

Hong Kong's foremost food authority, William Mark, loves anything with goose or duck and this may be one of his favorite recipes. As is typical of most Cantonese dishes, this duck stew has subdued and balanced flavors, so don't look for any chili punch here. The Chinese often eat their poultry with bones, for the bones add their own flavor and nourishment to the dish; Westerners might find it easier to bone the duck, in which case the meat tenderizes and cooks through more quickly, or to cut it into serving pieces. Cooked rice is the traditional accompaniment along with a vegetable stir-fry of Chinese broccoli or bok choy.

Sauce

2 tablespoons oyster sauce

1 tablespoon dark soy sauce

1 tablespoon Chinese rice wine

Stew

3 tablespoons cornstarch

2 tablespoons salt

One 3- to 4-pound duck, cleaned and cut into bite-sized pieces

2 tablespoons vegetable oil (preferably peanut), or more if needed

Six $1/2$-thick slices fresh ginger, chopped

3 cloves garlic, peeled and chopped

6 ounces bamboo shoots, cut into bite-sized pieces

8 dried Chinese mushrooms or shiitake mushrooms, soaked in hot water for 20 minutes, stems removed

1. To make the sauce, whisk together the oyster sauce, soy sauce, and wine. Set aside.

2. To make the stew, stir together the cornstarch and salt. Sprinkle over the duck pieces.

3. Heat the oil in a large wok or skillet over medium-high heat. Add the ginger and garlic, and stir-fry until golden, about 1 minute; transfer to a stockpot. Add the duck and stir-fry until slightly crisp, 5 to 8 minutes; transfer to the stockpot.

4. Add the sauce to the stockpot and enough water to cover the duck. Bring the mixture to a boil, reduce the heat to low, and cook, uncovered, until the duck is tender, 1 to $1^1/2$ hours. Stir in the bamboo shoots and mushrooms, and cook for 15 minutes more. Serve hot.

MAKES 3 TO 4 SERVINGS

"Three-Cup" Chicken

Chinese-Vietnamese cook Helene Sze McCarthy describes this fast-cooking Peking-style stew as a country dish, but because of its sweet and sour flavors, it has become a widespread favorite of city folk too. "It's easy to eat, easy to cook, and tasty with rice," she says.

It's also very versatile, and you can adjust the quantities of each ingredient to suit your mood. One of her favorite variations is to substitute a half cup sugar and a half cup oil for the cup of sugar. Another option is to substitute a half cup oil and a half cup wine for the cup of wine. But try this recipe first—it is delicious as is.

Cut the chicken up the Chinese way—that is, chop it into small serving pieces, bone and all. For example, cut a thigh piece in half, and a breast half into two or three pieces. Serve the chicken with plenty of rice.

1 cup sugar

1 cup soy sauce

1 cup Chinese rice wine or dry
　white wine

One 2- to 3-pound chicken, cleaned
　and cut into serving pieces

4 scallions, trimmed and sliced into
　2-inch lengths

One 3-inch piece fresh ginger,
　thinly sliced

4 cloves garlic, peeled and sliced

Combine the sugar, soy sauce, and wine in a large saucepan and bring the mixture to a boil. Add the chicken, scallions, ginger, and garlic, reduce the heat to low, and cook until the chicken is tender, about 30 minutes. Serve hot.

MAKES 4 TO 5 SERVINGS

Cornish Game Hen Soup

As she fussed about her Maryland kitchen preparing this dish, Bong S. Lee of Korea explained that it is a special cooling summer soup, delicate and nourishing, and a favorite with her family. But she added that it should be eaten only as a soup and must be accompanied only by rice—which for her, of course, means short-grain Korean rice. When prepared the traditional way with Korean ginseng, the soup also offers some health benefits, she said. But Mrs. Lee admitted that this is a costly ingredient—you'll need about 20 dollars' worth of ginseng for this dish—so consider the ginseng optional.

When you are cleaning the game hen, discard all the innards except the neck and kidneys, which you will use in the stuffing. If you like the taste of garlic, you may use an entire unpeeled head.

^{1}/$_2$ to ^{3}/$_4$ cup short-grain Korean or
   Japanese rice

1 Cornish game hen, cleaned, trimmed
   of all visible fat, with neck and kidneys reserved

8 cloves garlic, peeled

8 Chinese dates, soaked in hot water
   for 20 minutes and pitted

One 3-inch piece Korean ginseng
   (optional)

1 thin slice fresh ginger

8 cups water

Salt and freshly ground black pepper
   to taste

1. Pour the rice into a large bowl and rinse until the water runs clear. Drain. Spoon the rice into the cavity of the hen. Stuff in the garlic, dates, ginseng if using, ginger, and reserved neck and kidneys.

2. Fill the stockpot with the water and gently lay the hen in it (be careful not to dislodge the stuffing). Do not close the cavity with a skewer, as this would prevent the stuffing from flavoring the water. Rest the lid on the pot so it is slightly ajar to allow steam to escape. Bring the water to a boil and cook over medium heat, 45 minutes to 1 hour, or until the hen is tender. With a thick towel, wipe the foam from the side of the pot as the hen cooks.

3. Ladle the liquid from the pot into each soup bowl. Slice some of the hen from the bones and set in the bowl. Scoop some of the stuffing into the bowl, being sure to include some of each ingredient. Season with salt and pepper and serve hot.

MAKES 2 SERVINGS

Imperial Korean Chicken Stew

As Marylander Bong S. Lee explained, dishes from the Imperial courts of ancient Korea are elegant and beautiful, and this chicken stew, with its assortment of fresh chilies and beloved Korean seasonings of black pepper, toasted sesame oil, and soy sauce, is one such royal dish. Mrs. Lee's mother learned about this when she was a guest at the Imperial Palace many years ago. After trial and error, her mother was able to duplicate this dish in her own kitchen, and she often served it to visiting dignitaries. Now her daughter re-creates it often for her own family in the United States.

As with all Korean dishes, the emphasis is on beauty, so Mrs. Lee says you must stir the chicken several times during cooking to prevent the meat from sticking to the cookpot and pulling off the bones, leading to an "ugly presentation." Serve this with a side dish of Korean Fried Tofu (page 244).

One 3- to 4-pound chicken

2 tablespoons freshly ground black pepper

3 tablespoons vegetable oil

5 cloves garlic, peeled, crushed, and minced

4 thin slices fresh ginger, crushed and minced

1 cup soy sauce

3 tablespoons toasted sesame oil

1½ cups water

3 scallions, trimmed and sliced into 3-inch lengths, greens included

1 carrot, peeled and thinly sliced on the diagonal

2 fresh red chilies, thinly sliced (optional)

2 green chilies, thinly sliced (optional)

2 teaspoons Korean red pepper powder

1. Using a sharp cleaver, cut the chicken, including the bones, into small serving pieces. Remove the skin and fat, if desired. Rinse the chicken under cold running water and pat dry. Repeat this procedure 3 times. Sprinkle the chicken with the pepper.

2. Heat the oil in a large saucepan over medium heat. Add the garlic and ginger, and stir-fry until just golden, about 1 minute. Stir in the soy sauce, sesame oil, and chicken pieces. Bring to a boil and cook for 10 minutes. Add the water, and rest the lid on the pot so it is slightly ajar to allow steam to escape. Reduce the heat to low and cook for 10 minutes. Stir in the scallions, carrots, red and green chilies if using, and red pepper powder, and cook until the chicken is tender and the liquid is partially reduced, about 10 minutes more. Serve hot.

MAKES 3 TO 4 SERVINGS

Noodles and Chicken in Broth

Tori Nanban

Noodle soups in Japan are standard fare and, certainly at one time, were the backbone of Japanese fast-food eating. For this nourishing dish, Yoko Morford combines soba with such classic seasonings as soy sauce, dashi *(Japanese First Stock, page 34), and mirin, the sweet Japanese cooking wine that makes any food more elegant.*

$^1/_4$ **pound boneless, skinless chicken breast, cut into strips**

1 teaspoon plus 2 tablespoons soy sauce

1 teaspoon plus 1 tablespoon mirin

1 cup *dashi* **(Japanese First Stock, page 34)**

4 scallions, trimmed and diagonally sliced

3 ounces dried soba, cooked (see page 303)

1 cup 2-inch pieces loosely packed spinach, steamed until wilted

$^1/_4$ **teaspoon** *shichimi*

1. Place the chicken in a saucepan with 1 teaspoon of the soy sauce and 1 teaspoon of the mirin. Let marinate for 20 minutes.

2. Stir the *dashi*, the remaining 2 tablespoons soy sauce, and the remaining 1 tablespoon mirin into the chicken marinade. Bring to a boil. Stir in the scallions and cook for 2 minutes.

3. Put the cooked noodles in the bottom of a soup bowl and arrange the spinach on top. Pour the hot broth and chicken over the top. Season with the *shichimi* and serve hot.

MAKES 1 SERVING

Japanese Chicken and Vegetables in One Pot

Mizutaki

If you have a yen for communal eating, this traditional Japanese one-pot meal should satisfy it. This country-style dish is often cooked and served in a clay pot in the middle of the table, but any other table-top cooking vessel is fine—electric pots are readily available and keep the soup at a constant temperature. As with other Japanese hot-pot dishes, you may use up any remaining broth by making a rice soup. You may also ladle some broth into a small bowl or cup during cooking, add some salt, and enjoy the soup alone during the meal.

Chicken Broth

4 chicken legs (thighs and drumsticks)
   with skin and bones, each cut into
   4 pieces
3 thin slices fresh ginger
5 cups water
2 tablespoons sake

Accompaniments

4 leaves Chinese (napa) cabbage
1/2 bunch spinach, rinsed, trimmed,
   and cut into bite-sized pieces
1/2 bunch edible chrysanthemum
   leaves (crown daisy)
12 dried shiitake mushrooms, soaked
   in hot water for 20 minutes
1 bunch enoki mushrooms, rinsed
2 large green onions or leeks, sliced
   on the diagonal into 1-inch pieces
1/2 pound firm tofu, cut into
   1-inch cubes
1 cup Ponzu Shoyu Dipping Sauce
   (see Note, page 33)
1 1/2 cups short-grain rice, cooked
   (3 cups cooked) (see page 4)
2 large eggs, lightly beaten
1/2 cup finely chopped scallions
Assorted Japanese pickles (optional)

1. To make the chicken broth, combine the chicken, ginger, water, and sake in a tabletop cooking vessel. Bring to a boil and skim off the foam. Reduce the heat to medium-low and cook until the chicken is cooked through, about 20 minutes.

2. To serve, take the pot to the table and keep the liquid at a simmer. Arrange the cabbage, spinach, chrysanthemum leaves, shiitake mushrooms, enoki mushrooms, green onions or leeks, and tofu on the same or on separate platters. Place a small serving dish with the ponzu sauce on the table. Set the accompaniments on the table with serving utensils or chopsticks. Let people cook their own food and eat it at their leisure. Cooked ingredients should be dipped into the ponzu sauce before eating.

3. After eating, remove any ingredients from the cooking liquid and stir in the rice. Cover the pot and let boil until the rice is heated through, about 3 minutes. Remove the lid and quickly stir in the eggs. Remove the pot from the heat, sprinkle the rice with the scallions, and serve as a soup course. Pass around an assortment of Japanese pickles, if desired.

MAKES 4 TO 6 SERVINGS

Japanese-Style Chicken Curry

While Japanese cooking offers many exciting dishes, few Westerners would think that curry is one of them. But as I learned one afternoon, Japanese generally like curries and have even invented and packaged their very own curry mixture. This, explains Sachi Yamada and her daughter Nancy, comes in a soft foil packet and is sold at Japanese groceries. She assured me that the paste produces a delicious curry; nonetheless she has created her own chicken curry recipe.

The flavorings are far less complex than those used in most other Asian curries, but this curry does call both for a commercial Indian curry mixture and for the Indian spice mixture known as garam masala, used in many North Indian dishes. There are infinite masala possibilities, and if you want to mix your own—which is what most Indian women do—the Garam Masala recipe (page 29) is a good starting place.

Mrs. Yamada's recipe is versatile, for you can substitute boneless country-style spareribs or squares of firm tofu for the chicken. But if chicken is your choice, you can use chicken parts, boning and cubing the meat, or a whole chicken, chopping the chicken, bones and all, into small serving pieces.

One 3- to 4-pound chicken, cleaned
   and cut into serving pieces
1/4 cup Indian curry powder
2 tablespoons Ghee (page 17) or
   vegetable oil, or more as needed
5 medium onions, peeled and chopped
2 tablespoons all-purpose flour
5 cups Basic Chicken Stock (page 19)
3 large carrots, peeled and
   diagonally sliced
6 medium potatoes, peeled and cubed
1 zucchini or Oriental eggplant,
   thinly sliced
Juice of 1/2 lemon
1 tablespoon Worcestershire sauce
2 teaspoons ground coriander
1 teaspoon ground cumin
1/2 apple, peeled and grated
1/2 cup plain yogurt or sour cream
Pinch of sugar
Salt to taste
2 teaspoons Garam Masala (page 29)

1. Place the chicken in a bowl and sprinkle the curry powder over the meat. Set aside.

2. Heat the ghee or oil in a large saucepan over medium heat. Add the onions and flour, and cook, stirring occasionally, about 15 minutes, or until just golden. Stir in the stock, reduce the heat to medium-low, and cook until the onions almost disintegrate, about 30 minutes.

3. Add the chicken pieces and carrots, and cook for 15 minutes. Stir in the potatoes, zucchini or eggplant, lemon juice, Worcestershire sauce, coriander, and cumin, and cook until the chicken is tender, about 15 minutes more. Remove from the heat. Stir in the apples and yogurt or sour cream. Season with the sugar and salt, and sprinkle with the garam masala.

MAKES 4 SERVINGS

Filipino Green Papaya Soup

Tinola

Known as tinola, *this classic Filipino soup-stew of chicken and young chili leaves has a delicate flavor gently soured by the elongated green papaya, a popular Southeast Asian fruit that is very different from the smaller Mexican or South American papayas. Green papaya is sturdy enough for importing and is easy to find at Asian markets in this country, but chili leaves, with their delightful, somewhat peppery aroma and flavor, are really only at hand where chili plants grow. Young leaves are preferable because they are tender, but you may use any chili leaves you can find.*

According to the Filipina cook Pinkie Imson, your chicken stock should be flavorful; otherwise you should enhance the flavor by adding chicken bouillon cubes.

2 tablespoons vegetable oil

$^1/_2$ head garlic, cloves separated, peeled, and sliced

1 medium onion, peeled and diced

1 tablespoon minced fresh ginger

$1^1/_2$ to 2 pounds chicken thighs, with bones, cut in half

3 cups Basic Chicken Stock (page 19)

1 small young green papaya or chayote, peeled, seeded, and cut into bite-sized pieces

$^1/_4$ cup young chili leaves (optional)

Fish sauce to taste

Heat the oil in a large stockpot over medium heat. Add the garlic and onion and cook, stirring often, until browned and soft, 8 to 10 minutes. Stir in the ginger and chicken pieces and cook, stirring, for 2 minutes. Stir in the stock, reduce the heat to medium-low, and cook until the chicken is tender, about 15 minutes. Add the papaya or chayote and cook 15 to 20 minutes, or until tender. Stir in the chili leaves, if using, and fish sauce, and serve hot.

MAKES 3 TO 4 SERVINGS

Chicken Adobo

A popular chicken stew in the Philippines, and one that many claim to be the national dish, chicken adobo is a sour-salty mixture of vinegar and soy sauce that captures the Filipinos' love of this flavor combination. The dish is also immensely practical for the tropics, because the vinegar acts as a preservative and, say some, a large pot of adobo will keep for days without refrigeration. While there are many variations on the adobo theme, adding sugar to the mix apparently is not one of them, although that is how my family first ate and loved adobo in Hong Kong, with enough sugar added to counter the vinegar.

My Filipina friend Pinkie Imson says that the kind of vinegar you use is important, and she always keeps a bottle of apple cider vinegar handy because it imparts a better flavor and color to the finished dish. The flavor of the entire dish improves if you make this one day before eating it. Cooked rice as an accompaniment adds a degree of sweetness to the chicken.

1½ to 2 pounds chicken pieces with bones, or pork loin roast with bones, or a combination, cut into small pieces

1 cup vinegar, preferably apple cider vinegar

¾ cup soy sauce, preferably light

1 head garlic, cloves separated, peeled, and crushed

1 bay leaf

1 teaspoon black peppercorns

¼ cup vegetable oil

1. Place the chicken in a large bowl and stir in the vinegar, soy sauce, garlic, bay leaf, and peppercorns. Cover the bowl and set aside for at least 1 hour, up to 3 hours—the longer the meat marinates, the better the flavor.

2. Remove the meat from the marinade and reserve the marinade for later use. Heat the oil in a large wok or saucepan over medium heat. Add the chicken and cook about 10 minutes, or until browned on all sides. Stir in the marinade, reduce the heat to low, and cook about 30 minutes, until the chicken is tender and the sauce thickens. Serve hot.

MAKES 4 SERVINGS

Filipino Chicken and Vegetable Stew

Apritadang Manok

Filipina cook Evelyn Manuel makes this casual Filipino meal often for her carry-out restaurant in Virginia. Feel free to adjust quantities—for example, if you want a soupier dish, simply add more water. For a more authentic flavor, use a Filipino brand of soy sauce, but a Japanese or Chinese soy sauce is certainly fine too.

$1\frac{1}{2}$ pounds chicken wings and thighs

1 tablespoon cornstarch

$1\frac{3}{4}$ cups water, or more if needed

1 teaspoon vegetable oil, or more
   if needed

1 medium onion, peeled and diced

1 clove garlic, peeled and diced

2 tomatoes, diced

1 large potato, peeled and cubed

1 carrot, peeled and thinly sliced

$\frac{1}{4}$ cup soy sauce

1 tablespoon tomato paste

$\frac{1}{2}$ teaspoon achiote

$\frac{1}{2}$ green bell pepper, cut into
   thin strips

$\frac{1}{2}$ red bell pepper, cut into thin strips

1. Bring a large stockpot of water to a boil. Add the chicken and cook for 3 minutes.

2. Stir together the cornstarch and 1 cup of the water.

3. Heat the oil in a large stockpot over high heat. Add the onion and garlic, and cook, stirring often, until brown, about 5 minutes. (Add more oil if the mixture seems dry.) Stir in the tomatoes and cook until softened, 2 to 3 minutes. Stir in the chicken, potatoes, carrots, cornstarch mixture, soy sauce, tomato paste, and achiote. Reduce the heat to low, and cook for 10 minutes. Stir in the remaining $\frac{3}{4}$ cup water, the green peppers, and the red peppers. (Add more water if the mixture seems dry.) Cook until the chicken is tender, about 10 minutes more. Serve hot.

MAKES 2 TO 3 SERVINGS

Pagoda Memories—
Burma (Myanmar), Laos,
Cambodia, and Vietnam

Nestled between China and India, Burma and the former Indo-Chinese countries of Laos, Cambodia, and Vietnam have been strongly influenced by their giant Asian neighbors, and these influences often show up in the kitchen. For example, the Chinese have donated techniques such as stir-frying and ingredients like noodles; the Indians have given generously of their passion for curries and their ability to extract the utmost flavor from commonplace ingredients. To many Westerners, however, the cuisines of these four countries remain unfamiliar, partially because for so many decades they have been virtually closed to outsiders. But times have changed, and the contemporary traveler just beginning to fully explore these once inaccessible lands is finding some unspoiled culinary treasures.

Burma (Myanmar)

How the Burmese love their rich, pungent curries—and currylike dishes—and their full range of soups: clear soups, rich soups, spicy soups! Of the many meals we ate in Rangoon recently, more than half featured curries. Assuredly, the other half highlighted soups of one kind or another. We breakfasted on Coconut Noodles and on Mohinga (pages 48 and 160); brunched on Fiery Fish Curry (page 171); lunched on curries and soups at a local open-air restaurant called Shwe Ba; and dined at a friendly Burmese Bahá'í's house on a chicken curry (page 65). Vegetables, rice, noodles, and tea formed the backdrop for these numerous meals.

Just how much the Burmese value these foods struck home after touring the kitchen at

Shwe Ba. Our friend Daw Anna Khin-Khin Kyawt led us out back, where dozens of enormous ceramic vats, each large enough to hold a goat, were bubbling with curries. The cooks smiled as they lifted off the vats' wooden lids and revealed the steaming contents. Later, as we ate a dark duck curry, a chilied prawn curry, and a salad of fermented bean sprouts, lettuce, mint, steamed watercress, and bitter gourd (also known as bitter melon—a very popular vegetable throughout Asia), an electric fan blew paper napkins around—and unfortunately blew away some of the curry fragrance.

If you can say the Burmese love curries and soups, you can also say in truth that they love food: Daw Anna led us through many local wet markets, but none so memorable as the nameless community market in the shadow of the great, gilded Shwedegon pagoda. Unfortunately, it has closed since my last visit. This used to be country marketing at its best: Fish were so fresh they wriggled out of their bins and somersaulted into the aisles. A coconut grinder used to operate a rackety machine that bored through the fresh coconut meat and spewed out milk in a steady stream of white liquid. Fruits and vegetables, familiar and strange, formed a colorful jigsaw pattern at every stall. With armloads of ingredients for the makings of a multicourse Burmese meal, we would pick our way back to Daw Anna's car and speed home to cook.

Laos

Today's Laos exists as a landlocked country caught between five Asian neighbors. Yesterday's Laos exists as a kingdom only in the memories of such people as the venerable Bounsou Sananikone, a Laotian woman who fled her country in the mid-1970s to come to America.

She has spoken often of her picturesque homeland, with its gentle people and beguiling customs, and has taken me among her people to participate in their Buddhist celebrations and to feast on traditional Lao food: its "sticky" rice and grilled sausages, its lusty noodle soups, and its fiery chili-based condiments.

Bounsou Sananikone once lent me a book that put her words into context. In the mid-1950s, a Frenchman named René de Berval collected a series of essays about Laos and called his book *Kingdom of Laos, The Land of the Million Elephants and of the White Parasol*. The photos and line drawings have captured the soul of this country's ancient beauty, which seems so very remote from modern life.

Lao cooking today is still very much rooted in the traditions and customs that prescribe long, slow cooking: ingredients just picked from the vine or the twig, an abundance of fish and game, and a liberal sprinkling of chilies and fish sauce to enliven flavors.

At the heart of every Lao meal are the complex soups—or *kaengs*—and souplike dishes of chicken, of meat, of fish, and of such vegetables as bamboo shoots, all usually served over a bed of rice noodles. As Bounsou Sananikone recalls, "We used to eat every day a very simple soup called 'boiling beef' soup. But at every meal [lunch or dinner], we eat soup, whether from fish, or beef, or pork bones, or chicken, or duck . . . A meal without soup is considered an incomplete meal."

If you ever sit down to a traditional Lao meal, you'll find an economy of ingredients, for Lao cooks cleverly use every scrap and morsel of food—from intestines, hides, and hooves to stems, flowers, and leaves. You'll enjoy foods with very distinctive combinations of flavors and textures—for example, the Lao pairing of sour rattan and mild bamboo shoots. You'll learn to dine the Lao way by forming the sticky rice into bite-sized morsels and eating them with mouthfuls of shredded green papaya salad or a Lao noodle soup.

It is a cuisine of great economy, yet great dignity—and the Lao meal, even if it is humble, is a tribute to both host and guest.

Cambodia

The author of the treasured *The Cambodian Cookbook of H.R.H. Princess Rasmi Sobhana* states unequivocally that Cambodian cuisine is "one of detail, small amounts of many ingredients being first finely pounded in a mortar, cooked individually and eventually added to the main dish. The typical Cambodian stove is a charcoal brazier and all food is cooked fresh daily according to the Buddhist religion."

What this book doesn't convey—even among its recipes for spiced snipe, sautéed sparrow, and stuffed cuttlefish—is the sense that soups and curries play a key role in this cuisine. As one Cambodian restaurant owner in Virginia, Yann Ker, explained to me, "A typical meal would include one soup, one stir-fry, and one grilled dish with rice. Soup is always there, and is considered a main-course dish. Soup serves as a liquid, like Westerners drink sodas, water, and beer. So when we eat dry food, something washes it down. That's how Cambodians eat soup."

The book also does not immediately impress readers with the subtleties of Cambodian seasonings, nor how rich and varied ingredients can be. Bora Chu's Coconut Red Curry Noodles (page 165) is just such an example with its layers of sweet, hot, and sour flavors and crunchy and chewy textures.

But unlike some of their southern neighbors, such as the Thais and Malaysians, Cambodians steer clear of chili madness, so chilies come into only limited play in the Cambodian kitchen. Even Mrs. Chu downplayed the chili role, for in her red curry paste, she suggested the use of a mild Mexican Anaheim chili to add flavor and color—but not heat.

Seated in the Virginia home of Mrs. Chu, and watching how she assembled her red curry, I learned that as a girl in Cambodia she was expected to really understand ingredients: "Mom said, 'Cook by eye, not by taste.' So I learned that if a curry is bubbling, it may need more salt." Such early training produces cooks who prepare flawless meals of rice or noodles, surrounded by dishes that are basic, flavorful, and wholesome.

Vietnam

You might find many ways to characterize Vietnamese cooking, but I would summarize it this way: soups. As are their Cambodian and Lao neighbors, Vietnamese are passionate about their soup pots. In fact, there are probably not many other countries where vendors each day ready their soups by dawn to meet the breakfast crowd and keep the pot boiling for those who may then return for lunch or a mid-afternoon or evening bowl of soup.

As much as anything else, Vietnamese soup making has become an art form. And it is not at all surprising that Westerners—who have fallen in love with the Vietnamese *pho*, a robust, full-meal beef-and-noodle soup from Hanoi—now flock to *pho* restaurants in suburban and urban America.

Even Vietnamese girls, who will never receive professional praise for their soups, learn its art early. As Helene Sze McCarthy, my Chinese-Vietnamese friend from Haiphong, explained over a platter of stir-fried bamboo shoots, steamed rice, cups of chrysanthemum tea, and a hot-and-sour shrimp soup (page 177), soup-making skills come early. As we ate, my friend explained that basic soup lessons included such tips as never, ever cover a soup when it is simmering or it will turn cloudy, always use cleaned and washed bones, and skim the scum from the surface for the clearest soup.

Of course, Vietnamese cooking is not just about soups. An artful and beautiful cuisine, it runs along geographical lines and as the topography varies, so do cooking styles—from the hearty, simple meals of the North to the lighter, vegetable-filled soups and stir-fries of the South. Yet as a general rule, everywhere dishes star freshly caught seafood, a variety of crisp herbs and vegetables used to garnish and embellish them, and rice and noodles. Everything is carefully prepared and carefully arranged, so even the eating of Vietnamese food is both refined and delicate and something of an art form and ritual in itself. Even wrapping up foods in the traditional rice papers requires skill and precision to avoid messy eating.

As Helene Sze McCarthy remembers her family meals in Haiphong, the food was presented on small, beautiful plates and dishes and served on shiny brass trays. And then, everyone in the family sat around on the gleaming wooden floors "like Buddhas," drinking the soup and "eating little bits of this, little bits of that with chopsticks for picking up our choices . . . everything chopped up very small . . . very beautiful."

Meating Asia: Beef, Lamb, Pork, and Goat

"Good meat results in good soup."

—Chinese proverb

Meating Asia: Beef, Lamb, Pork, and Goat

"Good meat results in good soup."

—Chinese proverb

Lamb in a Saffron, Apricot, Coconut, and Poppy Seed Curry

Shahjehani Qorma

Cooking is usually not haphazard in an Indian kitchen: Philosophy, logic, and sound nutritional sense go into the composition of almost every dish. And this elegant lamb curry is proof of that—see "The Tale of Shahjehani Qorma" (below) for the story behind this dish. But beyond science and logic, this sumptuous offering is a gastronomic masterpiece, fit for the king for whom it was created.

When you set about preparing this, you should keep several things in mind: For one, you'll need to allow some time ahead of the actual cooking to prepare the thickened yogurt, though you may be able to find commercially prepared thick yogurt in some health food markets. You will also need to allow time for the meat to marinate. If you like the musky flavor of goat, you may use that instead of the lamb. The recommended accompaniments—probably suggested for their complementary nutritional merit as much as for their texture and flavor—for this curry are steamed broccoli and freshly cut-up melon and papaya. And as always with a curry, you may certainly serve this with rice.

Shahjehani Paste

12 dried apricots, soaked in hot water
    for 20 minutes and chopped
1½ cups shredded unsweetened
    dried coconut
12 almonds, skinned
One 1½-inch piece fresh ginger, sliced
12 pistachios, skinned
About ½ cup water
½ teaspoon ground cumin
½ teaspoon ground turmeric
½ teaspoon freshly ground
    black pepper
Salt to taste
3½ cups thickened yogurt (see Note)

Curry

2¼ pounds boneless lamb, cut into
    2-inch cubes
½ cup Ghee (page 17) or
    vegetable oil
2 cups chopped onions

1. To make the Shahjehani paste, combine the apricots, coconut, almonds, ginger, and pistachios in a blender. Add just enough water to process, and blend until smooth. Add the cumin, turmeric, pepper, and salt, and blend until the spices are incorporated. Whisk the thickened yogurt in a large bowl until creamy and stir in the paste.

2. To marinate the meat for the curry, place the lamb in the bowl with the yogurt mixture and turn to coat. Cover and let marinate in the refrigerator for 2 hours.

3. Meanwhile, make the dry masala by pulverizing the chilies, cardamom, cloves, cinnamon, mace, nutmeg, and poppy seeds in a spice grinder or blender.

4. To make the curry, heat the ghee or oil in a large saucepan over medium heat. Add the onions and cook, stirring, about 10 minutes, or until golden. Add the marinated meat and marinade and cook, stirring often, until the liquid begins to boil, about 10 minutes. Stir in the masala. Reduce the heat to low, cover, and cook, stirring occasionally, 20 to 25 minutes, or until the meat is tender. (Add more water if the sauce becomes too thick—it should

2 teaspoons saffron threads, soaked
   in 2 tablespoons warm water for
   10 minutes and ground to a paste

Dry Masala

4 dried red chilies
10 green cardamom pods, roasted
   (see page 11)
10 whole cloves, roasted (see page 11)
Six 1-inch pieces cinnamon stick
2 blades mace, roasted (see page 11),
   or 1 teaspoon ground mace
$^1/_4$ whole nutmeg, roasted (see page
   11), or 1 teaspoon ground nutmeg
$1^1/_2$ tablespoons poppy seeds

resemble a thick pancake batter.) Stir in the saffron and cook, uncovered, for 15 minutes more. Spoon equal portions of meat onto the center of each plate and spoon the sauce on top. Serve hot.

MAKES 4 TO 6 SERVINGS

Note: To make $3^1/_2$ cups thickened yogurt, scoop 4 cups yogurt into a colander lined with several layers of cheesecloth. Let the yogurt drain for about 1 hour to make $3^1/_2$ cups. For other purposes, you can turn the yogurt into a "cheese" by continuing to drain it to the desired thickness.

The Tale of Shahjehani Qorma

Indian food historian J. Inder Singh Kalra has trekked across his country and written about almost every aspect of his beloved cuisine. And this is the story he has researched about the recipe known as Shahjehani Qorma:

"This is the delicacy Shah Jehan—the builder of the Taj Mahal—was fed by his *hakeem* (doctor of the Unani school of medicine) and *rikaabdaar* (chef) during his imprisonment by his son Aurangzed, the last Moghul emperor. The various ingredients that go into its making provide a harmonious blend of the therapeutic with the aesthetic. Yogurt, while improving taste, eases respiration, is an excellent digestive, and reduces phlegm and prevents cough. Cloves not only prevent deterioration, but are said to actually improve eyesight. Besides, they clear congestion and purify blood. That they freshen the mouth is no secret. Cinnamon helps build up the appetite, clear the windpipe, is considered an excellent deworming agent, and is said to possess aphrodisiac qualities. Red chilies, black pepper, mace, and nutmeg are all hot spices. The coolant in the masala comes in the form of poppy seeds. The combination of masala provides energy, reduces mental stress, and according to practitioners of traditional medicine on the Subcontinent, encourages the formation of bone marrow. Consumed in the prescribed quantities, they induce sound sleep. Turmeric is an all-purpose healer of wounds and brings relief to aching joints. Coconut eases renal pain and purifies blood. Finally, apricots in their dried form, prevent thirst and you can gauge the fruit's importance when you consider that Shah Jehan was given minimal quantities of water. Apricots are also anti-pyretic."

Lamb and Mango Curry

A tall young Sikh, Raminder Malhotra, has earned his reputation as a leading chef in New Delhi by producing superlative grilled meats and velvety curries—all from the minute kitchen of his dhaba *(roadside stand). A protégé of India's super epicure, J. Inder Singh (Jiggs) Kalra, Malhotra manages a staff of about a dozen boys who chop chilies, mince fresh coriander, and grind ginger and garlic into a paste while sitting on the dusty sidewalk—a memorable experience to watch, especially as several cows saunter by.*

One of his more outstanding dishes is this curry from the city of Hyderabad. It pairs the musky, earthy flavor of lamb with the pronounced sweetness of mangoes in a curry gravy that has just a hint of chili fire. Indians might choose to use goat instead of lamb, and for a change of pace, you may want to try it out. As for the mangoes, this must be a seasonal dish, for it needs the fully ripe mango when it is at its sweetest and best. Too often supermarket mangos are both hard and sour—these are not worthy of this curry. Ordinarily, this curry, when served with rice, the Indian bread naan, *and a salad or vegetable dish, would scantily serve four. But mango lovers will devour this, so you may wish to increase the quantities.*

¹/₂ cup Ghee (page 17) or vegetable oil

1³/₄ pounds onions, peeled and sliced

1³/₄ pounds boneless lamb roast, cut into 1¹/₂-inch cubes

2¹/₂ tablespoons Ginger Paste (page 28)

1¹/₂ tablespoons Garlic Paste (page 28)

2 teaspoons Indian red chili powder

1 teaspoon ground turmeric

Salt to taste

3 cups water

4 ripe mangoes, peeled, seeded, and cut into 1-inch cubes

1 tablespoon cumin seeds, roasted (see page 11)

2 green chilies, seeded and chopped

¹/₄ cup chopped fresh coriander leaves

1. Heat the ghee or vegetable oil in a large wok or saucepan over medium heat. Add half the onions and cook, stirring, until golden, 15 to 20 minutes. Add the lamb and the remaining onions and cook, stirring, until the meat is browned, about 5 minutes. Add the ginger, garlic, red chili powder, turmeric, and salt and cook, stirring often, until the meat is well coated, about 5 minutes. Stir in 2 cups of the water. Reduce the heat to low, cover, and cook, stirring occasionally, 30 to 40 minutes, or until the meat is tender.

2. Increase the heat to medium, stir in the mango, and cook, uncovered, stirring often, for 5 minutes. Stir in the remaining 1 cup water. Reduce the heat to medium-low and cook, stirring occasionally, for 10 minutes. Stir in the cumin, chilies, and coriander, and cook for 5 minutes more. Serve hot.

MAKES 4 SERVINGS

On Cooking with Yogurt

The Indians' lavish use of yogurt in cooking and at mealtimes far surpasses the Western concept of yogurt as a snack. Perhaps Westerners would be more inclined to cook with yogurt, too, if we understood more about its properties—and if we, like the Indians, made our yogurt from scratch and from full-fat buffalo milk, which yields a thick and creamy product. But for cooking, many commercial Western yogurts, with their additives and low fat content, do not thicken or enrich a curry gravy in quite the same way as their richer Indian cousin.

One problem with cooking yogurt is its tendency to break down when heated to a boil. Anne Willan explains in *La Varenne Pratique* that cultured milk products, such as yogurt, tend to separate when heated, and thus should be added toward the end of cooking. Tom Stobart writes in *The Cook's Encyclopedia* that yogurts made from goat's milk are stable if boiled "carefully." In many cases, Indian recipes call for the addition of yogurt in an early step, so cooks may want to learn how to stop their yogurt from separating.

Several experts suggest helpful remedies to prevent yogurt breakdown. For one, always use the freshest yogurt possible; if using a commercial product, check the expiration date on the container. Ideally, your yogurt should be only three or four days old. Never stir cold yogurt into a hot dish—instead, bring the yogurt to room temperature and stir it into the dish at the last moment of cooking. Indian cook and author Julie Sahni advises mixing some sour cream with yogurt for added richness, and perhaps that will help prevent its breakdown.

Alternatively, say some experts, you can stabilize yogurt and prevent it from separating by mixing it with cornstarch diluted in water—my Indian friend B. Runi Mukherji-Ratnam says to use arrowroot starch instead for a better consistency—in the ratio of 1 cup yogurt to 1 tablespoon cornstarch mixed with $1/4$ cup water.

But with all of that said, I remember watching a young Delhi chef in a *dhaba* (roadside stand) outside the city unwrap his fresh yogurt from its cheesecloth sack and stir it directly into his bubbling lamb curry near the end of its cooking. Magically, the yogurt was immediately assimilated and the dish we later ate—Fragrant Lamb Curry, known as *rogan josh* (page 106)—was sublime. No stabilizers here.

Burmese Lamb and Noodle Curry

Panthay Khauk-swe

Another way to serve Burmese-style noodles, (see also Burmese Coconut Noodles, page 48 and Burmese Chicken and Noodle Curry, page 50) this combines egg noodles and lamb or goat meat, and because of its intrinsic heat, it might very well inspire plenty of brow mopping—the seasoning paste contains a generous number of chilies. Cook Devyani Hinshaw learned this recipe as a child in Calcutta from her Anglo-Burmese tutor. But she has undoubtedly refined the original recipe, since like most Asian cooks, she stirs, tastes, and adds ingredients as she goes along.

If you decide to use lamb, you may want to boil the meat first in water tinted with 1 tablespoon ground turmeric for about 15 minutes—this removes the "lamby" taste. A medium-wide egg noodle works well here. And of course, you can always cut back on the number of chilies. My Burmese friend Than Than Yi says this is a Muslim Indian dish from the southern Shan states in Burma, and that panthay khauk-swe *is typically made elsewhere with chicken.*

Seasoning Paste

8 cloves garlic, peeled

2 large onions, peeled and quartered

8 large dried red chilies, soaked in hot
　water for 20 minutes

About $\frac{1}{2}$ cup water

Curry

$\frac{1}{4}$ cup vegetable oil

1 tablespoon mustard oil

$1\frac{1}{2}$ tablespoons Roasted Red Chili
　Powder (page 16) or cayenne pepper

$\frac{1}{2}$ teaspoon ground turmeric

3 cups water

Salt to taste

2 pounds boneless lamb roast or goat
　leg, cut into $1\frac{1}{2}$-inch cubes

1 tablespoon gram flour (besan)

3 cups coconut milk

1. To make the seasoning paste, combine the garlic, onions, and chilies in a blender. Add just enough water to process, and blend until smooth.

2. To make the curry, heat the vegetable oil and mustard oil in a stockpot over medium heat until it just begins to smoke. Remove from the heat and set aside to cool.

3. Reheat the oils over medium heat. Add the seasoning paste and cook, stirring, about 5 minutes, or until fragrant. Stir in the red chili powder or cayenne pepper, turmeric, 1 cup of the water, and salt. Add the meat, increase the heat to high, and cook, stirring often, until the mixture thickens, about 15 minutes. Stir in the flour, the remaining 2 cups water, and the coconut milk. Reduce the heat to low and cook, stirring occasionally, 30 to 40 minutes, or until the lamb is tender.

Accompaniments

1 pound dried egg noodles, cooked
(see page 302)

2 large onions, peeled and very
thinly sliced

3 fresh red chilies, very thinly sliced

1 cup fresh coriander leaves

3 limes, quartered

3 hard-boiled eggs, shelled
and quartered

1 bunch scallions, trimmed and
thinly sliced

4. To serve, place the cooked noodles—make sure they are hot—and the other accompaniments in individual serving bowls and place them on the table. Pour the curry into a tureen and serve at the table: Place a portion of noodles in each soup bowl and ladle the curry over the noodles. Pass around the accompaniments.

MAKES 4 TO 6 SERVINGS

Fragrant Lamb Curry

Rogan Josh

One of the great dishes of the Indian curry kitchen, rogan josh *balances the spiciness of cinnamon, cardamom, and cloves with the musky tones of lamb and asafoetida. The latter, a very common Indian flavoring agent, lends an elusive and earthy undertone to many curries, which would somehow taste flat without it.*

The chef who provided this recipe, Raminder Malhotra, calls for an Indian food coloring agent called rattanjot, *which is a deep orange. It is not readily available, so plan to use a substitute. Red food coloring or cayenne pepper will have a similar though less dramatic effect. He also suggests a tip for making a velvety-smooth sauce: After the final 30 minutes of cooking, remove the meat from the mixture and pour the sauce through a fine-mesh strainer into a separate saucepan. Return the gravy to the heat and bring it to a boil. Reduce the temperature to low and cook, stirring occasionally, until the sauce is thickened.*

Americans who have sampled Indian food may be familiar with this dish, a glorified and glamorous spin on lamb stew. But this version, served with Indian masala tea and plenty of hot, fresh Indian bread, is irresistible.

Seasoning Mixture

1 tablespoon fennel seeds, roasted
   (see page 11) and ground

2 teaspoons ground ginger

1 1/2 teaspoons Indian red chili powder

1 teaspoon ground coriander

2 tablespoons red food coloring

1/2 cup water

Curry

1/2 cup Ghee (page 17) or
   vegetable oil

12 green cardamom pods

6 whole cloves

Three 1-inch pieces cinnamon stick

3 bay leaves

1/2 teaspoon asafoetida powder mixed
   with 2 tablespoons water

2 large onions, peeled and thinly sliced

2 1/4 pounds boneless lamb, cut into
   1 1/2-inch cubes

1. To make the seasoning mixture, stir together the fennel, ginger, chili powder, coriander, food coloring, and water.

2. To make the curry, heat the ghee or oil in a large saucepan over medium-low heat. Add the cardamom, cloves, cinnamon, and bay leaves, and cook, stirring, 3 to 5 minutes, or until the cardamom begins to darken. Stir in the asafoetida paste. Add the onions and cook, stirring, 7 to 10 minutes, or until golden. Remove the onions from the pan and set aside on a plate. Increase the heat to medium. Cook the meat, in batches, until browned on all sides. Remove from the pan and set aside on a plate. Reduce the heat to medium-low and stir in the garlic, ginger, and salt. Cook for 1 minute. Add the meat. Reduce the heat to low, cover, and cook, stirring occasionally, for 20 minutes. Remove the cover, increase the heat to medium, and stir-fry the meat until all the liquid is evaporated. Stir in the seasoning mixture and stock, and bring to a boil. Reduce the heat to low and cook, uncovered, until the meat is tender, about 30 minutes.

5¹/₄ teaspoons Garlic Paste (page 28)

3¹/₂ teaspoons Ginger Paste (page 28)

Salt to taste

3¹/₂ cups Basic Chicken Stock (page 19) or Basic Lamb Stock (page 20)

1 cup plain yogurt, lightly whisked

1 teaspoon Garam Masala (page 29)

3. Remove the pan from the heat, stir in the yogurt, and return to the heat. Cook, stirring often, until heated through, about 5 minutes. Stir in the onions and garam masala, and serve hot.

MAKES 4 TO 6 SERVINGS

Lamb Curry with Vegetables

Baoli Handi or Gosht Subz Bahaar

As with many Indian curries, this one has its very own legend, says Indian food historian J. Inder Singh Kalra: "The Begum Hazrat Mahal, the Queen of Oudh (Avadh), created baoli handi *as the main course for a midsummer's day picnic by her favorite step well, or* baoli." *But you do not need to wait for a hot summer day's picnic to enjoy this lamb dish (you may also use goat) with its smattering of vegetables for color, texture, and flavor—and the Kayasth people of Kashmir believe the vegetables provide a cooling effect to offset the "heating" of the mutton. As in many other curries, yogurt thickens and enriches the sauce. The queen may have served this dish with rice, but egg noodles and a crisp green salad make fine accompaniments as well.*

2 tablespoons plus ¼ cup vegetable oil
  (preferably peanut), or more if needed

½ cup cubed potatoes

½ cup cubed carrots

¼ cup 1-inch-long pieces green beans

¼ cup peas

3 green cardamom pods

2 black cardamom pods

3 whole cloves

One 1-inch piece cinnamon stick

1½ pounds boneless lamb, cut into
  1½-inch cubes

3½ teaspoons Ginger Paste (page 28)

5 teaspoons Garlic Paste (page 28)

1 teaspoon ground coriander

1 teaspoon ground turmeric

Salt to taste

1 cup plain yogurt, lightly whisked

2½ teaspoons Fried Onion Paste
  (page 28)

1 teaspoon Indian red chili powder

1½ cups water

½ teaspoon ground black cardamom

½ teaspoon ground cinnamon

½ teaspoon ground cumin

2 drops *kewra*

1. Heat 2 tablespoons of the oil in a large saucepan over medium heat. Add the potatoes, carrots, green beans, and peas, and cook, stirring, about 2 minutes, or until softened. Transfer the vegetables to a plate.

2. Heat the remaining ¼ cup oil in the saucepan over medium heat. Add the green cardamom pods, black cardamom pods, cloves, and cinnamon, and cook, stirring, 2 or 3 minutes, or until the green pods darken. Add the meat, increase the heat to medium-high, and stir-fry to sear and seal in the juices, 3 to 4 minutes. (Add more oil if the mixture seems dry.) Add the ginger and garlic, and cook, stirring, for 1 minute. Add the coriander, turmeric, and salt, and cook, stirring, for 1 minute more. Reduce the heat to low, cover, and cook, stirring occasionally, for 15 minutes.

3. Remove the saucepan from the heat, stir in the yogurt, and return to the heat. Increase the heat to medium and cook for 5 minutes. Stir in the fried onion paste and cook, stirring, for 5 minutes. Stir in the red chili powder and cook, stirring constantly, for 1 minute. Stir in the water. Reduce the heat to low, cover, and cook, stirring occasionally, 15 minutes more. Add the vegetables, bring to a boil, and remove from the heat. Stir in the cardamom, cinnamon, cumin, and *kewra*. Serve hot.

MAKES 4 TO 6 SERVINGS

Vibrant Lamb and Beet Curry

Chukander Gosht

Shredded beets give this pungent, rich curry its high drama, because they color the sauce a violet-magenta—and they also sweeten it. The cook, Baasim Zafar, uses a large quantity of oil for cooking the onions and meat and for binding all the flavors together, but you could cut back on the quantity and still get good results. Goat is an option here instead of lamb, for a very traditional Indian meal.

1½ cups vegetable oil

1 large onion, peeled and
   finely chopped

1½ teaspoons finely minced garlic

1 teaspoon finely minced fresh ginger

2 pounds boneless lamb or goat, cut
   into 1-inch cubes

2 teaspoons Indian red chili powder

1½ teaspoons ground turmeric

1 teaspoon ground coriander

1 teaspoon ground cumin

Salt to taste

2 cups water

¼ cup plain yogurt

1½ pounds beets, peeled and shredded

1 bunch fresh coriander, rinsed and
   chopped

1. Heat the oil in a stockpot over medium heat. Add the onion and cook, stirring often, 10 to 15 minutes, or until golden. Stir in the garlic, ginger, and meat, and cook, stirring often, until the meat is browned, about 10 minutes. Stir in the chili powder, turmeric, ground coriander, and cumin until combined. Stir in the salt, water, and yogurt, reduce the heat to medium-low, and cook until the oil rises to the surface, 15 to 20 minutes.

2. Stir in the beets, cover, and cook for 5 minutes more. Add the fresh coriander and mix well. Cover, remove from the heat, and set aside for 10 minutes before serving. Serve hot.

MAKES 4 TO 6 SERVINGS

Sri Lankan Black Beef Curry

Several different elements—such as toasting the rice and coconut and using an already toasted curry powder—work in tandem to darken the color of this Sri Lankan dish from Felicia Wakwella Sørensen's book, The Exotic Tastes of Paradise, The Art of Sri Lankan Cooking. *The resulting full-flavored curry should end up with a thick sauce, so only add the extra half cup water if the beef needs further cooking and tenderizing.*

As with most of the rest of Asia, Sri Lanka is a rice-eating country, so rice—and a dish of steamed vegetables—would suit this curry well.

1 tablespoon long-grain rice

1 tablespoon shredded
  unsweetened coconut

2 tablespoons Fragrant Curry Powder
  (page 30)

1/4 cup tamarind juice

2 pounds boneless chuck or stewing
  beef, cubed

2 green chilies, thinly sliced

3 cloves garlic, peeled and chopped

3 thin slices fresh ginger,
  finely chopped

One 2-inch piece lemon grass,
  trimmed

One 2-inch piece cinnamon stick

3 whole cloves

1 teaspoon Indian red chili powder

1/2 teaspoon freshly ground
  black pepper

1 1/2 cups water

2 teaspoons salt

2 tablespoons vegetable oil

6 shallots, peeled and sliced

6 curry leaves or 3 bay leaves

1. Heat a small skillet over medium heat until hot. Add the rice and coconut, and cook, stirring often, about 3 minutes, until light brown. Stir in the curry powder and cook, stirring often, 2 to 3 minutes more, until dark coffee in color. Spoon this mixture into a spice blender, add the tamarind juice, and blend until smooth.

2. Place the beef, seasoning paste, chilies, garlic, ginger, lemon grass, cinnamon, cloves, chili powder, pepper, and water in a large wok or saucepan and bring to a boil. Reduce the heat to low, cover, and cook about 45 minutes, until the meat is tender. Stir in the salt and remove from the heat.

3. Heat the oil in a large skillet over medium heat. Add the shallots and cook, stirring often, until golden brown, about 5 minutes. Stir in the curry or bay leaves and cook for 1 to 2 minutes. Pour this mixture into the beef curry, return the wok to the heat, and bring to a boil. Serve hot.

MAKES 4 TO 6 SERVINGS

Nepalese Lamb Curry

Jack Katayal of the Katmandu Restaurant in Washington, D.C., offers this typical curry from the mountain kingdom of Nepal. The combination of onions, garlic, and ginger plus the various seasoning ingredients produces an immensely satisfying and flavorful lamb dish that would be pleasing with either rice or boiled potatoes as an accompaniment.

Curry Paste

3 medium onions, peeled
  and quartered

3 cloves garlic, peeled

One 1-inch piece fresh ginger

3 whole cloves, crushed

About $1/2$ cup water

Curry

$3/4$ cup vegetable oil, or more if needed

2 bay leaves

$1^1/2$ teaspoons Indian red chili powder

1 teaspoon ground turmeric

$1/4$ teaspoon cumin seeds

Salt to taste

2 medium tomatoes, chopped

1 cup water

2 pounds boneless lamb roast, cut into
  $1^1/4$-inch cubes

$2^1/2$ tablespoons white vinegar

2 medium potatoes, peeled, boiled, and
  cut into $1^1/4$-inch cubes

1. To make the curry paste, combine the onions, garlic, ginger, and cloves in a blender. Add just enough water to process and blend until smooth.

2. To make the curry, heat the oil in a large saucepan over medium heat. Add the curry paste, bay leaves, chili powder, turmeric, cumin, and salt, and cook, 4 to 5 minutes, stirring, or until fragrant. (Add more oil if the mixture seems dry.) Stir in the tomatoes and water, and cook, stirring occasionally, for 5 minutes. Stir in the lamb. Reduce the heat to low, cover, and cook, 30 to 45 minutes, or until the meat is tender.

3. Stir in the vinegar and potatoes, and cook, uncovered, for 5 minutes. Serve hot.

MAKES 4 TO 6 SERVINGS

Burmese Sour Pork Curry

Wet-thar-hin-lay

Sour and citrusy, this simple curry shows its Indian roots with the use of mango pickle, a mouth-puckering condiment available at Indian grocers. The cook who provided this recipe, Daw May Khin Maung Than, suggests serving this with plain rice. For a fancier meal, use Burmese Coconut Rice (page 229).

Curry Paste
10 cloves garlic, peeled and minced
3 stalks lemon grass, trimmed
   and sliced
One 1¹⁄₂-inch piece fresh ginger
1 teaspoon Roasted Red Chili Powder
   (page 16) or cayenne pepper
About ¹⁄₂ cup water

Curry
1 pound lean boneless pork, cut into
   1-inch cubes
Pinch of salt
1 tablespoon fish sauce
4 large onions, peeled and cubed
¹⁄₂ cup vegetable oil
3 cups water
1 tablespoon mango pickle or
   tamarind juice
15 small white onions, peeled

1. To make the curry paste, combine the garlic, lemon grass, ginger, and red chili powder or paprika in a blender. Add just enough water to process, and blend to a coarse paste.

2. To make the curry, place the pork into a large bowl and sprinkle with the salt and fish sauce. Stir to coat the pork cubes, then stir in the curry paste and cubed onions.

3. Heat the oil in a large saucepan over medium heat. Add the pork mixture and cook, stirring, until the meat begins to brown, about 5 minutes. Add the water, ¹⁄₂ cup at a time, stirring after each addition. Stir in the mango pickle or tamarind juice and small white onions, reduce the heat to low, and cook about 30 minutes, until the onions and pork are tender.

MAKES 4 SERVINGS

Burmese Meatball Curry

Amae-thar-lone

This no-frills dish offers a flavorful spin on an all-time favorite: meatballs. For Burmese, says cook Than Than Yi, this comprises a main course in a typical, everyday family meal and is delicious served over steamed rice.

1 pound lean ground beef

3 cloves garlic, peeled and minced

1 large egg

$^1/_2$ teaspoon salt

$^1/_4$ teaspoon freshly ground
   black pepper

$^1/_4$ teaspoon Garam Masala (page 29)

$^1/_4$ teaspoon ground turmeric

$^1/_4$ cup flour

$^1/_2$ cup vegetable oil

1 cup peeled and chopped onions

1 teaspoon paprika

$^1/_2$ cup chopped tomatoes

$^3/_4$ cup water

1. Combine the beef, garlic, egg, salt, pepper, garam masala, turmeric, and flour. Form into 1-inch balls.

2. Heat the oil in a large saucepan over medium heat. Add the meatballs, a few at a time, and fry about 5 minutes, until lightly browned on all sides. Transfer the meatballs to paper towels to drain.

3. Add the onions to the saucepan and cook until golden, 3 to 5 minutes. Stir in the paprika, tomatoes, and $^1/_4$ cup of the water. Cook, stirring occasionally, until the mixture thickens, 7 to 10 minutes.

4. Add the meatballs and the remaining $^1/_2$ cup water, bring the mixture to a boil, and cook for 5 minutes more. Serve hot.

MAKES 3 TO 4 SERVINGS

Pickled Bok Choy and Pork Soup

Nguyen Ly, a Vietnamese studying at an American university, told me over tea one day that her young son—even when faced with an assortment of fast-food choices in the United States—prefers this family-style soup of North Vietnam. While its slightly sour taste may not mean "comfort food" to a Westerner, it is both agreeably refreshing and, when served with rice, a complete meal.

2 tablespoons vegetable oil

1 shallot, peeled and sliced

$^1/_2$ pound boneless pork roast (with some fat), cut into long, thin strips

2 heads pickled bok choy, rinsed, squeezed dry, and shredded (see Note)

3 large tomatoes, each cut into 5 or 6 sections

$^1/_2$ teaspoon sugar

Salt to taste

3 green chilies, thinly sliced, or to taste

1. Heat the oil in a large saucepan over medium heat. Add the shallots and cook, stirring, until fragrant but not golden, about 1 minute. Add the pork and cook, stirring, until it begins to brown, about 5 minutes.

2. Stir in the bok choy and tomatoes, and cook, stirring, 2 to 3 minutes more, until the tomatoes begin to soften. Stir in the sugar and salt, and cook, stirring, until well combined, 4 to 5 minutes more. Add enough water to cover, reduce the heat to low, and cook until the pork is cooked through, about 20 minutes more. Garnish with the green chilies and serve hot.

MAKES 2 TO 3 SERVINGS

Note: You can find pickled bok choy or cabbage at a well-stocked Asian market, sold in a jar or from a large earthenware crock.

Vietnamese Beef Stew Pot

For this delicious stew, the Chinese-Vietnamese cook Helene Sze McCarthy always discards the pieces of garlic and ginger after the first cooking stage. She then adds the remaining seasonings in the final cooking stage so that the individual flavors of the meat and carrot remain intact. She suggests using a less tender cut of beef that requires lengthy cooking, though she says that a pork roast or a 3- to 4-pound chicken cut into serving pieces is a good alternative. The trick is to add no salt or soy sauce until the last minute, or the meat will toughen. Serve with side dishes of French bread for dunking into the gravy and sliced fresh lemons for squeezing fresh juice over the meat.

2¹/₂ pounds boneless chuck, cubed
¹/₄ cup vegetable oil
¹/₄ cup tomato paste
5 cloves garlic, peeled
One 3-inch piece fresh ginger, smashed
1 large carrot, peeled and diagonally sliced
3 to 4 green chilies, thinly sliced
3 to 4 tablespoons fish sauce
Soy sauce to taste
Salt to taste
Fresh lemon slices

1. Place the beef in a large stockpot and add enough water to cover. Bring the water to a boil and cook the meat until the juices are no longer pink, about 15 minutes. Discard the water, cover the meat with fresh water, and set aside.

2. Heat the oil in a large wok or skillet over medium heat. Add the tomato paste, garlic, and ginger, and cook, stirring often, 5 to 7 minutes, until fragrant. Discard the garlic and ginger, and spoon the tomato paste into the water with the beef.

3. Return the stockpot to the heat and bring the water to a boil. Reduce the heat to low and cook, uncovered, until the beef is tender, about 3 hours.

4. Meanwhile, put the carrots and enough water to cover in a large saucepan and bring to a boil. Cook about 6 minutes, or until the carrots are just crisp-tender. Drain the carrots and cool under running water. Set aside until the last few moments of cooking the beef.

5. When the beef is tender, stir in the carrots, chilies, fish sauce, soy sauce, and salt. Cook for 2 minutes. Serve hot and pass the lemon slices.

MAKES 4 TO 6 SERVINGS

Vietnamese Vinegar Beef

The Mongolian Hot Pot (page 280) spawned a family of cook-alikes, since virtually every Asian country has its own version of ingredients cooked in liquid at the table. In this Vietnamese version, very thinly sliced beef is quick-cooked in a hot vinegar-based broth. Rather than being unpleasantly sour, the cooked beef is only mildly astringent and complements the vegetables, noodles, and dipping-sauce accompaniments.

My Chinese-Vietnamese friend Helene Sze McCarthy introduced me to this unique dish, teaching me how to cook, wrap, and eat all the various components. As with many Vietnamese dishes, using softened rice-paper wrappers to make edible packets is a key part of eating and enjoying this meal. For instructions on using these delicate, yet chewy, wrapping papers, see "Using Rice-Paper Wrappers" (below).

When you present this dish, be sure to include fresh coriander, mint, and Thai basil—these are almost mandatory! If you can find it, use Vietnamese mint, or rau ram; otherwise, substitute Thai mint. Mix the dipping sauce to taste—it combines the sweet, sour, and salty flavors that Vietnamese love.

Stock

1 cup water, or more as needed

1/3 cup white vinegar, or more as needed

2 tablespoons shredded fresh ginger

Dipping Sauce

1/2 cup plus 2 tablespoons water

1/3 cup fish sauce

1/4 cup sugar

3 tablespoons minced garlic

Juice of 1 lime

Ingredients for Wrapping

1/2 pound lean top round, very
   thinly sliced

12 to 16 triangular rice-paper wrappers

1/4 pound rice vermicelli, cooked (see
   page 302)

10 sprigs fresh coriander

2 carrots, peeled and cut into long, very
   thin strips

1 cup thinly sliced cucumbers

1/4 pound bean sprouts

1 cup Thai basil leaves

1 cup Thai mint leaves

1. To make the stock, combine the water, vinegar, and ginger in a tabletop cooking vessel. Heat the stock at the table until boiling.

2. To make the dipping sauce, combine the water, fish sauce, sugar, garlic, and lime juice. Transfer to a serving dish and place at the table.

3. Arrange the ingredients for wrapping on a separate platter and offer each person chopsticks—each diner uses chopsticks to pick up and swish the beef through the hot stock. (Add more water and vinegar as needed.) Because it is so thin, the beef cooks in seconds. Each person wraps the beef and other ingredients as desired in the rice-paper wrappers and dunks the package into the dipping sauce before eating.

MAKES 3 TO 4 SERVINGS

Using Rice-Paper Wrappers

Vietnamese rice-paper wrappers make edible envelopes for fillings that may include grilled meats, cooked seafood, and a variety of raw greens and herbs. Because they have virtually no flavor—and hence do not compete with other foods—and because they add a distinctive chewy texture, these wrappers make for yet another sensual element at the Vietnamese table.

Made of rice flour and water, these wrappers when dried are brittle and semi-translucent and are patterned with a distinctive crosshatch design that the moist wrappers pick up as they dry on bamboo mats. Before use, the wrappers need to be softened, which may be done in one of several ways: by dipping each wrapper quickly in warm or cold water, by brushing them with beaten whole eggs, by brushing the surface of the wrapper with moistened fingers, or by wrapping them in moist towels. They are ready for use when they are soft and pliable. Available in circular or triangular shapes, the wrappers are sold at most Asian markets and keep indefinitely in a cupboard.

Filling the wrappers for neat eating is another trick altogether, and if you have ever watched someone practiced in this art eat without spilling food, you'll understand how efficient and neat the wrapping becomes. To fill the triangles, place a mouth-sized portion of food in a line parallel to and near the rounded end and make the first fold over, enclosing the food. Fold in each side to the center, then continue rolling the wrapper tightly, jelly-roll fashion, to the tip. For filling circles, the principle is the same, except that you are rolling not toward a tip of a triangle but toward the opposite rounded edge of the circle. If wrapped tightly enough, each roll stays firmly closed for neat eating.

Cambodian Pork, Peanut, and Coconut Milk Soup

Nga Tang

A sweet-salty and very rich soup, this is a favorite of the Cambodian cook Bora Chu and her family. She prefers to make her own coconut milk rather than using the canned or frozen varieties so that she can have only the thickest milk from the first pressing of the coconut meat. She also varies this dish by using shrimp instead of pork, or by combining the two. If you want to use shrimp alone, precook the shrimp until just pink, then add them during the last 5 minutes of cooking.

For an authentic Cambodian rendition, sliver the lime leaves as thin as threads and hand slice the peanuts on an angle so that they resemble slivered almonds. To save time, you may use the commercially prepared fried garlic and fried shallots, but remember these do not have the same lively flavor as the freshly cooked ingredients. Use bread, shrimp crackers, or fried rice cakes for dunking into the soup during the meal.

$3/4$ cup vegetable oil

2 shallots, peeled and thinly sliced

5 cloves garlic, peeled and thinly sliced

$1/2$ pound ground pork

2 teaspoons ground turmeric

3 tablespoons sugar, or more to taste

10 kaffir lime leaves, very thinly sliced

$1/3$ cup fish sauce

$2^1/_2$ to 3 cups thick coconut milk (see page 6)

1 cup roasted peanuts (see page 11), thinly sliced

French bread slices, fried shrimp crackers (see Note on page 79), or fried rice cakes (see Note)

1. Heat the oil in a large wok or skillet over medium heat. Add the shallots and cook, stirring, about 3 minutes, or until golden. Add the garlic and cook, stirring, until golden, about 1 minute more. Transfer the shallots and garlic to a plate. Pour off some of the oil in the wok, leaving about 3 tablespoons.

2. Return the wok to the heat and add the pork; stir with a fork to break apart any clumps. Sprinkle with the turmeric and stir to blend. Stir in the sugar, lime leaves, fish sauce, and 2 cups of the coconut milk. Reduce the heat to medium-low and cook until the pork is no longer pink, about 5 minutes. Stir in the peanuts and half of the fried shallots and garlic. Cook for 4 minutes more. Stir in the remaining $1/2$ cup of the coconut milk and the remaining fried shallots and garlic (add more coconut milk for a more liquid soup). Cook until hot, about 5 minutes more. Serve immediately with bread, crackers, or rice cakes.

MAKES 2 TO 3 SERVINGS

Note: Fried rice cakes look like Rice Krispies that have been glued together into a small square. They are tasteless but pick up the flavors of whatever they are dunked in. Fried rice cakes are sold at Asian markets.

Malaysian Sweet Onion and Beef Stew

Chili Jintan

This lusty, rugged dish, with its dark color and sweet-hot bite, calls for large sweet onions that cook slowly and caramelize, a process that brings out their natural sugars. The fire comes from the substantial quantity of dried chilies; for these, use the long varieties packed in cellophane and sold at Indian or pan-Asian groceries. The black Indonesian soy sauce is a must here, for it gives the dish its dark tint and adds yet another layer of sweetness. The cook, Majmin Hashim of Kuala Lumpur, Malaysia's capital city, says that calves' liver is a fine substitute for the beef. Serve this with rice or egg noodles and plenty of chilled beer or wine.

$^1/_4$ cup vegetable oil

3 large onions, peeled and sliced

10 to 12 dried red chilies, roasted
(see page 7)

2 teaspoons fennel seeds, roasted
(see page 11)

1 teaspoon cumin seeds, roasted
(see page 11)

10 curry leaves

4 green cardamom pods

One 2-inch piece cinnamon stick

4 whole cloves

1 pound boneless top round, cut into
$^3/_4$-inch-wide strips

2 cups water, or more if needed

2 tablespoons black soy sauce

1 tablespoon tamarind juice

1 tablespoon minced fresh ginger

1 teaspoon sugar (optional)

1. Heat the oil in a large wok or skillet over medium heat. Add half of the onions and cook, stirring often, until golden brown, about 10 minutes.

2. Meanwhile, pulverize the chilies, fennel, and cumin in a spice grinder or blender. Stir this mixture into the onions along with the curry, cardamom, cinnamon, and cloves. Add the beef, remaining onions, and water, and stir until thoroughly combined. Reduce the heat to medium-low and cook, uncovered, stirring often, until the beef is tender, about 1 hour. (Add more water if the mixture seems dry.) Stir in the soy sauce, tamarind juice, ginger, and sugar, if using. Cook for 15 minutes more. Serve hot.

MAKES 4 SERVINGS

Malaysian Rendang

Both the Malaysians and Indonesians claim rendang *as their own, but regardless of its origins, a traditional* rendang *is a "dry stew," cooked so long that almost all the liquid has evaporated and the mixture becomes pastelike. Any remaining paste provides a thick coating for the meat and is intensely flavored, to say nothing of chili hot. Some versions are slightly "wetter" than others, but the dish's overall dryness acts as a preservative of sorts, since many home cooks swear that a* rendang *keeps well for up to one month without any refrigeration. This, of course, suited tropical life before electricity.*

My Malaysian friend Majmin Hashim is generous in her use of shallots and says the more shallots you use, the better. You can also substitute chicken cut into serving pieces for the beef, but first the chicken must be slow-roasted in a wok or skillet without any added fat or liquid so that the meat becomes firm and dries out. This recipe calls for a Malaysian fruit called asam kuping, *which provides a certain tartness to the dish. It is unavailable in the West and has no substitution, so simply prepare the dish without it. Typically this dish is cooked in an uncovered wok with a large surface area, allowing the liquid to evaporate more quickly. The sauce tends to splatter as it cooks, so you may want to set this on a back burner away from other dishes.*

Seasoning Paste

8 to 10 fresh red chilies

One 1-inch piece fresh ginger,
  chopped

One $1/2$-inch piece galangal,
  thinly sliced

About $1/2$ cup coconut milk

Stew

$1^1/2$ cups coconut milk

10 to 12 shallots, peeled and
  thinly sliced

3 stalks lemon grass, trimmed and very
  thinly sliced

4 cloves garlic, peeled and minced

1 kaffir lime leaf, shredded

1 turmeric leaf, shredded (optional)

$1^1/2$ pounds boneless beef stew meat,
  cut into cubes

3 cups water

$3/4$ cup shredded unsweetened coconut,
  toasted until golden, and pounded
  with a mortar and pestle

1. To make the seasoning paste, combine the chilies, ginger, and galangal in a blender. Add just enough coconut milk to process and blend until smooth.

2. To make the stew, combine the seasoning paste, coconut milk, shallots, lemon grass, garlic, lime leaf, turmeric leaf, beef, and water in a large wok or saucepan. Stir together thoroughly. Cook over medium-low heat, uncovered, stirring occasionally, for $1^1/2$ hours. Stir in the toasted coconut and cook, stirring often toward the end of the cooking time, until the liquid has almost completely evaporated and the mixture is very thick, about $1^1/2$ to 2 hours more. Serve hot or at room temperature.

MAKES 4 SERVINGS

Maj-min Hashim's "Special Noodles"

Popular with the cook's family, this dish resembles the traditional Malaysian laksa *with its use of noodles as a base for a succulent coconut gravy. As with all* laksas, *this is a full meal in a bowl, ideal for lunch or supper.*

3 tablespoons vegetable oil, or more
    if needed

5 shallots, peeled and sliced

2 cloves garlic, peeled and sliced

2 teaspoons chopped fresh ginger

8 dried red chilies, or to taste, soaked
    in hot water for 20 minutes and
    pounded or ground in a blender

2 stalks lemon grass, trimmed
    and minced

2 tablespoons Malaysian yellow soybean
    paste (*taucheo*)

1 cup roasted peanuts, coarsely chopped

$^{1}/_{2}$ pound boneless top round, cut into
    $^{1}/_{2}$-inch cubes

4 cups water

1 cup coconut milk

$^{1}/_{2}$ cup cubed potatoes

$^{1}/_{2}$ pound medium shrimp, shelled
    and deveined

$^{1}/_{2}$ pound Fried Tofu (page 18)

Accompaniments

1 pound fresh egg noodles, cooked
    (see page 303), or $^{1}/_{2}$ pound dried
    egg noodles, cooked (see page 302)

$^{1}/_{2}$ pound bean sprouts, blanched in
    boiling water for 1 minute

$1^{1}/_{4}$ cups Fried Shallots (page 17)

1 cucumber, peeled and cut into
    thin strips

3 tablespoons thinly sliced scallions

5 green chilies, thinly sliced, or to taste

2 limes, quartered

1. Heat the oil in a stockpot over medium heat. Add the shallots, garlic, and ginger, and cook, stirring, about 5 minutes, or until golden. (Add more oil if the mixture seems dry.) Stir in the chilies, lemon grass, and soybean paste, and cook, stirring, until fragrant, about 5 minutes. Stir in the peanuts and meat, and cook, stirring, for 4 minutes. Add the water and coconut milk, reduce the heat to low, and cook for 15 minutes. Add the potatoes and cook until tender, 8 to 10 minutes more. Stir in the shrimp and tofu, and remove from the heat.

2. To serve, arrange portions of the noodles, bean sprouts, shallots, cucumbers, scallions, and chilies in individual soup bowls. Ladle in the hot gravy, squeeze in some lime juice, and serve.

MAKES 4 SERVINGS

Malaysian Fiery Noodles and Sweet Potato Curry

An intensely hot and rich curry, ideal for warming the cockles of your heart, this dish needs some advance planning because it calls for cooked and mashed sweet potatoes. These are essential for the overall effect, since they both thicken and sweeten the potent curry sauce. You can shorten preparation time by prebaking the potatoes a day or so ahead, scooping the flesh from the skins and mashing it, and storing the puree until ready to use. Of course, you can quick-cook the potatoes in a microwave oven. This is another of Majmin Hashim's wonderful traditional Malaysian dishes and is excellent with steamed spinach or a light salad of tart greens.

3 tablespoons vegetable oil

5 shallots, peeled and diced

2 cloves garlic, peeled

2 teaspoons chopped fresh ginger

8 dried red chilies, roasted and ground

½ pound boneless beef roast or flank
    or top round steak, sliced into thin
    2-inch-long strips

6 black peppercorns, crushed

4 cups water

1 cup cooked mashed sweet potatoes

Salt to taste

Accompaniments

1 pound fresh egg noodles, cooked (see
    page 303), or ½ pound dried egg
    noodles, cooked (see page 302)

2 cups shredded lettuce

1 bunch scallions, trimmed and
    thinly sliced

1 cucumber, thinly sliced

½ pound bean sprouts, blanched in
    boiling water for 1 minute

Garnishes

3 to 4 green chilies, thinly sliced, or
    to taste

1 cup Fried Shallots (page 17)

1. Heat the oil in a large wok or skillet over medium heat. Add the shallots, garlic, and ginger, and cook, stirring, until golden, about 5 minutes. Stir in the ground chilies, beef, peppercorns, and water. Reduce the heat to low and cook until the beef is tender, about 30 minutes. Stir in the sweet potatoes and salt, and cook until the mixture is thickened, 10 to 15 minutes.

2. To serve, arrange portions of the noodles, lettuce, scallions, cucumbers, and bean sprouts in individual soup bowls. Ladle in the hot sweet potato mixture, garnish with the chilies and shallots, and serve.

MAKES 2 TO 3 SERVINGS

Thai Curried Noodle Soup

Nick Srisawat, owner of the Tara Thai restaurants in the Washington, D.C., metropolitan area, explained that this soup is a typical, traditional noodle dish that vendors sell as street food in Thailand—and it captures many of the flavors that make Thai cooking so alluring. The soup also shows its Indian influence with the addition of curry powder and its Chinese roots with the use of noodles. As for the noodles, Mr. Srisawat suggests using the thin flat rice noodles Thais use for making the popular noodle dish pad Thai.

3 tablespoons vegetable oil

2 tablespoons Thai Red Curry Paste
(page 25)

4 cups coconut milk

1 tablespoon curry powder

1 pound boneless lean round steak,
cubed or sliced into short, thin strips

6 dried red chilies, roasted and ground
(see page 7)

2 tablespoons fish sauce, or more to
taste

3 tablespoons sugar

Accompaniments

3/4 pound rice stick noodles, cooked
(see page 302)

1 pound bean sprouts, blanched in
boiling water for 1 minute

1 tablespoon shredded preserved
Chinese cabbage

1 cup cubed pressed firm tofu
(see Note)

1 cup roasted peanuts, crushed

1 tablespoon minced garlic, fried
until golden

2 tablespoons chopped scallions

2 tablespoons chopped fresh coriander
leaves

2 hard-boiled eggs, shelled
and quartered

1. Heat the oil in a large saucepan over medium heat. Add the curry paste and cook, stirring, about 5 minutes, or until fragrant. Stir in the coconut milk and the curry powder, and bring to a boil. Add the beef, reduce the heat to low, and cook, uncovered, until the meat is very tender, about 45 minutes. Stir in the ground chilies, fish sauce, and sugar, and remove from the heat.

2. Divide the noodles and bean sprouts among individual soup bowls. Layer each serving with a portion of cabbage, tofu, peanuts, and garlic. Ladle the soup and beef into each bowl. Garnish with the scallions, coriander leaves, and eggs, and serve immediately.

MAKES 4 SERVINGS

Note: For this recipe, the tofu should be pressed before cubing to remove excess moisture. To do so, slice the tofu in half horizontally and press it between layers of paper towels. Change the towels and repeat the process until most of the excess water has been removed.

Thai Beef Soup with White Radishes

Tom Nuea Savoey

The cook who provided this recipe, Sarnsern Gajaseni of The Thai Cooking School at The Oriental, Bangkok, explains that you can vary this soup by using six or eight chicken thighs or drumsticks in place of the beef. But should you select beef, use a tough cut that can stand up to a long boiling time—this produces a tastier soup—and keep skimming the surface to produce a clear broth. This dish is suitable for a light supper if served with a garlicky bread, but Thais would use this as part of a much more complete meal that would include a curry, rice, possibly a grilled meat, and fruit.

5 cups water, or more if needed

2 cups sliced brisket of beef

2 cups thinly sliced or diced daikon

3 tablespoons tamarind juice

3 tablespoons fish sauce

1 tablespoon palm sugar or dark
  brown sugar

9 green chilies, or to taste

1 teaspoon salt

3 tablespoons rice vinegar

1. Pour the water into a large stockpot and add the beef. Cook over medium-low heat 15 to 30 minutes, or until the beef is tender and the liquid is slightly reduced. Stir in the daikon, reduce the heat to medium-low, and cook until the daikon is soft, about 10 minutes. (Add more water if the mixture seems dry.) Stir in the tamarind juice, fish sauce, and sugar.

2. Meanwhile, pound the chilies and salt together. Moisten with the vinegar. Serve this with the soup and spoon it in to add some chili zest. Serve hot.

MAKES 4 TO 6 SERVINGS

Rich Mutton Korma

To most Westerners, the word "mutton" means the meat from old sheep. But in India, mutton generically refers to the meat from both young goats and young lamb. And mutton as goat meat is commonly eaten in the Indian Subcontinent. The young Indian cook who provided this recipe, Baasim Zafar, here calls for using goat in this family recipe, but a mild and tender spring lamb will certainly be a fine substitute.

This stew has plenty of liquid for mopping up with Indian breads such as naan, roti, *and onion* kulcha. *But if you cannot find these, pita bread is a good alternative.*

³/₄ cup vegetable oil

2 medium onions, peeled and
   thinly sliced

2 tablespoons minced garlic

1¹/₂ tablespoons minced fresh ginger

2 pounds boneless goat leg, cut into
   1-inch cubes

³/₄ cup plain yogurt

4 teaspoons ground coriander

2 teaspoons Indian red chili powder

Salt to taste

One 3-inch piece cinnamon stick

4 bay leaves

8 green cardamom pods

10 whole cloves

1 teaspoon black peppercorns

³/₄ teaspoon mace

¹/₄ teaspoon ground nutmeg

1 cup water

6 drops *kewra*

1. Heat the oil in a stockpot over medium heat. Add the onions and cook, stirring often, 10 to 15 minutes, or until golden. Transfer the onions to paper towels to drain. Stir in the garlic and ginger, and cook, stirring, for 30 seconds. Remove from the oil. Add the meat and cook, stirring often, about 15 minutes, or until all the excess liquid is evaporated.

2. Add 2 tablespoons of the yogurt and cook, stirring constantly, 7 to 10 minutes, or until slightly thickened. Stir in the coriander, chili powder, and salt. Stir in the remaining yogurt and enough water to cover the meat. Reduce the heat to medium-low and cook until the oil rises to the surface of the stew, 15 to 20 minutes. Add the cinnamon and bay leaves and cook for 3 minutes.

3. Meanwhile, combine the fried onions, cardamom, cloves, peppercorns, mace, and nutmeg in a blender. Add just enough liquid from the stew to process and blend until smooth. Stir into the stew with the 1 cup water and cook about 10 minutes, or until slightly thickened. Add the *kewra*, cover, and cook the stew for 10 minutes more. Serve hot.

MAKES 6 SERVINGS

Mussaman Curry with Beef

Gaeng Mussaman Nua

Southern Thailand is home to a large Muslim population, explains Nick Srisawat, owner of Tara Thai restaurants in the Washington, D.C., metropolitan area. They popularized this curry dish, which is generally made with beef, and less often with chicken and lamb, but never with pork. The Mussaman (also spelled Masaman) curry depends for its multilayered flavor on spices such as cinnamon, cardamom, nutmeg, cloves, and mace—all brought to Thailand by the Muslim traders—which have set this curry apart from all other Thai curries. A slightly sweet dish, it also calls for a generous helping of chilies in the curry paste, as well as peanuts and potatoes in the curry itself. The final flavor is soured a bit by tamarind juice. Prepare the curry paste several hours ahead of time to allow the flavors to mature.

½ cup Mussaman Curry Paste
   (page 26)

2½ cups coconut milk

1 pound boneless sirloin, cubed

6 bay leaves

5 green cardamom pods, roasted
   (see page 11) and seeded

One 3-inch piece cinnamon stick

3 tablespoons palm sugar or dark
   brown sugar

1 tablespoon unsalted peanuts

2 medium potatoes, peeled and cubed

10 shallots or 2 medium onions, peeled
   and sliced

¼ cup fish sauce

2 tablespoons tamarind juice

Combine the curry paste and 1 cup of the coconut milk in a large saucepan over medium heat. Cook until about 5 minutes, or until fragrant. Stir in the beef and cook, stirring occasionally, for 10 minutes. Stir in the remaining 1½ cups coconut milk, bring to a boil, and cook, stirring occasionally, for 10 minutes. Stir in the bay leaves, cardamom, cinnamon, sugar, peanuts, potatoes, shallots or onions, fish sauce, and tamarind juice, and cook until the beef and potatoes are tender, 15 to 20 minutes more. Serve hot or at room temperature.

MAKES 4 SERVINGS

Sumatran Beef and Noodle Soup

Soto Minang

West Sumatrans who live in the highland areas, such as the mountain town of Bukittinggi, often prepare this filling beef soup. Irmansjah Madewa, the manager of the Hotel Pusako in Bukittinggi at the time of my visit, offered me the recipe for this soup, which may serve as a luncheon main course or a robust addition to a multicourse dinner.

8 cups Basic Beef Stock (page 19)

³/₄ pound boneless top round roast

8 stalks lemon grass, trimmed and
   lightly pounded

8 Indonesian or Western bay leaves

Four 2-inch pieces fresh ginger, diced

One 1-inch piece galangal,
   thinly sliced

4 teaspoons minced garlic, fried
   until golden

1 teaspoon ground mace

¹/₄ cup vegetable oil, or more if needed

4 medium potatoes, peeled and cubed

³/₄ pound rice vermicelli

Salt and freshly ground black pepper
   to taste

Garnishes

¹/₂ cup Fried Shallots (page 17)

1 leek, trimmed, rinsed, and
   thinly sliced

1 stalk celery, trimmed and
   thinly sliced

4 green chilies, sliced, or to taste

1. Combine the stock and beef in a large saucepan and bring to a boil. Reduce the heat to medium-low and stir in the lemon grass, bay leaves, ginger, galangal, garlic, and mace. Cook until the beef is tender, 15 to 20 minutes. Transfer the meat to a cutting board. Reduce the heat to low and let the broth continue to simmer. When the beef is cool enough to handle, cut it into cubes.

2. Heat the oil in a large wok or skillet over medium heat. Add the meat and cook, stirring often, until browned, 5 to 10 minutes. Transfer to a plate. Add the potatoes and cook until golden, about 10 minutes. (Add more oil if the mixture seems dry.)

3. Meanwhile, soak the vermicelli in hot water for 15 minutes. Drain and trim into 4- or 5-inch pieces. Place equal portions of the noodles and meat into individual soup bowls.

4. Strain the broth through a fine sieve and discard the solids. Season with salt and pepper. Ladle the broth into each bowl and add the fried potatoes, fried shallots, leeks, celery, and chilies.

MAKES 4 SERVINGS

Indonesian Lamb Curry

Gulai Kambing

This succulent concoction calls for using lamb chops, a costly ingredient for a curry dish, but you can trim the price by using blade or shoulder chops instead. Sumatrans like this dish hot, says the cook who provided this recipe, Mrs. Hanief Djohan, but add the chilies to suit your taste.

Curry Paste

3 to 10 fresh red chilies

4 shallots, peeled and chopped

4 cloves garlic, peeled

5 macadamia nuts or candlenuts

One 1-inch piece fresh ginger

One $^1/_2$-inch piece galangal

About $^1/_2$ cup coconut milk

Curry

$^1/_3$ cup vegetable oil

1 stalk lemon grass, trimmed and stem
   end crushed

6 kaffir lime leaves, halved

2 turmeric leaves (optional)

2 Indonesian bay leaves

1 teaspoon salt

$^1/_2$ teaspoon ground turmeric

8 cups Basic Chicken Stock (page 19)
   or water

$2^1/_2$ cups coconut milk

$1^1/_2$ pounds lamb chops, bone in,
   trimmed of fat

1. To make the curry paste, combine the chilies, shallots, garlic, nuts, ginger, and galangal in a blender. Add just enough coconut milk to process, and blend until smooth.

2. To make the curry, heat the oil in a large wok or saucepan over medium heat. Add the curry paste and cook, stirring, until fragrant, 3 to 5 minutes. Add the lemon grass, lime leaves, turmeric leaves if using, bay leaves, salt, and ground turmeric. Stir in the stock or water and coconut milk, and bring to a boil, stirring constantly. Add the lamb. Reduce the heat to low, cover, and cook, stirring occasionally, until the lamb is tender and a layer of oil forms on the surface, 1 to $1^1/_2$ hours. Serve hot.

MAKES 4 SERVINGS

Sumatran Coconut and Chili Beef Curry

I met Irmansjah Madewa on the Indonesian island of Sumatra when he was the manager of the mountaintop Hotel Pusako in the town of Bukittinggi. We sat and discussed local curries, and he gave me the recipe for this dish, which brings together many of the elements—chilies, coconut milk, garlic, and Indonesian bay leaves—typical of Indonesian cooking. Chances are the local cooks would use water buffalo, but this version uses beef. You may use chicken instead, but plan on a shorter cooking time.

Curry Paste

5 dried red chilies, soaked in hot water
    for 20 minutes
2 stalks lemon grass, trimmed and
    thinly sliced
4 shallots, peeled and quartered
One 4-inch piece fresh ginger,
    chopped
4 cloves garlic, peeled
1 tablespoon ground turmeric
About $1/2$ cup coconut milk

Curry

$1/4$ cup vegetable oil
$2^1/2$ cups coconut milk
2 pounds boneless beef roast, trimmed
    and sliced $1/4$-inch thick into
    $1^1/2 \times 3$-inch pieces
1 turmeric leaf (optional)
3 kaffir lime leaves, halved
2 Indonesian bay leaves
1 teaspoon ground coriander
Salt to taste

1. To make the curry paste, combine the chilies, lemon grass, shallots, ginger, garlic, and turmeric in a blender. Add just enough coconut milk to process, and blend until smooth.

2. To make the curry, heat the oil in a large wok or skillet over medium heat. Add the curry paste and cook, stirring, about 5 minutes, or until fragrant. Stir in the coconut milk, beef, turmeric leaf if using, lime leaves, bay leaves, coriander, and salt. Reduce the heat to medium-low and cook, uncovered, 30 to 40 minutes, or until the beef is tender and the sauce is thickened.

MAKES 4 TO 6 SERVINGS

Stewed Young Jackfruit

The cook who provided this recipe, Hanny Nabiela Sugianto, calls this unusual Indonesian dish panci *or perhaps* pangsit *(we could not decide on the spelling), but it does not fit the description of* pangsit *as a dish of fried minced pork and shrimp given in Sri Owen's classic book on Indonesian cooking,* Indonesian Food and Cookery. *Instead, this is a substantial stew that pairs jackfruit, a tropical fruit that grows abundantly in Indonesia, with meat.*

The recipe calls for fresh young jackfruit, which we found in piles at Hanny's local market in the town of Medan on Sumatra. But chances are that most Westerners will find jackfruit available only in cans or jars, packed in a sugar syrup or water. For this recipe, use the unsweetened jackfruit if you can find it. Whether you use the preferred young fresh jackfruit or the canned version, the fruit must cook with the meat for the full 5 hours without stirring—the meat should cook until it falls apart. Part of the cooking liquid is coconut water, the liquid you hear splashing around inside a coconut when you shake it. Should you have fresh coconuts on hand, you can extract this clear liquid by cracking the coconut open and catching the water as it pours out. An easier way to get coconut water is to look for it in cans at an Asian market. However, this product has sugar added, so reduce the palm sugar accordingly. Hanny Nabiela Sugianto served this with several other dishes, including rice, a watercress salad, and sweet jasmine tea.

3 pounds young jackfruit, peeled and
    sliced, pits removed, or two
    1¼-pound cans jackfruit, preferably
    water-packed

One 2-pound boneless beef roast or
    2 pounds assorted chicken pieces

10 shallots, peeled and sliced, skins
    reserved and wrapped in cheesecloth

15 Indonesian or Western bay leaves

4 cloves garlic, peeled and sliced

1 cup palm sugar or dark brown sugar

3½ tablespoons ground coriander

8 cups coconut milk

6 cups coconut water or water

Salt and freshly ground black pepper
    to taste

3 fresh red chilies, thinly sliced

3 green chilies, thinly sliced

Combine the jackfruit, beef or chicken, shallots, shallot skins (which will help color the stew), bay leaves, garlic, sugar, coriander, coconut milk, and coconut water or water in a stockpot. Cook over low heat, uncovered, for 5 hours. Before serving, discard the shallot skins. Season with salt and pepper, and garnish with the chilies. Serve either hot or cold.

MAKES 6 TO 8 SERVINGS

Mu-Shu Pork Soup

According to the cook who provided this recipe, Joyce Piotrowski, the Chinese learned centuries ago that marinades seal in meat juices, making the meat seem more tender than it actually is. The effect of the "marinade" here happens in the pan during cooking, not during any lengthy soaking time in which the meat is tenderized. This light and delicate soup does not call for added salt, because the chicken stock should provide enough. The wok should be so hot that there is an explosion of fragrance when you add the oil and meat. If you serve this as the main course for a light supper, offer spring rolls or steamed dumplings to round out the meal.

Meat Marinade

2 teaspoons Chinese rice wine

1 teaspoon cornstarch

One 1-inch-thick center-cut pork chop, partially frozen and cut into thin strips

Soup

1 tablespoon vegetable oil

One 1-inch piece fresh ginger, cut into thin strips

1 clove garlic, peeled and smashed

3 scallions, trimmed and thinly sliced

4 small cloud ear mushrooms, soaked in hot water for 20 minutes and cut into strips

1 bunch spinach, rinsed and trimmed

6 cups Basic Chicken Stock (page 19)

1 tablespoon cornstarch

1 teaspoon toasted sesame oil

1 teaspoon Szechuan peppercorns, crushed

2 large eggs, beaten

1. Combine the rice wine and cornstarch in a bowl. Add the sliced pork and stir to coat.

2. Heat a large wok or skillet over high heat for several minutes. Add the oil and pork, and stir-fry until the meat turns white, 2 to 3 minutes. Transfer the meat to a plate. Add the ginger and stir; add the garlic and stir; add the scallions and stir; add the mushrooms and stir; and add the spinach and stir until it is wilted. Return the meat to the pan and add the stock. Combine the cornstarch, sesame oil, and peppercorns. Moisten with a little stock and stir into the soup. Bring the mixture to a boil.

3. Just before serving, add the eggs in a thin trickle, stirring constantly, to form "threads" in the soup. Ladle into individual bowls and serve hot.

MAKES 2 SERVINGS

Cantonese Mutton Stew

Hong Kong's ultimate gastronome, William Mark, once held a Cantonese banquet at the now-demolished King Bun restaurant in Hong Kong for several acquaintances, and I was lucky enough to attend. He ordered a mutton stew as the banquet's star—preceded by an array of less important courses—and this garlicky, gingery dish has left an indelible impression on me. In fact, if I were faced with ordering my last meal, this mutton stew would be on the menu.

In the sauce, you may substitute rosemary, sage, or tarragon for the lime leaves, but then the result will not be particularly Cantonese. You may also use canned rather than fresh water chestnuts. The fermented bean curd in this dish bears a remarkable similarity to Roquefort cheese, so don't be surprised by its "cheesy" taste. William Mark notes that smashing the ginger before trimming it releases its juices.

8 cups water

2 pounds boneless lamb, cut into
   1-inch cubes

1/2 pound fresh ginger, peeled,
   smashed, and cubed

1/2 cup peanut oil, or more if needed

2 tablespoons Chinese rice wine
   or sherry

One 5-ounce can water chestnuts,
   drained

2 pieces fermented red bean curd

2 tablespoons minced garlic

Sauce

2 pieces fermented white bean curd

4 fresh red chilies, shredded

5 kaffir lime leaves, shredded

1. Bring the water to a boil in a large saucepan. Add the lamb and ginger, and cook until the juices are no longer pink, about 10 minutes. Drain and transfer the lamb to paper towels.

2. Heat a large wok or skillet over high heat. Add the oil and lamb, and stir-fry until lightly browned. Stir in the wine and transfer the lamb to the saucepan. Add the ginger to the wok, reduce the heat to medium, and stir-fry about 2 minutes, or until lightly browned. Transfer the ginger to the saucepan.

3. Add more oil to the wok if needed, then stir-fry the water chestnuts, bean curd, and garlic until fragrant, about 2 minutes. Return the lamb and ginger to the pan and stir-fry about 3 minutes more, or until fragrant. Transfer the contents of the wok to the saucepan and add enough water to cover. Cook the mixture, uncovered, over low heat about 45 minutes, or until the lamb is very tender.

4. Just before serving, make the sauce by placing the bean curd, chilies, and lime leaves in a small saucepan. Add 1 cup of the gravy from the meat mixture and cook over medium heat, stirring constantly, until slightly thickened, about 5 minutes. Pour over the lamb and serve immediately.

MAKES 4 SERVINGS

Hot Pot of Pork Ribs and Eggplant in Spicy Plum Sauce

Chef Chow Chung, of the Hyatt Regency Hong Kong, served me this one noontime and I would have asked for seconds if I hadn't worried about his losing face, because I suspected there were none. In its balance of sweet and slightly sour, this hot-pot concoction must be mainly Cantonese in heritage. It's important to use meaty ribs, so do not substitute the regular Western-style spareribs. You need to cut through the bones, so you may want to ask your butcher to do this. Because this dish is so delicious, you might want to double the recipe for leftovers, or for generous entree portions for rib-lovers.

1/2 pound country-style spareribs, cut in half crosswise

1 1/2 teaspoons cornstarch

1/2 cup vegetable oil

1/2 pound Oriental eggplant, peeled and cubed

4 cloves garlic, minced

One 1-inch piece fresh ginger, minced

1/2 fresh red chili

1 tablespoon chopped scallions

1 1/2 teaspoons plum sauce

1 teaspoon Chinese yellow soybean paste (*mien see*, see Note)

1 teaspoon sugar

1/3 teaspoon salt

1/2 teaspoon Chinese rice wine

1/2 cup Basic Beef Stock (page 19)

Dash of toasted sesame oil

2 tablespoons water

1. Cut the spareribs into single- or double-rib portions and sprinkle them with 1/2 teaspoon of the cornstarch. Set aside.

2. Heat the vegetable oil in a large wok or skillet over high heat. Carefully add the spareribs and eggplant, and cook until they begin to brown, about 1 minute. Using tongs, transfer the ribs and eggplant to a plate.

3. Add the garlic, ginger, chili, scallions, plum sauce, soybean paste, sugar, and salt. Stir-fry until fragrant, 2 to 3 minutes. Add the spareribs and eggplant, and stir-fry until crisp, about 5 minutes. Pour in the rice wine, stock, and sesame oil. Reduce the heat to low, cover, and cook, about 15 minutes, or until the pork is tender. Mix the remaining 1 teaspoon cornstarch with the water and stir into the mixture. Bring the mixture to a boil and cook, uncovered, about 5 minutes, until thickened. Serve hot.

MAKES 2 SERVINGS

Note: For this recipe, if you cannot find yellow soybean paste, also known as yellow bean sauce, look for Malaysian *taucheo* or Indonesian *tau co* or substitute a mixture of white and dark miso.

Stewed Pork Rolls with Garlic Leaf

A succulent Chinese pork stew combining bamboo shoots, mushrooms, rice wine, and garlic, this dish would be at home at an emperor's banquet. It is truly elegant, but it also requires time, effort, and nimble fingers for tying the garlic leaves around the pork bundles. The cook who provided the recipe, Joyce Piotrowski, admits that it is tricky business to present neat meat packages, but here, the end really justifies the means.

With these delicate pork bundles, you might consider serving such non-Chinese accompaniments as roasted potatoes and leeks for their complementary flavors. A chilled white wine would be the perfect finishing touch.

**1 large stalk green garlic leaf
or 1 leek and 4 cloves garlic,
peeled (see Note)**

1 pound boneless center-cut pork loin

**3 canned bamboo shoots, cut into
$^1/_4 \times {}^1/_4 \times$ 3–inch strips (for a total
of 6 pieces)**

**3 dried Chinese mushrooms, soaked in
hot water for 20 minutes, stems
removed, cut into $^1/_4$-inch-wide
strips (for a total of 12 pieces)**

**6 scallions (white part only), trimmed
to 3 inches long**

$^1/_3$ cup soy sauce

1 tablespoon Chinese rice wine

**3 tablespoons peanut oil, or more
if needed**

3 tablespoons sugar

$^1/_4$ cup Chinese rice vinegar

**3 cups Basic Pork Stock (page 20)
or water**

1 teaspoon toasted sesame oil

1. Cook the garlic leaf in boiling water until just softened, about 3 minutes.

2. Slice the pork crosswise into 6 pieces (about $^1/_3$-inch-thick each). Pound each slice with the flat side of a meat pounder or cleaver until it is doubled in size.

3. Working with 1 slice at a time, lay the pork on a flat surface. Place 1 strip of bamboo shoot, 2 slices of mushroom, and 1 scallion on the pork. Wrap the pork around the filling as if you were making an envelope—that is, fold the bottom corner over the filling first, then roll the left-hand corner and the right-hand corner to the center and, finally, fold the top corner toward the center. Make sure the ends are firmly tucked in. Repeat with the remaining ingredients. Tie each roll around the middle with a strip of garlic leaf or leek. Knot the leaf and trim off the ends.

4. Combine the soy sauce and rice wine in a bowl. Add the pork rolls and let marinate for 10 minutes.

5. Heat the peanut oil in a large wok or saucepan over medium heat. Add the rolls and cook, turning occasionally, until browned on all sides, 4 to 6 minutes. Add the sugar, vinegar, stock, remaining marinade, and garlic cloves if using the leek. Reduce the heat to medium-low and cook for 20 minutes. Drizzle with the sesame oil just before serving. Serve hot.

MAKES 4 TO 6 SERVINGS

Note: Not to be confused with garlic chives, which is not a substitute, garlic leaf is the green part of the garlic bulb that grows above ground. Because it is strong and flavorful, garlic leaf is ideal for tying up these bundles. However, if you cannot buy or pick your own garlic leaf, the green part of a leek makes a good substitute:

Trim off and discard the white part of the leek. Halve the green part, rinse well, and cook in boiling water until softened, 1 to 2 minutes. Cut the leek lengthwise into $1/4$-inch-wide strips. Use these to tie up the pork. Add the garlic to the cooking liquid in the final step.

Satay Beef and Bean Thread Hot Pot

Chef C.K. Chan, of Sheraton Hong Kong Hotel & Towers, offered me this hot pot for lunch one day, and it's safe to speculate that this one-pot stew was probably inspired by the fragrant satays of Thailand and Malaysia. But here the meat is not grilled but stir-fried. Remember that bean thread (glass) noodles are tricky to work with because they are so brittle and tough when dry. To make cutting easier, purchase a brand of noodles tied up with string or a rubber band. Soak the tied noodles, then cut softened noodles afterward.

The original recipe calls for superior stock, an elegant Chinese soup stock that traditionally requires many hours of cooking and various preparation steps, although some modern chefs have created shortcuts for making this stock (see Chinese Superior Stock, page 23). You may use beef stock as a substitute, but it lacks the refined flavor of superior stock. The original recipe also calls for Yunnan ham, a specialty cured meat that is not readily available in the West, but rich Virginia ham is an acceptable substitute.

For an authentic presentation, spoon the stew into a Chinese casserole cookpot—the ceramic ones with the brown-glazed interior sold at Asian markets. Since you have the starch and meat in one dish, accompany this with stir-fried greens, such as spinach or Chinese broccoli.

$^3/_4$ **pound boneless rump roast, sliced into $1^1/_2 \times 3$–inch strips**

2 tablespoons cornstarch

2 tablespoons vegetable oil

2 scallions, trimmed and cut into 3-inch lengths

One 1-inch piece fresh ginger, thinly sliced

2 ounces dried shiitake mushrooms or Chinese mushrooms, soaked in hot water for 20 minutes

4 cups Basic Beef Stock (page 19)

2 ounces bean thread (glass) noodles, cut into 3-inch lengths

$^1/_2$ **teaspoon Chinese rice wine**

$^1/_2$ **teaspoon soy sauce**

Salt to taste

1 teaspoon Chinese-style satay sauce (see Note)

Pinch of MSG (optional)

1. Sprinkle the beef with the cornstarch.

2. Heat a large wok or skillet over high heat until hot. Add the oil, meat, scallions, and ginger, and stir-fry until slightly crisp, 2 to 3 minutes. Add the mushrooms and stir-fry until softened, 2 to 3 minutes more. Add the stock and noodles, reduce the heat to medium, and cook until the noodles are softened, 2 to 3 minutes. Stir in the wine, soy sauce, salt, satay sauce, and MSG if using. Serve hot.

MAKES 3 TO 4 SERVINGS

Note: Chinese satay sauce is a commercial product available in an Asian grocery. If you want a zestier flavor, marinate the meat in some of the satay sauce before sprinkling it with cornstarch and stir-frying it.

Spicy Stuffed Szechuan Eggplant

A remarkably rich and savory stew, this eggplant and pork entree packs a mighty wallop. It also requires a little extra work, but the combinations of flavors and textures are wonderful and make it all worthwhile.

The cook who provided this recipe, Joyce Piotrowski, calls for using pork tenderloin. When she fixes this dish, she minces the meat by hand. You can also prepare the meat in a food processor, though the texture will not be the same. The eggplant slices should be lightly and quickly browned on both sides so they do not absorb too much oil. Egg or rice noodles make a fine accompaniment. Also serve plenty of chilled beer or wine.

1 large eggplant (about 2 pounds)

2 tablespoons salt

1/2 pound ground or minced
    pork tenderloin

1 scallion, trimmed and minced

2 tablespoons soy sauce

1 tablespoon Chinese hot soybean
    paste (*lat chu jeung*, see Note)

1 large clove garlic, peeled
    and smashed

1 teaspoon freshly grated ginger

1 teaspoon hot chili oil

1 1/2 cups Basic Pork Stock (page 20)
    or Basic Chicken Stock (page 19)

1 tablespoon rice vinegar

1 teaspoon sugar

1/2 teaspoon Szechuan peppercorns

1/2 teaspoon toasted sesame oil

1/2 cup vegetable oil, or more if needed

1. Peel the eggplant and slice it crosswise into 1/2-inch-thick slices. Cut each slice in half and, using a small, sharp knife, make a pocket in the straight side of each slice. Sprinkle with salt and set aside in a colander to drain for 1 hour to extract the bitter juices. (You do not need to rinse the eggplant, as the juices rinse off the salt.)

2. Meanwhile, make the filling by combining the pork, scallions, soy sauce, soybean paste, garlic, ginger, and 1/2 teaspoon of the chili oil.

3. Combine the stock, rice vinegar, sugar, peppercorns, sesame oil, and the remaining 1/2 teaspoon chili oil in a large saucepan over medium heat. Cook until heated through, about 3 minutes.

4. Pat the eggplant dry with paper towels. Divide the filling mixture among the eggplant slices and stuff each cavity with a portion.

5. Heat a large wok or saucepan over high heat. Add the vegetable oil and cook the eggplant until browned, about 5 minutes per side. (Add more oil if needed.) Pour in the stock mixture, reduce the heat to medium-low, and cook about 15 minutes, or until the eggplant slices are tender. Serve hot.

MAKES 4 TO 6 SERVINGS

Note: If you can tolerate very spicy food, increase the amount of Chinese hot soybean paste—also known as chili soybean paste—to suit your taste.

Lion's Head Stew

This unusual stew consists of spoon-shaped meatballs that, when draped with a green vegetable, resemble a lion's head with mane—thus giving the dish its name. Besides the visual effect, this stew has other pluses. For one, it stores well so it can be made several days in advance. For another, you can vary the main ingredients by substituting beef for the pork and fresh mushrooms for the dried black mushrooms.

Aileen T'sing, of the Towngas Cooking School in Hong Kong, says that for the right consistency you should mince the meat by hand—a Chinese cleaver does a fine job, but any large, sharp knife should produce the right consistency. Of course, you may also ask your butcher to grind the meat for you. For an authentic presentation, serve this in a clay pot.

Meatballs

1/2 pound minced or ground
   pork tenderloin

1 egg white, beaten until frothy

1/2 teaspoon sugar

Salt to taste

Toasted sesame oil to taste

Freshly ground black pepper to taste

1 tablespoon dark soy sauce

1 teaspoon Chinese rice wine

Stew

4 1/4 cups vegetable oil

Two 1/4-inch-thick slices fresh ginger,
   smashed

1/2 pound Chinese (napa) cabbage,
   stem end trimmed

6 dried Chinese mushrooms or
   shiitake mushrooms, soaked in hot
   water for 20 minutes, stems
   removed, thinly sliced

1/4 cup sliced bamboo shoots

2 cups Basic Chicken Stock (page 19)

2 tablespoons cornstarch

1 teaspoon soy sauce

1 teaspoon water

1. To make the meatballs, combine the pork, egg white, sugar, salt, sesame oil, and pepper in a medium bowl. Form into 2 equal-sized balls and set in the bowl. Sprinkle with the dark soy sauce and wine, and let marinate for 20 minutes.

2. Meanwhile, heat 1/4 cup of the oil in a large wok or skillet over medium heat. Add the ginger and stir-fry 2 to 3 minutes, or until browned and fragrant. Stir in the cabbage, mushrooms, bamboo shoots, and stock. Remove from the heat.

3. Coat the meatballs with 5 teaspoons of the cornstarch. Heat the remaining 4 cups oil in a large saucepan over medium heat. Place the meatballs in the oil and deep-fry 7 to 10 minutes, or until browned. Transfer to paper towels to drain.

4. Add the meatballs to the stock, return the wok to the heat, and bring the mixture to a boil. Reduce the heat to medium-low and cook, stirring often, about 10 minutes, or until slightly thickened.

5. Meanwhile, dissolve the remaining 1 teaspoon cornstarch in the soy sauce and water. Stir into the stew and cook, stirring often, until thickened, 4 to 5 minutes. Serve hot.

MAKES 2 SERVINGS

Tibetan Pulled Noodle Soup

Tantog

Picture yourself on a frozen mountain slope in the Himalayas, and you'll understand why this hearty Tibetan soup is so popular there. The traditional recipe calls for using yak meat and broth. But as Tibetan cook Tseten Wangchuk, who now lives in the United States, noted when he gave me this recipe, yak is not a meat sold at Western supermarkets. For a reasonable facsimile, he would use the more available buffalo, but of course, beef and beef stock will do fine.

Since the translation of tantog is "pulled noodle," you'll need to make your own noodles for this dish, but these are surprisingly easy to fix from everyday ingredients you'll have on hand. This is a meal in a bowl and needs only some hot tea or coffee as the final touch. Of course, if you are not sitting on a snowy peak, a hearty red wine would suit this dish well.

$^1/_2$ cup vegetable oil

$1^1/_3$ cups all-purpose flour

$^1/_2$ cup water

1 pound boneless chuck, trimmed
   and cubed

2 large onions, peeled and chopped

7 cups Basic Beef Stock (page 19)

$^3/_4$ cup peas

20 spinach leaves, rinsed and trimmed

Salt and freshly ground black pepper
   to taste

1. Pour the oil into a large wok or skillet. Stir together the flour and water to make a soft dough. Cut this mixture into 8 or 10 small cubes, dip into the oil, and set aside for 1 hour.

2. Meanwhile, heat the oil over medium heat. Add the meat and onions, and cook, stirring often, about 15 minutes, or until well browned.

3. Pour the stock into a large saucepan and bring to a boil. Pull each cube of dough to form a thin, flat "noodle" about 2 inches long. Drop the noodles into the bubbling stock one at a time. Add the browned meat and onions, peas, spinach, salt, and pepper. Cook until the noodles float to the surface. Ladle into individual serving bowls and serve hot.

MAKES 4 SERVINGS

Tibetan New Year's Stew

Lapu Gaptso

Tibetan cook Tseten Wangchuk said this meaty stew is eaten every New Year's morning in his country. As a celebratory dish, it's a robust offering that brings together chilies, ginger, onions, and, if you were in Tibet, yak meat and yak butter.

If there is any stew left over for another day, remove any radish pieces before reheating and cook them in oil. Sprinkle both sides with salt, pepper, and hot chili sauce and serve them as a side dish. Mugs of hot tea enriched with milk and sugar would be typical, but steins of chilled beer would soothe the palate.

1 cup (2 sticks) unsalted butter, or
  more if needed

2 large onions, peeled and cubed

8 to 12 dried red chilies

One 3-inch piece fresh ginger,
  thinly sliced

2 pounds beef chuck or chuck blade
  roast, with bone, cut into large
  pieces (the size and thickness of half
  a hand)

3 cups water

Salt and freshly ground black pepper
  to taste

3 daikon, peeled and cut into
  1 × 3-inch pieces

1. Heat ³/₄ cup of the butter in a large saucepan over medium-high heat. Add the onions, chilies, and ginger, and cook, stirring often, about 10 minutes, or until the onions are golden. Remove from the pan and set aside on a plate. Add the meat and cook, stirring often, until browned on both sides. (Add more butter if the mixture seems dry.) Stir in the water and return the vegetables to the pan. Reduce the heat to low so the water barely simmers and cook, uncovered, until the meat is very tender, about 2¹/₂ hours.

2. Season the stew with salt and pepper, and stir in the daikon. Cook until the daikon pieces are tender, about 10 minutes more. Just before serving, place the remaining ¹/₄ cup butter on top of the stew and stir it in as it melts. Serve hot.

MAKES 4 TO 6 SERVINGS

Korean Rice Cake Soup

Dtuk Kuk

Served as a special treat on New Year's Day for breakfast or lunch, this main-dish Rice Cake Soup is made of heen dtuk—dtuk *means any kind of Korean snack made of rice;* heen dtuk *means white-rice cake, explained the cook who provided this recipe, Hira Lee. These "cakes" have a curious chewy texture that makes them addictive.*

This is a simple soup to put together, which is reason enough to celebrate. But there is no reason to wait for New Year's Day to enjoy it—in fact, many Korean restaurants serve this year-round.

¹/₄ **pound lean ground beef**

1 scallion, trimmed and thinly sliced

2 tablespoons chopped garlic

1 tablespoon soy sauce

1 teaspoon toasted sesame oil

7 cups Basic Beef Stock (page 19)

6 cylindrical sticks of rice cake,
   diagonally sliced about 1 inch thick,
   or 36 rice-cake ovals

1 teaspoon freshly ground black pepper

Salt to taste

1 large egg, well beaten

1 tablespoon crumbled nori
   (Japanese seaweed)

Pinch of sesame seeds

1. Combine the chopped beef, scallions, garlic, soy sauce, and sesame oil in a bowl.

2. Pour the stock into a large saucepan and bring to a boil. Add the beef mixture, rice cakes, pepper, and salt. Reduce the heat to low and cook, stirring occasionally, until the beef is no longer pink, about 10 minutes.

3. Pour the egg through a fine-mesh sieve into the hot stock. (As the egg streams into the saucepan, it will cook instantly, making thin "threads" in the liquid.) Garnish the soup with the nori and sesame seeds. Serve hot.

MAKES 3 TO 4 SERVINGS

Rice Cakes

Korean cook Hira Lee reminisced about rice cakes as a delicacy from her childhood. "In wintertime when everything was frozen," she said, "we would take the long ones for a snack. We used to have a little portable stove, and sitting around the stove, we used to bake them over the charcoal. It turns out as a really good snack for cold winter nights." Street hawkers in Korea still sell these cakes today, cooked with chili-laden hot paste.

Korean Shredded Meat Soup

As I watched Korean cook Bong S. Lee prepare this soup, I wondered how boiling a whole flank steak could produce anything savory and satisfying. But the surprise here comes not so much from the flank-steak broth, but from the seasonings and accompaniments, and the way the meat gets shredded.

The main flavors come from sesame seeds—used so generously that they float to the surface of the soup—and from the hot seasoning sauce, which gets its punch from Korean red pepper powder. This sauce is delicious, if you like things hot, and you should make plenty for leftovers to use for zipping up cooked rice or Fried Tofu (page 18). Serve this soup with a mixture of cooked white rice and barley that you spoon into the soup as you eat it, and follow the soup with a tart green salad.

8 cups water

1 1/2 pounds flank steak

1/4 cup soy sauce

2 tablespoons toasted sesame oil

3 teaspoons Korean red pepper powder
   (see Note)

2 teaspoons sesame seeds

1 teaspoon Garlic Paste (page 28)

1 teaspoon freshly ground black pepper

1 bunch scallions, trimmed and
   diagonally sliced

1 daikon, peeled and cubed

Salt to taste

1/2 cup Hot Pepper Seasoning Paste
   (page 35)

1. Pour the water into a stockpot and add the meat. Bring the water to a boil, reduce the heat to medium-low, and cook the steak, uncovered, until the water is slightly brown and the meat is tender, about 1 1/2 hours. Remove the steak from the broth and set aside. Let the broth cook over very low heat until you are ready to eat. When the meat is cool enough to handle, shred it finely with your fingers.

2. Place the meat shreds in a large bowl and add the soy sauce, sesame oil, red pepper powder, sesame seeds, garlic paste, and black pepper. Add the white parts of the scallions and reserve the green ends. Toss, preferably with your hands, to distribute the seasonings. Stir in the daikon, sliced scallion greens, and salt.

3. To serve, put a portion of the meat mixture into each bowl and ladle the broth over the meat. Pass around the soup with the hot pepper seasoning paste.

MAKES 4 TO 6 SERVINGS

Note: The cook stresses that the red pepper powder must be fresh, because as it ages, it loses its potency—so ask your Korean grocer about the freshness of the supply.

Korean Beef and Bean Paste Stew

Doenjang Chiggye

When Hira Lee gave me this recipe, she assured me that this rich-tasting and inexpensive dish is a favorite at her home. It combines the flavor of mild soybean paste, or doenjang, *with beef and with the piquancy of Korean green chilies, which are longer, milder, and plumper versions of the more familiar Thai finger hot chilies. Serve this with rice and vegetables.*

Marinade

2 scallions, trimmed and thinly sliced

3 cloves garlic, peeled and chopped

2 tablespoons soy sauce

1 teaspoon sugar

1 teaspoon sesame seeds

1 teaspoon toasted sesame oil

$^1/_2$ teaspoon freshly ground
   black pepper

Stew

1 tablespoon vegetable oil

$^1/_3$ pound lean boneless top round, cut
   into $1 \times ^1/_2$-inch pieces

2 tablespoons Korean soybean paste
   (*doenjang*) or dark brown or red miso

1 tablespoon toasted sesame oil

$1^1/_2$ teaspoons chopped garlic

$^1/_3$ medium potato, peeled and cubed

$^1/_2$ large onion, peeled and cubed

$^1/_3$ zucchini, cubed

2 Korean green chilies,
   diagonally sliced

$1^1/_2$ cups boiling water

2 tablespoons chopped scallions

2 to 3 slices Japanese fish cake
   (*kamaboko*), optional

1. To make the marinade, combine the scallions, garlic, soy sauce, sugar, sesame seeds, sesame oil, and pepper in a bowl. Add the beef and turn to coat. Set aside for 10 minutes.

2. To make the stew, heat an earthenware or other heat-proof pot over medium heat and add the oil. When the oil is hot, add the beef and the marinade and stir-fry for 2 minutes. Stir in the soybean paste, sesame oil, garlic, and potatoes, and cook for 1 minute. Add the onions, zucchini, and chilies, and cook, stirring often, until slightly softened, 5 to 10 minutes. Add the boiling water. Reduce the heat to medium-low, partially cover, and cook until the flavors are well blended, about 5 minutes more. Stir in the scallions and fish cake if using. Serve hot.

MAKES 2 TO 3 SERVINGS

Korean Short Rib Beef Soup

Kalbi Tang

This very popular soup is probably one of the few Korean dishes Westerners know well, since it is served at most Korean restaurants in the West. Its appealing heartiness comes from beef short ribs, a meat Westerners and Koreans alike love, and the addition of garlic, onions, soy sauce, and toasted sesame oil enhances the soup's flavor.

Despite the long list of ingredients, this is really a simple dish to prepare. If you want something fast, forego the long soaking time for the fast boiling of the meat. The soaking or boiling of the meat is necessary to produce an ultra-clear broth, the sign of a successful kalbi tang.

You must remember several steps, however. For one, the ribs need to be scored all over so that the meat falls easily from the bones as you eat them. For just the right cut, buy your short ribs from a Korean butcher or market. Otherwise, do as I did and use the standard short ribs from your local market.

The Korean cook who provided this recipe, Young-mi Pierce, offers other tips for best results. For one, the best garlic flavor comes from mashing and mincing the cloves by hand, not chopping them in a food processor.

To serve this full-meal soup, don't worry about other courses, but do be sure to offer salt, pepper, and chopped onions at the table, along with a bowl of Hot Pepper Seasoning Paste (page 35). Accompany this with rice and various types of kimchi, *the Korean fermented pickled cabbage.*

Soup

4 pounds beef short ribs, trimmed of
    all visible fat
6 quarts water
5 Korean green onions or leeks,
    trimmed, rinsed, and
    diagonally sliced
1 head garlic, cloves separated, peeled,
    smashed, and minced
One 1-inch piece fresh ginger
1 daikon, peeled
Pinch of MSG (optional)

1. To make the soup, slice the rib bones apart, if attached, and score the ribs on all sides. Place the ribs and enough water to cover into a large stockpot and refrigerate overnight; discard the soaking water the next morning. Alternatively, fill the stockpot three-quarters full with water and bring to a boil. Add the ribs and cook until the juices are no longer pink, about 3 minutes. Discard the cooking water.

2. In the stockpot, combine the ribs, water, 2 of the green onions or leeks, 2 teaspoons of the minced garlic, and ginger. Bring to a boil and cook for 10 minutes. Add the daikon, reduce the heat to medium-low, and cook, uncovered, until the meat can easily be pulled from the bones, about 1¹/₂ hours. Stir in the MSG if using.

Seasoning Mixture

¹/₄ cup chopped Korean green onions
  or scallions

¹/₄ cup minced garlic

¹/₄ cup soy sauce

2 tablespoons salt

2 teaspoons toasted sesame oil, or more
  to taste

2 teaspoons sesame seeds, or more
  to taste

2 tablespoons freshly ground
  black pepper

Garnishes

2 eggs, separated (see Note)

1 tablespoon vegetable oil

2 Korean green onions or scallions,
  very thinly sliced

3. Meanwhile, make the seasoning mixture by combining the green onions or scallions, garlic, soy sauce, salt, sesame oil, sesame seeds, and pepper in a large bowl.

4. When the beef is cooked, transfer the ribs to the bowl with the seasoning mixture. Remove and dice the daikon. Add it to the ribs along with the remaining green onions or leeks and minced garlic. Carefully mix this together so the meat does not fall off the bones. Return the meat mixture to the stockpot, partially cover the pan, and cook for 15 minutes more.

5. Meanwhile, for the garnishes, stir, but do not beat, the egg yolks and whites separately. Heat the oil in a skillet over medium heat. Reduce the heat to low, pour in the yolks, and cook until firm. Slide this "omelet" out of the skillet and repeat the procedure with the whites. Slice the omelets into decorative strips. When the soup is ready, garnish it with the strips of egg and green onions or scallions. Serve hot.

MAKES 4 TO 6 SERVINGS

Note: For making the omelet, use a rectangular Japanese omelet pan if you have one. Otherwise, heat a small round skillet, add the oil, and trim the cooked omelet into a rectangular shape, then into thin diagonal strips.

Korean Kimchi Stew

A typical stew of Korean pickled cabbage—more commonly known as kimchi—*and pork offers Westerners a sampling of traditional Korean ingredients and flavors. While pickled cabbage turns up in many Asian kitchens, it's a safe bet that Koreans have elevated this particular item to an art form. Traditionally, Korean families made hundreds of pieces of* kimchi *in the fall for winter use. When spring came, the unused* kimchi *may have become too sour to eat on its own, so the thrifty housewife turned it into a stew—hence the development of this dish. You may use the whole* kimchi *(available premade at Korean or Asian markets) or the* kimchi *that is sliced into long strips. You will need one small or medium* kimchi *for this dish.*

One of the reasons Koreans used pork, says the cook who gave me this recipe, Hira Lee, is because the meat provided energy and fat in winters to ward off the cold; a modern Korean family might use Spam instead of pork.

Marinade

2 scallions, trimmed and thinly sliced

3 cloves garlic, peeled and chopped

2 tablespoons soy sauce

1 teaspoon sugar

1 teaspoon sesame seeds

1 teaspoon toasted sesame oil

1 teaspoon grated fresh ginger

$1/2$ teaspoon freshly ground black
   pepper

Stew

1 small or medium *kimchi*

$1/3$ pound boneless pork, sliced into
   $1 \times 1/2$-inch strips

2 tablespoons toasted sesame oil

2 cups boiling water

1 tablespoon chopped garlic

3 tablespoons chopped scallions

1. To make the marinade, combine the scallions, garlic, soy sauce, sugar, sesame seeds, sesame oil, ginger, and pepper in a medium bowl. Add the pork and turn to coat. Set aside for 15 minutes.

2. To make the stew, heat an earthenware or other heat-proof pot over low heat. When the pot is hot, increase the heat to medium-low and add the *kimchi*, pork, and sesame oil. Cook, stirring often, until the pork is no longer pink, about 10 minutes. Pour in the boiling water, increase the heat to medium, and cook for 5 minutes. Reduce the temperature to medium-low and stir in the garlic and scallions. Cook until the flavors are well blended, 2 to 3 minutes more. Serve hot.

MAKES 4 TO 6 SERVINGS

Japanese Pork and Vegetable Miso Soup

Ton Jiru

Yoko Morford loves this soup any time of year but remembers it most fondly as that filling and nourishing substance she craved during her various pregnancies. Then she would cook up gallons of the soup, and the result was she had plenty of leftovers for her neighbors.

Unless you cook and eat traditional Japanese food, you are apt to run across some unfamiliar ingredients in this recipe. For example, kabocha *pumpkin is a richly flavored, deep orange vegetable available at Japanese and Korean markets. You can substitute Western pumpkin instead.* Sato imo *is a Japanese field yam with starchy flesh that is very similar to a potato. It is sold at Japanese and Korean markets, but you may substitute a baking potato instead.* Gobo *(or burdock), a member of the aster family, is a long, slender root harvested year-round, but those available in early spring are considered the tastiest. The Japanese consider burdock highly effective in preventing geriatric disorders, says the cook. Since the shopping and preparation are time-consuming, why not double or triple the amount of the soup you prepare? It can be frozen for up to one month.*

¹/₃ pound thinly sliced boneless pork, cut into long ¹/₃-inch-wide strips

1 cup bite-sized *kabocha* pumpkin pieces

¹/₂ cup peeled bite-sized *sato imo* pieces

¹/₂ cup bite-sized daikon pieces

¹/₄ cup bite-sized carrot pieces

1 ounce burdock, peeled and diagonally sliced about ¹/₃ inch thick

2 ounces deep-fried tofu, cut into bite-sized pieces (see Fried Tofu, page 18)

1 piece *konnyaku*, sliced and cut into bite-sized pieces

¹/₂ packet instant Japanese soup base (*dashi-no-moto*) dissolved in 5 cups water

1 tablespoon mirin

¹/₃ cup red miso

1 scallion, trimmed and finely chopped

Sprinkle of *shichimi*

1. Set the pork in a colander and run very hot water over it to remove excess fat. Combine the pork, pumpkin, *sato imo*, daikon, carrots, burdock, tofu, *konnyaku*, and *dashi-no-moto* in a large saucepan and bring to a boil. Reduce the heat to medium-low and cook, skimming often, until the pork and vegetables are tender, about 20 minutes. Stir in the mirin. Place the miso in a fine-mesh strainer and dip it into the soup so only the fine part of the miso seeps through and dissolves into the soup.

2. Remove the soup from the heat and garnish with the scallions and *shichimi*. Serve hot.

MAKES 4 SERVINGS

Shabu-Shabu

This dish earns the name "shabu-shabu" from the sounds meat slices make as you swish them through the cooking liquid. This one-pot meal is considered elegant for entertaining guests, says Yoko Morford, partly because of the expensive and high-quality beef you need for the dish. Each person cooks for himself at the table in this communal meal of thinly sliced meat and vegetables. Two dipping sauces are traditionally served with this meal: Ponzu Shoyu Dipping Sauce (page 33) and gomadare sauce (described below).

Presentation, as in most Japanese meals, is very important. For this meal, Yoko Morford arranged paper-thin slices of beef and an assortment of vegetables—cabbage leaves, decorative carrot slices, bundles of cabbage-wrapped cooked spinach, jícama sticks, enoki mushrooms, fresh shiitake mushrooms, and edible chrysanthemum leaves—on one platter in an artful way. As for the vegetables, her choice is only a guide, for you can select any combination of Japanese vegetables you wish. For the mushrooms and the chrysanthemum leaves, select 1/4 to 1/2 pound of each. See "On Eating Shabu-Shabu" (below) for directions on composing, cooking, and eating this meal.

Cooking Liquid

6 cups water
One 3-inch-square piece dried *kombu*
(Japanese seaweed)

Soup Ingredients

1 1/2 cups Japanese rice, cooked
(see page 4)
1 1/2 pounds boneless sirloin,
thinly sliced
1/2 pound firm tofu, cubed
1 daikon, peeled, diagonally sliced into
1/2-inch-thick pieces, and quartered
2 carrots, peeled, diagonally sliced
into 1/2-inch-thick pieces, and
quartered or cut with a flower-
shaped cookie cutter
1 bunch enoki mushrooms, rinsed
12 shiitake mushrooms, rinsed
1 bunch edible chrysanthemum leaves
(crown daisy)
1 head Chinese (napa) cabbage, outer
leaves discarded, firm central core
cut into bite-sized pieces

1. To make the cooking liquid, pour the water into a large tabletop cooking vessel. Add the *kombu* and let it soak for 30 minutes. Discard the *kombu*. Take the cooking vessel to the table and bring the liquid to a boil. Let simmer until you are ready to eat.

2. For the soup ingredients, place the rice in a serving bowl. Arrange the remaining ingredients on the same or on separate platters. Set the bowl and platters on the table along with serving utensils or chopsticks.

3. Stir together the ponzu sauce, daikon, and *shichimi* in a serving bowl.

4. To make the *gomadare* dipping sauce, combine the *dashi*, sesame seeds, mirin, vinegar, miso, sugar, and soy sauce in a blender and process until smooth. Transfer to a serving bowl.

5. Set the dipping sauces on the table. Let people cook their own food and eat it at their leisure. The cooked meat should be dipped into the *gomadare* sauce and the vegetables should be dipped into the ponzu sauce before eating.

Accompaniments

1 cup Ponzu Shoyu Dipping Sauce
(see Note, page 33)

¹/₄ cup grated daikon

1 teaspoon *shichimi*

1 cup *dashi* (Japanese First Stock,
page 34)

¹/₂ cup sesame seeds, roasted
(see page 11)

¹/₃ cup mirin

¹/₃ cup rice vinegar

2 tablespoons white miso

2 tablespoon sugar

1 tablespoon soy sauce

2 large eggs, lightly beaten

¹/₂ cup finely chopped scallions

Assorted Japanese pickles (optional)

6. After eating, remove any remaining meat slices or vegetables from the cooking liquid and add the cooked rice. Cover the pot and let boil for about 5 minutes. Remove the lid and stir in the eggs quickly. Remove the vessel from the heat, sprinkle the rice with the scallions, and serve. Pass around an assortment of Japanese pickles, if desired.

MAKES 4 TO 6 SERVINGS

On Eating Shabu-Shabu

Let people cook and eat their selection of beef at their leisure, slice by slice. But as they fill up on the beef, add the vegetables and any remaining meat to the bubbling liquid. As ingredients cook, guests remove them from the cooking liquid with chopsticks and dip them into the appropriate dipping sauce—the meat into a sesame-miso dipping sauce called *gomadare* (above), the vegetables into a ponzu sauce (page 33) filled with finely grated daikon and *shichimi*, a seven-spice seasoning powder—before eating.

Although Yoko Morford prefers ending the meal by cooking the rice in the liquid and making a mild rice soup out of this, she explains that there is another option: You may serve and drink the broth at the end of the meal, or cook noodles in the hot broth and serve both noodles and broth together in individual soup bowls.

Beef and Vegetables in Soy Sauce

Sukiyaki

The cook who provided this recipe, Yoko Morford, calls it her own "homestyle" recipe, one which she must make often because she recited it to me without referring to any notes. She did not give any quantities—the amounts are my suggestions. Use a tabletop cooking vessel or electric frying pan or wok for cooking this communal meal and let people help themselves.

The success of this famous dish—and it is a bit of a stretch to call this simmered beef and vegetable dish a stew—depends on using the best-quality beef available. If you have a Korean or Japanese market nearby, you will find the appropriate beef sliced to the correct thickness.

Before eating, the Japanese traditionally dip the cooked meat and vegetables into a beaten raw egg—the egg partially cooks on the surface of the hot food and gives each bite an intriguing texture. The egg also acts as a dipping sauce, since no other is served with sukiyaki. Use the raw egg at your own discretion, as it may be contaminated with salmonella. If you have any cooked leftovers, heat them up for another meal. Warmed sake, chilled white wine, or Japanese green tea make ideal beverages for this classic dish.

One 1 × 1–inch piece beef suet or
   1 tablespoon vegetable oil

1¹/₂ to 2 pounds well-marbled, high-
   quality steak, such as Delmonico,
   very thinly sliced

¹/₃ to ¹/₂ cup sugar

¹/₂ cup soy sauce, or more as needed

¹/₄ cup sake, or more as needed

¹/₂ pound firm tofu, cubed

1 pound *shirataki* noodles, drained
   and rinsed

6 ounces dried somen, cooked
   (see page 303)

¹/₂ pound dried shiitake mushrooms,
   soaked in hot water for 20 minutes
   and stems removed

¹/₂ pound spinach, rinsed, trimmed,
   and cut into bite-sized pieces

1 bunch edible chrysanthemum leaves
   (crown daisy)

¹/₂ head Chinese (napa) cabbage,
   thinly sliced

1. Heat the suet in a skillet until it is melted, and use the resulting fat to grease the cooking vessel. Alternatively, use a paper towel to wipe the vegetable oil around the bottom and sides of the cooking vessel.

2. Heat the cooking vessel and add several slices of the beef. Brown the slices and sprinkle them with 1 tablespoon of the sugar, 1 tablespoon of the soy sauce, and 1¹/₂ teaspoons of the sake. Bring this mixture to a boil over high heat. Remove the beef and eat immediately. Dip it into the beaten egg before eating, if desired. Repeat this process (adding more soy sauce, sake, sugar, and beef) until all the meat is finished before adding and cooking the other ingredients.

3. Add the tofu, noodles, and vegetables, placing them in different areas of the vessel, and sprinkle with more sugar, soy sauce, and sake during the cooking (in the ratio of 2 tablespoons sugar, 3 tablespoons soy sauce, and 2 tablespoons sake). Taste the liquid as you cook and adjust to your liking. You may also use several tablespoons water to replenish some of the liquid, if you wish. Add more ingredients as needed.

Dipping Sauce for Meat

1 whole raw egg per person, served in individual cups for beating at the table (optional)

4. At the end of the meal, place the noodles in the center of the skillet and add more sugar, soy sauce, and sake. Heat before eating.

About *Sukiyaki*

Although *sukiyaki* is not a traditional Japanese dish with a long pedigree, it certainly seems to be one of Japan's most famous and popular dishes, at least among Westerners. How it came into being is anybody's guess, but the tales are certainly colorful. As one of the stories goes, Japanese farmers created *sukiyaki* by cooking their meat either on the end of a shovel or a plough. Another tale relates how poachers had to quick-cook their illicit kill and used the end of a hoe as a cooking pan held over an open fire. Today's *sukiyaki* cooks use a shallow pan for cooking the very thinly sliced beef.

Although recipes for *sukiyaki* exist, cooks say it is virtually impossible to prepare this dish incorrectly, no matter what you do, since the recipe is only a guideline and the ingredients and quantities can be changed to suit your taste. Even the cooking liquid can vary according to tastes. One cook says she flavors her liquid with mirin, a pinch or two of sugar, and soy sauce. Another describes how her mother made the cooking liquid with about 1 tablespoon each of sugar, soy sauce, and sake. She cooked the beef first, and replenished the liquid as needed, and when people were ready to start cooking any of the other ingredients, she arranged them in separate portions in the cookpot. Not surprisingly with such a flexible recipe, there are several styles of this dish, including a Kanto-style (Tokyo area), Osaka-style, and Kansai-style version.

Filipino Beef and Sausage Stew

Caldaretta

Owner of a Filipino market and carry-out, Evelyn Manuel demonstrated how to make this rather simple and flavorful stew, which ideally should contain tender sirloin rather than a tougher cut of beef that needs longer cooking. She suggests goat as an alternative to beef, if you feel like experimenting with a more exotic cut of meat. Note the inclusion of green olives here, an addition that suggests some of the Spanish heritage of this simple stew.

1 tablespoon vegetable oil

$1/4$ cup cubed onions

$1^1/4$ pounds boneless sirloin or
   top round steak, cut into
   $2 \times 1/4$-inch strips

3 ounces chorizo, sliced

2 tomatoes, cubed

$1/4$ cup soy sauce

$2^1/4$ cups water

1 tablespoon achiote, diluted in
   $1/4$ cup water

1 cup cubed potatoes

1 cup cubed carrots

1 cup cubed red bell peppers

$1/2$ cup pitted green olives

Heat the oil in a large saucepan over medium heat. Add the onions and cook until golden, 3 to 5 minutes. Add the sirloin, chorizo, and tomatoes, and cook, stirring often, until browned, 3 to 4 minutes. Stir together the soy sauce and water, and gradually pour into the saucepan, $1/4$ cup at a time, stirring constantly as you pour. Add the achiote mixture. When all the liquid is added, reduce the heat to low, cover, and cook until the meat is tender, 15 to 20 minutes. Stir in the potatoes, carrots, peppers, and olives, and cook, uncovered, until the vegetables are tender, about 20 minutes. Serve hot.

MAKES 4 SERVINGS

Filipino Pork and Liver Stew

Menudo

The classic version of this Filipino pork-and-liver stew usually contains garbanzo beans, but the Filipina cook who gave me this recipe, Pinkie Imson, has omitted them here. Instead, you'll find raisins for a touch of sweetness and a variety of vegetables that make this a hearty meal in a bowl. She suggests using commercially prepared liver paste instead of cooking and pounding liver the traditional way—it makes fixing this dish much faster and simpler.

2$^1/_4$ cups water

1 pound lean boneless pork shoulder, cubed

2 tablespoons vegetable oil, or more if needed

1 medium onion, peeled and diced

$^1/_2$ head garlic, cloves separated, peeled, and minced

4 tomatoes, diced

1 red bell pepper, cubed

1 green bell pepper, cubed

2 potatoes, peeled and cubed

2 tablespoons raisins

1 teaspoon black peppercorns

1 bay leaf

$^1/_2$ pound chicken liver or pork liver, thinly sliced, or two 4$^1/_2$-ounce cans liver paste, cubed

1 tablespoon achiote or 1 teaspoon cayenne pepper

Salt to taste

Fish sauce to taste

1. Combine 2 cups of the water and the meat in a large saucepan and bring to a boil. Reduce the heat to medium-low and cook for 10 minutes. Remove from the heat.

2. Heat the oil in another large saucepan over medium heat. Add the pork cubes (reserve the stock) and brown the meat on all sides. (Add more oil if the mixture seems dry.) Transfer the pork to a plate.

3. Add the onions and garlic to the saucepan and cook, stirring often, until golden, 5 to 10 minutes. Add the tomatoes, reduce the heat to low, and cook, stirring occasionally, until thickened, about 15 minutes. Add the peppers, potatoes, raisins, peppercorns, bay leaf, and reserved pork and stock. Cook until the potatoes are tender, 10 to 15 minutes. Add the sliced liver or cubed liver paste and cook until slightly thickened, 5 to 10 minutes.

4. Just before serving, stir together the achiote or cayenne pepper and the remaining $^1/_4$ cup water. Stir into the stew along with the salt and fish sauce. Serve hot.

MAKES 3 TO 4 SERVINGS

Straits Laced—
Malaysia and Singapore

On the map of Southeast Asia, an exclamation point of land jutting into the South China Sea forms the two countries of Singapore and peninsular Malaysia. Their political affiliation ended in the late 1940s when the British departed, but many people still think of these two countries as the flip side of the same coin. Nothing could be farther from reality.

True, they share the same fishing waters, and many of their customs and peoples bear a striking resemblance. But Malaysia stands like a towering giant above tiny Singapore, attracting visitors to enjoy its steamy jungles and sparkling white beaches, its steel-framed urban centers and its cool mountain retreats—and it can draw upon its vast natural resources to contribute to the diverse Malyasian cookpot.

With only 618 square kilometers of its own, on the other hand, Singapore and its nearly 3 million people rely on other sources of inspiration to frame its destiny. As the city-state undergoes its relentless facelift, officials know enough to retain traces of antiquity for culture and tourism's sake. They also have a stake in retaining Singapore's world-class reputation as the ultimate restaurant.

Singapore

For such a tiny country, it's a wonder that Singapore has forged such a giant gastronomic reputation. Yet as Asia's crossroads and main shopping mecca, it is an island home to such groups as Malays, Chinese, Indians, Arabs, and Europeans and hosts millions of tourists annually. With this population to feed, Singapore's talented cooks have turned the tables to offer what can only be called a feeding frenzy.

As Singapore glorifies the likes of Shanghainese or Hokkien, colonial British or McDonald's meals, native Singaporeans also know to look down the back alley or to cross to the other side of town to find the perfect platter of local chili crabs or bowl of Hainanese chicken rice, another local favorite. For even in the face of a continual culinary onslaught, Singapore has developed its own favorites, dishes that tap into the Malay, Chinese, and Indian influences that are the hallmark of local cooking.

Take the Steamboat (page 267), for example, one of the wonders of Singapore's soup world and a probable descendant of the Malaysian version. Or the *murtabagh*, the Indian flat bread folded over a curried beef-and-egg filling. You'll find it best as served at Newton Circus, a center for diehard gluttons, where several stands are manned by Indian cooks—called *mamak roti*, or men who specialize in this paper-thin bread. One serving of *murtabagh* with chilled beer should satisfy, but other stalls offer more local favorites: Chinese *mee* (noodle) soups; Malaysian jumbo tiger prawns in their jade-green-and-black shells grilling over hot coals; and fresh ripe mango or durian readied to order.

Perhaps the best way for the visitor to discover the country's great culinary riches is to find local resident Geraldene Lowe, a Singaporean steeped in local lore. On one of her famous walking tours, you will see the city from an insider's perspective, glimpsing the royal palace of the last king of Singapore (who at the time of the tour happened to still be in residence); or watching one of the last weavers of the tiny palm-frond baskets for holding steamed rice; or stopping for a cold drink or hot bowl of fish ball soup at one of Singapore's oldest and most famous sidewalk eateries; or climbing the stairs of an Indian café for a lunch of *murtabagh* and fiery curries; or browsing through one of the last of the old-fashioned cookware stores on Beach Road.

And, if your luck holds, you may get to meet Aziza of Aziza's or Violet Oon, another of Singapore's notable food ladies. And you may get a nighttime view of the waterfront area with its old-fashioned eating center, where hawkers offer such temptations as fried noodles, bowls of soup, and glasses of Singapore's sweet and gingery *teh halia*, or pulled tea.

As night dwindles and the last bowl of soup is drunk, the sated, surfeited, and satisfied Singaporean can head to bed, secure in the knowledge that tomorrow dawns another day—for eating.

Malaysia

To me, Malaysian cooking is best summed up in two words: chilies and coconut milk. In ways that challenge simple creativity, the average Malaysian cook has used these two basic ingredients to turn curries, soups, and souplike dishes into bowls of creamy fire.

Who, one wonders, would ever think to slow-cook pieces of chicken or beef in a chilied coconut milk base until the meat dries out and absorbs the seasonings' flavors? What emerges after about four hours of cooking is the famed Malaysian *rendang* (page 120)—a dry stew so potent that chili lovers can become quick-fix addicts. It has its practical side, for the cooking preserves the meat, which can last without refrigeration for up to one month.

Indeed, once you select any part of the Malaysian banquet, you are hooked. But figuring out which dish belongs to which ethnic group becomes something of a puzzle for the outsider, for Malaysian cooking is its own melting pot.

Three main ethnic groups—the Chinese, the Indians, and the indigenous Malays—make up the country's population, and as one might imagine, each group has put its own spin on ingredients:

The Chinese love pork, but the Islamic Malays forbid its use. The Hindu Indians do not eat beef. The Chinese rarely cook with coconut milk. The Peranakans, a subgroup on Malaysia's resort island Penang and in Singapore of Chinese-Malay families, have created their own Nonya style of cooking, borrowing the best of both worlds to create Chinese dishes that sparkle with assertive Malaysian seasonings. And finally, there are the Malaysian dishes themselves that all three communities have come to serve at their own tables. An outgrowth of so much cultural intermingling, these include the *satays, po piahs* (spring rolls), coconut rice, and noodle dishes.

But wherever you look or eat, the ubiquitous soup pot bubbles forth with potent, turmeric-washed curries; flavorful vegetable, seafood, and meat soups; and the souplike dishes known as *laksas* (page 183). For the foreign visitor, the *laksa* may seem like the ultimate soup with its noodles and its abundance of ingredients and garnishes. To the Malaysian, *laksas* are a convenient way to flavor and eat noodles, which may account for the seemingly endless variations.

Perhaps the ultimate Malaysian soup feast is the steamboat meal (for information about steamboats, see page 269). A close relative of the Chinese Mongolian Hot Pot (page 280), the steamboat takes its cue from the abundance of local foodstuff, starring fresh seafood and market-crisp vegetables and herbs. The steamboat was all anyone talked about, said my sister, Mary Hager, of a business trip to Malaysia not so long ago. The dinner, she remembered, was ambrosial: "There were at least 50 different items on display to pick from: shrimps, prawns, shellfish, vegetables, noodles and noodles, chickens, quail eggs. . . ."

Even at their home base, Malaysians crave their own foods. As Maryland resident Sherina Massoumi, originally from Petaling Jaya, Malaysia, noted: "Food is very important in Malaysian life and culture. When my sisters and I were in boarding school [in Malaysia], we would come home on weekends and that was a special deal with special foods. I would especially like the Laksa Johore [also known as Johore Laksa], one of my most favorite things. . . . Just the smells [of food] always bring me back home."

Netting the Sea

"A bowl of fish soup isn't worth more than a few cents; Yet, made as in the days of the former capital, it brings smiles to the imperial face . . ."

—from a Ming Dynasty poem

Burmese Fish and Rice Noodle Soup

Moke-Hin-Khar

Spelled in Burma as moke-hin-khar, *but pronounced and spelled in the West as* mohinga, *this potent soup is made with fresh fish in a rich broth and served over rice noodles. Although you might expect every household to have its own version, the recipes I received from two Burmese cooks, Than Than Yi and Daw May Khin Maung Than, were very similar.*

The soup calls for at least one ingredient that may be unfamiliar to you: the inner core of the banana tree trunk. This, says Burmese cook Than Than Yi, is virtually unavailable in the West unless you have friends who will cut down part of their banana tree, peel and boil the stalks, and give or mail the core to you.

You'll also need to learn the Asian trick of hollowing out a stalk of lemon grass: Use a sharp knife to slit the length of the stalk and pull aside the tough outer layers. Cut out the tender inner core and use that for pounding into the seasoning paste. The outer stalk is now pliable enough to be knotted into a loop and dropped into the liquid to add extra flavor.

When you serve the soup, arrange the accompaniments in individual bowls and place them at the table. See "About Mohinga," *below, for more information about this dish.*

Seasoning Paste

3 stalks lemon grass, trimmed and cut
　　into 1-inch pieces
One 1-inch piece fresh ginger
5 cloves garlic, peeled
About $1/2$ cup water

Soup

$1/3$ cup yellow split peas (*chana dal*),
　　rinsed, picked clean, and soaked in
　　cold water to cover for 6 to 12 hours
$15^1/2$ cups water
1 cup vegetable oil
10 to 12 medium onions, peeled
　　and sliced
$1^1/2$ tablespoons paprika or
　　cayenne pepper
2 teaspoons Roasted Red Chili Powder
　　(page 16) or cayenne pepper

1. To make the seasoning paste, combine the lemon grass, ginger, and garlic in a blender. Add just enough water to process, and blend until smooth.

2. To make the soup, combine the split peas and $1^1/2$ cups of the water in a saucepan and bring to a boil. Reduce the heat to medium-low and cook until soft, about 45 minutes. Transfer the peas and cooking liquid to a blender or food processor and puree.

3. Meanwhile, heat the oil in a large wok or skillet over medium heat. Add the onions and cook, stirring often, about 10 minutes, or until very soft and golden,. Stir in the seasoning paste, paprika or cayenne pepper, chili powder or cayenne pepper, turmeric, and 2 tablespoons of the fish sauce. Remove from the heat and set aside.

1 teaspoon ground turmeric

2 tablespoons plus $^{1}/_{2}$ cup fish sauce

7 stalks lemon grass, inner core
removed, outer stalk tied into a knot
(see Headnote)

20 pearl onions or 5 small white
onions, peeled

1 cup rice flour (see Note)

1 to 2 pounds catfish fillets, or other
firm-fleshed fish fillets, skin
removed, sautéed in oil (see Note)
and flaked

Pinch of MSG (optional)

Salt and freshly ground black pepper
to taste

Accompaniments

1 pound rice vermicelli, cooked
(see page 302)

10 to 15 Fried Split Pea Fritters
(page 162)

7 hard-boiled eggs, shelled and sliced

1 cup chopped fresh coriander leaves

1 cup sliced scallions

$^{1}/_{2}$ cup Roasted Red Chili Powder
(page 16) or cayenne pepper

4. Combine 12 cups of the water and lemon grass in a stockpot and bring to a boil. Stir in the onions and reduce the heat to medium-low. Whisk together the rice flour, pureed split peas, and remaining 2 cups water until smooth. Whisk this mixture into the stockpot and cook for 10 minutes. Stir in the fried onion mixture, flaked fish, remaining $^{1}/_{2}$ cup fish sauce, MSG if using, salt, and pepper. Cover and cook until slightly thickened, about 10 minutes more.

5. Pour the hot soup into a tureen. To serve, divide the noodles among serving bowls and ladle the soup over the noodles. Pass around the accompaniments.

MAKES 8 TO 10 SERVINGS

Note: Although rice flour is readily available at Asian markets, I recommend making your own for this dish, roasting the rice before pulverizing to add more flavor. Use 2 cups long-grain rice and dry-roast it in a hot skillet, stirring constantly to prevent burning. When the grains begin to brown, remove from the heat, cool, and pulverize in a blender or spice grinder.

Note: To cook the catfish fillets, heat 3 tablespoons oil in a large skillet. Add the fillets and cook until opaque in the center, about 2 minutes per side.

About Mohinga

Mohinga, the healthful, delicious, and filling national dish of Burma, is sold everywhere, at least in Rangoon. Several Burmese acquaintances who now live in the United States remember when hawkers sold *mohinga* on every street corner in Rangoon. Not only is this a popular street food, but the Burmese often make it at home for breakfast, and it is an ideal party dish when you want to serve a filling meal without spending a great deal of money.

Fried Split Pea Fritters

Parc-chan-kyaw

An accompaniment to mohinga *and sometimes to* ohn-no-khauk-swe, *these split pea fritters make a crispy garnish for this wholesome and hearty main dish. Besides, they are a great snack food. They must be very thin—after frying, they resemble very delicate savory cookies. If the batter does not form a thin layer in the hot oil, thin out the remaining batter with a little water. As you cook them, keep adjusting the heat—if the pan gets too hot, the split peas will burst apart.*

$1/2$ cup yellow split peas (*chana dal*), rinsed and picked clean

$1/2$ teaspoon baking soda

3 tablespoons rice flour

1 tablespoon sticky (glutinous) rice flour

$1/2$ teaspoon salt

Pinch of ground turmeric

$1/2$ cup water

2 cups vegetable oil, or more if needed

1. Put the split peas in a large bowl with the baking soda and enough water to cover. Let soak for 6 to 12 hours. Drain and rinse. Transfer to a medium bowl.

2. Stir in the rice flour, sticky rice flour, salt, turmeric, and water.

3. Heat the oil in a large wok or skillet over medium heat. Use a tablespoon to scoop the batter into the hot oil; you may fry several at one time. Fry until each fritter is crisp and golden on both sides. Transfer to paper towels to drain. Add more oil, if needed, and repeat with the remaining batter.

MAKES 10 TO 15 FRITTERS

Indian Prawn and Okra Curry

A potent, fiery curry just barely smoothed by coconut milk, this Indian dish calls for using extra-large shrimp (prawns). I splurged on the 16- to 20-per-pound jumbo size, although the smaller extra-large or large sizes are fine. The cook who provided this recipe, J. Inder Singh Kalra, also calls for using okra—be sure to select okra that are truly plump and fresh. In a pinch, you may need to substitute frozen okra, but it's safe to say it will not be as good. The accompaniments of steamed rice, a salad with yogurt, and a variety of Indian breads turn this into a feast.

Curry Paste

8 dried red chilies, roasted
   (see page 7)
2 tablespoons coriander seeds, roasted
   (see page 11)
1 teaspoon cumin seeds, roasted
   (see page 11)
About ³/₄ cup water
One 2-inch piece fresh ginger, sliced
5 cloves garlic, peeled

Curry

¹/₄ cup vegetable oil, preferably peanut
1¹/₄ cups finely chopped onions
1¹/₂ pounds extra-large shrimp, shelled
   and deveined
¹/₂ cup thin coconut milk
   (see page 6)
¹/₄ cup water
¹/₂ pound okra, stems removed
¹/₂ cup chopped tomatoes
¹/₂ cup thick coconut milk
   (see page 6)
3 tablespoons tamarind juice
2 green chilies, halved lengthwise and
   seeded
Salt to taste

1. To make the curry paste, combine the chilies, coriander, and cumin in a blender. Add just enough water to process, and blend until coarsely chopped. Add the ginger, garlic, and just enough water to process, and blend until smooth. Strain through a fine-mesh sieve.

2. To make the curry, heat the oil in a large wok or saucepan over medium heat. Add the onions and cook, stirring often, 10 to 15 minutes, or until golden brown. Add the curry paste and cook, stirring, about 3 minutes, until fragrant. Add the shrimp and cook, stirring, about 2 minutes, until they begin to turn pink. Add the thin coconut milk and water, and bring to a boil. Stir in the okra and tomatoes, reduce the heat to medium-low, and cook until the okra is tender, about 5 minutes. Stir in the thick coconut milk, tamarind juice, chilies, and salt. Bring the mixture to a boil, stirring often. Remove from the heat and serve.

MAKES 4 SERVINGS

Cambodian Green Curry Noodle Soup

Kaffir lime leaves, lime rind, and Cambodian Green Curry Paste (page 36) give this soup its pale green color and citrusy accent. The starch is provided by noodles rather than the more commonplace rice. Here the cook, Bora Chu, uses Japanese somen, since she cannot find the kind of rice noodles she once used in Cambodia. But she prepares them Cambodian style: After boiling the noodles, she drains them in a colander, rinses them with cold water, gently wrings them out, coils them together in tidy bundles, and arranges them, pinwheel fashion, in overlapping layers on a platter. (For cooking instructions, see page 303. For coiling the noodles, see page 165.) In a Cambodian marketplace, she says, these coils would be arranged on a bamboo tray.

Cambodians consider this more of a snack than a real meal, but all the components are here for a substantial repast. For extra zing, serve this with whole fresh green chilies or ground dried red chilies, or both.

10 cups Basic Chicken Stock (page 19)

10 kaffir lime leaves, or more to taste

Rind of 1 kaffir lime

1 to 2 tablespoons sugar

1 tablespoon Cambodian fish paste
    (*prahok*), or more to taste (optional)

2 cups Cambodian Green Curry Paste

$^1/_2$ pound catfish fillets, roasted or
    broiled (see Note on page 161), and
    finely minced

1 cup coconut milk

Accompaniments

1 pound somen, cooked and coiled

1 bunch scallions, trimmed and
    diagonally sliced

$^1/_2$ cup coarsely chopped roasted
    unsalted peanuts

10 green or red chilies, sliced, or
    $^1/_2$ cup Roasted Red Chili Powder
    (page 16) or cayenne pepper

$^1/_4$ pound bean sprouts or green
    cabbage, thinly sliced

2 cups thinly sliced fresh banana flowers

2 cucumbers, peeled and thinly sliced

$^1/_4$ pound long beans, trimmed and cut
    into 3- or 4-inch lengths

1. Bring the stock, lime leaves, and lime rind to a boil in a large stockpot and cook for 10 minutes. Skim off any fat. Stir in the sugar and fish paste, if using.

2. Put the curry paste into a small bowl and stir in some of the hot stock to dilute it. Stir into the stock, reduce the heat to medium-low, and cook until slightly thickened, about 10 minutes. Stir in the fish and coconut milk, and cook until heated through, about 5 minutes.

3. Ladle the soup into a tureen. Arrange the noodles on one platter and the garnishes on another. To serve, place a portion of noodles in each soup bowl, ladle some soup over the noodles, and garnish each serving as desired. Serve hot.

MAKES 8 SERVINGS

Cambodian Coconut Red Curry Noodles

This thick and potent curry soup, an outstanding dish of exquisite flavors, becomes strictly vegetarian if you make the Cambodian Red Curry Paste (page 37) without the fish.

The accompaniments are a very important part of the dish, and the ones listed below are those Bora Chu often serves with noodles. If she were in Cambodia, she says, fresh banana flowers would be part of the selection. But in the West, use whichever Asian leafy greens you want.

Soup

6 cups thick coconut milk (see page 6)

3 1/2 cups Cambodian Red Curry Paste

1/2 cup palm sugar or dark brown sugar

1/4 cup fish sauce

1 teaspoon Thai or Malaysian
    shrimp paste

1/2 pound salmon fillets, grilled or
    broiled, and chopped

1 1/2 cups shrimp powder

8 kaffir lime leaves

Rind of 1 kaffir lime

Accompaniments

1/2 pound dried somen, cooked (see
    page 303) and coiled (see Note)

1/2 bunch watercress, blanched in
    boiling water for 30 seconds

2 cups shredded green papaya or chayote

1/4 pound bean sprouts, blanched in
    boiling water for 1 minute

1 cup Thai basil leaves

1 cucumber, cut into long, thin strips

2 cups sliced red cabbage or
    Chinese cabbage

Garnishes

1/2 cup sliced green chilies

1/4 cup Roasted Red Chili Powder
    (page 16) or cayenne pepper

2 limes, each cut into 4 wedges

1. Bring 1/2 cup of the coconut milk to a boil in a stockpot. Stir in 1/2 cup of the curry paste, the sugar, fish sauce, and shrimp paste. Reduce the heat to medium-low and cook, stirring occasionally, about 10 minutes, or until fragrant and oil appears on the surface. Stir in the remaining 3 cups curry paste, the fish, shrimp powder, lime leaves, and lime rind, and cook, stirring occasionally, 10 minutes more. Stir in the remaining 5 1/2 cups coconut milk and cook, stirring often, until heated through, 5 to 10 minutes more. Discard the lime leaves and lime rind.

2. Pour the soup into a tureen, arrange the noodles on a platter, mound the vegetables and green papaya or chayote in a big serving bowl, and arrange the garnishes in individual serving bowls. Alternatively, place a portion of the noodles into an individual bowl, place a selection of vegetables on the noodles, and ladle a serving of the curry over the noodles. Garnish each serving with sliced green chilies and red chili powder, and squeeze lime juice on top.

MAKES 4 TO 6 SERVINGS

Note: After boiling the noodles, drain them in a colander, rinse with cold water, and gently wring out the excess moisture. Then coil them together in tidy bundles. Bora Chu showed me the traditional method of doing this: Grasp a clump (about 1/2 inch in diameter) of cooked and cooled noodles and gently wrap or loop the noodles over your index finger. Then slide the clump off, gently press to flatten, and place on a serving plate.

Bengali Mustard Fish

A beloved Bengali dish, this pungent and piquant stewlike dish has a heady aroma that lures the hungry to the table. The Bengali cook who provided this recipe, Runi Mukherji-Ratnam, says this needs a firm-fleshed, oily fish to stand up to the assertive flavors of mustard seeds, mustard oil, and green chilies. I used swordfish with fine results. She also noted that a Bengali cook would use mustard oil for all the cooking, but since it is costly, she suggested using it only for the second stage of cooking to retain some of the oil's characteristic flavor. To cut its pungency, you need to heat mustard oil until very hot and then cool it before using it for cooking.

For a shortcut version, you can brown the fish in vegetable oil, add the water, and stir in a mixture of 1 cup mustard seeds, 2 to 3 halved green chilies, and 1 teaspoon tomato paste. Runi Mukherji-Ratnam warns not to omit the green chilies, because the mustard seeds will taste bitter. For a change of pace, substitute hard- or soft-shell crabs for the fish. These need a quick boil rather than a quick pan-fry for the first cooking step. Whichever version of this recipe you use, it will capture your taste buds.

1 cup mustard oil or vegetable oil

2 tablespoons *panch phooran*

2 pounds 1-inch-thick firm-fleshed,
 oily fish steaks, such as shad, carp,
 or mackerel

1/2 to 3/4 cup black mustard seeds,
 soaked in 1 cup warm water for
 20 minutes

2 to 3 green chilies

1 to 1 1/2 cups water

1 teaspoon tomato paste (optional)

1/2 to 1 teaspoon ground turmeric

Salt to taste

1. Heat the oil in a large wok or skillet over medium heat until it just begins to smoke. Remove from the heat and set aside to cool.

2. Reheat the oil over medium heat and stir in 1 tablespoon of the *panch phooran*. Set the fish on top of the spices and cook until browned, about 5 minutes per side. Transfer the fish to paper towels to drain. Set the oil aside.

3. Combine the mustard seeds and chilies in a spice grinder or blender. Blend, gradually adding enough water to form a smooth paste, until the mixture increases to three times its original volume. (The consistency of the final mixture should resemble a thin pancake batter.) If you are using the tomato paste, add it now and blend until just combined.

4. Transfer 1/4 to 1/2 cup of the oil—being careful not to include any of the cooked spices, which will settle to the bottom of the oil—to another large wok or skillet over low heat. Add the remaining 1 tablespoon *panch phooran* and arrange the fish steaks in a single layer. Cook until fragrant, about 5 minutes.

5. Pour the mustard seed paste over the fish, sprinkle with the turmeric and salt, and cook until the water evaporates, leaving a mustard-seed sauce, about 10 minutes. Serve hot.

MAKES 4 TO 6 SERVINGS

Note: *Panch phooran* is a special spice mixture that contains equal amounts of the following: mustard seeds, fenugreek seeds, anise or fennel seeds, cumin seeds, and dill or caraway seeds. The seeds should be roasted separately and cooled before use.

Prawn Chili Curry

Sri Lankan cook Felicia Wakwella Sørensen combines hot, sour, and spicy flavors for an appealing shrimp (prawn) curry. The heat, which comes from the green chili and the red chili powder, can be tamed by accompanying this with plenty of chilled drinks—iced tea, iced coffee, wine, or beer. Serve rice and several vegetable dishes alongside this curry.

Curry Paste

6 shallots, peeled and sliced

1 green chili, stem removed

3 cloves garlic, peeled

3 thin slices fresh ginger

1 cup water

Curry

$1/4$ cup tamarind juice

6 curry leaves or 3 bay leaves

One 2-inch piece cinnamon stick

1 to 2 teaspoons Roasted Red Chili
   Powder (page 16)

1 teaspoon salt

$1/4$ teaspoon fenugreek seeds

2 pounds large shrimp, shelled and
   deveined

1. To make the curry paste, combine the shallots, chili, garlic, and ginger in a blender. Add just enough water to process, and blend until smooth. Stir in the remaining water.

2. To make the curry, transfer the curry paste to a large wok or saucepan. Stir in the tamarind juice, curry leaves or bay leaves, cinnamon, chili powder, salt, and fenugreek. Bring to a boil, reduce the heat to medium-low, and cook, 5 to 7 minutes, or until thickened and all the moisture has evaporated. Stir in the shrimp and cook until just pink, 3 to 4 minutes. Serve hot.

MAKES 4 TO 6 SERVINGS

Chilied Nepalese Fish Curry

Although one does not necessarily associate the landlocked, mountainous country of Nepal with seafood, this fish curry comes from this inland country. Showing off its possible Indian heritage, the curry brings together the fire of chilies and red chili powder and the soothing appeal of yogurt and sour cream. The cook who provided this recipe, Jack Katayal, says that any kind of fish fillets with a flavor that can stand up to the chilies is fine to use.

Curry Paste

2 small onions, peeled and chopped

4 green chilies, stems removed

4 cloves garlic, peeled

One 1^1/$_2$-inch piece fresh ginger

2 tablespoons ground turmeric

1^1/$_2$ tablespoons Roasted Red Chili
Powder (page 16)

1^1/$_2$ teaspoons ground coriander

About ^{1}/$_2$ cup water

Curry

2^1/$_2$ pounds firm-fleshed fish
fillets, such as cod or catfish,
skin removed, thinly sliced

2 teaspoons salt

1 tablespoon fresh lemon juice, or
more to taste

^{3}/$_4$ cup unsalted butter

^{1}/$_4$ cup plain yogurt

^{1}/$_4$ cup sour cream

1. To make the seasoning paste, combine the onions, chilies, garlic, ginger, turmeric, chili powder, and coriander in a blender. Add just enough water to process, and blend until smooth.

2. To make the curry, place the fish in a large glass or enamel baking dish. Sprinkle the surfaces of the fish with salt and lemon juice. Spoon the seasoning paste over the fish and spread to cover both sides. Cover the dish with plastic wrap and set aside for 15 minutes.

3. Melt the butter in a large saucepan over medium heat until sizzling. Add the fish and yogurt, and stir to mix well. Reduce the heat to low, cover, and cook until the fish is opaque in the center, about 20 minutes. Stir in the sour cream, cover, and cook for 5 minutes more. Serve hot.

MAKES 4 TO 6 SERVINGS

Delicate Burmese Crab Curry

The cook who provided this recipe, Daw Mya Mya Gyi, says that this mild curry can feature crabmeat, shrimp, or scallops when whole fresh crabs are not in season. Because eating whole crabs can be a messy affair, plan this for an al fresco meal and offer plenty of paper napkins—and plenty of chilled beer to drink. A tossed salad and several cold vegetable dishes would suit the crab curry well.

6 large live crabs

2 tablespoons vegetable oil, or more
   if needed

1 large onion, peeled and chopped

3 cloves garlic, peeled and crushed

1 tablespoon grated fresh ginger

2 tablespoons minced fresh
   coriander leaves

$1/2$ teaspoon ground cumin

$1/2$ teaspoon cayenne pepper

$1/4$ teaspoon ground turmeric

2 plum tomatoes, chopped

1 cup boiling water, or more if needed

Salt and freshly ground black pepper
   to taste

Lemon wedges

1. Bring a large pot of water to a boil. Add the crabs and cook for 1 minute. Drain. When cool enough to handle, cut the bodies in quarters and crack the claws. Set aside.

2. Heat the oil in a large wok or skillet over medium heat. Add the onions and cook, stirring, about 5 minutes, or until translucent. Stir in the garlic and ginger, and reduce the heat to medium-low. Stir in the coriander, cumin, cayenne pepper, and turmeric, and cook, stirring, 3 to 4 minutes, or until fragrant. (Add more oil if the mixture seems dry.) Stir in the tomatoes and water, increase the heat to medium, and bring to a simmer. Add the crabs. Reduce the heat to medium-low, cover, and cook about 10 minutes, or until the crabs turn orange. (Add more boiling water if the sauce becomes too thick.) Stir in the salt and pepper, and serve immediately with the lemon wedges.

MAKES 2 TO 3 SERVINGS

Burmese Fiery Fish Curry

One early morning in Rangoon, Anna Khin-Khin Kyawt led my friend and me through one of the city's numerous wet (fresh) markets—this one, her favorite place to buy fresh fish. Dressed in the traditional longhi—a long-skirted garment that resembles a sarong—she guided us up and down the aisles of the marketplace. Before the market closed down, she used to stop there often during the week to pick up needed staples, such as fresh coconut milk, vegetables, and, of course, freshly caught fish. Although she could have sent her household servants to shop, she often made the trip herself so she could pick out the very best the vendors were selling.

From the many mounds of wriggling fish, Anna selected a local variety called butterfish—something she also called the "king of the fish," explaining that the firm, rich flesh resembles lobster, which you may substitute in this recipe. (Monkfish is also a fine alternative.) Back at her family's lakeside home, she then proceeded to show me the traditional way of preparing this curry, cooking it over a charcoal fire on the back verandah. The servants pounded the ingredients for the curry paste with a mortar and pestle, and the thunking sound reverberated in the quiet country morning. Anna meanwhile prepared the other courses for the family's main meal. In a little less than an hour, all of us sat down to a five-course dinner of chicken curry, this spectacular fish dish, rice, and two different vegetables.

Curry Paste

5 dried red chilies, soaked in hot water
    for 20 minutes
3 large shallots, peeled and chopped
1 head garlic, cloves separated
    and peeled
4 or 5 whole sprigs of fresh coriander
About $\frac{1}{4}$ cup water

Curry

2 pounds firm-fleshed fish fillets, such
    as monkfish, skin removed, cubed
1 tablespoon ground turmeric
1 tablespoon salt
$\frac{1}{2}$ cup vegetable oil, or more if needed
1 cup water
$\frac{1}{2}$ cup chopped fresh coriander leaves

1. To make the curry paste, combine the chilies, shallots, garlic, and coriander in a blender. Add just enough water to process, and blend until smooth.

2. To make the curry, place the fish in a large bowl. Stir together the turmeric and salt, and sprinkle over the fish.

3. Heat the oil in a large saucepan over medium heat. Add the curry paste and cook, stirring, 5 to 7 minutes, or until fragrant. Add the fish and cook, stirring, until the paste clings and forms a crust, about 5 minutes more. Add the water. Reduce the heat to low, cover, and cook, stirring occasionally, for 15 minutes. Remove the cover and cook until thickened, 5 to 10 minutes more. Sprinkle with the coriander leaves and serve.

MAKES 4 TO 6 SERVINGS

Fish Curry with Lemon Grass

When the Burmese cook Daw Mya Mya Gyi gave me this recipe, she explained that not only does it combine many of the favorite Burmese flavors—onion, garlic, ginger, and lemon grass—but that it also comes together very quickly, a bonus for busy cooks. Although rice would be a typical starch, you may serve Asian wheat or rice noodles and offer several vegetable dishes as well.

1 pound catfish or cod fillets, or other firm-fleshed fish fillets, skin removed, cut into 1¹/₂-inch-long strips

¹/₄ cup fish sauce, or more to taste

¹/₄ cup vegetable oil

1 large onion, peeled and chopped

4 cloves garlic, peeled and minced

1 tablespoon grated fresh ginger

1 stalk lemon grass, trimmed and thinly sliced

¹/₄ teaspoon ground turmeric

¹/₄ teaspoon cayenne pepper

2 plum tomatoes, chopped

¹/₄ to ¹/₂ cup boiling water, if needed

1 tablespoon chopped fresh coriander leaves, or more to taste

1. Place the fish in a bowl and add the fish sauce. Set aside.

2. Heat the oil in a large saucepan over medium heat. Add the onions and cook, stirring, until translucent, about 5 minutes. Add the garlic and ginger and cook, stirring, about 2 minutes, or until golden. Stir in the lemon grass, turmeric, and cayenne pepper. Add the tomatoes and cook, about 10 minutes, or until slightly thickened. (Do not let the sauce stick to the pan—if it does, loosen by stirring in some of the boiling water.) Add the fish, turn to coat the pieces with the sauce, and cook until the fish is opaque in the center, about 10 minutes. Garnish with coriander leaves and serve immediately.

MAKES 2 TO 3 SERVINGS

Laotian Bamboo Shoots and Fish Soup

This exotic dish, which combines catfish, bamboo shoots, and stems from an indigenous Lao plant called yanang, *typifies how the Laotians use all the natural ingredients they have at hand. For example, bamboo grows abundantly in Laos and cooks have plenty of very young shoots, which are used for this soup, at their disposal, explains my Lao friend Bounsou Sananikone. She also says that yanang, the woody stem of a climbing plant with the botanical name* Tiliacora triandra, *is abundant and imparts to any dish the slightly sour taste that Laotians love. Fortunately for the Lao living in the West,* yanang *comes frozen or water-packed in cans.*

Seasoning Paste

3 stalks lemon grass, trimmed
    and sliced

4 to 5 green chilies

4 shallots, peeled and sliced

2 tablespoons sticky (glutinous) rice,
    soaked in cold water for 20 minutes,
    soaking water reserved

About $^1/_2$ cup water

Soup

4 cups water

$^1/_4$ cup tamarind juice

1 pound catfish fillets, or other firm-
    fleshed fish fillets, skin removed, cut
    into strips

One 20-ounce can bamboo shoots,
    rinsed and shredded

$^1/_2$ pound *yanang*

1 bunch watercress, rinsed and trimmed

1 cup Thai mint leaves

$^1/_4$ pound enoki mushrooms, rinsed

$^1/_2$ ounce dried cloud ear mushrooms,
    soaked in hot water for 20 minutes

12 young pumpkin leaves (optional)

2 tablespoons fish sauce

1. To make the seasoning paste, combine the lemon grass, chilies, shallots, rice, and soaking water in a blender. Add just enough water to process, and blend until smooth.

2. Pour the water and tamarind juice into a large saucepan and bring to a boil. Reduce the heat to low and add the fish, bamboo shoots, *yanang*, watercress, mint leaves, enoki mushrooms, cloud ear mushrooms, pumpkin leaves if using, and fish sauce. Cook for 5 minutes. Stir in the seasoning paste and cook for 10 minutes more. Serve hot.

MAKES 4 TO 6 SERVINGS

Cambodian "Fondue"

If you trace the journey of the Chinese Mongolian Hot Pot (page 280) through Asia, you'll find that every country seems to have adapted this sensible way of cooking and eating to fit into its own culture and cuisine. And while the method is similar—cooking at the table in a tabletop cooking vessel—the results are always different.

For the Cambodian version, you cook just the meat in the cooking liquid (water or chicken broth); the vegetables are eaten raw. If you like squid, allow two small squid per person. For a more flavorful cooking liquid, use the dipping sauce in place of 6 cups of plain water. The amounts that Cambodian cook Sokheng N. Kheang suggests for both cooking and dipping are included in parentheses. Use the lesser quantities if you are using the sauce just for dipping.

Dipping Sauce and/or Cooking Liquid

2 (or 5) shallots, peeled and sliced

4 tablespoons minced garlic (or 1 head
   of garlic, cloves separated, peeled,
   and minced)

1 cup (or 3 cups) sugar

2 tablespoons (or $^1/_3$ cup) salt

$1^3/_4$ cups (or 6 cups) water

$^3/_4$ cup (or 2 cups) white vinegar

$^1/_3$ cup (or 1 cup) fish sauce

Soup

$1^1/_2$ pounds thinly sliced boneless
   top round

1 pound large shrimp, shelled
   and deveined

8 small squid, cleaned (see Note) and
   cut into bite-sized pieces

1. Pour the cooking liquid—either water or the combination of shallots, garlic, sugar, salt, water, vinegar, and fish sauce—into a tabletop cooking vessel and bring to a boil.

2. Transfer the cooking vessel to the table and keep the liquid at a simmer. If you are using just water as the cooking liquid, whisk together the dipping sauce ingredients in a separate serving bowl.

3. Arrange the beef, shrimp, and squid on a large serving platter. Arrange the cabbage leaves, bean sprouts, cucumbers, and noodles on another platter. Place the garnishes in serving bowls. Take the platters and serving bowls to the table.

**1 head Chinese (napa) cabbage,
separated into leaves, tough
ends trimmed**

**$^1/_2$ pound bean sprouts, blanched in
boiling water for 1 minute**

**3 cucumbers, peeled and cut into
thin strips**

**$^1/_2$ pound thin rice vermicelli, cooked
(see page 302)**

1 cup roasted peanuts, finely chopped
1 cup fresh mint leaves

4. Let people cook the meat using chopsticks, a wire-mesh basket, or a fork. Then use the cabbage leaves as wrappers: Place a portion of noodles, vegetables, meat or seafood, and garnishes on a leaf. Wrap up snugly and dip into the cooking liquid before eating. The cooking liquid may be drunk as soup after eating.

MAKES 4 SERVINGS

Note: To clean fresh or thawed squid, hold the body in one hand and the head portion with the tentacles in the other (hold behind the eyes). Detach the head by gently pulling it off the body; the intestines will come out at the same time. Peel off the outer skin and pull out and discard the cartilage-like backbone. Rinse the interior of the body thoroughly and slit it open lengthwise. Carefully trim the tentacles off the head portion in front of the eyes, taking care not to rupture the ink sac. Rinse the tentacles thoroughly before slicing.

Fish Soup with Pineapple and Tomatoes

This delicious soup with its play of sweet against sour flavors can be served as an appetizer, but in Cambodia, it would be the main course. To vary the dish, you can also use chicken or shrimp, explains the cook who provided this recipe, Sokheng N. Kheang.

3 tablespoons vegetable oil

1¹/₂ pounds red snapper, rockfish, mud fish, or catfish fillets, skin removed, cut into 2-inch-long pieces

8 cups Basic Fish Stock (page 21) or Basic Chicken Stock (page 19)

3 tablespoons fish sauce

2¹/₂ tablespoons tamarind juice

2¹/₂ tablespoons sugar

2¹/₂ teaspoons salt

¹/₄ fresh pineapple, skinned, cored, and cubed

¹/₂ Chinese bitter gourd, peeled and cubed (optional)

4 large tomatoes, chopped

1 to 2 tablespoons Fried Garlic (page 18)

1 cup Thai basil leaves

1. Heat the oil in a large skillet over medium heat. Add the fish and cook until golden, 2 to 3 minutes per side. Transfer to paper towels to drain.

2. Pour the stock into a large saucepan and bring to a boil. Add the fish, fish sauce, tamarind juice, sugar, and salt. Return to a boil and add the pineapple and bitter gourd. Reduce the heat to medium-low and cook until the gourd is softened, about 10 minutes. Add the tomatoes and cook until softened, 2 to 3 minutes more. Remove from the heat and garnish the soup with the fried garlic and basil leaves. Serve hot.

MAKES 4 TO 6 SERVINGS

Vietnamese Hot and Sour Soup

Who does not love the interaction of the sweet-sour flavors that you find in this light, delicate soup? The ingredient proportions really depend on the flavors you like best and on how sweet or sour you want the final flavor.

Be sure to add the bean sprouts, tomatoes, and shrimp just before serving—too much cooking softens the sprouts and tomatoes and toughens the shrimp. Bring this soup to the table in a tureen, or serve it in individual soup bowls and pass around a side dish of sliced chilies in fish sauce, which you may sprinkle on as an added garnish. The cook who provided this recipe, Helene Sze McCarthy, suggests also using pork fat drippings—fried until golden brown—as a last-minute garnish for this soup. The pork fat, she says, "perks up the flavor."

Serve the soup with cooked rice as an accompaniment, or spoon the rice into the soup and eat the two together. You may eat this as an appetizer or a light supper—at a Vietnamese table, this soup would be just one of several courses served at one time.

4 to 5 cups Basic Chicken Stock
    (page 19)
2 stalks lemon grass, trimmed and cut
    into thirds
2 tablespoons vegetable oil
4 cloves garlic, peeled and sliced
1 cup chopped fresh pineapple
2 tablespoons sugar, or more to taste
$^1/_2$ to 1 cup tamarind juice
$^1/_4$ cup fish sauce
$^1/_2$ pound okra
2 cups thinly sliced celery
1 pound large shrimp, shelled
    and deveined
About $^1/_4$ pound bean sprouts
1 large tomato, cut into eighths
Fresh mint leaves
Fresh coriander leaves

1. Pour the stock into a large saucepan and bring to a simmer. Add the lemon grass and cook for 5 minutes. Remove from the heat and discard the lemon grass.

2. Heat the oil in a large wok or skillet over medium heat. Add the garlic and cook, stirring, about 2 minutes, or until browned. Stir in the pineapple and sugar, and cook 3 to 4 minutes, or until the sugar is dissolved. Stir into the stock and bring to a simmer. Stir in the tamarind juice, fish sauce, okra, and celery. Reduce the heat to medium-low and cook until the okra is tender, 6 to 8 minutes. Add the shrimp, bean sprouts, and tomatoes, and cook until the shrimp begins to turn pink, about 2 minutes. Taste and add more sugar and tamarind juice, if desired. Remove from the heat, garnish with the mint and coriander leaves, and serve hot.

MAKES 4 SERVINGS

Vietnamese Crab and Tomato Soup

Bún Rieu

According to my Vietnamese friend David Quang, making this soup the old-fashioned way means catching the crabs, steaming them, and cracking the shells open to pick out the meat, something he was asked to do as a child. Today, he says, most Vietnamese cooks—especially in the West—simply buy already prepared lump crabmeat for this very typical soup. That means his busy wife can prepare this often. He notes that you can add more or less crabmeat, depending on your budget. This soup with its herb garnishes is substantial enough to work as a main course.

9 cups Basic Pork Stock (page 20) or
   Basic Chicken Stock (page 19)

3 pounds tomatoes, cubed

3 eggs

$^1/_2$ to 1 pound lump crabmeat,
   picked clean

1 tablespoon fish sauce

$1^1/_2$ teaspoons Chinese or Vietnamese
   shrimp paste, or more to taste

1 pound rice vermicelli, cooked
   (see page 302)

$^1/_4$ pound bean sprouts

$^1/_2$ cup fresh mint leaves

$^1/_2$ cup Thai basil leaves

1. Bring the stock to a boil in a large saucepan. Stir in the tomatoes and return to a boil. Reduce the heat to medium-low and cook for 10 minutes.

2. Beat the eggs in a bowl. Add the crabmeat, fish sauce, and shrimp paste. Stir into the soup and cook until heated through, 5 to 10 minutes.

3. To serve, place a portion of noodles in each serving bowl and ladle the soup over the top. Arrange the bean sprouts, mint, and basil on a plate and pass around the table for garnish.

MAKES 4 TO 6 SERVINGS

Vietnamese Seafood Rice Soup

Chao Tom

As Vietnamese cook Suòng Thomas says, like other Asians, the Vietnamese make a soup out of rice (for recipes and more information on Asian rice soups, see page 236) and use the hot rice soup, which should be the consistency of thick gruel, as a cooking medium for the raw seafood. You can vary the main recipe by adding seasoned ground pork instead of seafood. She adds that many Vietnamese cooks brown the rice for about 5 minutes before boiling it. The browning adds both flavor and aroma to the dish.

With some minor adjustments, the Vietnamese use this soup as a remedy for fevers and colds: Stir an egg into the hot rice, letting the heat of the soup cook it. Serve this mixture with plenty of black pepper.

6 cups water, or more if desired

$^1/_2$ cup long-grain rice

$^1/_2$ to $^3/_4$ pound medium shrimp, shelled and deveined (see Note)

3 tablespoons chopped scallions

3 tablespoons chopped fresh coriander leaves

1 tablespoon fish sauce, or more to taste

1 teaspoon minced fresh ginger

Salt and freshly ground black pepper to taste

1. Bring the water to a boil in a large saucepan. Stir in the rice. Reduce the heat to low, cover, and cook until the rice reaches the desired consistency, about 1 hour. (Add more water for a soupier consistency, if desired.)

2. Add the seafood and cook until opaque in the center, about 5 minutes. Add the scallions, coriander, fish sauce, ginger, salt, and pepper. Serve immediately.

MAKES 2 TO 4 SERVINGS

Note: You may use whole shrimp or make it into a paste the Vietnamese way: Using the flat side of a cleaver, mash the shrimp. Combine the resulting shrimp paste with black pepper, fish sauce, and sugar to taste and form this mixture into small balls. Add them to the rice after it reaches the desired consistency.

Thai Fiery Seafood Soup

Poh Taek

Many years ago, my family and friends sat beachside in Pattaya, Thailand, drinking chilled beer and eating the restaurant's specialty, a firebrand seafood soup. Thick with whole and sliced fresh chilies and chunky with fresh shrimp, baby squid, and baby octopus, the soup was intensely hot—so hot that each of us wept from the sting of the chilies. But the soup was a masterpiece of seafood pleasures.

For the best seafood flavor, make a delicate base by making a stock from the shells of the shrimp. However, to simplify preparation, you may use water instead. With my version of this fiery soup—which has gone through many trials and errors—you need to serve plenty of icy drinks and have lots of napkins on hand (to mop up perspiration!). We had nothing else for dinner that night, but grilled fish, rice, and fruit would work well with this soup. If you prefer, you may certainly throw in baby squid and octopus instead of sliced adult squid.

1 pound large shrimp, shelled and deveined, shells reserved

8 cups water

7 fresh red and green chilies, diagonally sliced, or to taste

2 stalks lemon grass, trimmed and thinly sliced

3 thin slices galangal

2 cloves garlic, peeled and minced

1/4 cup fresh lime juice

2 tablespoons fish sauce

1 pound squid, cleaned (see page 175) and cut into thin rings

1/2 cup chopped fresh coriander leaves

2 scallions, trimmed and thinly sliced on the diagonal

1. To make the stock, combine the shrimp shells and water in a stockpot and bring to a boil. Reduce the heat to medium and cook for 15 minutes. Strain through a fine-mesh sieve and discard the shells.

2. Return the stock to the saucepan and add the chilies, lemon grass, galangal, garlic, lime juice, and fish sauce. Cook over medium-low heat for 10 minutes. Stir in the shrimp and squid, and cook until the shrimp are pink, about 5 minutes more.

3. Garnish the soup with the coriander leaves and scallions, and serve immediately.

MAKES 4 TO 6 SERVINGS

Malaysian Shrimp and Tofu Soup

Sup Tauhu

Were it not for the addition of the fish, this nourishing soup would be a vegetarian's dream, as tofu is really the star of the dish. I haven't experimented, but you could omit all the seafood and boost the number of vegetables for an all-veggie meal.

The original recipe calls for a fish named ikan kurau, *or threadfin fish, but since you are not likely to find it in the West, you may use any firm-fleshed white fish instead—or simply increase the quantity of shrimp and omit the fish altogether. For added punch, serve this with a side dish of hot chili sauce or sliced green chilies and with a sprinkle or two of fish sauce or soy sauce.*

Stock

3 tablespoons vegetable oil

$^1/_2$ pound large shrimp, shelled, deveined, and halved lengthwise, shells reserved

2 tablespoons minced garlic

Two $^1/_8$-inch-thick slices fresh ginger

2 shallots, peeled and sliced

1 tablespoon fish sauce

Sugar to taste

6 cups water

Soup

3 tablespoons vegetable oil

4 cloves garlic, peeled and minced

Eight 3×3-inch cubes soft tofu

$^1/_2$ pound firm-fleshed fish fillets, such as catfish, skin removed, chopped

$^1/_2$ cup chopped celery

$^1/_2$ cup chopped scallions

Salt and freshly ground black pepper to taste

1. To make the stock, heat the oil in a stockpot over medium heat. Add the shrimp shells and garlic, and cook, stirring, until fragrant, 3 to 4 minutes. Add the ginger, shallots, fish sauce, sugar, and water. Bring to a boil, reduce the heat to medium-low, and cook for 15 minutes. Strain through a fine-mesh sieve and discard the solids. Set aside.

2. To make the soup, heat the oil in a large wok or skillet over medium heat. Add the garlic and cook, stirring, until golden, 2 to 3 minutes. Stir in the stock and bring to a boil. Add the tofu, reduce the heat to low, and cook for 20 minutes. Add the shrimp and fish, and cook until the shrimp are pink and the fish is opaque in the center, 5 to 6 minutes more. Stir in the celery, scallions, salt, and pepper, and cook for 4 minutes more. Serve hot.

MAKES 4 SERVINGS

Malaysian Noodles with Fish and Vegetables

Asam Laksa

One of Malaysia's staple dishes, this "soup," which Malaysians think of as vegetables and noodles with gravy, has rice noodles as its basis. Over each portion of noodles comes a generous scoop of a slightly soured "gravy" rich with chilies and fish and accented by a variety of accompaniments used for texture and flavor. For extra punch, you can also garnish the soup with salt, a black shrimp paste known as petis *that you dilute with water and pour over the noodles, and sliced fresh chilies. The cook who provided this recipe, Majmin Hashim, calls this a healthful dish. Westerners might find a large helping or two with plenty of noodles meal enough, but a grilled meat or chicken and rice are delicious accompaniments.*

Seasoning Paste

8 shallots, peeled and sliced

3 cloves garlic, peeled

1 stalk lemon grass, trimmed and sliced

1 thin slice galangal

5 fresh red and green chilies, or to taste

1/2 teaspoon Malaysian or Thai shrimp paste

About 1/2 cup water

Soup

3 tablespoons vegetable oil

1 pound firm-fleshed fish fillets, such as mackerel or catfish, minced

1 Indonesian bay leaf

Salt to taste

6 cups water

1/2 cup tamarind juice

Accompaniments

1 pound fresh rice noodles, rinsed, or 1/2 pound dried rice vermicelli or rice stick noodles, cooked (see page 302)

2 cups mint leaves

1 onion, peeled and sliced

1/2 pound bean sprouts, blanched in boiling water for 1 minute

1 cucumber, peeled, seeded, and sliced into long, thin strips to resemble noodles

2 cups cubed fresh pineapple

3 fresh red and green chilies, sliced

1 tablespoon Malaysian black shrimp paste (*petis*) mixed with 1/2 cup water (optional)

1. To make the seasoning paste, combine the shallots, garlic, lemon grass, galangal, chilies, and shrimp paste in a blender. Add just enough water to process, and blend until smooth.

2. To make the soup, heat the oil in a large wok or saucepan over medium heat. Add the seasoning paste and cook, stirring, until fragrant, about 5 minutes. Add the fish, bay leaf, salt, water, and tamarind juice. Bring to a boil, reduce the heat to medium-low, and cook for 10 minutes.

3. To serve, put a portion of noodles, mint leaves, onion, bean sprouts, cucumber, and pineapple in each bowl. Ladle in the liquid, and garnish with chilies and diluted black shrimp paste, if using.

MAKES 4 TO 6 SERVINGS

Malaysia Takes to *Laksas*

Over a lengthy dinner, I listened to two Malaysians discussing the merits of their favorite *laksa*. But what I wanted to know was, what are *laksas*?

Lacking any direct English translation, a *laksa* could be called a soup, or maybe a stewlike dish, but strictly speaking, a Malaysian—or a Singaporean, for that matter—might just think of a *laksa* as a way to eat round rice noodles moistened with a savory sauce or gravy. Then, of course, non-Malaysians are confronted with the bewildering array of Malaysian *laksas*, including the Penang *laksa*; Johore *laksa*; curry noodles, which are also a *laksa*; Asam *laksa*, which turns out to be similar to Penang *laksa*; *laksa lemak*; and Kelantan *laksa*. And so it goes.

To clarify the *laksa* riddle, I asked my Malaysian friend Harris Lokmanhakim to help sort it out, and this is what he e-mailed me about the differences between a Penang *laksa* and an Asam *laksa*:

> "Asam *laksa* is a chicken or fish broth sour soup that can vary by cooks. The chief ingredients are tamarind and lemon grass in a red chili paste soup. There aren't many vegetables in this other than greeny, leafy garnishing [sic] like parsley. I have only had this dish as an entree, but then, as you know, a Malaysian entree is shared at the table and not served individually.

> "Penang *laksa* is a fish (mackerel here in the United States) broth soup where the fish meat has been stewed and separated and remains suspended in the broth . . . I recall some tamarind and limes. This dish is usually served with rice noodles and a plethora of raw vegetables. Take a serving of noodles, and choose any amount of the following . . . bean sprouts (roots removed), julienned cucumbers, deep-fried tofu strips, Chinese parsley [fresh coriander], spring onions . . . then ladle in a helping of the fish broth soup. One optional condiment is hea-ko (*petis*), a potent, black-as-molasses paste made from shrimp heads. The northern states even use rice vermicelli instead of rice noodles. . . . This is an individual dish unlike Asam *laksa* that is served as an entree."

Spicy Malaysian Prawn Soup

Sup Udang

The chefs at the Parkroyal Hotel in Kuala Lumpur, Malaysia, have created this take on the traditional Malaysian soup—and this adaptation comes to the table as a fragrant seafood offering redolent of garlic and ginger. If you want a meatier dish, up the number of shrimp (prawns), and for more texture, increase the amount of bean thread (glass) noodles.

1¼ pounds medium shrimp, shells intact, rinsed

3 tablespoons vegetable oil, or more if needed

2 to 3 shallots, peeled and chopped

5 cloves garlic, peeled and minced

One 1-inch piece fresh ginger, chopped

1½ tablespoons Malaysian Soup Spices (page 32)

4 cups Basic Fish Stock (page 21) or Basic Chicken Stock (page 19), or more if needed

3 stalks lemon grass, trimmed and lightly pounded

1 ounce bean thread (glass) noodles, soaked in hot water for 15 minutes

Salt and freshly ground black pepper to taste

Pinch of MSG (optional)

1. With a sharp knife, slit the shrimp shells along the back, and trim off the head and legs. Leave the tail and shell intact.

2. Heat the oil in a stockpot over medium heat. Add the shallots, garlic, and ginger, and cook, stirring often, 3 to 4 minutes, or until golden. Stir in the soup spices and stock. Bring to a boil and cook, stirring, for 1 minute. Stir in the shrimp, lemon grass, noodles, salt, pepper, and MSG if using. Reduce the heat to low and cook 5 minutes more.

MAKES 4 SERVINGS

Malaysian Coconut Milk and Seafood Soup

Laksa Lemak

This rich and creamy laksa *is a specialty of Malaysian cook Majmin Hashim, and her daughter Zuraidah finds it hard to limit herself to only one or two bowls at a time. Because this* laksa *has all the components—vegetables, meat, and starch—of a full meal, you may want to accompany this with only drinks and a light dessert.*

Seasoning Paste

12 or more dried red chilies, soaked in
   hot water for 20 minutes

3 stalks lemon grass, trimmed and sliced

1 large onion, peeled and quartered

6 macadamia nuts

One 3-inch piece galangal, sliced

1 tablespoon minced fresh turmeric or
   1 teaspoon ground turmeric

2 teaspoons coriander seeds, roasted
   and ground (see page 11)

1 teaspoon Malaysian or Thai
   shrimp paste

About $1/2$ cup coconut milk

Soup

$1/4$ cup vegetable oil

$1^1/2$ pounds large shrimp, shelled
   and deveined

Salt to taste

6 to 7 cups coconut milk

$3/4$ pound mackerel or catfish fillets,
   skin removed, minced

Accompaniments

1 pound fresh wide rice noodles, rinsed,
   or $1/2$ pound dried rice stick noodles,
   cooked (see page 302)

$1/2$ pound bean sprouts, blanched in
   boiling water for 1 minute

3 cucumbers, peeled and shredded

6 fresh red and green chilies, thinly sliced

1. To make the seasoning paste, combine the chilies, lemon grass, onion, macadamia nuts, galangal, turmeric, coriander, and shrimp paste in a blender. Add just enough coconut milk to process, and blend until smooth.

2. To make the soup, heat the oil in a large stockpot over medium heat. Add the seasoning paste and cook, stirring, until fragrant, 3 to 4 minutes. Add the shrimp and salt, and cook, stirring, for 5 minutes. Stir in 5 cups of the coconut milk and bring to a boil. Add the fish, reduce the heat to medium-low, and cook for 3 minutes. Stir in the remaining coconut milk and cook the mixture until heated through, about 10 minutes more. Remove from the heat.

3. To serve, put a portion of noodles and bean sprouts in each bowl. Ladle in the liquid and garnish each serving with the cucumbers and chilies.

MAKES 4 TO 6 SERVINGS

Fragrant and Fiery Malaysian Noodle Soup, Penang Style

Penang Laksa

This popular noodle dish, which is a close relative to asam laksa, *probably originated on the island of Penang, Malaysia, and may have as many variations as there are cooks. This recipe from the Parkroyal Hotel in Kuala Lumpur, Malaysia, calls for a fragrant herb called* daun kesum, *which resembles a cross between basil and mint. Since it is virtually impossible to find in the West, substitute mint. It also calls for using buds from flowering ginger, also an unlikely find in the West. Unfortunately, there are no substitutes, so you may have to do without. The cook here calls for a daunting number of chilies; once again, let your fire quotient be your guide.*

Seasoning Paste

20 dried red chilies, soaked in hot
   water for 20 minutes

³/₄ pound shallots, peeled and chopped

4 stalks lemon grass, trimmed
   and sliced

8 thin slices galangal

One 1-inch piece fresh turmeric or
   2 teaspoons ground turmeric

1 teaspoon Malaysian or Thai
   shrimp paste

About ³/₄ cup water

Soup

2 teaspoons vegetable oil, or more
   if needed

2 pounds mackerel fillets, skin
   removed, minced

10 sprigs *daun kesum* or mint

1 ginger bud, halved (optional)

2 teaspoons sugar

1 teaspoon salt

6 cups Basic Fish Stock (page 21)
   or water

4 cups tamarind juice

1. To make the seasoning paste, combine the chilies, shallots, lemon grass, galangal, turmeric, and shrimp paste in a blender. Add just enough water to process and blend until smooth.

2. To make the soup, heat the oil in a large saucepan over medium heat. Add the seasoning paste and cook, stirring, until fragrant, about 5 minutes. Add the fish and cook for 5 minutes more. (Add more oil if the mixture seems dry.) Add the mint, ginger bud, if using, sugar, salt, stock or water, and tamarind juice, reduce the heat to medium-low, and cook for 30 minutes longer.

3. To serve, arrange portions of the noodles, pineapple, lettuce, onion, cucumber, mint leaves, ginger bud if using, and chilies in individual soup bowls. Ladle in the hot soup. Combine the shrimp paste and boiling water, and drizzle over each portion. Serve immediately.

MAKES 4 TO 6 SERVINGS

Accompaniments

$1^{1}/_{4}$ pounds fresh rice noodles, rinsed
   (see page 302), or $^{3}/_{4}$ pound dried rice
   stick noodles, cooked (see page 302)
3 cups shredded fresh pineapple
1 head lettuce, shredded
1 large onion, peeled and thinly sliced
1 cucumber, peeled and shredded
$2^{1}/_{4}$ cups mint leaves
1 ginger bud, thinly sliced (optional)
4 fresh red chilies, thinly sliced
1 tablespoon Malaysian or Thai shrimp
   paste, or more to taste
$^{1}/_{2}$ cup boiling water

Malaysian Hot, Sweet, and Sour Noodle Soup, Kelantan Style

Kelantan Laksa

Yet another version of laksa, *this recipe from Norhayati Ibrahim, who grew up in the Malaysian state of Kelantan, plays hot against sweet and sour. The recipe calls for slices of* asam gelvaor, *which is dried tamarind. You are not likely to find this at any Asian market, so use tamarind juice instead for the needed sourness. The cook says she uses either fresh or canned mackerel with equally good results. She also serves a chili sauce condiment, such as the Indonesian* sambal oelek *or the chunky Vietnamese chili sauce, at the table to add fire.*

1 pound mackerel fillets, skin removed,
   cubed
1 large onion, peeled and thinly sliced
4 cloves garlic, peeled and sliced
One $1/2$-inch piece fresh ginger,
   minced
2 cups coconut milk
$1^1/2$ cups water
$1/2$ cup tamarind juice
1 teaspoon oyster sauce
$1/2$ teaspoon freshly ground black pepper
Sugar to taste
Salt to taste
$1/2$ pound fresh wide rice noodles,
   rinsed (see page 302), or $1/4$ pound
   dried rice stick noodles, cooked
   (see page 302)

Accompaniments

10 lettuce leaves, thinly sliced
1 cucumber, peeled and finely chopped
$1/2$ pound bean sprouts, blanched in
   boiling water for 1 minute
2 carrots, peeled and grated
$1/2$ teaspoon Malaysian or Thai shrimp
   paste mixed with 2 tablespoons water
Indonesian chili paste (*sambal oelek*) or
   Vietnamese chili sauce to taste

1. Combine the fish, onions, garlic, ginger, coconut milk, and water in a large saucepan and bring to a boil. Reduce the heat to medium-low and cook for 5 minutes. Stir in the tamarind juice, oyster sauce, pepper, sugar, and salt. Remove from the heat.

2. To serve, arrange portions of the noodles, lettuce, cucumbers, bean sprouts, carrots, shrimp paste, and chili paste or sauce if using, in individual soup bowls. Ladle in the hot soup and serve.

MAKES 3 TO 4 SERVINGS

Red Fish Curry

In Sri Lanka, cooks often use a sour ingredient called gamboge, *which apparently does not grow in the West. So, as a substitute, cook Felicia Wakwella Sørensen in her book* The Exotic Tastes of Paradise, The Art of Sri Lankan Cooking, *suggests using tamarind juice for its souring effect. This is a light and spicy curry for which rice noodles—or, of course, rice—would make a pleasant foil.*

1¹/₂ pounds firm-fleshed fish fillets, such as red snapper, skin removed, cubed

6 shallots, peeled and sliced

2 green chilies, sliced

6 curry leaves or 3 bay leaves

3 cloves garlic, peeled and sliced

3 thin slices fresh ginger

1¹/₂ teaspoons tamarind juice or *gamboge*

1 tablespoon paprika

1¹/₂ teaspoons salt

1 to 2 teaspoons Indian red chili powder

¹/₄ teaspoon fenugreek seeds

1¹/₂ cups water

Place all ingredients in a large saucepan and bring to a boil. Reduce the heat to low and cook until slightly reduced and the fish is opaque in the center, about 10 minutes. Serve hot.

MAKES 4 TO 6 SERVINGS

Thai Herbed Soup with Vegetables and Shrimp

Gaeng Liang

As Sarnsern Gajaseni, of The Thai Cooking School at The Oriental, Bangkok, demonstrated this refreshing and rather wholesome soup in class, he explained that this basically all-vegetable soup works well with an assortment of vegetables, including mushrooms, zucchini, snow peas, and ears of baby corn. If you decide to use green beans, blanch them in boiling water for 2 minutes to soften, then loop them into a knot for a prettier presentation. He also assured us that we can stop our eyes from tearing when we chop onions or shallots: Blanch or freeze them before chopping. Or you can do as some Thais—bite on a spoon, presumably wooden, while you chop. This soup is equally delicious served hot, warm, or at room temperature.

Soup

5 shallots, peeled and chopped

1 tablespoon chopped coriander root

1 tablespoon, plus 1 teaspoon
   black peppercorns

1 teaspoon salt

1/2 cup water

1/2 cup shrimp powder

1/2 cup minced fresh shrimp

5 cups Basic Chicken Stock (page 19)
   or water

2 to 5 cups sliced fresh vegetables, such
   as squash, spinach, and blanched
   green beans

1 tablespoon green peppercorns,
   lightly crushed (optional)

1/4 pound large shrimp, shelled
   and deveined

2 cups Thai basil leaves

2 tablespoons fish sauce

1 tablespoon black peppercorns

1. To make the soup, combine the shallots, coriander root, 1 teaspoon black peppercorns, salt, and water in a blender and blend to a coarse paste. Transfer to a large bowl and stir in the shrimp powder and minced shrimp.

2. Bring the stock or water to a boil in a large saucepan. Stir in the shrimp mixture and return to a boil. Reduce the heat to low, add the vegetables and green peppercorns if using, and cook until just tender, 7 to 10 minutes. Stir in the shrimp, basil, fish sauce, and peppercorns. Serve immediately.

MAKES 4 TO 6 SERVINGS

Spiced Soup of Grilled Prawns

Tom Klohng Goong Pow

Grilled shrimp (prawns) are the focal point of this soup, and their smoky flavor is buttressed by the taste of grilled garlic, shallots, and chilies. All this makes for a remarkably unusual soup that celebrates the art of direct wood-fire cooking. For an even smokier taste, instructor Sarnsern Gajaseni, of The Thai Cooking School at the The Oriental, Bangkok, suggests using the grilled shrimp shells—just wrap them in cheesecloth, plunge into the broth, and remove and discard before serving.

The recipe calls for fresh prig khee nu, *or bird's eye chilies, but you may substitute Thai finger hot chilies, which are slightly milder. And you can intensify and sharpen flavors by adding some Chili Jam (page 27).*

3 fresh coriander roots

24 black peppercorns

5 cups water

6 large shrimp, grilled (see Note), shelled, deveined, and halved lengthwise, shells reserved

7 shallots, roasted and peeled (see page 8), sliced

1/2 cup sliced lemon grass

3 large dried red chilies, roasted (see page 7), seeded, and chopped

5 cloves garlic, roasted and peeled (see page 8)

3 thin slices galangal

3 to 4 tablespoons fish sauce

3 to 4 tablespoons fresh lime juice

1 cup straw mushrooms

2 tablespoons finely shredded kaffir lime leaves

7 fresh red or green chilies, thinly sliced

1. Pound together the coriander root and peppercorns to form a paste.

2. Pour the water into a stockpot and bring to a boil. Stir in the shrimp shells, shallots, lemon grass, chilies, garlic, and galangal, bring to a boil, and cook for 5 minutes. Strain through a fine-mesh sieve and discard the solids. Return the liquid to the stockpot. Reduce the heat to low and stir in the fish sauce, lime juice, coriander root paste, shrimp, and mushrooms. Return to a boil and remove from the heat.

3. Ladle the soup into bowls and sprinkle with lime leaves and chilies.

MAKES 2 TO 3 SERVINGS

Note: Grilling the shrimp, as with any other ingredient, adds a wonderful smoky flavor to the finished dish. To grill, cook the shrimp over medium-hot coals until pink, 2 to 3 minutes per side. Alternatively, you may broil the shrimp 4 to 6 inches from the heat, but they will lack the smoky flavor.

Thai Curried Vegetables and Prawns

Gaeng Som Goong

Translated as "sour-tasting prawn curry," this country-style dish may be a single course as part of a larger meal or, Western-style, the main course for a light luncheon. When instructor Sarnsern Gajaseni, of The Thai Cooking School at The Oriental, Bangkok, demonstrated this dish, he used Chinese (napa) cabbage and a handful of flowers from trees that grow in Bangkok as vegetables, since that was what was available. You may use any combination of vegetables you wish (see Note), and you can add extra crunch and flavor by including scoops of shredded raw Asian green papaya or watermelon rind with the vegetables. For a meatier dish, boost the amount of shrimp (prawns) you use. For an entirely different result, replace the water or fish stock with coconut milk, use only string beans and watercress for vegetables, and add chopped fresh pineapple.

1 cup water

6 large shrimp, shelled and deveined, or $1/4$ pound firm-fleshed fish fillets, such as red snapper or catfish, skin removed, minced

9 large dried red chilies, soaked in hot water for 20 minutes

7 shallots, peeled

$1/2$ stalk lemon grass, trimmed and sliced

3 tablespoons chopped galangal

2 cloves garlic, peeled

1 teaspoon shredded kaffir lime rind

1 teaspoon Thai or Malaysian shrimp paste

$1/2$ teaspoon salt

Soup

5 cups Basic Fish Stock (page 21) or water

3 cups chopped or sliced vegetables

5 tablespoons tamarind juice

$1/4$ cup fish sauce

1 teaspoon palm sugar or dark brown sugar

$1/2$ pound large shrimp, shelled and deveined

1. Bring the water to a boil in a large saucepan. Add the shrimp or fish and cook for 5 minutes. Transfer to a plate. When cool enough to handle, mince the shrimp or fish.

2. To make the curry paste, combine the chilies, shallots, lemon grass, galangal, garlic, lime rind, shrimp paste, and salt in a blender. Add just enough water from the cooking to process, and blend to a coarse paste. Add the cooked shrimp or fish and blend until smooth.

3. Bring the stock or water to a boil in a large saucepan. Add the curry paste, vegetables, tamarind juice, fish sauce, and sugar, and stir until the sugar is dissolved. Reduce the heat to low and cook 5 to 7 minutes, or until the vegetables are crisp-tender. Stir in the whole shrimp and cook until just pink, 2 to 3 minutes more. Serve hot.

MAKES 3 TO 4 SERVINGS

Note: Vegetable options can include cauliflower, Chinese (napa) cabbage, string beans, baby corn, gourd, spinach, winged beans, pickled vegetables, and zucchini.

Shrimp and Coconut Soup, Medan Style

Soto Medan

An Indonesian cook from Sumatra, Hanny Nabiela Sugianto, prepared this rich chicken soup for lunch one day at her home in the coastal city of Medan. Since it is typical of the area, the soup is usually served with shrimp; but it's also versatile, for you can use chicken parts or sliced beef instead. After all, with coconut milk forming the base of the dish, it's hard to go wrong. Because a bowlful is satisfying, plan a light meal around the soup and offer a fragrant tea for the beverage. The cook served a very floral jasmine tea that she'd bought in her open-air market that morning.

Seasoning Paste

3 onions, peeled and sliced

7 shallots, peeled and sliced

2 tablespoons minced fresh ginger

1 teaspoon crumbled saffron threads

About $^3/_4$ cup coconut milk

Soup

3 tablespoons vegetable oil

$1^1/_4$ pounds large shrimp, shelled and deveined

3 to $3^1/_3$ cups coconut milk

$^1/_2$ teaspoon crumbled saffron threads

Salt and freshly ground black pepper to taste

Garnish

$^1/_2$ cup Fried Shallots (page 17)

$^1/_2$ cup diced celery

1. To make the seasoning paste, combine the onions, shallots, ginger, and saffron in a blender. Add just enough coconut milk to process, and blend until smooth.

2. Heat the oil in a large saucepan over medium heat. Add the seasoning paste and cook, stirring, about 5 minutes, or until fragrant. Add the shrimp and cook, stirring, until just pink, 2 to 3 minutes. Stir in the coconut milk, saffron, salt, and pepper. Reduce the heat to low and cook until heated through, about 10 minutes. Garnish the soup with the shallots and celery, and serve immediately.

MAKES 3 TO 4 SERVINGS

Vietnamese Snail Noodle Soup

Do not think French and escargots when you think about this soup. This purely Vietnamese dish calls for tiny shellfish—"snails"—such as periwinkles or "apple snails" available frozen at Asian markets. The cook who provided this recipe, Helene Sze McCarthy, says to serve this soup with a bowl of the pale grey Vietnamese shrimp paste, used for seasoning at the table. For the stock, she calls for either a mushroom stock or a pork stock.

6 tablespoons vegetable oil

3 ounces tomato paste

1 tablespoon sugar

One 1-pound package frozen periwinkles, thawed and rinsed

6 cups mushroom stock (see Note) or Basic Pork Stock (page 20)

Two 16-ounce cans plum tomatoes, diced

Accompaniments

6 to 8 ounces rice vermicelli, cooked (see page 302)

1 bunch scallions, trimmed and cut into 3-inch lengths

$^1/_4$ pound bean sprouts

Sprigs of mint

Fresh coriander stalks

3 tablespoons Vietnamese or Chinese shrimp paste

Lemon wedges

1. Heat the oil in a large wok or saucepan over medium heat. Add the tomato paste and sugar, and cook, stirring constantly, for about 5 minutes. Add the periwinkles and 3 cups stock and cook 5 minutes more, or until heated through.

2. Meanwhile, in a separate pan, combine the remaining 3 cups stock and tomatoes. Cook over medium heat for 7 to 10 minutes, until heated through.

3. To serve, divide the noodles among individual soup bowls. For each bowl, ladle in a portion of the tomato mixture and top with a portion of the snail mixture. Serve hot and pass around the remaining accompaniments.

MAKES 4 SERVINGS

Note: To make the mushroom stock, boil 2 pounds of mushrooms in 8 cups water for 10 minutes, then strain.

Indonesian Tuna and Coconut Curry

Freshly cooked tuna, simply grilled or combined with other ingredients as in this simple curry, is one of Neptune's wonders. The trickiest part of this dish—the recipe for which Irmansjah Madewa gave me—is finding the best tuna on the market. Anything less could be tough and flavorless. Because the coconut milk makes this a rich course for a meal, accompany the tuna with rice and a light salad or a bowl of diced fruit.

Curry Paste

10 shallots, peeled

5 cloves garlic, peeled

One 1-inch piece fresh ginger

1 teaspoon ground turmeric

About $^1/_2$ cup coconut milk

Curry

2 tablespoons vegetable oil

$2^1/_2$ cups coconut milk

$^1/_2$ cup tamarind juice

1 stalk lemon grass, trimmed and cut
into 2-inch lengths

2 Indonesian bay leaves

2 kaffir lime leaves, halved

1 turmeric leaf (optional)

2 pounds tuna steaks or red snapper
fillets, skin removed, cubed

3 tomatoes, each cut into 8 wedges

1. To make the curry paste, combine the shallots, garlic, ginger, and turmeric in a blender. Add just enough coconut milk to process, and blend until smooth.

2. To make the curry, heat the oil in a large wok or saucepan over medium heat. Add the curry paste and cook, stirring, about 5 minutes, or until fragrant. Stir in the coconut milk, tamarind juice, lemon grass, bay leaves, lime leaves, and turmeric leaf. Reduce the heat to low and cook until the sauce begins to thicken, about 20 minutes. Stir in the fish and cook until opaque in the center, about 10 minutes. Stir in the tomatoes and cook for 5 minutes more.

MAKES 4 TO 6 SERVINGS

Chinese Shrimp Soup with Sizzling Rice

The Chinese have perfected, and perhaps even invented, how to make rice sizzle—seeming almost to explode. But don't worry, there's no kitchen hazard here, only a carefully contrived way to deep-fry chunks of cooked rice into sizzling "croutons."

Getting rice to sizzle properly is a two-step process that begins with drying out pieces of cooked rice for several days. (You'll need the rice that sticks to the bottom of a pan after boiling.) Then, when you are ready to sizzle, heat the oil, put the pieces of rice into wire-mesh scoops, and dip into the hot oil for a few minutes—the rice should actually "explode" when it hits the oil, says the cook who provided this recipe, Joyce Piotrowski. After removing and draining the rice, it goes into a large soup tureen and, when covered with the hot soup, its sizzling is dramatic.

Shrimp Marinade

2 teaspoons cornstarch

1 tablespoon Chinese rice wine

$^1/_2$ teaspoon salt

Pork Marinade

1 teaspoon cornstarch

2 teaspoons soy sauce

Soup

$3^1/_4$ cups vegetable oil,
    preferably peanut

$^1/_2$ pound large shrimp, shelled,
    deveined, and halved lengthwise

$^1/_2$ pound lean pork tenderloin, cut
    into very thin strips

2 scallions, trimmed and cut into very
    thin strips

5 dried Chinese mushrooms, soaked
    in hot water for 20 minutes, stems
    removed, cut into very thin
    2-inch lengths

1. To make the shrimp marinade, combine the cornstarch, wine, and salt. Add the shrimp and stir to coat.

2. To make the pork marinade, combine the cornstarch and soy sauce. Add the pork and stir to coat.

3. To make the soup, heat $^1/_4$ cup of the vegetable oil in a large saucepan over medium-high heat. Add the shrimp and stir-fry until pink, 1 to 2 minutes. Transfer the shrimp to a bowl. Add the pork and stir-fry until no longer pink, about 2 minutes. Transfer the pork to the bowl with the shrimp. Add the scallions and mushrooms, and stir-fry until softened, 2 to 3 minutes. Stir in the stock and bring to a boil.

4. Combine the cornstarch and water in a bowl. Stir in the ketchup, soy sauce, vinegar, sesame oil, and peppercorns. Carefully pour this mixture into the stock to prevent splattering and cook until thickened, about 5 minutes. Stir in the peas, shrimp, and pork, and return to a boil.

4 cups Chinese Chicken Stock
   (page 22)

3 tablespoons cornstarch

$^{1}/_{4}$ cup water

$^{1}/_{4}$ cup ketchup

1 tablespoon soy sauce

1 tablespoon red rice vinegar

2 teaspoons toasted sesame oil

$^{1}/_{2}$ teaspoon Szechuan peppercorns

$^{1}/_{4}$ cup peas

1 cup Special Crispy Rice pieces
   (page 198), see Note

5. Meanwhile, heat the remaining 3 cups vegetable oil in a deep-fryer or stockpot to about 370°F. (The oil is hot enough when a grain of rice dropped in explodes.) Add the rice pieces all at once and fry until golden. Quickly remove the rice pieces from the oil so they don't burn, and arrange in the bottom of a heatproof tureen or bowl. Pour the hot soup over the rice—this mixture should crackle and sizzle—and serve immediately.

MAKES 4 TO 5 SERVINGS

Note: If you wish to make your own rice for sizzling, follow the recipe for Special Crispy Rice. Or, if you have a well-stocked Chinese market nearby, you should be able to buy rectangular pieces of the rice there, sold loose in a cellophane bag.

Special Crispy Rice

1 cup rice
1¹/₂ cups water

1. Combine the rice and water in a large saucepan with a tight-fitting lid. Cook over high heat until the rice forms "dragon's eyes" (when steam holes appear in the surface of the rice, the bubbles look like bulging eyes), about 5 minutes. Cover the pan and reduce the heat to very low. If you are using an electric burner, transfer the pan to a cool burner. Cook for 25 minutes, turn off the heat, and let the rice cool completely. (You can refrigerate it, or do as the Chinese and let it sit out overnight.)

2. The next day, break the crusted rice into 2-inch pieces and arrange on a cookie sheet. Dry the rice thoroughly in a 200°F oven for 2 hours.

MAKES 2¹/₂ CUPS RICE

Chinese Squid Flower Soup

Part of the magic of Chinese cooking comes from the chef's ability to do more than just cook—that is, the chef must put together a menu to tempt the eyes with vivid colors and fanciful shapes, and to appeal to the palate with pleasing flavors, explains cook Joyce Piotrowski. Her squid flower soup, with its vegetable cutouts (she suggests using the Chinese-patterned metal cutters that look like cookie cutters) and subtle flavors, fits the prescription for good Chinese cooking.

This recipe calls for special handling of the squid. After cleaning it (see page 175), score the tender part, or underside, in a crosshatch design. When the squid cooks, the scores will open to form an eye-catching diamond-shaped pattern.

This light and delicate soup is perfect followed by a more assertive seafood dish or a grilled fish or pork entree served with stir-fried vegetables and rice.

Marinade

1 teaspoon grated fresh ginger

1 tablespoon Chinese rice wine

Soup

1 pound squid, cleaned (see page 175)
  and cut into fillets, or $^3/_4$ pound
  squid fillets

2 tablespoons cornstarch

$6^1/_4$ cups Basic Chicken Stock
  (page 19)

2 tablespoons soy sauce

2 tablespoons oyster sauce

1 teaspoon sugar

Salt to taste

1 small carrot, peeled, thinly sliced,
  and cut into thin decorative shapes,
  such as triangles, circles, or flowers

1 small turnip, peeled, thinly sliced,
  and cut into thin decorative shapes,
  such as triangles, circles, or flowers

$^1/_2$ cup snow peas, diagonally sliced
  into bite-sized pieces

1 fresh red chili, very thinly sliced

$^1/_2$ cup fresh coriander leaves

1. To make the marinade, combine the ginger and wine in a medium bowl.

2. To make the soup, score the squid by placing each fillet on a cutting board with the soft inner side up. Hold the cleaver or knife at a 25-degree angle to the cutting board and lightly slice into the fillet every $^1/_{16}$ inch. Do not cut through the fillet. Turn the fillet a quarter turn and repeat the scoring—this will produce a crosshatch pattern. Cut the fillets into 2-inch-square pieces. Add the squid to the marinade and stir to coat.

3. In a small bowl, combine the cornstarch and $^1/_4$ cup of the stock.

4. Combine the remaining 6 cups stock, the soy sauce, oyster sauce, cornstarch mixture, sugar, and salt in a large saucepan over medium heat and bring to a boil. Add the carrots, turnips, snow peas, chilies, and coriander leaves. Reduce the heat to low and cook until the vegetables are crisp-tender, about 5 minutes. Stir in the squid and increase the heat to medium. When the mixture comes to a boil, remove from the heat and serve immediately.

MAKES 4 TO 6 SERVINGS

Braised Prawns with Bitter Gourd

While Chef Chow Chung, of the Hyatt Regency Hong Kong, produced this slightly bitter stewlike dish one lunchtime, he explained that bitter gourd, also called bitter melon, is popular with the Chinese, though Westerners may find that its flavor takes some getting used to. As I later learned, besides its culinary benefits, bitter gourd has some health benefits: It purifies the blood and cools the system.

In this dish, the bitter taste is offset by sweet, fresh shrimp (prawns) and a variety of typical Chinese seasonings, including oyster sauce, ginger, and rice wine. You should keep the shrimp shells intact for a prettier presentation.

¹/₂ **pound large shrimp (prawns), shells intact, rinsed**

1 bitter gourd, the size of a large cucumber

1 tablespoon salt

3 tablespoons vegetable oil

Six ¹/₂-inch-long pieces scallions

¹/₂ **fresh red chili**

3 cloves garlic, peeled and minced

1 teaspoon Chinese yellow soybean paste (*mien see*)

¹/₂ **teaspoon minced fresh ginger**

¹/₃ **cup Basic Chicken Stock (page 19)**

1 teaspoon oyster sauce

¹/₂ **teaspoon dark soy sauce**

¹/₂ **teaspoon sugar**

Dash of Chinese rice wine

1 teaspoon cornstarch mixed with 1 teaspoon water

1. With a sharp knife, slit the shrimp shells along the back and trim off the head and legs. Leave the tail and shell intact.

2. Cut the bitter gourd in half, remove the seeds, and cut into large pieces. Transfer the gourd to a large bowl, sprinkle with the salt, and add enough water to cover. Let soak for 5 minutes. Drain and rinse well.

3. Heat the oil in a large wok or skillet over medium-high heat. Add the shrimp and stir-fry until just pink, about 1 minute. Remove the shrimp from the oil. Add the scallions, chilies, garlic, soybean paste, and ginger, and stir-fry for 2 minutes. Add the bitter gourd and stir-fry for 2 minutes more. Stir in the stock, oyster sauce, soy sauce, sugar, and wine, and cook until heated through, about 5 minutes.

4. Return the shrimp to the wok and stir in the cornstarch mixture. Bring to a boil and cook until slightly thickened, about 5 minutes more. Serve hot.

MAKES 2 SERVINGS

Korean Hot-Spicy Crab Soup

The Korean cook Hira Lee gives you several options with this typical Korean soup, and those depend on how hot you like things. You can start with the mild soybean paste known as doenjang, *or you can turn up the heat by adding Korean ground hot red pepper to the soup. For a very hot result, and a version this cook serves, try the hot soybean paste known as* kochujang *stirred with the milder* doenjang.

6 large live crabs

6 cups water

2 tablespoons Korean soybean paste (*doenjang*), or 1$^1/_2$ tablespoons Korean hot soybean paste (*kochujang*) and 1$^1/_2$ teaspoons *doenjang*

2 tablespoons soy sauce

2 onions, peeled and cut into 8 wedges

2 carrots, peeled and thinly sliced

1 Korean zucchini or Western zucchini, cubed

6 scallions, trimmed and diagonally sliced

4 Korean green chilies or Anaheim chilies

3 cloves garlic, peeled and sliced

1. Place the crabs in a large pot, cover well with water, and bring to a boil. Cook for 1 minute. Drain. When cool enough to handle, cut the bodies in quarters and crack the claws. Set aside.

2. Bring the 6 cups water to a boil in a large stockpot. Add the soybean paste and soy sauce, and boil until dispersed in the water. Add the crabs, onions, carrots, zucchini, scallions, chilies, and garlic. Reduce the heat to low and cook 10 to 15 minutes, or until the crabs turn orange and the vegetables are tender. Serve in large soup bowls with rice as an accompaniment.

MAKES 4 SERVINGS

Japanese Clam Soup

Imagine the gentlest of seaside beaches and the softest of breezes, and you have the essence of this delicately flavored soup. It showcases tiny clams quick-cooked in a kelp-based broth—and it is a favorite of a very elegant Japanese friend of mine who treasures its subtle flavor.

4 cups water

8 small clams, scrubbed

One 4-inch piece dried *kombu* (Japanese seaweed), rinsed briefly

3 stalks Japanese parsley (*mitsuba*) (see Note)

1 tablespoon sake

1 tablespoon mirin

1 tablespoon soy sauce

Salt to taste

1. Bring the water to a simmer in a large saucepan over medium-high heat. Add the clams and *kombu*, and cook until the clams open, 3 to 5 minutes. Discard any clams that don't open. Remove the *kombu* and stir in the parsley, sake, mirin, soy sauce, and salt.

2. Ladle the soup into bowls and distribute the clams among them.

MAKES 3 TO 4 SERVINGS

Note: Japanese parsley, or *mitsuba*, is usually used as a garnish, but it is added to this soup for flavor.

Japanese Egg and Noodle Soup

Nabeyaki Udon

One day, thinking of the Japanese movie Tampopo—*which celebrates the joys of noodle-soup making in Tokyo—I asked my Japanese friend Yoko Morford if she had a recipe for traditional Japanese noodle soup. Since soup shops are nearly everywhere in Tokyo, I thought a recipe would be easy to come by. Not so. As Yoko Morford explained, these shops serve soups based on the Chinese noodles, ramen. So, strictly speaking, these are not really Japanese soups. But, she added quickly, the Japanese do have their own very delicious noodle soups based on udon—and this is one of them.*

Stock

1½ cups *dashi* (Japanese First Stock,
    page 34)

2 tablespoons soy sauce

1 tablespoon mirin

Soup

2 tablespoons soy sauce

2 tablespoons mirin

1 dried shiitake mushroom, soaked
    in hot water for 20 minutes and
    stem removed

3 bamboo shoots, thinly sliced

½ pound fresh udon or 3 to 4 ounces
    dried udon, cooked (see page 303)

1 large shrimp, shelled, deveined, and
    tempura-fried (see Note)

1 slice Japanese fish cake

1 cup spinach, rinsed, trimmed, and
    steamed until wilted

1 large egg

1 teaspoon shichimi

1. To make the stock, combine the *dashi*, soy sauce, and mirin in a small saucepan. Bring to a boil and remove from the heat.

2. To make the soup, combine 1 tablespoon of the soy sauce and 1 tablespoon of the mirin in another small saucepan over medium heat and bring to a boil. Add the shiitake mushroom and cook for 3 minutes. Remove the mushroom and set aside. Add the remaining tablespoon soy sauce, 1 tablespoon mirin, and bamboo shoots, and cook for 3 minutes. Remove from the heat.

3. Place the noodles in the bottom of a heatproof clay pot with a lid. Top with the shrimp, mushroom, bamboo shoots, fish cake, and spinach. Pour the stock into the pot, cover, and bring to a boil. Crack the egg into the soup. Reduce the heat to low, cover, and cook until the egg is firm, 2 to 3 minutes. Ladle into bowls, sprinkle with the shichimi, and serve immediately.

MAKES 1 SERVING

Note: To prepare the shrimp, prepare a tempura batter from a commercial mix and deep-fry the shrimp until golden.

Japanese One-Pot Seafood Stew

Yose-nabe

A dish that hardworking Japanese fishermen developed, this is a no-frills seafood stew that is both flavorful and nutritious. It is usually cooked at the table in a tabletop cooking vessel. Loosely translated, its name means "a gathering up of numerous ingredients," and traditionally, this has meant adding even fish fins to the pot.

The cook who provided this recipe, Frank Kuge, says that the quantity (and combination) of ingredients is really a matter of common sense and of what is available at the market—hence, the amounts listed are only approximate, for you can expand and contract the contents as you wish. The dish is a close relative of Chanko-nabe *(page 274), because you may use all kinds of vegetables and seafood. The principal difference seems to be that sumo wrestlers do not traditionally eat* Yose-nabe, *whereas* Chanko-nabe *is their dietary mainstay. (For more information about Sumo wrestlers and their food, see page 275.) With this stew, serve rice and hot sake.*

8 cups *dashi* (Japanese First Stock, page 34)

6 tablespoons sake or mirin, or more to taste

Salt to taste

1 pound firm-fleshed fish fillets or steaks, such as cod or swordfish, skin removed, cut into 1-inch cubes

8 small clams, scrubbed

8 large shrimp, shelled and deveined

1/2 pound firm tofu, cut into 8 equal-sized cubes

1/2 ounce *harusame*, soaked in hot water for 15 minutes

10 Chinese (napa) cabbage leaves (see Note)

10 spinach leaves, rinsed and trimmed

10 mushrooms, rinsed

4 stalks celery, thinly sliced

1. Heat the *dashi* in a large saucepan over medium heat until it begins to boil. Stir in the sake or mirin and salt, and pour 6 cups of the *dashi* into a tabletop cooking vessel. Transfer the cooking vessel to the table and keep the liquid at a simmer. (You may need to replenish the stock as it boils away.)

2. Arrange the seafood, tofu, noodles, and vegetables by category on a serving platter. Pour the dipping sauce into a bowl and ladle in 1/3 cup of the hot *dashi*. Set the platter and bowl on the table.

3. Let people cook the food and help themselves, using chopsticks or other serving utensils, at their leisure. (Discard any clams that don't open after 5 minutes of cooking time.) They should dip the ingredients into the sauce before eating.

4 scallions, trimmed and cut into
2-inch lengths
2 carrots, peeled and cut into
2-inch strips

1/2 cup Ponzu Shoyu Dipping Sauce
(see Note, page 33)

4. When all the food has been cooked, serve the remaining broth in individual soup bowls.

MAKES 4 TO 6 SERVINGS

Note: The cook suggests a fancy presentation by rolling the cabbage and spinach leaves together in the following manner: Blanch the cabbage leaves in boiling water until soft, about 2 minutes. Squeeze out the water and lay flat. Blanch the spinach leaves in boiling water for about 1 minute and squeeze out the water. Lay a spinach leaf inside a cabbage leaf and roll them up. Slice each roll into bite-sized pieces and place in the cooking vessel. (If you use spinach separately, you should blanch it anyway to get rid of some of its dark green color, which would darken the clear broth.)

Japanese Custard Soup

Chawan-mushi

Friends Peter and Diana Semon ran a Japanese inn and restaurant in New York for several years and found that this custard soup was one of the most requested dishes on their menu. Perhaps it's the gentle, comforting combination of unsweetened egg custard in a mildly flavored broth that has so much appeal. Or perhaps Westerners and Japanese alike find this a nourishing appetizer with its combination of vegetables, seafood, and broth. Whatever the reason, the Japanese often describe this as a "solid soup"—the custard is steamed until firm, but the accumulated liquids make this soupy. It may be served hot or chilled, depending on the time of year.

6 large shrimp, shelled and deveined

$1/2$ cup sake

$1/4$ cup diced chicken breast

$1/4$ cup plus 2 teaspoons soy sauce

4 cups *dashi* (Japanese First Stock, page 34)

1 teaspoon mirin

1 teaspoon salt

4 large eggs, lightly beaten

18 gingko nuts

Garnishes

3 scallions, trimmed and thinly sliced

6 watercress leaves

1. Soak the shrimp in the sake for 15 minutes. Soak the chicken in $1/4$ cup of the soy sauce for 15 minutes.

2. While the shrimp and chicken are soaking, combine the *dashi*, the remaining 2 teaspoons soy sauce, mirin, and the salt in a large bowl. Gently stir in the eggs. Strain through a fine-mesh sieve.

3. Divide the shrimp, chicken, and nuts among the custard cups and pour the egg mixture on top. Cover each cup with foil or plastic wrap and set on the steaming rack of a large steamer pot. Fill the bottom section with water, cover, and bring to a boil. Reduce the heat to medium and steam the custards until firm, 15 to 20 minutes. Test for doneness by inserting a bamboo skewer into the center of the custards; they are ready if the skewer comes out clean. Garnish with the scallions and watercress, and serve hot.

MAKES 4 TO 6 SERVINGS

Japanese Tabletop Seafood Soup

Uo suki

The cook who provided this recipe, Yoko Morford, describes this as a seafood version of sukiyaki *(page 150).*
But unlike the beef in sukiyaki, *the seafood is marinated, and the marinade, not a dipping sauce, imparts*
the seasoning; it also becomes the cooking liquid. As with other cook-at-the-table dishes, the food arrange-
ment on platters is very important and should be attractive. Use chopsticks for dipping the ingredients into
the simmering liquid, and drink the cooking liquid as broth after all the food has been cooked.
Traditionally, this dish is eaten before the rice, which is later served with pickles.

Marinade

3 cups *dashi* (Japanese First Stock,
    page 34)

1 cup sake

³/₄ cup mirin

¹/₂ cup soy sauce, preferably Japanese

3 tablespoons sugar

Soup

¹/₂ pound red snapper fillets, or other
    firm-fleshed fish fillets, skin
    removed, cut into bite-sized pieces

¹/₂ pound boneless yellowtail or tuna,
    cut into bite-sized pieces

4 large shrimp, shelled and deveined

4 clams or oysters, scrubbed

1 squid, cleaned (see page 175) and cut
    into bite-sized pieces

¹/₂ pound firm tofu, cut into
    8 equal cubes

4 Chinese (napa) cabbage leaves

4 thick scallions, trimmed and diago-
    nally sliced into 2-inch lengths

3¹/₂ ounces edible chrysanthemum
    leaves (crown daisy)

5 ounces *shirataki*, cooked (see page
    303), or rice vermicelli, cooked
    (see page 302)

1. To make the marinade, combine the *dashi*, sake, mirin, soy sauce, and sugar in a glass or an enamel dish. Add the fish and shellfish, and turn to coat. Let marinate for about 10 minutes.

2. Pour the marinade into a tabletop cooking vessel and bring to a boil. Transfer the cooking vessel to the table and keep the liquid at a simmer.

3. Arrange the tofu, vegetables, noodles, and marinated seafood on separate platters. Place the platters on the table.

4. Let people cook their own food using chopsticks or other serving utensils and eat it at their leisure.

MAKES 4 TO 6 SERVINGS

"River Bank" Oyster Stew

Kaki Dote-nabe

According to the cook who provided this recipe, Sachi Yamada, this hearty winter stew was constructed to resemble, with a bit of imagination, a sand bank at a beach or by a river. If this sounds difficult to visualize, consider how the cook assembles the dish: The insides of an earthenware pot (or other tabletop cooking vessel) are coated with both red and white miso. One color is spread around the side of one half of the pot, the other around the other half—this "sand bank" gradually dissolves into the liquid as the stew cooks. But even better, the miso adds a deep, salty flavor to the oysters, making this a delectable main course served with rice and a cucumber or seaweed salad. Serve with warm sake.

$1/4$ cup red miso

1 teaspoon sake

$1/4$ cup white miso

1 pound fresh shucked oysters

One 6-ounce cake tofu, broiled (see
  Note) and cubed

1 bunch Japanese parsley or spinach,
  rinsed and trimmed

1 bunch scallions, trimmed and cut
  into 3-inch lengths

4 cups *dashi* (Japanese Second Stock,
  page 34) or 1 packet instant Japanese
  soup base (*dashi-no-moto*) dissolved
  in 4 cups water

1. Stir together the red miso and $1/2$ teaspoon of the sake. Smear in one side of the pot. Stir together the white miso and the remaining $1/2$ teaspoon sake. Smear in the other side of the pot.

2. Put half of the oysters, the tofu, parsley or spinach, and scallions in the center of the pot. Pour in the *dashi* and bring to a boil. Transfer the cooking vessel to the table and keep the liquid at a simmer. Let people help themselves, using chopsticks or other serving utensils, and eat the ingredients at their leisure. (Be careful not to let the oysters overcook.) Add more oysters as needed. Serve the remaining broth as a soup, if desired.

MAKES 4 SERVINGS

Note: Although grilled or broiled tofu, or *yakidofu,* is available at many Asian markets, you can make your own by pressing firm tofu between layers of paper towels to remove excess water and then broiling it until golden; alternatively, lightly brush the tofu with oil and pan-grill it over high heat.

Macanese Seafood Soup

Sopa de Marisco

With this seafood soup recipe from the Macau Tourist Information Bureau you can capture all the flavors of the Euro-Chinese cooking of Macau, since the dish features many of the kinds of seafood caught in the surrounding waters of the South China Sea. Although the recipe serves six as a first-course soup, you may wish to use this as a light main-course dish for three or four served with a salad and bread.

¹/₄ cup olive oil

2 onions, peeled and chopped

2 large tomatoes, cored and quartered

4 cloves garlic, peeled and chopped

1 green chili, thinly sliced

3 sprigs parsley, chopped

3 sprigs fresh coriander, chopped

1 tablespoon brandy

1 tablespoon dry white wine

1 pound assorted shellfish and fish
   (shrimp, mussels, clams, squid, and
   firm-fleshed fish fillets), shelled or
   cleaned, diced

1 bay leaf

6 cups plus 2 tablespoons water

²/₃ cup all-purpose flour

1 cup heavy cream

Salt to taste

1. Heat the oil in a large saucepan over medium heat. Add the onions, tomatoes, garlic, chili, half of the parsley, and half of the coriander and cook, stirring, until the vegetables are softened, about 5 minutes. Stir in the brandy, wine, shellfish and fish, and bay leaf. Cook, stirring, until heated through, 3 to 4 minutes. Add 6 cups of the water and bring to a boil. Let cook for 5 minutes.

2. Stir together the remaining 2 tablespoons water and the flour and pour slowly into the pan. Stir well to break up any lumps. Reduce the heat to low and cook until the clams and mussels open and the other seafood is opaque in the center, about 10 minutes. (Discard any clams and mussels that don't open.)

3. Stir in the cream, salt, the remaining parsley, and the remaining coriander. Serve immediately.

MAKES 3 TO 6 SERVINGS

Braised Mussels with Portuguese Ham

Served at the Hotel Lisboa in Macau, this full-flavored soupy dish pairs the delicate, sea-bound flavors of mussels with the assertive saltiness of cured ham.

3 tablespoons olive oil

2 medium onions, peeled and shredded

1 tablespoon minced garlic

1 medium green bell pepper, shredded

1 small red chili, shredded

2 pounds mussels, scrubbed

1 cup dry white wine

1/2 pound Portuguese ham or Parma ham, shredded

1/2 cup chopped Italian (flat-leaf) parsley

1. Heat the oil in a skillet over medium heat. Stir in the onion and garlic, reduce the heat to medium-low, and cook, stirring, until softened, about 5 minutes. Stir in the green peppers, red chili, mussels, and wine. Cover and cook, stirring often, until the shells open, about 10 minutes. (Discard any mussels that don't open.) Stir in the ham and cook until heated through, about 5 minutes more.

2. Garnish with the parsley just before serving.

MAKES 4 SERVINGS

Essay 4:

Chili Exotics— Thailand and Indonesia

Most Asians love chilies, but the Thais and Indonesians surely must rank chilies next to rice as divine. Consider the local markets, where hawkers sell tangles of chilies piled so high they topple over. Consider their basic curry seasonings, a paste of chilies pounded with cooler companions. Or consider the many ways they can electrify their foods with a spoonful of chili paste—Indonesia's *sambal oelek* and Thailand's *nam prik phao*, for example, condiments that they now bottle and ship to chili heads everywhere.

It's not that Thai and Indonesian food is always hot. But for chili exaggeration, several of their dishes come to mind, including a grilled chicken dish called *ayam rica-rica* from Indonesia's island of Manado that calls for 40 chilies (that's about half a pound!) and Thailand's Fiery Green Curry with Roast Duck (page 76), with a curry paste made from 25 chilies. And in countries where chilies come as a standard ingredient, beware.

That makes the point. Local cooks have a zeal for chilies.

Thailand

While many Westerners think of curry as a powder, says cooking teacher Sarnsern Gajaseni of The Thai Cooking School at The Oriental, Bangkok hotel, Thais define curry as a combination of ingredients cooked in a rich, thick, spicy sauce based on a ground paste of chilies and other seasonings. In vibrant colors from yellow and red to green, curries are often the centerpiece of Thai meals.

As he gets down to basics, Gajaseni explains he learned about Thai curries and the basic pastes at his mother's mortar and pestle, so he never really measures anything: "My mother never told me a quantity. When I saw her pounding, she would tell me, 'Just add.' I helped my mother so many times, I just know.'" That approach is typical. To a Thai, the components and texture of the basic paste dictate the quality—and flavor—of the eventual curry.

The Thai cook composes the paste of ingredients that come from the Thais' five main seasoning categories: salty (as with fish sauce, salted eggs, shrimp paste, soybean paste), sour (tamarind, lime juice, vinegar), sweet (palm sugar, granulated sugar, sweet soy sauce), spicy (fresh or dried chilies or black or green peppercorns), and herbs (garlic, shallots, coriander). Gajaseni throws in a sixth "miscellaneous" category with only one entry: coconut milk.

Next, the cook decides whether his curry will be oil-based (a "country" curry—gutsy, hot, pungent); coconut-based (a "city" curry—more refined, subtler, subdued); or a combination of thick coconut milk and oil (a "suburban" curry, a good backdrop for any kind of meat).

Third, the cook debates whether to use fresh green chilies, for a green curry; red chilies, for a red curry (never mix red or green chilies, he warned); or some other basic ingredient, such as turmeric, to produce a yellow curry—a Southern favorite.

Gajaseni offers a few other curry-making tips: Tradition dictates the use of an odd number of ingredients (15 chilies, 9 peppercorns, 7 spoonfuls of palm sugar, for example); otherwise, it is believed, the dish will be unbalanced and will not turn out well. He quickly added, "Thais also use odd numbers elsewhere, as in Buddhist amulets worn around the neck. These are only in odd numbers."

One final thought: The cook must select the curry's main ingredient. Will it be something assertive, such as beef (the Thais would use water buffalo) or milder-tasting chicken or duck? That helps determine ingredient quantities, for the cook must keep flavors balanced and bring back the basic sweetness of a curry paste by, for example, using more shallots or adding some sugar to a curry paste for beef.

After making all these decisions, the cook pounds together or processes the paste ingredients, and in a traditional home this pounding once played an important matrimonial role, explains my Thai friend and cooking teacher, Nongkran Daks. In villages, men would stroll past a girl's house, and if the pounding were slow, that meant she was lazy, she says. If the pounding were quick and rhythmic, that meant she was energetic, and, hence, good marriage material.

When the paste is ready, cooking may begin. But not every Thai agrees on the next step. For example, Nongkran Daks simply combines the curry paste with some of the other ingredients and begins the simmering process. Others insist on frying the paste first to develop its flavor. Whether you use oil or thick coconut milk for frying depends on whether you eventually want a gutsy or a milder dish—that is, you would never fry a "country" curry paste in coconut milk, says Gajaseni. If you do fry the paste, he adds, make sure an oil slick has risen to its surface—do not skim the oil off—for this means it has cooked long enough. Add ingredients—such as lime and basil leaves or fish sauce—that do not need cooking just before serving.

How long do you fry? According to Nick Srisawat, owner of several Tara Thai restaurants, popular Thai restaurants in the Washington, D.C., metropolitan area, "You know when your curry paste is ready . . . when you sneeze."

And always use a fresh paste for your curries. Of course, having said that, Gajaseni admits that not everyone will assemble a from-scratch curry paste. Some may opt to use a commercial paste instead, the flavor of which can be freshened by blending in chilies, several shallots, and several cloves of garlic.

Just as fussy about their soups, Thais have a soup vocabulary that might seem a bit baffling. A popular seasoned soup is *tom nuea savoey (tom* means "bring a liquid to a boil"), which is really a simple soup with meat, or *nuea*, and *savoey*, meaning "pertaining to royalty." For an herbed soup, there is *gaeng liang*. *Gaeng* is more complex than *tom*, and *liang* means "cool," so you end up with a rather medicinal mixture with plenty of herbs to cool you down.

For spiced soups, there is the very complex *tom khlong goong pow*. *Tom khlong* refers to a type of spiced soup with roasted herbs (shallots, garlic, and chilies), and *goong* means prawns. And, of course, there is the popular soup *tom yam goong*, or spiced prawn soup. Since *yam* means salad, expect to find a handful of fresh vegetables, such as bean sprouts and snipped coriander, in a bowl of this soup.

Once you've crossed into chili territory and feel comfortable with the often-blazing Thai cooking, you may end up craving a dish or two of curry or soup. For me, it's Crispy Duck and Noodle Soup (page 74) and Fiery Green Curry with Roast Duck (page 76). Now *that* is comfort food.

Indonesia

I once thought Balinese food defined Indonesia's cooking, until I learned that the Balinese are Hindu and eat pork, forbidden elsewhere in Muslim Indonesia. Since Indonesia is a collection of more than 13,000 islands spread out over 3,000 miles, it is easy to see why no single island dish can capture the spirit of the Indonesian kitchen—except perhaps their *soto ayam*, or chicken soup (page 78), which may be about the closest thing to a national dish there is. In fact, my two Indonesian cookbooks from Jakarta call it "Indonesian chicken soup," and that's enough indication that this wholesome and nourishing dish finds a welcome place at everyone's table.

Indonesians take to soups much as they take to chilies, and the traditional main meal of supper is not complete without a bowl of either *soto* or *sup*. Although the distinction between the two seems blurry, apparently *sotos* are robust and lively, whereas *sups* depend on a well-seasoned broth to show off their few ingredients. Perhaps the chunkier *sotos* more closely resemble stews. Curries—or *gulai* or *karis*—on the other hand are hearty, sometimes stewlike dishes and an important component of the Indonesian meal.

While no island dish can sum up this cuisine, the island of Sumatra is a good place to learn something about the Indonesian appetite for Tuna and Coconut Curry (page 195), Stewed Young Jackfruit (page 130), the salad *gado-gado*, and sweetened black rice. In the central market of the mountain town Bukittiniggi, in West Sumatra, shoppers head down a gentle slope through lanes of dry goods, food stalls, fruit hawkers, and cooking utensils to a thriving wet (fresh) market at the base of a flight of stairs, where five pounds of fresh Sumatran coffee costs about one U.S. dollar and where every fresh fruit, vegetable, and chili for local consumption is for sale.

At dawn, the cooking stalls start selling bowls of oxtail soup with celery, tomato, and fried shallots, accompanied by deep-fried dumplings, and chili-red bowls of jackfruit stewed with meat and shallots and brightened with pink rice crackers. A stroll back up the hill in the early morning light will mean that shoppers can stop at a vendor selling sweet *murtabagh* folded with peanuts, sugar, black rice, and grated chocolate; tropical fruits such as rambutan, durian, jackfruit, odd-shaped bananas, and guavas; fried bananas; and something called *kwai*, or brown sugar with coconut milk, sticky rice, and salt. The choices seem endless, and the vendors and cooks in their stalls are eager to make sales.

As you walk and snack, you can see the *nasi kapau*, or savory foods stalls, setting up for business at midmorning, just after shoppers have eaten their fill of breakfast. And you can try to figure out just where it was your companion mentioned finding delicious goat's head soup, gouramy's (fish) head soup, and some cooked red rice, which is nicknamed "Indonesian vitamins."

Mostly Meatless

"Bean curd, if good, is better than bird's nest. And better than sea slugs, if these are not first rate, is a dish of bamboo shoots."

—Yuen Mai

4

Indian Hot and Sour Onions

Kandha Ki Subzi

A Rajasthani dish, this recipe proves that a few seasonings can turn onions into a blaze of flavors. Indian gastronome J. Inder Singh Kalran calls for using small whole onions, the next size up from tiny pearl onions.

1 teaspoon mango powder (*amchur*)

³/₄ teaspoon ground coriander

¹/₂ teaspoon ground cumin

¹/₂ teaspoon Indian red chili powder

¹/₂ teaspoon ground turmeric

Pinch of black rock salt

2¹/₄ pounds small white onions, peeled but left intact

Curry Sauce

3 tablespoons vegetable oil

2 teaspoons cumin seeds

5 teaspoons Garlic Paste (page 28)

2¹/₂ teaspoons Ginger Paste (page 28)

2 green chilies, stems removed, seeded, and finely chopped

1 teaspoon ground coriander

¹/₂ teaspoon Indian red chili powder

1 teaspoon ground turmeric mixed with 3 tablespoons warm water

1 pound tomatoes, peeled, seeded, and chopped, or one 14-ounce can tomato sauce

1 tablespoon chopped fresh coriander leaves

Salt to taste

1 cup water

Pinch of green cardamom powder, black cardamom powder, ground cinnamon, ground cloves, and ground mace

Fresh coriander leaves

1. To make the filling, combine the mango powder, coriander, cumin, chili powder, turmeric, and rock salt in a small bowl.

2. Make a crisscross incision on the top of each onion. Push equal quantities of the filling into the slits with your fingertips. Set the onions aside for 30 minutes and reserve any extra filling to stir into the curry sauce.

3. To make the curry sauce, heat the oil in a large wok or saucepan over medium heat. Add the cumin seeds and stir-fry until they begin to crackle. Add the garlic paste and ginger paste, and cook, stirring, until the moisture evaporates, 2 to 3 minutes. Add the green chilies and stir-fry for 1 minute. Add the coriander, chili powder, and turmeric, and cook, stirring, for 1 minute. Add the tomatoes and coriander leaves, and cook, stirring, until the tomatoes are completely soft and mashed, about 5 minutes. Stir in the onions, salt, and water, and bring to a boil. Reduce the heat to medium-low, cover, and cook until the onions just begin to soften, about 10 minutes. Sprinkle the onions with the green cardamom, black cardamom, cinnamon, cloves, and mace. Stir the mixture and remove from the heat. Garnish with the coriander leaves and serve hot.

MAKES 6 SERVINGS

Indian Spinach and Dal Curry

With its combination of tart spinach and mild lentils (also known generically as "dal" in India), this recipe from J. Inder Singh Kalra and Pushpesh Pant will suit the palates of vegetarians seeking a different way to serve dal; it is also a flavorful complement to an Indian grilled meat, such as a barbecued leg of lamb.

$^2/_3$ cup yellow lentils (*toor dal*), rinsed and picked clean

$^1/_2$ teaspoon ground turmeric

$3^1/_2$ cups water

$^1/_4$ teaspoon asafoetida

3 tablespoons vegetable oil, preferably peanut

2 dried red chilies

1 teaspoon mustard seeds

$^1/_2$ teaspoon cumin seeds

4 to 6 cloves garlic, peeled and crushed

$1^1/_4$ cups chopped onions

1 large tomato, cubed

4 green chilies, halved lengthwise and seeded

1 pound spinach, rinsed, stems intact

Salt to taste

12 curry leaves

1. Combine the lentils, $^1/_4$ teaspoon of the turmeric, and 3 cups of the water in a large saucepan and bring to a boil. Reduce the heat to medium-low and cook until softened, about 10 minutes. Stir in the asafoetida, reduce the heat to low, and cook, mashing the lentils against the sides of the pan with a spoon until the lentils begin to soften, 10 to 15 minutes more. Remove from the heat.

2. Heat the oil in a large wok or saucepan over medium-high heat. Add the dried chilies and stir-fry until they begin to darken. Remove from the pan and set aside. Add the mustard and cumin, and stir-fry until they begin to crackle. Remove from the pan and set aside. Add the garlic and stir-fry until golden. Remove from the pan and set aside. Add the onions and stir-fry for 1 minute. Return the chilies and garlic to the pan. Add the remaining turmeric, tomato, and green chilies, and stir-fry until the tomato softens, 2 to 3 minutes. Stir in the spinach and salt, increase the heat to high, and stir-fry until the spinach begins to release its juices, about 2 minutes. Reduce the heat to low, cover, and cook, stirring occasionally, until the stalks of the spinach are softened, about 5 minutes. Stir in the lentils and add the remaining $^1/_2$ cup water. Increase the heat to high and bring to a boil. Stir in the curry leaves and cook until wilted. Stir in the mustard and cumin seeds. Serve hot.

MAKES 3 TO 4 SERVINGS

Eggplant and Coconut Curry with Peanuts and Sesame Seeds

Baghare Baingan

A curry from Hyderabad, India, this multiflavored vegetable dish pulls out all the stops, and the result is a mixture that is hot yet sweet, textured yet soft. So much is going on here that this dish holds center stage at any meal.

Baghare baingan is traditionally made with Indian red onions, which are the size of large shallots and are sweet and mild. I have been told that Korean markets carry onions that are similar, but if you cannot find these, use large shallots or small yellow onions.

The original recipe calls for 24 eggplants and the cooks who created it—J. Inder Singh Kalra, Pushpesh Pant, and Raminder Malhotra—mean a certain Indian eggplant, which is small and round. Since these are not readily available in the West, Mr. Kalra suggests using 8 to 12 of the slender, long, purple Oriental ones. Bengali cook B. Runi Mukherji-Ratnam says that she often uses the small round Italian eggplants for her Indian cooking.

Traditionally, says Mr. Kalra, the cook makes large quantities of this curry gravy at one time so that there is always some ready to use as a base for other curries, including sweet tamarind, okra, or green chili curry. If you choose to make this with chilies, prepare them the same way as the eggplant—that is, make a crisscross incision on the top of each chili—then remove the seeds, fry them, and simmer them in the curry gravy. This curry will keep for a week in the refrigerator if it has been cooked properly, since a layer of oil will rise and seal its surface.

Curry Paste

³/₄ cup shredded unsweetened coconut

2 cups chopped onions

¹/₂ cup roasted peanuts

¹/₄ cup sesame seeds

About ³/₄ cup water

Curry

8 to 12 Oriental eggplants

2 cups mustard oil or vegetable oil

2¹/₂ tablespoons Garlic Paste (page 28)

2¹/₂ teaspoons Ginger Paste (page 28)

1 teaspoon ground turmeric

1. To make the curry paste, heat a skillet over very low heat until hot. Add the coconut and roast until fragrant. Transfer to a blender. Repeat this process with the onions, peanuts, and sesame seeds, roasting each ingredient separately until fragrant and transferring to the blender. Add just enough water to process, and blend until smooth.

2. To make the curry, slice off the stem end of the eggplants and make a crisscross incision from the top of each eggplant to three-quarters of the way to the base.

3. Heat the oil in a large wok or skillet over medium heat. Add the eggplants and cook until softened, 3 to 4 minutes. Transfer to paper towels to drain. Strain off all but ¹/₂ cup of the oil; reserve 1 teaspoon for later use.

1 teaspoon Indian red chili powder
mixed with 2 tablespoons
warm water

³/₄ cup fresh tomato puree (made
from 4 fresh tomatoes) or canned
tomato puree

Salt to taste

¹/₄ cup tamarind juice

1²/₃ cups water

¹/₂ teaspoon ground cumin

One 1-inch piece fresh ginger, cut into
thin strips

¹/₂ teaspoon mustard seeds

16 curry leaves

4. Reheat the oil in the wok over medium heat. Add the garlic paste and ginger paste, and stir-fry for a few seconds. Add the turmeric and red chili powder, and cook, stirring, for 3 minutes. Add the curry paste and cook, stirring, until fragrant. (Add a little water, if needed, to prevent the mixture from sticking.) Add the tomato puree and cook for 2 minutes. Stir in the salt and tamarind juice, and cook, stirring often, for 5 minutes. Add the water, bring to a boil, and reduce the heat to low. Add the eggplants and cook until tender, 15 to 20 minutes. Sprinkle with the cumin and ginger.

5. Reheat the reserved 1 teaspoon of oil in a skillet over medium heat. Add the mustard seeds and stir-fry until the seeds begin to crackle. Add the curry leaves, stir once, and pour over the curry. Serve hot.

MAKES 4 TO 6 SERVINGS

Vietnamese Vegetarian Hot and Sour Soup

From the owner of the Cafe Dalat Vietnamese restaurant in Arlington, Virginia, this light and delicate dish is a vegetarian take on the shrimp-filled Vietnamese Hot and Sour Soup (page 177).

1½ cups water

1 tablespoon sugar

1 tablespoon fish sauce

½ cup broccoli florets

⅓ cup bean sprouts

1 clove garlic, peeled, chopped, and fried until golden

1 thin crosswise slice fresh pineapple, cut into bite-sized pieces

⅓ stalk celery, thinly sliced

½ tomato, thinly sliced

4 small straw mushrooms, rinsed

¼ zucchini, thinly sliced

⅔ cup cubed firm tofu

2 tablespoons gluten

½ cup pineapple juice

½ teaspoon tamarind juice

Juice of ½ lemon, or more to taste

¼ teaspoon Vietnamese chili sauce, or more to taste

1 scallion, trimmed and thinly sliced

1. Bring the water to a boil in a large saucepan over medium heat. Add the sugar, fish sauce, broccoli, and bean sprouts. Cook until the vegetables are tender, about 5 minutes. Remove the vegetables from the water and transfer to a large bowl. Add the garlic to the vegetables.

2. Add the pineapple, celery, tomato, mushrooms, zucchini, tofu, gluten, pineapple juice, and tamarind juice to the saucepan. When the water returns to a boil, stir in the lemon juice and chili sauce. Pour into the bowl with the vegetables and stir to combine. Garnish with the sliced scallion and serve.

MAKES 1 SERVING

Red Lentils with Pumpkin, Buttermilk, and Mint

The Bengali cook B. Runi Mukherji-Ratnam serves this creamy red-orange, very thick soup often on cool fall days. When the temperature really plummets, she turns up the heat by cooking and grinding the chili with the lentils rather than adding the chili at the end. But don't reserve this marvelous full-meal dish for cold weather—just serve it at room temperature with chilled buttermilk on warmer days. The dish has the taste and texture of a chunky pumpkin pie that is loaded with sensational flavors.

1 cup red lentils (*masoor dal*), rinsed and picked clean

4 cups water

One 2-inch piece fresh ginger, cut into thin strips

2 tablespoons shredded fresh mint leaves, plus several whole leaves for garnish

1 tablespoon chopped fresh coriander leaves, plus several whole leaves for garnish

$1/2$ teaspoon light brown sugar

$1/2$ teaspoon ground turmeric

1 small pumpkin or winter squash (such as acorn or butternut), peeled and cut into $1/2$-inch cubes (about $1^1/2$ cups)

2 tablespoons Ghee (page 17) or vegetable oil

1 dried red chili, crumbled

1 teaspoon cumin seeds

1 teaspoon Mughlai garam masala (see Note)

Salt and freshly ground black pepper to taste

1 cup buttermilk

1. Combine the lentils and water in a large saucepan and bring to a boil. Reduce the heat to medium-low and cook until softened, 25 to 30 minutes. Transfer the lentils to a blender or food processor, add just enough of the cooking water to process, and blend until smooth.

2. Return the lentils to the saucepan and stir in half of the ginger, 1 tablespoon of the shredded mint, the chopped coriander, brown sugar, turmeric, and squash. Cook over medium-low heat until the squash is tender, 20 to 25 minutes.

3. Heat the ghee or vegetable oil in a skillet over medium heat. Add the remaining ginger and cook, stirring, for 2 minutes. Add the chili and cook, stirring, for 1 minute. Add the cumin and cook, stirring, until fragrant, about 1 minute. Add the remaining shredded mint to the skillet and stir into the squash mixture. Stir in the garam masala and season with salt and pepper.

4. To serve, ladle the soup into 4 individual bowls and swirl $1/4$ cup of the buttermilk into each serving. Garnish with the fresh coriander and mint leaves.

MAKES 4 SERVINGS

Note: To make this garam masala, Ms. Mukherji-Ratnam combines 1 tablespoon whole cloves, one 2-inch piece cinnamon stick, 1 teaspoon black peppercorns, and 1 heaping tablespoon green cardamom pods. Roast each spice individually (see page 11) and shell and discard the cardamom pods. Pulverize the spices in a spice grinder or blender. Add $1/2$ teaspoon nutmeg to the ground spices and combine well.

New Potatoes with Yogurt Sauce

The Bengali cook B. Runi Mukherji-Ratnam passed this recipe on with its simply seasoned yogurt sauce. She says this need not be a last-minute dish: You may prepare the dish ahead of time and set it aside, covered, until mealtime. Reheat the potatoes in a microwave, but be careful not to overcook them. What makes this potato dish so delicious is the contrast between the sweetness of the potatoes and the spicy sourness of the yogurt sauce. She uses the tiniest new potatoes and pierces their skins so they absorb the seasoning flavors; if you use larger potatoes, you may want to slice them in half or quarters.

1½ pounds small new red or
    white potatoes

1 clove garlic, peeled

1 tablespoon Ghee (page 17) or butter

4 green cardamom pods

4 whole cloves

1 teaspoon ground cinnamon

1 bay leaf

Salt to taste

1 cup plain yogurt, whisked
    until creamy

1 teaspoon cumin seeds, roasted and
    ground (see page 11)

1. Bring a large saucepan of water to a boil. Add the potatoes and garlic, and boil until the potatoes are almost tender, about 20 minutes. Drain the potatoes and cover to keep warm.

2. Melt the ghee or butter in the saucepan over low heat. Add the cardamom, cloves, cinnamon, and bay leaf, and stir-fry until fragrant. Add the warm potatoes and sprinkle with salt. Stir in the yogurt and cook until the yogurt is warm, 2 to 3 minutes. Transfer to a serving dish and sprinkle with the cumin before serving.

MAKES 4 SERVINGS

Nepalese Dal and Tomato Stew

My friend Pat Bonifer-Tiedt spent time in Nepal in the Peace Corps, and she brought back this hearty, folksy stew. It's simple to prepare and combines layers of complementary flavors, from garlic and onions to ginger and ground turmeric. This dish goes well with yogurt and some puffy tandoori bread.

2 medium tomatoes, quartered

1/2 cup yellow split peas (*chana dal*), rinsed, picked clean, and soaked in cold water to cover for 6 to 12 hours

1 medium onion, peeled and chopped

Salt to taste

3 cups water

3 tablespoons vegetable oil

1 teaspoon grated fresh ginger

1/2 teaspoon ground turmeric

1/2 teaspoon ground cumin

1/2 teaspoon mustard seeds

1/4 teaspoon Indian red chili powder

3 cloves garlic, peeled and chopped

1 tablespoon chopped fresh coriander leaves

8 bay leaves

1. Combine the tomatoes, split peas, onion, salt, and water in a large saucepan and bring to a boil. Reduce the heat to medium-low and cook until the split peas are soft, 25 to 30 minutes. Transfer to a blender or food processor, add just enough of the cooking water to process, and blend until smooth.

2. Heat the oil in a wok or large saucepan over medium heat. Add the ginger, turmeric, cumin, mustard seeds, and chili powder, and cook, stirring, until golden and fragrant, about 5 minutes. Add the garlic, coriander, and bay leaves and cook, stirring, for 2 minutes. Stir in the pureed split peas and tomatoes, bring to a boil, and cook for 1 minute. Serve hot.

MAKES 2 SERVINGS

South Indian Red Lentil Broth

Rasam

An integral part of many South Indian meals, explains the cook, B. Runi Mukherji-Ratnam, rasam literally means "juice." It may be either the leftover liquid of a sambar *(a spicy lentil dish) or prepared as a separate entity.* Rasam *is served with meals to moisten cooked rice or dry curries, or it may be eaten separately as an appetizer, a soup, or a tart, refreshing drink. Ms. Mukherji-Ratnam finds American coriander too bland, so she intensifies the musky coriander taste by adding its stems and roots.*

Seasoning Paste

1 to 4 dried red chilies, soaked in hot
    water for 20 minutes
1 tablespoon yellow split peas (*chana
    dal*), rinsed
1 tablespoon coriander seeds, roasted
    (see page 11)
1 teaspoon cumin seeds, roasted
    (see page 11)
About ¹/₂ cup water

Broth

7 cups water
¹/₂ cup red lentils (*masoor dal*), rinsed
    and picked clean
1 large bunch coriander, rinsed
2 large cloves garlic, unpeeled
1 tablespoon coriander seeds
1 tablespoon black peppercorns
3 tomatoes, cored
1 teaspoon ground turmeric
1 tablespoon Ghee (page 17) or
    vegetable oil
1 teaspoon mustard seeds
1 teaspoon cumin seeds
¹/₄ teaspoon asafoetida
¹/₄ cup tamarind juice or juice of
    2 lemons
Salt and freshly ground black pepper

1. To make the seasoning paste, combine the chilies, split peas, coriander seeds, and cumin seeds in a spice grinder or blender. Add just enough water to process until smooth.

2. To make the broth, combine the water, lentils, fresh coriander, garlic, coriander seeds, and peppercorns in a large saucepan and bring to a boil. Reduce the heat to medium-low, cover, and cook until the lentils begin to soften, about 15 minutes. Reduce the heat to low, stir in the tomatoes and turmeric, and cook, uncovered, until the tomatoes fall apart, about 15 minutes. Stir in the seasoning paste. Strain through a coarse sieve into a serving bowl, pushing the tomato pulp and lentils through the holes.

3. Heat the ghee or oil in a small saucepan over medium heat. Add the mustard seeds, cumin seeds, and asafoetida, and stir-fry until the seeds begin to crackle. Stir into the lentil mixture along with the tamarind juice or lemon juice. Season with salt and pepper.

MAKES 4 TO 6 SERVINGS

Bengali Vegetable Curry

This versatile dish works well with almost any vegetable combination, such as eggplant, potatoes, and squash. Although broccoli is not generally used in India, the cook who provided this recipe, B. Runi Mukherji-Ratnam, finds its addition delicious. She also likes to add mint leaves and a pinch of sugar for extra zip. Serve this dish—which resembles a very thick, rich soup—with warm rice and Indian bread.

Seasoning Mixture

1/2 cup shredded unsweetened coconut

3 green chilies, seeded

1/2 cup water

Curry

1/2 cup yellow split peas (*chana dal*), rinsed, picked clean, and soaked in cold water to cover for 6 to 12 hours

2 1/2 cups water

1 bunch broccoli, chopped into bite-sized pieces

2 tomatoes, cored and chopped

1 teaspoon *sambar* powder (see Note)

1/2 cup water, or more if needed

1 teaspoon ground turmeric

Salt to taste

2 teaspoons cumin seeds, roasted (see page 11)

1. To make the seasoning mixture, combine the coconut, chilies, and water in a blender, and blend until smooth.

2. To make the curry, combine the split peas and water in a large saucepan and bring to a boil. Reduce the heat to medium-low and cook until softened, 25 to 30 minutes. Add the broccoli, tomatoes, and *sambar* powder. (Stir in the water if the mixture seems dry.) Reduce the heat to low, cover, and cook about 8 minutes. Stir in the seasoning mixture, turmeric, and salt, and cook, uncovered, until the coconut aroma is no longer apparent, about 5 minutes. Garnish with the cumin seeds and serve.

MAKES 3 TO 4 SERVINGS

Note: There are many different variations on *sambar* powder. In this recipe, the cook calls for a spice mixture of equal parts of roasted and ground coriander seeds and cumin seeds.

Fiery Nepalese Stew

Amti

My friend Pat Bonifer-Tiedt brought this recipe back from Nepal. It cooks up into a very thick, fragrant dish and its flavors are wonderful, but be wary: If you use the full complement of chilies, the result is fiery. A filling main-course soup or stew, amti *would make an ideal fireside supper if accompanied by a tossed green salad and hot, crusty bread.*

1¹/₂ cups yellow lentils (*toor dal*), rinsed
  and picked clean

5 cups water, or more if needed

¹/₄ cup vegetable oil

1 teaspoon mustard seeds

6 green chilies, halved and seeded

1 large onion, peeled and diced

2 teaspoons salt

1 teaspoon ground turmeric

1 teaspoon paprika

¹/₄ teaspoon ground cinnamon

¹/₄ teaspoon ground cloves

¹/₄ teaspoon ground cardamom

Freshly ground black pepper to taste

2 tablespoons fresh lemon juice

1 teaspoon light brown sugar

1. Combine the lentils and 4¹/₂ cups of the water in a large saucepan and bring to a boil. Reduce the heat to medium-low and cook until soft, 25 to 30 minutes.

2. Meanwhile, heat the oil in a large wok or saucepan over medium heat. Add the mustard seeds and stir-fry until the seeds begin to crackle. Add the chilies and onion, and stir-fry 3 to 4 minutes, or until golden. Add the salt, turmeric, paprika, cinnamon, cloves, cardamom, and pepper, and stir-fry about 2 minutes, until fragrant.

3. When the lentils are cooked, stir in the spice mixture and the remaining ¹/₂ cup water. Cook, stirring occasionally, until well combined, 5 to 6 minutes. Stir in the lemon juice and brown sugar. Serve hot.

MAKES 4 TO 6 SERVINGS

Nepalese Tomato and Green Chili Soup

Pairing tomatoes and green chilies is a natural, and despite the heat of this delicious soup, you probably won't have any leftovers. You can turn this into a light lunch entree if you tag on a yogurt-based salad and some Indian bread. J. Inder Singh Kalra and Pushpesh Pant brought this recipe back from the Natuchghar restaurant at the Hotel Yak & Yeti in Katmandu, Nepal, and it will be a welcome addition for Americans who like excitement in their soup bowls. It serves four to five sparingly; you may wish to double the ingredients so you will have seconds, especially if there are chili lovers among you.

$^1/_4$ cup plus 3 tablespoons Ghee (page 17) or vegetable oil

2 small onions, peeled and diced

$3^1/_2$ teaspoons Garlic Paste (page 28)

$3^1/_2$ teaspoons Ginger Paste (page 28)

4 cups chopped tomatoes

$^3/_4$ cup chopped fresh coriander leaves

4 green chilies, halved lengthwise

2 tablespoons ground turmeric

2 tablespoons freshly ground black pepper

4 bay leaves

$4^1/_2$ cups Basic Chicken Stock (page 19)

2 tablespoons Garam Masala (page 29)

3 tablespoons all-purpose flour

$^1/_4$ cup chopped garlic

2 teaspoons cumin seeds, roasted (see page 11)

1. Heat $^1/_4$ cup of the ghee or oil in a large saucepan over medium heat. Add the onions, garlic paste, and ginger paste, and cook, stirring often, until the onions are golden, 15 to 20 minutes. Add the tomatoes, coriander, chilies, turmeric, pepper, and bay leaves, and cook, stirring occasionally, until the tomatoes are softened, about 5 minutes. Stir in the stock, reduce the heat to low, and cook, uncovered, for 1 hour.

2. Heat the remaining 3 tablespoons ghee or oil in a small saucepan over medium heat. Stir in the garam masala and flour. Pour $^1/_2$ cup of the hot soup into the mixture and stir until smooth. Stir into the soup and cook until thickened, 2 to 3 minutes. Garnish with the garlic and cumin seeds before serving.

MAKES 4 TO 5 SERVINGS

Singaporean Dal Rice

According to the Malaysian cook Aziza Ali, this dish is the ideal accompaniment to her Singaporean-Malay Chicken Curry (page 71). But vegetarians could accompany this with some greens or a salad and perhaps a bowl of minted yogurt. The cook also calls for using milk, but my guess is that coconut milk is more traditionally used.

Seasoning Paste

1 tablespoon minced fresh ginger

3 cloves garlic, peeled

About ¼ cup water

Dal Rice

⅓ cup yellow split and hulled mung beans (*moong dal*), rinsed and picked clean

3 cups water

3 tablespoons Ghee (page 17) or vegetable oil

2 cups basmati rice or other long-grain rice, soaked in cold water to cover for 1 hour, rinsed, and drained

1 cup milk

1 teaspoon ground cinnamon

1 teaspoon star anise seeds

Salt to taste

1. To make the seasoning paste, combine the ginger and garlic in a blender or spice grinder. Add just enough water to process, and blend until smooth.

2. To make the rice, combine the mung beans and 1¼ cups of the water in a large saucepan and bring to a boil. Reduce the heat to medium-low and cook until soft, 25 to 30 minutes.

3. Meanwhile, heat the ghee or oil in a large wok or skillet over medium heat. Add the seasoning paste and cook, stirring, until fragrant, about 5 minutes. Add the rice and cook, stirring constantly, until translucent, about 5 minutes.

4. Transfer the rice mixture to a large saucepan. Stir in the milk, the remaining 1¾ cups water, the cinnamon, star anise seeds, and salt, and bring to a boil. Reduce the heat to medium-low, cover, and cook until the rice is tender, 15 to 20 minutes. Just before serving, stir in the mung beans and heat through.

MAKES 4 SERVINGS

Burmese Coconut Rice

Ohn-hta-min

The coconut milk makes the rice ultra-rich, but the onions cut its richness. Serve this with crunchy, tangy vegetables for interesting contrasts in taste and texture. Keep an eye on the temperature—the coconut milk may scorch when the rice is nearly cooked, says the cook, Daw May Khin Maung Than.

4 cups long-grain rice, rinsed
6 cups coconut milk
1 large onion, peeled and sliced
3 tablespoons vegetable oil
1 tablespoon sugar
Pinch of salt

Combine all ingredients in a large saucepan and bring to a boil. Reduce the heat to low and cook, stirring often to prevent sticking and scorching, until the rice is tender, 15 to 20 minutes. (If the mixture seems dry, add water, a little at a time.) Use a fork to fluff up the rice and to prevent crushing the rice grains; use a slotted metal spoon to scoop the rice into each serving bowl. Serve hot.

MAKES 4 TO 6 SERVINGS

Dried Mushroom and Braissica Soup

Chef C.K. Chan, of the Sheraton Hong Kong Hotel & Towers, presented this soup with its delicate mushroomy flavor at an elegant lunch, and as we enjoyed it, we mulled over the meaning of "braissica." After much discussion, the chef decided that braissica [sic] was actually bok choy.

3/4 pound bok choy, rinsed and
   trimmed into bite-sized pieces

1 medium onion, peeled and
   thinly sliced

3 dried Chinese mushrooms, soaked in
   hot water for 20 minutes and stems
   removed, thinly sliced

Three 1-inch pieces fresh ginger

Salt to taste

6 cups Basic Beef Stock (page 19)

1/2 teaspoon Chinese rice wine

Combine the bok choy, onion, mushrooms, ginger, salt, stock, and wine in a large wok or saucepan over medium heat. Bring to a boil, reduce the heat to low, and cook until the flavors are intensified, about 40 minutes.

MAKES 3 TO 4 SERVINGS

Mrs. Yamada's Rice Soup

Mrs. Yamada prepares the following zosui *(cooked rice) recipe for her winter breakfasts—certainly more substantial than an egg on toast. She gives no ingredient amounts, since you may wish to breakfast solo or with the family. Quantities really depend on your appetite.*

2¹/₂ cups *dashi* (Japanese First Stock, page 34)

1¹/₂ cups cold cooked Japanese rice

Carrots, thinly sliced

Spinach leaves, rinsed

Dried shiitake mushrooms, stems removed, sliced

Shrimp or scallops (optional)

Scallions, chopped

Raw egg, beaten

Salt to taste

A few dashes soy sauce

Combine the *dashi* and rice, and cook, covered, over low heat until the rice becomes soft and the liquid is absorbed. Then add the carrots, spinach, mushrooms, and, if desired, shrimp or scallops. Cook until the ingredients are cooked through, about 5 minutes. Garnish with the scallions and stir in the egg, which cooks as it is stirred into the rice. Season with salt and soy sauce. Serve immediately.

MAKES 1 TO 2 SERVINGS

Korean Jott Jook

In this recipe, you must take the time to snap off the "eyes" of the pine nuts; otherwise they end up speck-ling—and blemishing—the appearance of the dish, says the cook who provided this recipe, Hira Lee.

5 pitted Chinese dates, or more
   to taste, very thinly sliced

About ¼ cup honey or syrup

1 cup pine nuts, black "eyes" removed
   (see Headnote)

10 cups water

2 cups short-grain sweet rice, soaked
   in cold water to cover for 2 hours
   and drained

1. Soak the dates in honey or syrup to cover for 20 minutes.

2. Grind the nuts and 1 cup of the water in a blender until smooth. Transfer to a bowl.

3. Grind the rice and 2 cups of the water in a clean blender until almost smooth—if you prefer a chunkier texture, blend the rice until coarsely chopped. Transfer to a large saucepan. Stir in the remaining 7 cups water and bring to a boil. Reduce the heat to medium and cook, stirring constantly to avoid clumping, until the rice paste becomes sticky, about 20 minutes. Reduce the heat to medium-low and gradually add the nuts, stirring constantly to avoid clumping. As soon as the mixture returns to a boil, remove from the heat. Garnish with the dates and serve.

MAKES 4 TO 6 SERVINGS

Tibetan "Rotting Cheese" Soup

Churu

"Overripe" sounds better than "rotting," since what you use for this dish is a pungent cheese, but Tibetan cook and Virginia resident Tseten Wangchuk could not think of any Western equivalent, with the possible exception of blue cheese, and that is what I used. Tibetan farmers apparently love this soup and often have it for lunch. If you like the flavor of blue cheese, you will adore this dish with its pungent flavor and its other layers of sweet and hot. Serve with a crusty bread, fruit, and white wine for a simple dinner, but add a roast and vegetables if you are feeding a hungry nonvegetarian crowd.

3 tablespoons butter

2 onions, peeled and chopped

3 dried red chilies, snapped into
   2 pieces

4$^1/_4$ cups water

$^1/_2$ pound Roquefort or other
   blue cheese

Paprika to taste

3 tablespoons barley flour (see Note)

1. Melt the butter in a large saucepan over medium heat. Add the onions and cook, stirring often, until browned, about 15 minutes. Add the chilies and 1 cup of the water and cook, stirring occasionally, for 5 minutes.

2. Crumble the cheese and stir into the soup. Cook, stirring constantly, until the cheese melts. Sprinkle with paprika and stir in 3 cups of the water. Combine the flour and remaining $^1/_4$ cup water. Stir into the soup and sprinkle with more paprika. Cook until slightly thickened, about 5 minutes more. Serve hot.

MAKES 3 TO 4 SERVINGS

Note: Barley flour is available at many Korean markets, but if you cannot find it, lightly toast barley grains and pulverize them in a blender.

Taiwanese Fermented Rice

To make the fermented rice, Bi Bi Kearney has provided the following recipe, which takes three days to make. You must use long-grain sticky (glutinous) rice only. The yeast used to ferment the rice comes in round balls that look a bit like moth balls—these are usually sold loose in jars at Asian markets. One ball equals about 1 tablespoon powdered yeast. Pound the yeast to pulverize it. Bi Bi Kearney has never tried Western packaged yeast, but it may work. She stressed that all utensils, including your hands, must be "squeaky" clean—that is, completely free of any greasy or oily residue—or the rice will not ferment properly.

5 cups uncooked long-grain sticky (glutinous) rice
1 ball Asian yeast

1. Soak 5 cups uncooked long-grain sticky (glutinous) rice in cold water to cover for at least 3 hours. Steam the rice over boiling water (you can use a Lao rice steamer or other steamer lined with cheesecloth) for 45 minutes over very high heat.

2. After steaming, rinse the rice under warm water to wash off any starchy residue. Continue rinsing until the water runs clear. Put the rice in a large glass or stainless steel bowl with a lid, or wrap the bowl securely in plastic wrap.

3. Crush the ball of Asian yeast and stir it evenly into the rice, using a ceramic or stainless steel spoon. Make sure that all the grains of rice are firmly pressed together so that the rice can ferment uniformly. Make a 1-inch-wide well in the center of the rice. Cover the bowl tightly, wrap it with a blanket or heavy towel, and put it in a warm place. (In Taiwan, in homes without furnaces, the cook wraps the rice in a heavy quilt.) You do not need to add any liquid to start the rice; it will produce its own liquid, which pools in the center well.

4. Do not touch or move the rice while it is fermenting. After three days, check the rice. If it has not exuded any sweet liquid—the liquid should taste "winey"—wait one more day. Should the liquid taste sour, that means the fermenting process was not successful: Either the utensils or your hands were not clean enough or the temperature of the "resting" place was not warm enough.

5. When the rice is ready—that is, the flavor is sweet and the rice has exuded some liquid—move the fermented rice and its liquid to a container with a tight-fitting lid and refrigerate. You must fill the container no more than three-quarters of the way; if you do not allow room for the rice to continue to expand, it could cause the lid to come off. To serve, scoop out desired portions and serve either hot or cold.

MAKES 4 TO 6 SERVINGS

Breakfast Barley-Rice Soup or Drink

Korean cook Bong S. Lee prescribes this refreshing pick-me-up for her family all year round, since it can be served warm in winter or over ice cubes for a cooling summer refreshment. Its light, delicate flavor of toasted barley softened by rice is delicious. But best of all, the cook says this soup makes people very healthy.

To make the soup, combine equal portions of toasted barley (this is available at Korean markets) and sticky (glutinous) rice in a blender or spice grinder and pulverize. Transfer to a pitcher and add water until the liquid is a pale golden color. Sweeten to taste with sugar. (Try a ratio of 1 tablespoon rice powder, 1 tablespoon barley powder, 1 tablespoon sugar, and 3 cups water.) Before serving, stir up the sediment from the bottom. In summer, serve in a bowl with cubes of ice. In winter, heat and pour into a soup bowl for drinking.

Asian Rice Soups

Asians love rice, and since it is their staple food, it's no wonder that most Asians—including the Chinese, Thais, Koreans, Japanese, Indonesians, Filipinos, and Vietnamese—have created a way to slow-cook rice into a thick soup.

Chinese Congee

Many of my most enduring memories of Hong Kong revolve around food, and I vividly remember walking in the early morning through Chinese marketplaces and watching the elderly Chinese, seated on folding stools at tiny round tables, eating bowls of steaming-hot *congee*.

Classified as both a soup and a gruel, or "soft rice," *congee* comes in many guises, depending on the ratio of rice to water and even on the type of rice, or combinations of rice, you select. *Congee* has many salutary benefits. It is thick, nourishing, and easy to digest, and some say a perfect means of cleansing the system.

As for gastronomy, by its very bland nature, *congee* (and similar rice soups) becomes the perfect foil for more dominant and dramatic ingredients, such as pickled fish or vegetables, barbecued pork, hard-boiled eggs with soy sauce, toasted sesame oil and peanuts, preserved turnips, and/or Chinese sausages. Of course, I suppose almost anything goes as a topping for *congee*. And, in the same vein, almost anything goes to cook with *congee*—from duck, pork, beef, chicken, and seafood to the bones of any of these creatures—some of which are added as you begin to cook the rice or, as with raw shrimp, at the end. Or, if you prefer, just cook the rice plain.

Since *congee* is simply a small portion of rice cooked in large quantities of water, there is really no recipe for it per se. You may use standard long-grain or short-grain rice, or a combination of the two, and cook the rice in the ratio of about 12 parts water to 1 part rice, although some suggest a ratio of 3 parts water to 1 part rice, as well as everything in between. You can soak the rice, but if you don't, you should rinse it until the water runs clear. Traditionally, the rice cooks over very low heat in a covered pot, usually for 3 to 4 hours. But many variations exist—for example, some recipes call for soaking the rice for several hours before cooking it, while others say to simmer it, covered or uncovered, for 2 to 3 hours.

Whether or not to cover the rice is debatable. Helene Sze McCarthy's recipe takes yet another approach. In any case, *congee* is ready when it has become a thickish, opaque-white liquid. If it is too thick for you at this point, thin by adding more water. And when it is ready, always serve it hot; leftovers will keep for several days if stored in a covered container in the refrigerator.

Mrs. McCarthy has her own very simple recipe for a *congee*-like Chinese rice soup she called *shao chau*—she wasn't sure of the spelling. For this, she uses only short-grain sticky (glutinous) rice (Japanese or Korean short-grain rice) and lets it cool down after cooking and before eating:

Combine $^1/_2$ cup rice in 10 cups water. When the water comes to a boil, let it cook, uncovered, for 20 minutes. Then cover the pot, turn off the heat, and let the rice stand for at least 10 minutes. Eat it when it cools slightly.

Mrs. McCarthy likes a very thin rice soup— "The thick one feels like your mouth is too full," she says. She also points out that when the rice is cooked for a shorter time, each grain stays intact. "This recipe is so simple," she says. "You leave it alone and when you come back home from work, you scoop out the rice and eat it with anything you want." Accompaniments for her include pickled cucumbers, pickled Chinese radish, preserved turnips, "salty" (fermented) bean curd, roasted peanuts, and/or Chinese barbecued pork *(char siew).* Or sometimes she adds half a pound of ground beef seasoned with salt, soy sauce, and toasted sesame oil with thinly sliced green onions and ginger to the rice soup when it is boiling and garnishes this dish with black pepper and fresh coriander before eating.

Everyone has different tastes, so be prepared to reduce the water-to-rice ratio, add more water to thin the *congee,* or cook it longer to thicken it. Personally, I prefer *congee* made from 10 parts water to 1 part rice (half short-grain rice, half long-grain rice). If you become a *congee* addict, you might explore the many ways that millions of Asians prepare this nutritious and filling soup (see below for the Japanese, Filipino, and the Korean versions).

Japanese Rice Soups

In Japan, rice soups are just as popular as elsewhere in Asia and are equally thrifty, since Japanese cooks make them from both leftover cooked rice *(zosui)* and from raw rice *(okayu),* explained a group of New York–based Japanese women, Yoko Auslander, Tomiko Baylis, Katsuko Inatome, and Sachi Yamada.

Apparently, *zosui* was created by peasants as a way to stretch their supply of cooked rice—and since the finished "soup" is both filling and tasty, it's easy to see why everyone has come to enjoy this dish. As for *okayu,* the Japanese have traditionally thought of it as a food for the infirm, because it is easy to digest. One woman recounted how her mother was routinely offered this thick gruel (it resembles the Chinese dish *congee*) after the birth of each of her children. She and her friends agreed that this tastes better if cooked over a charcoal fire. In fact, one of the women said, "In the olden days, the rice soup [the *okayu*] was much tastier, more economical, and more nutritious" than today. But no one could tell me quite why.

Mrs. Yamada adds that *zosui* may be prepared and eaten at any time of day, not just for breakfast, and that anything but beef can go into it— such as chicken, fish cakes, and *wakame* (Japanese seaweed). (See her recipe on page 231.) Yoko Auslander suggests adding ingredients such as chopped scallions, thinly sliced carrots, and sliced Japanese fish cakes at the beginning when you bring the *dashi* to a boil and before you add the cooked rice.

For the *okayu,* combine $^1/_4$ cup Japanese rice and 3 cups water in a large saucepan. Cook, uncovered, over low heat until all the water is absorbed and the mixture becomes a thick gruel, about 3 hours. This may be salted before serving.

Filipino Rice Soup

My friend Shirley Janairo Roth exclaimed that, oh, yes, Filipinos have their own version of the Chinese *congee*. Indeed, when you consider Filipino foods, of course you can trace the Chinese influence, especially in the use of soy sauce for seasoning so many of their dishes. Filipinos prepare *congee* the same way as the Chinese, but serve it, she said, in one of two ways: with a salty topping of fried salted fish (*theyo*) or cooked with chicken or tripe, or even with coagulated cow's blood.

Korean Jott Jook

As the Korean cook Hira Lee tells it, *jook* (also known as rice soup) is a soothing food that helps your stomach and is suitable for both old and young, even for toddlers being introduced to solid foods. "This helps them get acquainted with rice," she said, "before they are getting real rice." Unlike the Chinese and Japanese versions, the rice grains here are ground up, producing a silken-textured soup.

In the olden days, cooks had to grind the rice by hand. But modern cooks have electric gadgets that can puree soaked rice in minutes. Of course, you can vary the texture of this dish by only partially grinding the rice grains rather than pureeing them into a very smooth paste. During cooking, you may add other ingredients, such as ground barley or lentils. For a sweet dish, you may use red beans and sugar. If you wish, stir in a little salt at the end of the cooking time. (See recipe on page 232.)

Taiwanese Fermented Rice

Although it originated in Shanghai, says Bi Bi Kearney, the cook who provided the recipe (page 234), Taiwanese enjoy this invigorating souplike dish the same way Westerners enjoy hot chocolate—as a refreshing pick-me-up for breakfast or before bedtime. For a more substantial breakfast, drop in a few rice cakes before serving.

This soupy dish can also be served as a dessert, either hot or cold, and made even soupier with added water, if desired. Fermented rice is also sold in jars at some Asian markets as "Fermented Rice Soup" or "Sweet Rice Pudding."

Filipino Sautéed Mung Bean Stew

Mongo Guisado

Traditionally, says my Filipina friend Shirley Janairo Roth, this dish contains diced pork and shrimp, and this is the way she printed it in her book, Cooking the Filipino Way. *But here she turns the stew into a vegetarian offering, with mung beans providing the main protein source. You may cook the beans ahead of time—this way the dish can come together as a last-minute meal. It's a flavorful vegetarian entree made complete when served with cooked rice.*

1 cup whole green mung beans (*moong dal*), rinsed, picked clean, and soaked in cold water to cover for 6 to 12 hours

6 cups water

2 tablespoons vegetable oil

1 medium onion, peeled and sliced

2 cloves garlic, peeled and crushed

1 medium tomato, coarsely chopped

1 teaspoon salt

$^1/_4$ teaspoon freshly ground black pepper

$^1/_2$ pound spinach, rinsed and trimmed

1. Combine the beans and 4 cups of the water in a large saucepan and bring to a boil. Reduce the heat to low and cook until tender, about 30 minutes.

2. Heat the oil in a large saucepan over medium heat. Add the onion and garlic, and cook, stirring, until translucent, about 2 minutes. Stir in the tomato, salt, and pepper, and cook, stirring, for 1 minute. Stir in half the beans and cook for 2 minutes. Add the remaining half of the beans and 2 cups water. Stir in the spinach and cook until wilted, 1 to 2 minutes more. Serve hot.

MAKES 4 SERVINGS

Seaweed Cucumber Soup

For a hot-weather change of pace, consider Hira Lee's clear and invigorating Korean cold soup, rich in iron and vitamin C. Melting ice cubes provide the liquid, so you know it's going to be well chilled. Rice makes a nice counterpoint to the crunchy cucumbers and seaweed.

$^1/_3$ ounce *wakame* (Japanese seaweed)

2 cups water

2 medium pickling cucumbers, cut into thin strips

$^1/_2$ cup thin strips red bell pepper

1 tablespoon sliced scallions

1 tablespoon white vinegar

1 teaspoon soy sauce

2 teaspoons salt, or to taste

1 teaspoon sugar

4 or 5 ice cubes

1. Soak the *wakame* in cold water to cover until softened, 15 to 20 minutes.

2. Meanwhile, bring the water to a boil in a large saucepan. Add the softened *wakame*, reduce the heat to medium, and cook until tender, about 2 minutes. Remove from the water and, when cool enough to handle, slice into $^1/_2$-inch-wide strips.

3. Combine the cucumbers, pepper, scallions, vinegar, soy sauce, salt, sugar, and ice cubes in a large bowl. Stir in the *wakame* and serve.

MAKES 2 SERVINGS

Korean Summer Soy Soup

Let hot and humid weather do its worst, for this delicate, nutritious soup makes light of summer eating. The texture of the cooked beans is important, says the cook who provided this recipe, Hira Lee, because if the beans are overcooked, they will not have the desired rich flavor. The beans must still be firm to retain their fresh bean flavor.

1 cup dried soybeans, rinsed, picked
   clean, and soaked in cold water to
   cover for 6 to 12 hours

8 cups water

Salt to taste

1 egg, separated

1 tablespoon vegetable oil

$^1/_4$ pound somen, cooked
   (see page 303)

1 pickling cucumber, cut into
   thin strips

1. Combine the soybeans, 4 cups of the water, and salt in a saucepan and bring to a boil. Reduce the heat to medium and cook until just tender, 30 to 45 minutes. (Test the beans to make sure they are not overcooking; they must be tender but not mushy.) Drain. When cool enough to handle, rub the beans between your hands or fingers to detach the skins. Discard the skins.

2. Combine the beans and the remaining water in a blender or food processor, in batches if necessary, and blend until very smooth.

3. Beat the egg yolk and white separately. Heat the oil in a small skillet and cook the yolk and the white separately to make a thin omelet. When cool enough to handle, slice into very thin strips.

4. Put a portion of noodles in each bowl and ladle the bean soup over the noodles. Garnish with the thinly sliced egg white and yolk and the cucumber slices. Chill at least 1 hour before serving.

MAKES 2 TO 3 SERVINGS

Korean Tofu Stew

In olden days, Korean cooks made their tofu by hand. The task was time-consuming but, says Korean cook Bong S. Lee, the product was totally different from today's commercial tofu, and the soybean flavor was distinct and pronounced. Luckily, there is enough of a market today for the classic product so that freshly made tofu is still produced and sold in many Korean villages.

Ms. Lee explains you can make your own chili soybean paste with cooked and mashed soybeans, Korean red pepper powder, salt, and crushed, raw, sweet short-grain rice. Alternatively, you may buy a commercial hot soybean paste, known as kochujang. *You can turn this stew into something very different by adding* kimchi *and extra sliced beef to the basic recipe—the cook emphasizes that there is no ironclad recipe for making Korean tofu stew. This dish needs no other accompaniment than rice.*

1 tablespoon toasted sesame oil

1 thin slice boneless beef or pork (optional)

2 cloves garlic, peeled, smashed, and minced

Freshly ground black pepper to taste

3 cups water, or more if desired

2 tablespoons Korean hot soybean paste (*kochujang*) or 1 tablespoon red miso

$^1/_2$ pound firm tofu, cut into 1-inch cubes

Salt to taste

Heat the sesame oil in a saucepan over medium heat. Add the meat if using, garlic, and pepper, and cook, stirring, until the meat is browned, about 5 minutes. Add 2 cups of the water and the *kochujang* or miso and stir until the paste is dissolved. Reduce the heat to low and cook until heated through, about 5 minutes more. Stir in the tofu, remaining 1 cup water, and salt. (Add more water for a thinner stew, if desired.) Bring to a boil and cook for 5 minutes more.

MAKES 2 SERVINGS

Green Curry with Tofu

Gaeng Keow Wan Jae

According to Nick Srisawat, owner of the Tara Thai restaurants in the Washington, D.C., metropolitan area, the words keow *and* wan *mean "green" and "sweet," respectively. The green chilies in the curry paste add a pleasantly mild bite offset by the blandness of the tofu and the creaminess of the coconut milk. Serve this temperate curry with rice and hot tea for lunch or dinner.*

$^1/_2$ cup Thai Green Curry Paste
   (page 25)

3 cups coconut milk

1 pound Fried Tofu (page 18)

1 cup bamboo shoots

8 golf-ball-sized Thai eggplants,
   quartered

$^1/_4$ cup fish sauce

3 tablespoons palm sugar or dark
   brown sugar

$^1/_2$ cup Thai basil leaves

1 tablespoon thinly sliced red chilies

Cook the curry paste in a large wok or saucepan over medium heat until fragrant, about 5 minutes. Add the coconut milk and stir well. Add the tofu, bamboo shoots, and eggplants, and cook, stirring occasionally, until the eggplants are tender, 5 to 7 minutes. Stir in the fish sauce, sugar, and basil. Garnish with the chilies before serving.

MAKES 4 SERVINGS

Korean Fried Tofu

Because this tofu dish from Bong S. Lee is so easy to prepare, and so packed with flavor, you may wish to serve it often as a nutritious centerpiece to a meal of steamed or stir-fried vegetables and rice. For non-vegetarians, it is the appropriate accompaniment to Imperial Korean Chicken Stew (page 88).

$^1/_2$ **pound firm tofu, cut into**
 $^1/_4$-inch-thick slices
$^1/_4$ **cup vegetable oil**
Korean Hot Pepper Seasoning Paste
 (page 35) to taste
3 tablespoons water or soy sauce

1. Press the tofu between layers of paper towels. Change the towels and repeat the process until most of the excess water has been removed.

2. Heat the oil in a large wok or skillet over medium heat. Add the tofu slices and cook, turning often, until golden, about 2 minutes per side.

3. Spread the seasoning paste on top of each piece of tofu. Add the water or soy sauce and cook for 3 minutes. Reduce the heat to low and cook until the liquid is evaporated, about 10 minutes. Remove the tofu from the heat and carefully layer it on a serving platter.

MAKES 2 TO 4 SERVINGS

Stewed Bean Curd in Hot Pot

Because of the nutritional and gastronomic attributes of bean curd (tofu), many vegetarians—and non-vegetarians, for that matter—think of it as an ideal food. For this stew, Chef C.K. Chan, of the Sheraton Hong Kong Hotel & Towers, comes up with a dish that captures the heart and soul of a simple Chinese meal with mushrooms, bamboo shoots, and Chinese rice wine. Vegetarians can substitute water for the beef or chicken stock.

1 tablespoon vegetable oil

1 pound firm tofu, cubed

12 mushrooms, rinsed and thinly sliced

6 dried Chinese mushrooms, soaked in
   hot water for 20 minutes and
   stems removed

One 5-ounce can bamboo shoots,
   rinsed and drained

$1/2$ carrot, peeled and thinly sliced

5 cups Basic Beef Stock (page 19) or
   Basic Chicken Stock (page 19)

1 tablespoon Chinese rice wine

1 teaspoon toasted sesame oil

Salt to taste

Pinch of MSG (optional)

Heat the vegetable oil in a large wok or skillet over medium-high heat. Add the tofu and stir-fry for 1 minute. Add the fresh mushrooms, dried mushrooms, bamboo shoots, and carrot, and stir-fry for 1 minute. Stir in the stock, reduce the heat to low, and cook until the vegetables are tender, about 5 minutes. Stir in the wine, sesame oil, salt, and MSG if using. Serve hot.

MAKES 4 SERVINGS

Filipino Mixed Vegetable Stew

Coconut milk both sweetens and enriches this vegetable stew, which is good served either hot or cold, says the cook who provided this recipe, Evelyn Manuel. Westerners may find the cook's recommended amount of shrimp paste—3 tablespoons—overpowering. I used only 1 teaspoon and found that ample. I also added more liquid than the recipe calls for, because I wanted a soupier dish. Serve this with rice and a meat entree, if desired.

2 cups coconut milk

2 tablespoons vegetable oil

$^1/_4$ cup minced onions

4 Oriental eggplants, cut into
   1-inch cubes

1 teaspoon Thai or Malaysian shrimp
   paste, roasted (see page 10)

1 teaspoon salt, or to taste

1 pound green beans, trimmed and cut
   into 2-inch lengths

$^1/_2$ pound okra, cut into
   bite-sized pieces

1 cup peeled and cubed
   butternut squash

1 cup shredded kale or spinach leaves

1 medium tomato, diced

1 teaspoon shredded fresh ginger

1. Pour the coconut milk into a large saucepan and cook over medium-low heat until slightly thickened, about 15 minutes.

2. Heat the oil in a large wok or skillet over medium heat. Add the onions and cook, stirring, until golden, 3 to 5 minutes. Stir in the coconut milk, eggplants, shrimp paste, and salt, and cook until the eggplant is softened, about 5 minutes. Stir in the beans, okra, and squash, and cook until tender, about 15 minutes. Stir in the kale or spinach, tomato, and ginger, and cook for 5 minutes more.

MAKES 4 TO 6 SERVINGS

Chinese Walnut Cream

Ho T'ao Lao

Part of the beauty of this Northern Chinese dessert soup comes from its ivory-cream color—hard to achieve unless you have the patience to skin the walnuts. If you don't, the skins tint the soup a pale brown. In China, walnuts are sold with their skins already removed, but skinned nuts are relatively scarce in the West.

This version of the soup, from cook Joyce Piotrowski, also calls for the popular Chinese dates, or jujubes, and you must carefully remove their seeds. I tried pushing the dates through a strainer, but this was unsuccessful, so I ended up just removing the seeds by hand.

You may make this bland, yet nutty, soup two days before serving. Store it in the refrigerator and heat before serving.

1 cup Chinese dates, soaked in hot water for 20 minutes and pitted

1/2 cup walnuts, skinned (see Note)

1/4 cup sugar, or more to taste

3 1/2 cups water

1 tablespoon rice flour mixed with 1/4 cup water

1. Combine the dates in a saucepan with water to cover and bring to a boil. Cook for 5 minutes, drain, and let cool. Push the dates through a strainer to remove the seeds or remove the seeds by hand.

2. Combine the dates and walnuts in a blender and process until very smooth. Transfer to a large saucepan and stir in the sugar and the 3 1/2 cups water.

3. Set over medium heat and bring to a simmer, stirring constantly. Stir in the rice flour paste. Cook until the mixture has the consistency of a thick cream soup, about 5 minutes. Serve hot.

MAKES 2 TO 4 SERVINGS

Note: The cook says that skinning the nuts is easier after they have been blanched in boiling water for 2 minutes, but expect this to still be a long process. Use a utensil with a sharp tip, and it might help to start peeling at the point at which the shells split in two.

Chinese Cold Fruit Soup

This delicate liquid with its almond accent may be served as a light dessert; however, the Chinese often serve it as a palate cleanser after a particularly hot or salty dish. Then it is especially refreshing, says the cook who provided this recipe, Joyce Piotrowski.

One 20-ounce can lychees, drained

One 20-ounce can longans, drained

2 cups water

$^1/_2$ cup sugar

$^1/_4$ teaspoon almond extract

Stir together the lychees, longans, water, sugar, and almond extract in a bowl. Chill for at least 1 hour before serving.

MAKES 4 SERVINGS

Nepalese Egg Curry

My Peace Corps friend Pat Bonifer-Tiedt gave me this recipe, which she got from a friend in Nepal—and it's a favorite. You get wholesome, easy-to-eat eggs bathed in a gingery, coconut milk–based curry—the combination is outstanding. Don't think this is bland—the chilies, onions, and garlic are a power-packed trio.

For speedier preparation, make the curry sauce several days before serving and add the hard-boiled eggs in the final heat-up. The original recipe called for slicing the eggs in half lengthwise, but the cooked yolks crumble into the sauce and are messy, so I have left the eggs whole. It also called for 1 cup milk and 2 cups coconut milk, but I prefer using only coconut milk.

¹/₄ cup Ghee (page 17) or butter

2 large onions, peeled and chopped

4 cloves garlic, peeled and minced

2 to 3 green chilies, chopped

One 2-inch piece fresh ginger, minced

1 tablespoon all-purpose flour

1 teaspoon ground turmeric

3 cups coconut milk

Salt to taste

Juice of 2 lemons

1 tablespoon white vinegar

12 hard-boiled eggs, shelled

1. Heat the butter or ghee in a skillet over medium heat. Add the onions and garlic, and cook, stirring, 15 to 20 minutes or until golden. Remove from the skillet and set aside. Add the chilies and ginger to the skillet and cook, stirring, until the chilies are bright green, 1 to 3 minutes. Stir in the flour and turmeric, and cook for a few seconds. Stir in 2 cups of the coconut milk. Reduce the heat to medium-low and cook, stirring often, until reduced by half, about 20 minutes.

2. Stir in the remaining 1 cup coconut milk, the salt, and the reserved onions and garlic. Add the lemon juice, vinegar, and eggs. Cook until heated through, about 10 minutes.

MAKES 4 TO 6 SERVINGS

Vegetable Kurma

From Devagi Shanmugam, of the Thompson Cooking School in Singapore, this lusty vegetable stew shows off the fare typical of the Indian community in this Asian city-state. If you ever find yourself in Singapore with time on your hands, by all means take a walking tour of Little India, a series of stores, restaurants, spice markets, chili grinders, and jewelers, all in the radius of a few blocks. But if Little India is not on your itinerary, at least enjoy this vegetable dish and dream of faraway places.

Seasoning Paste

3 green chilies

6 cloves garlic, peeled

One 2-inch piece fresh ginger

About $1/2$ cup water

Curry

1 cup whole green mung beans (*moong dal*), rinsed, picked clean, and soaked in cold water to cover for 6 to 12 hour

6 cups water

3 tablespoons Malaysian Meat or Chicken Curry Powder (page 31)

Salt to taste

$3/4$ pound cauliflower florets

$1/2$ pound green cabbage, shredded

$1/2$ pound green beans, trimmed and cut into $1^1/2$-inch lengths

3 medium potatoes, peeled and diced

4 carrots, peeled and cubed

1 cup peas

2 tablespoons Ghee (page 17) or vegetable oil

1 large onion, peeled and sliced

5 green cardamom pods, crushed

Two 2-inch pieces cinnamon stick

2 sprigs curry leaves

5 whole cloves

1 cup coconut milk

1. To make the seasoning paste, combine the chilies, garlic, and ginger in a blender. Add just enough water to process, and blend until smooth.

2. To make the curry, combine the seasoning paste, mung beans, and water in a large saucepan. Set over low heat, cover, and cook until the beans are very soft, 45 minutes to 1 hour. Stir in the curry powder, salt, cauliflower, cabbage, green beans, potatoes, carrots, and peas, and cook until the vegetables are tender, 15 to 20 minutes.

3. Heat the ghee or oil in a large skillet over medium heat. Add the onion, cardamom, cinnamon, curry leaves, and cloves, and cook, stirring, until fragrant, about 5 minutes. Transfer to the simmering vegetables. Stir in the coconut milk and cook for 3 minutes before serving.

MAKES 4 TO 6 SERVINGS

Malaysian Vegetable and Coconut Milk Curry

Sayur Lodeh

Over a lunch at Fatima's—a restaurant that is legendary in Singapore, and where Fatima herself had done all the cooking for years—Singaporean Geraldene Lowe and I ate a wonderful meal of fried chicken with turmeric, wet chicken rendang, fried potato pancakes, achar (a cucumber pickle), mutton rendang, and sayur lodeh, a very typical Malaysian vegetable dish. (Incidentally, Fatima's always did a wonderful take-away business. The containers? Banana leaves.) Fatima herself sat down and talked about local cooking—and reeled off the recipe for this very traditional dish.

During our conversation, she gave me a few tips: You can make this dish soupier simply by adding more water; if you want a splash of color, add julienned carrots and sliced fresh red chilies; and serve the dish warm, or the ingredients will look "oily." With this meal we drank pitchers of iced tea, but chilled beer would go just as well.

Curry Paste

2 small onions, peeled and diced

2 stalks lemon grass, trimmed and
   thinly sliced

One 2-inch piece galangal

About ¹/₂ cup coconut milk

Soup

¹/₄ cup vegetable oil

2 teaspoons ground turmeric

1 heaping teaspoon dried
   shrimp, crushed

1 teaspoon Malaysian or Thai
   shrimp paste

3¹/₂ cups coconut milk

1 head Chinese cabbage, cored
   and shredded

1 small head cauliflower, broken
   into florets

1 pound long beans, trimmed and cut
   into 2-inch lengths

1¹/₂ pounds Fried Tofu (page 18)

Salt to taste

1. To make the curry paste, put the onions, lemon grass, and galangal in a blender. Add just enough coconut milk to process, and blend until smooth.

2. To make the soup, heat the oil in a large saucepan over medium heat. Add the curry paste and cook, stirring occasionally, until fragrant, about 5 minutes. Add the turmeric, dried shrimp, shrimp paste, coconut milk, cabbage, cauliflower, and beans, and bring to a boil. Reduce the heat to medium-low and cook until the vegetables are tender, about 15 minutes. Stir in the tofu and season with salt. Serve hot or cold.

MAKES 4 TO 6 SERVINGS

Malaysian Sweet Curry Pineapple

Pajri Nenas

If for nothing else, I wished I lived in Malaysia for its sweet tropical fruits. This recipe calls for the large, sweet pineapples from Sarawak, a state in Malaysia—a fruit few Westerners will be able to find easily. But fully ripe Hawaiian or other Western pineapples—and these must be the sweetest that you can find— are acceptable substitutes. This is a knockout dish, matching pineapple and coconut with the dusky flavors of curry seasonings. The recipe comes from the files of the Parkroyal Hotel, in Kuala Lumpur, Malaysia, where the chefs can definitely get their hands on Sarawak pineapples.

Curry Paste

$1/2$ cup shrimp powder

2 large shallots, peeled and chopped

8 cloves garlic, peeled

One 2-inch piece fresh ginger, sliced

About $1/2$ cup coconut milk

Curry

$1/4$ cup vegetable oil

2 tablespoons Malaysian Meat or
    Chicken Curry Powder (page 31)

$3^1/2$ cups coconut milk

2 large pineapples, peeled, sliced in
    half lengthwise, cored, and cut into
    1-inch-thick semicircles

1 cup shredded unsweetened coconut,
    toasted until golden

Salt and freshly ground black pepper
    to taste

Sugar to taste

1. To make the curry paste, combine the shrimp powder, shallots, garlic, and ginger in a blender. Add just enough coconut milk to process, and blend until smooth.

2. To make the curry, heat the oil in a large saucepan. Add the curry paste and cook, stirring, until fragrant, about 5 minutes. Stir in the curry powder, coconut milk, pineapple, coconut, salt, pepper, and sugar. Reduce the heat to medium-low and cook, stirring often, until the sauce thickens, 15 to 20 minutes. Serve hot.

MAKES 4 SERVINGS

Essay 5:

On Asia's Rim—
Korea, Japan, Taiwan, and
the Philippines

Steppingstones to mainland Asia, the countries of Korea, Japan, Taiwan, and the Philippines spread out from the chilly northernmost Sea of Japan down to the temperate South China Sea. Although they share a place on Asia's rim, they have little else in common, particularly in terms of their foods. For example, Koreans liberally douse their dishes with chilies, but their Japanese neighbors rarely do. The Filipinos love their Asian rice and soy sauce, but their main-course soups and stews taste Iberian. And Taiwan, Chinese to its roots, has contrived its own regional Chinese fare.

Korea

I had always found Korea, the Land of the Morning Sun, remote and unknowable until Hira Lee, a Korean woman living in Virginia, described her homeland. It's an Asian country with a Western attitude, she says, much like Los Angeles. Yet Korean cooking still seemed so unfamiliar.

I listened recently to my Bahá'í friend Vicki Sadrazadeh remembering Korea as her Asian home for many years. As she talked of the fruit and vegetable sellers at their stalls and the street vendors who began peddling their strawberries or pears at daybreak, she brought alive the Asian images of beautiful foods—grilled, baked, broiled, or fresh—offered for sale on street corners, down alleyways, and in colorful marketplaces. Then Korea and its foods began to take shape for me, and Hira Lee's words made sense: "Cooking is the basis of our tradition."

As almost everywhere in Asia, Korean meals center on rice, but there the similarities end. Seafood, chilies, beef, poultry, leafy and root vegetables, barley, and assorted seaweed make this cuisine a candidate for the contemporary Western diet. Indeed, Koreans prefer nibbling to devouring large quantities of food, sampling several exquisite and dainty offerings composed of beautifully cooked and arranged ingredients. These must be fresh, and the traditional cook will take great care to start a meal from scratch rather than to use processed foods.

Soup, served hot in winter and chilled in summer, and its companion, the Korean stew, find their regular place at the table. And no meal would be complete without *kimchi*, Korea's traditional fermented preserved cabbage, often heavily laced with hot chilies.

Because of their importance to the Korean diet, soups even have their own nomenclature. For example, hot soups may be thin and clear with vegetables and meat or fish (*kuk*), or they may be bracing and concentrated, with meat as the major ingredient (*tang*). To emphasize the complexities of characterizing Korean soups, Hira Lee adds, no one knows for sure what makes one soup a *kuk* or another a *tang*.

As for groups of stews, these have few Western counterparts, since the *chiggye* class is based on chili pastes or mild or hot soybean pastes, while the *jon-kol* stews, more like an American concoction, are often special-occasion dishes featuring everything from beef liver to cow intestines and requiring more elaborate preparations.

As my Korean sources noted, theirs is a beautiful and wholesome cuisine, with a proud heritage and noble history.

Japan

Delicate, ceremonial, picturesque, and seaweed-filled is one way of looking at Japanese food. But a few words by American journalist Mary Lord about eating in Tokyo paints another picture. "Slurp," she said. That was about the first sound she heard in that noodle-soup-mad city. And not just any noodles at that, but the Japanese version of the Chinese ramen. Dubbed (surely by foreigners) as "stamina ramen," this ubiquitous noodle soup bubbles and steams its way into every Japanese and foreign heart.

In fact, in Tokyo's frigid winter tableau, the only way to keep warm is to steam in a public bath or to slurp down a bowl of bubbling ramen soup, Lord says. "You put your face to the bowl—it's like a facial . . . the soup is really, truly scalding . . . . You bathe in this brothy, frothy steam and slurp." Fortunately for the chilled Tokyo-ites, ramen joints are on almost every corner.

Lord also describes how soup eating is an aesthetic experience, not just a nourishing one: "Soups for Japanese are like wine for the Western oenologist. The soup sits on the tongue; it has flavor that gets in the nose. They don't just down the soup and get on with the next course." Japanese have thousands of soups, all designed for some sort of eye appeal, a seasonal surprise, or a slightly different flavor, she says, and then praises the breakfast soup of hot miso and the raw egg on rice sprinkled with seaweed: "It is filling, salty, and jolts you awake."

And the Japanese please themselves with their hot dishes, which may be soup or stew, such as *oden, yosenabe,* shabu-shabu, and any one of the many *nabes* (one-pot stews). "*Nabe* dishes are like country stews," Lord says, but are popular even in the most upscale parts of town.

Los Angeles–based Japanese food expert Kinbo Mizutani explains the origin of the *nabes*: In the olden days, the Japanese house had one central fireplace, a square open pit, in the middle of the room. People sat around the fireplace—a source of heat for warmth and for cooking—and the cookpot was hung from the ceiling. Lacking burners or ovens, the cook had only one alternative: one-pot cooking.

Fortunately, Japanese cooks carried on with these dishes to develop an array of delicious one-pot meals. Take *oden* (a fish stew with plenty of vegetables), for example, sold at stands even in the flashy nightclub section of Tokyo. "Little old guys with pushscarts are selling this with fish cakes," says Lord, "cooked in this dashi broth. . . It's wonderful, hot, mushy. Each taste, each texture is different."

Taiwan

When Asian hands talk about favorite food haunts in Taipei, Taiwan's capital city, they become nostalgic and emotional. As for Taiwan's importance as a food mecca, one has only to watch the Taiwanese movie *Eat, Drink, Man, Woman*, which, among other things, celebrates the beauties of the local cuisine.

Opening shots depict the main character, a talented chef, preparing a sumptuous multicourse Sunday dinner for his family. But other shots of beautifully sliced, carved, stuffed, wrapped, fried, steamed, and basted foods punctuate the entire film. I watched this movie with my friend and professional chef Joyce Piotrowski. A student of Taiwan's leading food lady, Pei Mei, in Taipei, she had prepared practically every dish shown on screen and knew just what the chef was doing. As

we left the movie, we decided that such food is the stuff of gastronomic dreams.

The Philippines

It's been years since I sat in a Filipino taxi driving back to Manila from the International Rice Research Institute out in the countryside and enjoying a large wedge of *buko* pie. Made from the youngest and tenderest coconut meat, *buko* pies are rich, flanlike, and calorie-dense treats. And for me, they characterize the pleasures of the Filipino table. After all, what a delight to spoon into dishes that blend Asia and Spain in each mouthful!

But years have passed, and finding sources for good Filipino food outside of Asia is not always easy, unless you have a friend. I am lucky, for Shirley Janairo Roth, a longtime friend, lives nearby. And as a professional cook, she always has food on her mind. When she dabbles with her native dishes, I may end up with her leftovers. Just the other day, she gave me some dumplings and several dozen *lumpia* (Filipino spring rolls), a bowl of her *Mongo Guisado* Soup (page 239), and the remains of a vinegary Chicken Adobo (page 93).

She's just as generous with her knowledge as with her food: Now I know for sure that soy sauce, vinegar, tomatoes, garlic, and onions are the foundations for her endless soups and stews—integral parts of a Filipino meal. I also know that the *buko* pie is just one of a thousand different sweets—often made with coconut milk, sweet potatoes, and rice flour—that conclude a typical Filipino dinner.

Luckier than most, I also live near a Filipino market with carry-out service featuring traditional dishes. Owned and operated by Evelyn Manuel, the market is a great source for ethnic foods such as the *dinugan* (a dish with beef tripe, hog maws, pig ears, and beef blood); chicken curry; *sarsiado*; and the most popular of all, the *menudo*, a pork stew with potatoes and red and green bell peppers (page 153). If things go really well, maybe she will have fixed *ginataang halo-halo* (page 279), the popular dessert soup of coconut milk studded with chunks of banana, jackfruit, red yam, and rice balls (*bilo-bilo*) made from sticky rice flour.

Westerners who seek culinary glamour may find Filipino food too bland. But it is a cuisine that plays it straight, calling for many ingredients that are familiar to the Western palate.

Asian Feasts

For anyone who will cast aside gustatory fears and plunge right into the thick of kitchen things, Asian eating is spectacular. So if you are a Westerner ready to tie on your apron and cook Asian, this chapter holds a medley of wonderful dishes that require a little extra time and patience, along with an interest in exploring further the world of Asian foods.

Sri Lanka

Lampries: A Sri Lankan Feast

The Dutch used to govern Ceylon (now Sri Lanka). And, as the generations have passed, this meal—a *lampries*, or "full meal for a festive occasion"—has evolved into the Dutch interpretation of a Celanese curry dinner.

Traditionally, it consists of several different curries and a special rice moistened with coconut milk and wrapped around hard-boiled eggs. Then one curry, rice, eggs, and condiments are tucked neatly into a banana leaf wrapper, in which, during cooking, their flavors intermingle. When these steamy, savory packets are opened at the table, a heady drift of aromas escapes, luring the hungry to scoop out mouthfuls of this fragrant mixture and indulge. The meal is traditionally—and best—eaten with fingers and served with extra rice, a side dish of another kind of curry, and a cucumber *sambal*.

But surely the Dutch conceived *lampries* when each family had household help, for making this meal takes time. Two of us spent about five hours cooking and assembling it, but as we ate, we decided it had been time very well spent. The recipes for this particular meal serve six, but each recipe can be extended to accommodate a larger crowd; just be sure to have enough banana leaf on hand for wrapping. In fact, since this is so labor-intensive, it would make sense to double or triple the quantities and freeze the extras for another time. This was the advice of the Sri Lankan woman who gave me these recipes, and who wishes to remain anonymous. And she had household help!

Deep-Fried Hard-Boiled Eggs

¹/₄ cup salt
¹/₄ cup ground turmeric
3 hard-boiled eggs, shelled
3 cups vegetable oil

1. Combine the salt and turmeric in a small bowl. Dip in each egg and roll to coat well. Prick all over with a fork to prevent the egg from bursting open when deep-fried. Set aside.

2. Heat the oil in a deep saucepan over medium heat. Add the eggs and cook until browned and crisp, about 10 minutes

3. Transfer the eggs to paper towels to drain. Set aside.

MAKES 6 SERVINGS

Lampries Curry

This hearty mixture contains four different meats; however, the Muslims of Sri Lanka, who do not eat pork, would substitute mutton (or lamb) and beef for the pork and increase the amounts to compensate. My friend and I tested this recipe using just beef and the meat from a whole chicken—breast meat alone might become too dry.

The cook who gave me this recipe reminded me that in Sri Lanka, mutton means goat. She also suggested grinding the seasonings just before use—for example, using whole coriander seeds and roasting them before grinding. Incidentally, Sri Lankans use the same kind of red chili powder that Indian cooks do.

1 pound cubed chicken (white and
    dark meat)

1/4 pound cubed mutton

1/4 pound cubed pork loin

1/4 pound cubed top round

Salt to taste

5 green cardamom pods, seeded,
    pods discarded

4 cups water

1/4 cup shrimp powder

2 to 4 tablespoons Roasted Red Chili
    Powder (page 16), or more to taste

4 cloves garlic, peeled and minced

2 thin slices fresh ginger

1/4 teaspoon ground coriander

1/4 teaspoon black cumin seeds

1/4 teaspoon fennel seeds

1/4 teaspoon fenugreek seeds

1/4 teaspoon ground turmeric

3 tablespoons vegetable oil

10 shallots, peeled and diced

1 1/2 cups coconut milk, or more
    if needed

5 curry leaves

1. Place the chicken, mutton, pork, and beef in a large stockpot and add the salt, cardamom, and the water. Bring to a boil, reduce the heat to low, and cook for 30 minutes. Remove the meat and set aside until cool enough to handle. Reserve the stock for cooking the *lampries* rice (page 260).

2. Finely dice the meat and transfer to a large bowl. Stir in the shrimp powder, chili powder, garlic, ginger, coriander, cumin, fennel, fenugreek, and turmeric until well combined.

3. Heat the oil in a large wok or skillet over medium heat. Add the shallots and cook, stirring, until golden, about 5 minutes. Add the meat and cook, stirring often, for 5 minutes. Add the coconut milk and curry leaves, reduce the heat to medium-low, and cook until thickened, about 10 minutes. (Add more coconut milk if the mixture seems dry.) Set aside.

MAKES 6 SERVINGS

Lamprïes Rice

If you wish, you may cook the rice in an electric rice cooker after the first step.

¼ cup Ghee (page 17) or vegetable oil

½ cup diced shallots

5 green cardamom pods, seeded, pods discarded

One 2-inch piece lemon grass, trimmed and pounded

10 curry leaves

10 black peppercorns

2 teaspoons salt

2 cups long-grain white rice

4 cups liquid, including meat stock reserved from the *lampries* curry above

1. Heat the ghee or oil in a large saucepan over medium heat. Add the shallots and cook, stirring, about 5 minutes, or until golden. Add the cardamom, lemon grass, curry leaves, peppercorns, salt, and rice, and cook, stirring, until the rice is translucent, about 5 minutes more.

2. Stir in the stock and bring to a boil. Reduce the heat to low, cover, and cook until the rice is tender, 15 to 20 minutes. Set aside.

MAKES 6 SERVINGS

Frikkadels

From the Dutch term for "forced meatballs," frikkadels *are an essential part of this multiflavored curry meal. The cook who provided this recipe explains that in Sri Lanka the meat is minced by hand.*

Meatballs

1 pound lean beef, minced or ground
One thick slice white bread, crumbled
One 1-inch-thick slice fresh ginger, minced
1 tablespoon chopped red onions
2 cloves garlic, peeled and chopped
2 teaspoons Worcestershire sauce
1 teaspoon chopped fresh fennel bulb or 1 teaspoon fennel seeds, roasted (see page 11)
1 teaspoon black peppercorns
Pinch of ground cinnamon
Pinch of ground cloves
Salt to taste
1 large egg, lightly beaten
Juice of ¹/₂ lime

Coating

2 large eggs, well beaten
¹/₂ cup dry unseasoned breadcrumbs
¹/₂ cup Ghee (page 17) or vegetable oil, or more if needed

1. To make the meatballs, place the beef in a large bowl. Stir in the bread, ginger, onions, garlic, Worcestershire sauce, fennel, peppercorns, cinnamon, cloves, salt, beaten egg, and lime juice, and mix well. Shape the mixture into balls the size of a marble. (You should have about 60 meatballs.)

2. To make the coating, put the eggs in one bowl and the breadcrumbs in another.

3. Heat the ghee or oil in a large skillet over medium heat. Meanwhile, dip one-third of the meatballs into the eggs, then roll them in the breadcrumbs. Add the meatballs and cook until browned, 7 to 10 minutes. During cooking, shake the pan or stir the meatballs to brown evenly. Repeat this procedure with the remaining meatballs. Set aside.

MAKES ABOUT 60 MEATBALLS; 6 SERVINGS

Eggplant Pahi

Pahi is a mixture that is a cross between a pickle and a dry curry. This particular version is searingly hot, but oh, so good. Traditionally, Sri Lankans use an ingredient called maldifish, *which is known by several other names depending on where in Asia you happen to live. This predatory fish from Indian waters is also commonly known as "Bombay Duck," although it bears no resemblance to a duck. A very perishable fish, it is usually eaten dried and served as an accompaniment to curries. It is virtually impossible to find in the West, so use shrimp powder instead.*

4 medium Oriental eggplants

1 teaspoon crumbled saffron threads

Salt to taste

$^{1}/_{4}$ cup vegetable oil, or more if needed

1 tablespoon coriander seeds, roasted and ground (see page 11)

$1^{1}/_{2}$ teaspoons cumin seeds, roasted and ground (see page 11)

$^{1}/_{4}$ teaspoon fennel seeds, roasted and ground (see page 11)

$^{1}/_{2}$ cup white vinegar

$^{1}/_{2}$ cup tamarind juice

20 dried red chilies, seeded, roasted, and ground (see page 7)

3 green chilies, sliced

10 curry leaves

$^{1}/_{2}$ stalk lemon grass, trimmed and thinly sliced

4 cloves garlic, peeled and chopped

One 2-inch piece cinnamon stick

One 2-inch piece *pandan* leaf

1 tablespoon chopped red onions

1 tablespoon shrimp powder

1 tablespoon mustard seeds, roasted and ground (see page 11)

$^{1}/_{2}$ cup thick coconut milk (see page 6)

1 teaspoon sugar

1. Remove the stem end and slice the eggplants into long, thin strips that resemble thick French fries. (Do not remove the skin.) Combine the saffron and salt, and rub into the eggplant strips.

2. Heat the oil in a skillet over medium heat. Add the eggplant and cook, stirring occasionally, 7 to 10 minutes, or until golden. Remove from the heat.

3. Combine the coriander, cumin, fennel, vinegar, and tamarind juice in a large bowl. Stir in the ground chilies, chilies, curry leaves, lemon grass, garlic, cinnamon, *pandan* leaf, onions, shrimp powder, and mustard seeds. Add the eggplant and stir to mix well.

4. Combine the eggplant mixture and coconut milk in a large saucepan over medium heat and bring to a boil. Reduce the heat to medium-low and cook, stirring occasionally, for 15 minutes. Stir in the sugar and remove from the heat. Set aside.

MAKES 6 SERVINGS

Deviled Potatoes

2 medium potatoes, boiled until tender,
    peeled, and cubed
$^1/_4$ teaspoon fresh lime juice
Pinch of freshly ground black pepper
Pinch of saffron
$^1/_4$ cup vegetable oil, preferably
    corn oil
1 large red onion, peeled and sliced
$^1/_2$ teaspoon Roasted Red Chili
    Powder (page 16)
$^1/_2$ teaspoon salt

1. Stir together the potatoes, lime juice, pepper, and saffron.

2. Heat the oil in a large saucepan over medium heat. Add the onion and cook, stirring, 7 to 10 minutes, or until golden. Stir in the chili powder and salt. Add the potatoes and toss to gently mix. Cook for 3 minutes more. Remove from the heat and set aside.

MAKES 6 SERVINGS

Chili Sambal

Resembling a hot relish or condiment, this sambal *stores well in a tightly sealed container in the refrigerator. You may use any type of onion, including shallots, but the large red onion gives a good flavor. This* sambal *is both hot and sour. For a sweeter taste, add more sugar.*

2 tablespoons Ghee (page 17) or
    vegetable oil
2 large red onions, thinly sliced
3 cloves garlic, peeled and chopped
1 cup shrimp powder
$1^1/_2$ tablespoons Roasted Red
    Chili Powder (page 16)
Two 1-inch pieces cinnamon stick
Two 1-inch pieces *pandan* leaf
2 green cardamom pods
2 whole cloves
One $^1/_4$-inch-thick slice fresh ginger
$^1/_4$ cup tamarind juice
2 teaspoons fresh lime juice
1 teaspoon sugar
1 cup coconut milk

Heat the ghee or oil in a large wok or saucepan over medium heat. Stir in the onions, garlic, shrimp powder, chili powder, cinnamon, *pandan* leaf, cardamom, cloves, ginger, tamarind juice, lime juice, sugar, and coconut milk. Reduce the heat to low and cook until thickened, about 30 minutes. Set aside to cool.

MAKES 6 SERVINGS

Lampries Banana Leaf Packets

To assemble the packets, have ready, in addition to the recipes listed above:

6 tablespoons thick coconut milk
(see page 6)

6 pieces banana leaf, warmed (see
Note) and cut into 15 × 18–inch
pieces, trimmings reserved

1. Preheat the oven to 350°F. Slice each deep-fried egg in half lengthwise. Place each half, yolk side down, in each of six 4-ounce custard cups. Press the rice into each cup around the egg and top with a layer of rice. Spoon 1 tablespoon of the thick coconut milk over each and set the cups aside.

2. Working with 1 banana leaf at a time, lay the leaf on a flat surface. If the leaf is fragile, reinforce the section that covers the rice by placing a second and smaller portion of leaf on top. (This will prevent the rice from spilling out if the leaf tears.) Unmold a cup of rice into the center of each leaf.

3. For each packet, arrange in separate mounds in the following order, clockwise around the rice, about $1/2$ cup *lampries* curry, about 10 *frikkadels*, $1/2$ cup eggplant, a small scoop of deviled potatoes, and a small scoop of chili *sambal*.

4. For each packet, fold the two long sides of the leaf over the filling—if the leaf will not close, just cut off more banana leaf and use it to cover any openings. Close, or "stitch," the two open ends of the packet with toothpicks. Repeat the procedure for the remaining packets. You will probably have leftovers of some components of the meal; if so, make up extra packets with whatever is left over or serve the leftovers as is. (You can freeze the packets at this point for up to 3 months. Just thaw and reheat them before use.)

5. Arrange the packets on a wire rack in a baking pan. Fill the pan with water to 1 inch below the rack. Cover with a lid or a tent of aluminum foil and bake until steaming and heated through, about 30 minutes. Alternatively, steam the packets over boiling water for 30 minutes, replenishing the water as needed. Serve with the cucumber *sambal* alongside.

MAKES 6 SERVINGS

Note: In Asia, banana leaves—large, pliable, and aromatic leaves of the banana plant—are often used instead of foil to wrap foods prior to cooking. To the inexperienced, wrapping food in banana leaves can be tricky, especially since many types of packets require complex folds. Also, the banana leaves available in this country are usually frozen and even after thawing and warming remain brittle and tear or shred easily. I have been told that frozen leaves from the Philippines are the easiest to use.

To prepare banana leaves for wrapping, use scissors to cut away the spine and trim the leaves into usable sections. Wipe off any white spots and rinse the leaves in warm water. To soften, hold them over a lit gas burner for a few seconds or brush them across the top of heated electric burner coils. Or you can dip them quickly into a pot of very hot water or roast them briefly in a very hot oven until soft.

One cook suggests wrapping the banana leaf packets with parchment to ensure the contents are double-wrapped and cannot readily leak. You can also wrap the leaves with aluminum foil to prevent leaking, or use foil in place of the banana leaves altogether, but you will lose the subtle flavor the banana leaves impart as they cook. Banana leaves packed in sealed plastic bags keep indefinitely in the freezer.

Cucumber Sambal

1 cucumber, peeled and coarsely grated
1 teaspoon salt
8 shallots, peeled and thinly sliced
2 large green chilies, thinly sliced
1 tablespoon shrimp powder
$^1/_4$ cup thick coconut milk
   (see page 6)
Fresh lime juice to taste
Salt to taste

1. Sprinkle the cucumber with salt and set aside in a colander to drain for 10 minutes. Squeeze the cucumber well and pour off the excess water. (Do not rinse off the salt.)

2. Stir in the shallots, chilies, shrimp powder, and coconut milk until well blended. Season with lime juice and salt. Set aside.

MAKES 6 SERVINGS

Sri Lankan Coconut Custard

Wattalappan

The Sri Lankan cook who provided this recipe says this rich dessert makes the perfect finale to a lampries *meal. But don't wait to enjoy it until you construct a* lampries, *or any other curry dinner. Serve this anytime you want something stunning and elegant. Add more jaggery if you want a sweeter dessert.*

2 cups thick coconut milk
   (see page 6)
1 cup crushed jaggery or dark
   brown sugar
6 large eggs
$^1/_4$ teaspoon ground nutmeg
$^1/_4$ teaspoon ground cinnamon
$^1/_4$ teaspoon ground cardamom
Salt to taste

1. Combine the coconut milk and jaggery or brown sugar in a large saucepan over medium heat and bring just to a boil. Beat the eggs in a medium bowl, beat in $^1/_4$ cup of the hot coconut milk, and slowly press the eggs in a thin stream back into the coconut milk mixture, stirring constantly to prevent them from forming lumps. Strain the mixture into a large glass or enamel baking dish and stir in the nutmeg, cinnamon, cardamom, and salt.

2. Set the baking dish in a steamer and pour in about 2 inches of water. Cover the pot and let steam until the mixture is firm, about $1^1/_2$ hours. Alternatively, you may set the baking dish in a pan of water and bake in a preheated oven at 350°F until firm, about $1^1/_2$ hours.

MAKES 4 TO 6 SERVINGS

Singapore

Singaporean Steamboat

Because Singapore is a coastal city-state at the edge of the South China Sea, I think of any steamboat meal from there as primarily seafood, but of course, as served at the Harbour View Dai-Ichi Hotel, you can make of it what you will and can exclude seafood, meats, and poultry altogether in favor of something strictly vegetarian. However it is served and eaten, it's a magnificent meal served every evening at the hotel (at the time of this writing), and most assuredly elsewhere in the city, with more than enough choices to satisfy anyone's preferences and appetite.

The whole dining room becomes one large steamboat banquet table, with meats, vegetables, and seafood arranged by cooking-stock category—Chinese, Thai, chicken, satay, and ginseng are the basic stocks used. (The recipes for the chicken stock and the Thai stock are below.) At each section of the table, the chef sets out appropriate dipping sauces to complement the cooking stock. You ladle your selection into a small bowl or bowls and take this back to your table. You can use the sauces for dunking your cooked foods, or you can pour the sauces into the cooking stock for extra flavor.

The assortment of ingredients for cooking seems endless, and all patrons need to do is fill and refill their plates. It is perfectly fine to mix and match ingredients with each soup stock, so let your taste buds guide you. At the restaurant, you will also find steamed Chinese bread and slices of French bread; when you fix this at home, have some of each to offer your guests.

You cook your ingredients in a tabletop cooking vessel filled with the stock of your choice. Use chopsticks or small wire-mesh baskets to hold the food and plunge it into the bubbling liquid. By the end of the meal, your steamy cooking broth becomes very rich and loaded with flavor, and that is the perfect time to cook the noodles. Of course, once you have finished cooking and eating the noodles and other ingredients, you may drink the remaining rich liquid as a final bowl of soup. For more about steamboats, see "About the Steamboat," page 269.

Chicken Stock

20 cups water

1 pound chicken necks and backs

4 ounces soybean sprouts

3 tablespoons freshly ground white
pepper, or more to taste

2 ounces rock sugar or light
brown sugar

Pinch of salt

Pinch of MSG (optional)

Pour 8 cups of the water into a large stockpot and bring to a boil. Add the chicken bones and cook for 2 minutes. Remove the bones and discard the water. Refill the stockpot with the remaining 12 cups water and add the bones, bean sprouts, pepper, sugar, salt, and MSG if using. Bring to a boil, reduce the heat to medium-low, and cook for 1 hour. Strain through a fine-mesh sieve and discard the solids.

Ingredients suggested for chicken-stock steamboat cooking:

- Vegetables, including sliced scallions; leafy greens, such as Chinese (napa) cabbage, bok choy, and lettuce; okra, chilies, or bitter gourd stuffed with minced fish and tofu; sliced mushrooms; sliced tomatoes; and baby corn on the cob.
- Seafood, including shrimp; quartered crabs or crab legs; fish heads; sliced squid; fish balls; shrimp balls; octopus balls; fish fillets; thinly sliced abalone; and sea cucumbers.
- Meats, including thinly sliced beef roast (both marinated and plain); thinly sliced pork loin; thinly sliced boneless chicken breasts; and sliced pork livers.
- Noodles, including bean thread (glass) noodles; rice vermicelli; wide rice noodles; and narrow and wide egg noodles.

Dipping sauces:

Light soy sauce

Dark soy sauce with sliced fresh red chilies

Chinese chili sauce (*lat jiu jiang*) with sliced fresh ginger

Ponzu Shoyu Dipping Sauce (page 33)

Chinese satay sauce

Toasted sesame oil

MAKES 6 SERVINGS

About the Steamboat

Malaysians and Singaporeans alike adore the steamboat meal, and it sounds as though local cooks have similar ideas about its content and presentation. I asked a food-minded Malaysian friend, Harris Lokmanhakim, about steamboats in his country, and this was his reply:

"I don't know of the origins of this 'dish' but I can tell you what it is like in Malaysia. The name 'steamboat' is probably derived from the appearance of the specialized cooking instrument. At the middle of a large table sits a contraption that consists of a large 'Bundt pan' that sits over a burner. The middle hole acts as an exhaust funnel for the burner. This doughnut-shaped pan is filled with a chicken broth, sometimes fish broth, and should be within arm's reach of everyone at the table. Personal touches [for the broth] include adding cognac or just using water [for cooking in place of the broth or for thinning the broth]. Every restaurant and cook has his or her own concoction. The broth is brought to a gentle boil. This alone smells good. The table orders a bevy of dishes of meats, vegetables, [lots of] seafood, beefballs, fishballs, fishcakes, and quail eggs that are uncooked or in a few cases partly cooked. These ingredients are served on small plates that are usually arranged around the steamboat. Everyone takes an item, then places it in the steamboat to cook. The name steamboat incorrectly implies that the food is steamed; it is not. The food is dipped in this communal broth until cooked at the discretion of the individual. One can just throw the item in the broth with the hopes of fishing it out later (this is impossible if the steamboat is on a lazy Susan, common to many Chinese restaurants), or place it in a mini long-handled straining basket and leave that in the broth. Or lately the food has appeared on little bamboo skewers. The host or head of the table typically throws in half the ingredients and whatever you fish out is what you will eat. This is a real pot luck! There is a lot of flexibility to the individual. You can dip your item in a scrambled egg before cooking it. In the end, the broth takes on the flavorings of the foods and this in itself becomes a tasty soup."

Thai Cooking Stock

Tom Yam Stock

3 tablespoons vegetable oil

1 shallot, peeled and sliced

$1/2$ teaspoon Thai or Malaysian shrimp
    paste (optional)

3 green chilies, halved lengthwise

2 stalks lemon grass, trimmed
    and sliced

6 kaffir lime leaves, finely shredded

1 teaspoon rock sugar or light
    brown sugar

$1/2$ cup fresh coriander leaves

$1^1/_2$ pounds chicken necks and backs

3 tablespoons fish sauce

2 teaspoons chili oil

1 teaspoon fresh lemon juice

1 teaspoon Thai or other chili powder

$1/2$ cup Thai basil leaves

Pinch of MSG (optional)

10 cups water

Heat the vegetable oil over medium heat in a large stockpot. Add the shallots and cook, stirring, until golden, 1 to 3 minutes. Stir in the shrimp paste, chilies, lemon grass, lime leaves, sugar, and coriander leaves, and cook until fragrant, about 3 minutes. Add the bones, fish sauce, chili oil, lemon juice, chili powder, basil leaves, MSG if using, and water. Bring to a boil, reduce the heat to medium-low, and cook for 1 hour. Strain the stock through a fine-mesh sieve and discard the solids.

Ingredients suggested for Thai *tom yam* stock steamboat cooking:

- Leafy vegetables, such as Chinese (napa) cabbage, scallions, bok choy, and lettuce, thinly sliced or cut into bite-sized pieces.
- Seafood, including fish fillets, cut into bite-sized pieces; shellfish, such as shrimp and scallops; squid; fish cakes; fish balls; and shrimp balls.
- Meats, including thinly sliced boneless chicken breasts; thinly sliced beef roast (both marinated and plain); and thinly sliced pork loin.
- Noodles, including bean thread (glass) noodles; rice vermicelli; wide rice noodles; and wheat noodles.

Dipping sauces:

Chinese chili sauce (*lat jiu jiang*) with minced garlic
Toasted sesame oil
Chinese satay sauce

Items suggested for either chicken stock or Thai *tom yam* stock steamboat cooking:

Hard-boiled quail eggs	Fried shallots
Cubed tofu	Sliced green chilies
Fried tofu strips	Ground dried red chilies
Fried tofu skins	Octopus balls
Won tons	Carrot-and-fish rolls
Fried yams	Fish dumplings

To serve a steamboat:

Pour some of the stock into a large tabletop cooking vessel and bring to a boil. Transfer the cooking vessel to the table and keep the stock at a simmer. (Replenish the stock as it boils away.) Arrange the ingredients for cooking on a platter and pour the sauces into individual serving dishes. Place the bowls on the table for all to dip into and let people help themselves. Use chopsticks or small wire-mesh baskets to hold the food to be cooked: Submerge in the stock until cooked through, then dip in the sauce. Cook the noodles in the rich broth after cooking and eating the other ingredients. Eat the noodles and drink the broth.

MAKES 6 SERVINGS

Simplified Singaporean Steamboat

Back at my hotel in Singapore, a guest house just a block away from my favorite eating place, Newton Circus, a Singaporean-Cantonese guest named Shirley Yuen described over afternoon tea her version of a steamboat: Make a broth with some pork bones. Then arrange on a serving dish cubed tofu, cubed pork, cubed chicken, cabbage leaves, spinach leaves, shelled and deveined shrimp, cleaned and sliced squid, fish balls, and squid balls. The mild-tasting ingredients—the pork, chicken, cabbage, and spinach—should be cooked before the other ingredients. At the end, break an egg into the hot broth and stir in and cook some noodles.

Malaysia

A great cook in her own right in the Malaysian kitchen, Majmin Hashim of Kuala Lumpur, Malaysia, spent one entire afternoon teaching me how to assemble this very typical Malaysian curry meal. The special bread for it, the *roti canai*, takes great skill to shape and flatten properly. In Malaysia, a special *roti* man does the honors by stretching the dough out paper thin in an artful flourish before frying it. For easier preparation, Shirley Janairo Roth has provided a simpler Indian bread, a *paratha*, that is a reasonable facsimile of the Malaysian *roti canai*. You will need to buy *chapati* flour, or *atta*, the finely milled Indian flour used extensively in making unleavened breads. This is sold at Indian markets.

Majmin Hashim commented that with the curry, (*Dal Cha,* page 273), cooks may use any combination of fresh vegetables—except leafy greens, which are *never* used in this dish. The curry recipe makes six generous servings, but if you were Malaysian, you would multiply the quantity for any unexpected visitors who might arrive at mealtime. Guests must always feel welcome, Mrs. Hashim said.

Paratha

1 cup *chapati* flour, or *atta*

¹/₃ cup water

2 tablespoons Ghee (page 17) or
  butter, melted

1. Combine the flour and water in a large bowl. If it seems too dry, wet your hands with water and shake them off into the bowl. (This water should provide enough moisture for the dough.) Cover the bowl with plastic wrap and set aside for 1 hour.

2. Sprinkle a flat surface with flour and divide the dough into 6 equal-sized balls. Roll out a ball into a 7-inch circle, brush the surface with ghee or butter, and fold it in half to form a semicircle. Brush the surface again and fold in half again to form a cone. Brush the surface again and fold in half once more. Brush with ghee or butter and roll out. Repeat with the remaining balls.

3. Heat the skillet over medium heat. Brush the surface with ghee or butter. Add a piece of dough and cook until golden, about 1 minute. Flip over and cook until specks of brown appear, 30 seconds to 1 minute. (You may need to keep adjusting the heat so the skillet does not overheat and burn the bread.) Remove from the skillet and repeat with the remaining pieces of dough. (Brush the skillet with more ghee or butter, if necessary.)

MAKES 6 PARATHA

Dal Cha

1/2 cup yellow split peas (*chana dal*),
  rinsed, picked clean, and soaked in
  cold water to cover for 6 to 12 hours
4 1/2 cups water
2 tablespoons vegetable oil
4 shallots, peeled and sliced
4 cloves garlic, peeled and sliced
1 tablespoon chopped fresh ginger
Salt to taste
1/4 cup Malaysian Meat or Chicken
  Curry Powder (page 31)
4 whole cloves
4 green cardamom pods
One 1-inch piece cinnamon stick
1 pound boneless top round steak,
  cubed
1/2 cup coconut milk
1 potato, peeled and cubed
1 carrot, peeled, halved lengthwise, and
  sliced into 1-inch pieces
1 Oriental eggplant, cubed
1 cup cauliflower florets
1/4 pound long beans, trimmed and cut
  into 1-inch lengths
2 green chilies, sliced in half
  lengthwise and seeded
2 fresh red chilies, sliced in half
  lengthwise and seeded
1 large tomato, cubed
6 *Paratha* (page 272)

1. Place the split peas and 2 cups of the water in a large saucepan over medium heat and bring to a boil. Reduce the heat to medium-low and cook until soft, about 30 minutes.

2. Heat the oil in a large wok or saucepan over medium heat. Add the shallots, garlic, ginger, and salt, and cook, stirring often, until fragrant and the shallots are browned, about 5 minutes.

3. Stir together the curry powder and 1/4 cup of the water to form a paste. Stir into the shallot mixture along with the cloves, cardamom, and cinnamon. Add the meat and stir to coat. (To absorb all the flavors, the beef must be fully coated with the spices.) Combine the coconut milk and 1 1/2 cups of the water and stir into the wok along with the split peas. Reduce the heat to medium-low and cook until thickened, about 30 minutes.

4. Add the potato, carrot, and remaining 3/4 cup water and cook until tender, about 20 minutes. Add the eggplant, cauliflower, beans, green chilies, red chilies, and tomato, and cook until tender, about 10 minutes more.

5. To serve and eat this dish in the traditional way, place 1 piece of *paratha* on each plate or in each bowl and ladle a portion of curry to the side. Use the bread to scoop up mouthfuls of the curry, rather like using a large soup spoon.

MAKES 4 TO 6 SERVINGS

Japan

Sumo Wrestler's Fish Stew (Chanko-nabe)

There's something about the challenge of acquiring authentic recipes that makes writing this kind of cookbook an adventure. But acquiring a real *chanko-nabe* recipe—this is the famous stew eaten by sumo wrestlers—was more than I bargained for.

The hunt began after American journalist Jim Fallows described his *chanko-nabe* forays in Tokyo some years back. When he needed to satisfy an overwhelming craving for Western-style filling, bulky food, Fallows would take his sons to a restaurant run by retired sumo wrestlers—and sumo wrestlers are certainly known for their girth. The dish served there was like an Irish stew with fish, he says, and its main virtue was bulk. As Fallows remembers, *chanko-nabe* often contains many ingredients, including potatoes, rice, miso, and loads of seafood. The leftover hot broth is used for cooking noodles.

A Japanese chef in Washington assured me he had an authentic *chanko-nabe* recipe and would share it with me. After several lengthy conversations and a thorough revision of his original recipe, he finally confessed that he had not only never cooked *chanko-nabe*, he had never even eaten it.

Then followed a series of unsuccessful phones calls to a Japanese cultural office and to a leading Japanese restaurant in Washington. Next, I was put in touch with a Japanese restaurant in Orange County, California, that is reputedly frequented by sumo wrestlers traveling in the United States, but management never answered the phone. I faxed a Japanese publisher in Tokyo for permission to reprint a *chanko-nabe* recipe they had published 30 years ago—no response. Finally, on a whim, I asked San Francisco and Los Angeles telephone operators for numbers to any Japanese-American associations in their areas.

Success. A Japanese-American activist group in Los Angeles put me in touch with the Rokudan of Kobe restaurant in Los Angeles, which actually serves a version of *chanko-nabe*. The owner, Kimiko Gomyo, and a family friend, Kinbo Mizutani (a former chef and apparently a sumo fan), sat down and provided the following text and recipe. Of course, Mr. Mizutani explained, he could not give quantities, because that was really up to the cook to decide. Besides, he said, no restaurant *ever* serves the real *chanko-nabe* because it is too bland and it also is considered a "spiritual" food. In that vein, I felt it would not even be fitting to test this "spiritual" version of the recipe. This is the traditional version of *chanko-nabe*.

In his words, the story behind sumo, *chanko-nabe*, and a healthful way of eating stew:

Chanko and Sumo

Sumo dates back to the ancient Shinto ceremony of fertility—ritualistic wrestling matches between the God of East and the God of West represented by two sumo wrestlers.

Therefore, unlike Western sports of fighting such as wrestling or boxing, Sumo require the strict rituals before, during, and after each match. To be the Grand Champion (Yokozuna), one has to be not only the strongest but also has to be the man of integrity and honor as a Shinto priest.

Salt (solar dried natural sea salt) is used to purify the round Sumo link made of pounded sands encircled by rice straw bags with four outer corners representing the East, West, North, and South. Preceding each match, two Sumo wrestlers grab salt and spray them on the link followed by Shinto ritual of show of force and grace. At the end of each session, the Yokozuna gracefully dance.

The very solar dried natural sea salt is the essence of the Sumo wrestlers' daily diet called *Chanko*. *Chanko* is boiling water with a small amount of salt and plenty of vegetables with either seafood or poultry. Poultry and seafood is never used mixed which makes *Chanko* impure. Animal meat such as beef, pork are never used because they too are impure. Garlic or strong spices are not used because they will cause breath of impurity.

Like Shabu-Shabu [a] pot cooking salt water is brought to the boil and vegetables [and] either seafood or poultry are cooked in one giant pot and consumed as cooked to one's desire . . . At the end of the dinner, steamed rice is added to make rice porridge. Shiitake mushrooms and tofu (soybean cake) are also used frequently.

Each Sumo Gym (Housing 20 to 200 Sumo wrestlers) has their own House Specials and observes their traditions strictly. They are the recipes for victory, power, yet must be the religiously clean pure recipes.

Many Sumo fans dream of dining *Chanko* with Sumo wrestlers for they are the true heroes of power and spirits of the traditional Japan. But most of the fans are shocked when they have the true authentic Sumo *Chanko* for the lack of rich taste, though very tasty in a simple way. In other words, true *Chanko* is a food for victory and religious purification and is nutritiously complete but not necessarily the gourmet quality dinner to please the public.

After retirement, many Sumo wrestlers open up *Chanko-Nabe* restaurants to cater to Sumo fans with the sophisticated versions by adding such ingredients as dried kelp, dried bonito, dried anchovies for soup stock, beef or pork, or other tasty ingredients to please the average Sumo fan's appetite. Some *Chanko-Nabe* restaurants even add sake, mirin, shoyu, miso to the broth, and use ponzu sauce or even add garlic/ginger juice for dipping purposes. Exotic mushrooms [and a] wide array of fresh produce of the season are also added.

The authentic Sumo *Chanko* is very simple, pure, clean, nutritiously well-balanced, freshest foods cooked in a mild salt water (less than 0.3% salt) while restaurants' Chanko-Nabe is full of tastes with [a] rich array of ingredients in mixed use. They are both as old as Sumo itself and both are as traditional as they can be but two are very different.

Duck Chanko Authentic Sumo Style

Use tabletop gas or electric cooker; clay or cast-iron pots. The cook decides on quantities, according to whatever is available; this is well-balanced nutritionally. (One of many thousand recipes; [chanko-nabe is] not normally served at restaurants.)

Salt (solar dried natural sea salt)

Gallon of natural spring water

Sake

Cooking sake

Mineral water

Japanese Tokyo *Negi* (long leek)

Mochi (rice cake)

1 mallard duck, breast meat and bones, (domestic duck or free-range chicken may be used as a substitute)

Konbu, katsuo-bushi, niboshi, and/or dried anchovies, shiitake mushrooms to create enriched soup stock (optional)

Dried soba noodles

Tofu

Abura-age (fried thin tofu)

Yuba/Fupi (dried gluten film of soybean milk)

Namafu (fresh wheat gluten dough)

Fresh greens of the season (such as mustard greens, edible chrysanthemum [leaves])

Kabocha (Japanese chestnut pumpkin)

Wild mushrooms of the season (whatever are available)

Carrot/burdock root, both skinned

Snow pea pods

Hakusai Nappa [napa] (Chinese white cabbage)

Steamed rice

Chopped chives

Egg flower

1. One cup of natural sea salt with 5 to 6 cups of natural spring water brought to a boil to make saturated salt brine. Clean off the floating impurities then add $1/2$ to $3/4$ cup of sake and stir slowly after fire (boiling) is stopped. Let it cool off. This is called *mizushio* (watery salt) and is absolutely important to make a perfect clear soup stock. Keep it in glass bottle.

2. Three cups of cooking sake and 3 cups of mineral water mixed together and chilled in refrigeration. It is called *tamazake* (sake of jade).

3. Prepare plenty of ice cubes preferably made by natural spring water.

4. All ingredients are cut into proper bite-sizes.

5. Long onions are skewered and grilled lightly to bring aroma and sweetness. You may substitute with round regular onions. Take skewer off after grilling.

6. *Mochi* are cut to a small bite size and broiled to golden brown.

7. Duck meat sliced and blanched in a boiling cooking sake for 1 minute then washed in *tamazake* with ice cubes and cold water. [See Use of *tamazake*, below.]

8. Option: Duck bones are grilled and rinsed in a boiling cooking sake, then added to a pot of natural spring water to make a broth.

9. Option: *Konbu, katsuo-bushi,* dried anchovies, and dried shiitake mushrooms may be washed and left in the pot of mineral water overnight to create richer soup stock to be

added to duck stock. Shiitake mushroom stems must be removed after being soaked overnight. All the ingredients are removed from the stock immediately after water is brought to a boil. Total of one gallon or so of soup stock is needed to serve 5 to 6 people whether you use [step] 8 or 9, or a combination.

10. Now you have a soup stock. Add sake (about 10%) and small amount of *mizushio* [watery salt] to adjust the taste. (You may add soy sauce if you prefer.)

11. Soba noodle is to be partially boiled and washed/chilled.

12. Tofu is to be partially boiled slowly (70%) to squeeze out water, and cut into large dices then chilled.

13. *Abura-age* to be blanched in boiling water to take excessive oil out, then dried.

14. Dried *yuba* (*fupi*) to be soaked in water for a few hours then slowly boiled and cut into appropriate bite size (make rolls).

15. *Namafu* is to be poached and quickly chilled.

16. All the vegetables are washed and partially boiled after being cut to a bite size then washed in iced *tamazake*. [See Use of *tamazake*, below.]

17. *Hakusai Nappa* is to be rolled like a sushi roll and sliced like sushi bite sizes. By blanching each ingredient separately, the surfaces of the different ingredients are sealed, thus maintaining the individual aroma, flavor, taste, and texture, and that is the essence of *Chanko* cooking. The length of blanching are different by each different ingredients [the time is different depending on the ingredients]. Don't overcook. The purpose is to sear the surfaces and to slightly soften/harden the food as well as to bring out vivid colors. Neatly display all the ingredients, including the duck, on a bamboo basket with a large tray under to hold the water drips.

18. Prepare hot pot with soup stock [at] the dining table and add each ingredient to the boiling stock on an as-you-eat basis. Do not overload the pot with a lot of ingredients at one time. Just add a few, eat, clean the soup stock with fine-mesh wire ladle, then add some more ingredients as you cook and eat. Overloading the pot will lower the temperature of soup stock, thus making it murky, and the food will not taste crisp-clean with individual flavors. Murky soup makes murky tasting *chanko*. Add *tamazake* occasionally to adjust soup stock strength and to keep the constant temperature as soup stock tends to thicken as you cook.

19. Add soba noodles at the end of dinner, and you may add a little amount of ground white pepper and extra drops of mizushio [watery salt] to the stock.

20. Optional: Pour steamed rice in a bamboo or wire basket and wash with running cold water, then iced *tamazake*, then rinse off [with] water (this will wash away extra sticky starch from rice). Washed steamed rice may be added to the soup stock with small chopped chives and egg flower to make rice porridge for extra-hungry people.

Important: Only to use natural spring water for soup stock, *tamazake*, *mizushio*, and ice cubes are absolutely important as much as using the solar dried natural sea salt and the freshest ingredients. Do not use tap water and iodized salt for any cooking.

Use of *Tamazake*

1 cup chilled *tamazake*
1 tray ice cubes
1 quart chilled natural spring water

Mix these in a bowl, then drop hot food (such as blanched mallard duck breast fillets) into the bowl, wash vigorously stirring with chopsticks until duck completely cold. This will take cholesterol and excessive fat out of meat yet maintain duck taste and flavor.

The Philippines

Filipino Fruit and Coconut Soup

Ginataang Halo-Halo

I adore this soup, despite its high calorie count, for its coconut milk is filled with pieces of exotic fruit and small scoops of sticky (glutinous) rice flour cooked to the texture of tapioca. Equally delicious hot or cold, it is typically served hot, says the cook who provided the recipe, Evelyn Manuel. If you want to eat it cold, heat up the rice balls in boiling water before adding them to the soup, because they become rock hard when cold.

2 cups sugar

10 cups water

2 ripe plantains, peeled and sliced, or 2 bananas

1 large sweet potato, peeled and cubed

1 taro root, peeled, cubed, and steamed until tender

2 cups sticky (glutinous) rice flour mixed with 1 cup cold water

3 to 4 cups coconut milk

1/2 cup sago or small-pearl tapioca, cooked (see Note)

1 cup diced jackfruit

1. Bring 1/2 cup of the sugar and 4 cups of the water to a boil in a large saucepan. Add the plantains or bananas, sweet potatoes, and taro root, reduce the heat to medium, and cook until tender, about 20 minutes. Drain and transfer to a bowl.

2. Meanwhile, pour 4 more cups of the water into another large saucepan and bring to a boil. Form the rice flour paste into 1-inch balls and gently slide into the water with a slotted spoon. Cook until the balls float to the surface, about 5 minutes. Transfer to a colander to drain.

3. Bring the remaining 2 cups water to a boil in a large saucepan. Stir in the remaining 1 1/2 cups sugar and the coconut milk. Reduce the heat to medium-low and cook, stirring constantly, until the sugar is dissolved, about 5 minutes. Stir in the taro root, plantains, rice balls, sago or tapioca, sweet potatoes, and jackfruit. Cook for 5 minutes more and serve immediately.

MAKES ABOUT 8 SERVINGS

Note: Sago is a starchy product made from the sago palm and it resembles tapioca in shape and color. To cook sago, soak it in hot water for 15 minutes. Boil it in water, in the ratio of 1 part sago to 6 parts water, until transparent. As an alternative, you may also use noninstant tapioca and follow the cooking directions on the package.

Mongolian Hot Pot

A popular dish from Northern China, the Mongolian hot pot may well have been created by the nomadic peoples of the region many centuries ago. The Mongols bred and raised sheep that produced a lean meat and when thinly sliced and boiled in hot liquid, it made a delicious and hearty meal augmented with dumplings and sesame seed cakes. But Chinese food authority Kenneth Lo believes the dish is much more contemporary; he has written in his *The Encyclopedia of Chinese Cooking* that the dish Peking Mongolian (the Mongolian hot pot) was first enjoyed in Beijing in 1855 during the reign of the Manchurian Emperor Shan-feng.

Since lamb was the Mongols' meat of choice, one of the meal's Northern names is *shuan yang ro*, or "dipped sheep's meat." Another popular name is *huo-guo*, which means simply "hot pot." Farther south in China, this style of cooking is called *da-bin-lo*, or "beat the sides of the pot," referring to the sound of people's chopsticks retrieving food from the hot pot.

Apart from its colorful origins, what makes this meal so special is the authentic tiered brass or copper cooking vessel—probably of Mongolian design—with a base and grate for holding hot charcoal; a metal basin, or moat, that sits above the charcoal for holding and heating the cooking broth; and at the top tier, a squat, tapered chimney that fits through the moat and conducts the heat up through the broth. A simple cooking device that maintains a relatively high temperature, the hot pot is large enough for a crowd to gather around it at the table, allowing people to cook and keep warm at the same time.

Lamb is the traditional ingredient in the North. But in Hong Kong, people are likely to eat a Mongolian hot-pot meal that offers very thinly sliced beef or chicken, pig's liver or kidney, scallops, fish, clams, shrimp, oysters, and squid. And the hot pot's migration southward has changed the dish even more. For example, in Malaysia and Singapore—where the hot-pot-style meal is known as "steamboat" (see page 267)—almost anything goes, from beef and pork to quail eggs, crab legs, fish heads, okra, abalone, and sea cucumbers.

In Hong Kong, the Mandarin House Peking Restaurant serves this wintertime dish all year long, even in the dead heat of a Hong Kong summer. And their Mongolian Hot Pot may well be the restaurant's signature dish.

The wait staff carry out a tray containing 12 different seasoning ingredients, including cut-up chives, minced chilies, vinegar, sesame oil, fish sauce, Chinese rice wine, soy sauce, sugar, sesame paste, fermented red bean curd sauce, chopped green onions (scallions), and fresh coriander leaves.

The head waiter explains the procedure: Start with 2 spoonfuls of sesame paste as a seasoning base and scoop that into a small side dish. Mix in several splashes of other seasonings to suit your taste.

The liquid—in this case, plain water, although you may use chicken broth, if you prefer—should be bubbling hot. Use a wire-mesh spoon (sold in

Chinese or Asian markets) for holding your food and immerse the food into the hot liquid. Cook the meat or seafood first—selections could include very thinly sliced lamb, beef, chicken, pig's liver, or kidney, as well as scallops, fish, clams, shrimp, oysters, and squid. The meats cook quickly, probably within 30 seconds to 1 minute. Dip them into your seasoning sauce, replenishing the sauce as needed. Cook the vegetables—shredded Chinese (napa) cabbage, lettuce, and spinach—and noodles, tofu, and won tons after cooking the meat. Later, drink the very rich broth. For dessert, offer sweet plum tea and candied walnuts.

China

Hunanese Meatball Soup

In Hunan, cooks make a very special meatball soup that steams in small wooden barrels, a technique that produces an "ethereal, delicate meatball" in a very rich, clear broth, says the cook who provided this recipe, Joyce Piotrowski. But lacking the barrels, you may use a steamer container large enough to hold several small soup bowls, preferably with lids.

The chicken stock must be chilled and the surface fat removed before you start the steaming process. If you use warm stock, the meat will not form a solid "meatball." The cook also notes that when you combine the stock with the other ingredients, the mixture will look "terrible," but you should not worry. The meat magically pulls together to form the meatball. Cook this soup shortly before you plan to serve it, because it cannot be reheated; however, Joyce Piotrowski assures that the preparation steps can be done the day before serving.

Stock

4 pounds chicken necks and backs

3 scallions, trimmed

2 tablespoons Chinese rice wine

2 teaspoons sugar

Salt to taste

One 1 × 1–inch piece dried tangerine peel (see Note)

$^1/_4$ teaspoon five-spice powder

10 cups water

Soup

$2^1/_2$ pounds chicken thighs

1 pound pork tenderloin

$^1/_2$ chicken liver, minced

1 small onion, peeled and minced

8 water chestnuts, minced

4 dried Chinese mushrooms or shiitake mushrooms, soaked in hot water for 20 minutes, stems removed, minced

2 teaspoons soy sauce

1 teaspoon salt

$^1/_2$ teaspoon Szechuan peppercorns

$^1/_2$ teaspoon sugar

3 egg yolks

1. To make the stock, combine the chicken, scallions, wine, sugar, salt, tangerine peel, five-spice powder, and water in a stockpot and bring to a boil. Reduce the heat to low and cook, uncovered, for 3 hours. Strain into a large bowl and discard the bones and scallions. Refrigerate until thoroughly chilled. Skim off and discard the layer of fat on the surface.

2. To make the soup, remove the skin and bones from the chicken thighs and mince the meat with a cleaver. Combine the minced chicken with the pork and chicken livers, and mince them together with the cleaver. (It is preferable to do this by hand, as grinding or processing the meat with a blender or food processor will result in stringy meat.)

3. Add the meat, onion, water chestnuts, mushrooms, soy sauce, salt, peppercorns, sugar, and egg yolks to the bowl with the stock and stir to combine.

4. Fill soup bowls or cups with about 1½ cups of the soup. If the bowls have no lids, cover each tightly with plastic wrap. Place the bowls on a rack in a steamer and fill with water to 1 inch below the rack. Cover with a tight-fitting lid and cook until the meat forms a ball and the stock is clear, about 1½ hours. Replenish the water as needed. Alternatively, if your soup bowls have lids, place the bowls in a water bath and bake at 350°F for 1 hour, or wrap them in aluminum foil and follow the same procedure.

MAKES 6 SERVINGS

Note: Dried tangerine peel is available in many Asian markets. It comes packed in cellophane bags.

Thailand

Quail Curry

Gaeng Sut Nog Khing On

The Thais have created many unusual curries, and this version with tiny quail is one of their more interesting dishes. In fact, the Thai name for the curry translates loosely to "young minced bird curry with Chinese ginger," says Sarnsern Gajaseni of The Thai Cooking School at The Oriental, Bangkok, who provided this recipe. Although the recipe calls for quail, according to the cook you may substitute other exotica, such as boar, venison, frogs, snake, eels, or mice, or tamer meat such as chicken or pork. (If you make this with chicken or pork, omit the ginger.) When Thais use quail for this dish, they discard the head, feet, and feathers, but they chop up the rest, including the bones. The bones make the curry crisp and sweet, says the cook. In all honesty, I used chicken instead.

The cook precooks the coconut milk until the oil begins to separate from the liquid—this way the quails' dry meat picks up oil quickly and moistens it. Skim some oil off the surface to use for cooking the curry paste—when I prepared this recipe, the coconut oil did not form a layer of oil, so I cooked the curry paste in a small amount of thick coconut milk (see page 6) first.

To heighten the color of the paste, you may substitute one fresh red chili for one of the dried chilies. The paste should be so fine that when you smear some of it across your palm, a residue fills the lines on your hand. Mr. Gajaseni suggests blending the paste first, then pounding it with some salt and coriander and/or cumin seeds to help the pounding process. Serve this with rice and other components of a Thai meal, such as vegetables, fruit, and grilled meats, if desired.

Curry Paste

9 dried red chilies, soaked in hot water
   for 20 minutes

5 shallots, peeled and chopped

5 tablespoons thinly sliced lemon grass

7 cloves garlic, peeled

7 thin slices galangal

1 tablespoon chopped coriander root

1 teaspoon chopped kaffir lime rind

1 teaspoon white or black peppercorns

1 teaspoon Thai or Malaysian
   shrimp paste

About ¹/₂ cup thin coconut milk
   (see page 6)

1. To make the curry paste, combine the red chilies, shallots, lemon grass, garlic, galangal, coriander root, lime rind, peppercorns, and shrimp paste in a blender. Add just enough coconut milk to process, and blend until smooth.

2. To make the curry, bring the thin coconut milk to a boil in a large saucepan over medium heat. Reduce the heat to medium-low and cook, stirring often, 15 to 20 minutes, or until the mixture separates—a thin layer of oil should form on the surface—and the liquid thickens. Remove from the heat.

Curry

2½ cups thin coconut milk
  (see page 6)

1 cup thick coconut milk (see page 6)

15 quails, chopped (for a total of 2 cups
  chopped quail)

1 cup peeled and shredded fresh ginger

3 tablespoons fish sauce

1 teaspoon palm sugar or dark
  brown sugar

Garnishes

1 cup Thai basil leaves

½ cup cubed or sliced golf-ball-sized
  Thai eggplant

4 thinly sliced fresh red and
  green chilies

6 thinly sliced kaffir lime leaves

3. In a separate large saucepan, heat the thick coconut milk over medium heat and cook until a layer of oil forms on the surface and the coconut milk is reduced by half. Stir in the curry paste and cook about 5 minutes, or until fragrant. Add the quail, reduce the heat to medium-low, and cook, stirring often, until the quail is tender, about 10 minutes. (Add more oil from the reduced thin coconut milk to prevent the quail from sticking, if needed.) Stir in the ginger, fish sauce, and sugar. Pour in the remaining cooked thin coconut milk, including the oil, and cook until heated through, about 5 minutes more.

4. Garnish the curry with the basil leaves, eggplant, chilies, and lime leaves. Serve hot.

MAKES 4 TO 6 SERVINGS

Laos

Lao Chicken and Beef Stew

O Lam

According to the cook who provided this recipe, Phetsaphone Phanthavone, and to my Lao friend Bounsou Sananikone, this dish is a specialty of the cooks from the former royal city of Luang Prabang in northern Laos. This soup/stew differs from the plain O (see Lao Chicken and Vegetable Stew, page 68) because the meats, lemon grass, sticky rice, and chilies are grilled before going into the soup pot. You don't actually need a barbecue fire; if you have gas burners, cook the ingredients over the gas flame by threading them on thin skewers and turning them so they brown evenly. Otherwise, use the broiler in your oven to brown the ingredients. The stalks of lemon grass do not need to be skewered before grilling. Amazingly, you will be able to skewer the rice by compressing it into a ball first.

Lao cooks sometimes use birds, buffalo skin, or pork rind in the preparation and accent the dish with cloud ear mushrooms. According to René de Berval, commenting on Lao cooking in his book Kingdom of Laos, The Land of the Million Elephants and of the White Parasol, *a historic look at Lao cooking, "the dried skin of the Indian buffalo is a thing that is brought out with pride . . ." The recipe for this dish in the cookbook of Phia Sing, the former royal cook, calls for dried buffalo meat, dried buffalo skin, and crisp-fried pork skin.*

Here the cook uses a piece of beef skin (hide with hair scraped away and with the underlayer of fat intact), but only because buffalo is not available. You may substitute frozen pork skin sold at Asian markets or use Hispanic fried pork rinds and crumble them into the dish just before serving. Laotians also use fresh bark from the sakanh *tree (a variety typical of Laos in the area of Luang Prabang)—an ingredient that is considered "precious and typical"—and without it, you won't know the authentic taste. However, the bark is not available in the United States.*

2 stalks lemon grass, trimmed

4 fresh red chilies

2 tablespoons cooked sticky (glutinous) rice (see page 4), rolled into a ball

5 chicken pieces (legs, breast, and/or thighs), with bones

1 pound boneless beef roast, cooked and sliced

8 cups water

1. Preheat a grill or broiler. Cook the lemon grass stalks until the outer leaves begin to darken. Set aside until cool enough to handle, then slice. Thread the chilies on metal skewers and hold them over the fire or under the broiler, turning often, until the skins darken and blister. Set aside. Grill the ball of rice until the outer layer is blackened. Grill the chicken and beef for 2 to 3 minutes per side—just to give the exterior a smoky flavor. Set aside. When cool enough to handle, cut the chicken into small serving pieces and slice the beef.

10 golf-ball-sized Thai eggplants

1 ounce dried cloud ear mushrooms, soaked in hot water for 20 minutes, stems removed

One 4 × 8–inch piece frozen pork skin, boiled until softened (see Note) and thinly sliced

$1/2$ pound long beans, trimmed and cut into 2-inch lengths

1 cup chili leaves (optional)

$1/2$ cup Thai pea eggplants

$1/2$ cup fresh dill

3 scallions, trimmed and thinly sliced

2 tablespoons fish sauce, or more to taste

Salt to taste

Pinch of MSG (optional)

2. Bring 5 cups of the water to a boil in a large saucepan. Add the eggplant and cook until very soft, about 20 minutes.

3. Meanwhile, in a separate large saucepan, combine the mushrooms, lemon grass, and the remaining 3 cups water. Bring to a boil and let the mixture cook at a rapid boil for 10 minutes. Add the chicken and beef, and cook for 5 minutes.

4. Pulled the grilled rice ball apart, shape into marble-sized pieces, and drop it, piece by piece, into the saucepan with the meat. Add the pork skin and cook for about 5 minutes.

5. When the eggplants are soft, puree or mash them and stir into the saucepan with the meat. Add the beans, chili leaves if using, pea eggplants, dill, chilies, scallions, fish sauce, salt, and MSG if using. Cook, stirring often, until the vegetables are tender, about 10 minutes more. Serve hot.

MAKES 4 TO 6 SERVINGS

Note: To soften the pork skin, cook it in boiling water for several minutes. Some pork skin products come already shredded and need only to be cooked according to the package directions before use.

Nepal

A Nepalese Meal

One summer evening, Jamak and his relatives (a young Nepalese family who lives in Virginia) invited me to visit while the women prepared dinner—for most Westerners a rare chance for a brief, but intimate, look at Nepalese home cooking. Jamak's wife and sister-in-law explained as they chopped onions that a Nepalese cook is never supposed to taste while cooking, because she should understand ingredients so well that she intuitively knows the flavors are right. Serve this four-part feast with rice and *dal* as accompaniments.

Chicken Curry

This lively chicken curry calls for chicken thighs rather than breast meat. The turmeric adds both color and heat, and the other seasonings add layers of subtle flavors.

1 tablespoon vegetable oil, or more
   as needed
1/4 large onion, peeled and thinly sliced
10 to 12 chicken thighs, halved
   crosswise
1 teaspoon ground coriander
1 teaspoon ground cumin
2 teaspoons salt, or to taste
1 teaspoon ground turmeric
1 teaspoon minced fresh ginger
1 teaspoon minced garlic
Sprinkle of ground cinnamon

1. Heat the oil in a large wok or skillet over medium heat. Add the onion and cook, stirring often, about 5 minutes, or until golden. Transfer the onion to paper towels to drain.

2. Add the chicken and cook, stirring often, about 10 minutes, or until browned on all sides. Add more oil if needed. Mix together the coriander and cumin, and stir into the chicken along with the salt, turmeric, ginger, garlic, and fried onions. Reduce the heat to medium-low, cover, and cook, stirring occasionally, until the chicken is tender, 20 to 30 minutes. Stir in the cinnamon, cover, and cook for 10 minutes more. Serve hot.

MAKES 5 OR 6 SERVINGS

Potato Condiment or Pickle

Aloo Achar

Aloo *means potato, and* achar *is a food that is spicy hot, said Jamak's wife. When you prepare this, do not use too much turmeric, because it will turn the potatoes bitter. For a cooler dish in warm weather, you may substitute yogurt for the sesame seeds and chopped onions for the fenugreek seeds. This dish may be made up to three days before serving and refrigerated until ready to use. Serve this condiment with curry and rice.*

8 medium potatoes, boiled until tender, drained, cooled, peeled, and cut into eighths

1 tablespoon salt

2 to 3 teaspoons Roasted Red Chili Powder (page 16)

1 teaspoon ground turmeric

4 teaspoons black sesame seeds (see Note), roasted (see page 11)

³/₄ cup water

¹/₃ cup fresh lemon juice

2 tablespoons vegetable oil

1 teaspoon fenugreek seeds

4 to 6 green chilies, stems removed, broken in half

1. Place the potatoes in a large bowl and stir in the salt, red chili powder, and turmeric.

2. Pulverize the sesame seeds in a spice grinder or blender and sprinkle over the potatoes. Stir in the water and lemon juice.

3. Heat the oil in a large wok or skillet over medium heat. Add the fenugreek seeds and chilies, and cook, stirring, until dark brown, 2 to 3 minutes. Stir into the potato mixture. Serve hot or cold.

MAKES 5 OR 6 SERVINGS

Note: Black sesame seeds are readily available in Nepal but may be difficult to find in Western countries. If your Indian grocer or specialty food store does not carry them, substitute regular white sesame seeds. In Nepal, cooks use a large, flat stone—a special stone used only for this purpose—to crush sesame seeds into a paste. But in a Western kitchen, a Nepalese cook would probably use a blender or spice grinder to pulverize the roasted seeds.

Cauliflower and Tomato Curry

A succulent vegetable dish, this curry can stand on its own as a main course when accompanied by yogurt and cooked grains or Indian bread.

$^3/_4$ cup vegetable oil

$^1/_2$ large onion, peeled and thinly sliced

1 head cauliflower, cut into florets

2 large tomatoes, cubed

1 tablespoon salt

1 teaspoon ground turmeric

1 teaspoon ground cumin

1 teaspoon ground coriander

Chopped fresh coriander leaves

1. Heat the oil in a large wok or skillet over medium heat. Add the onions and cook until golden, about 10 minutes. Increase the heat to high, add the cauliflower, and cook, stirring often, until softened, about 10 minutes. Stir in the tomatoes and cook for 3 minutes more. Stir in the salt, turmeric, cumin, and coriander. Reduce the heat to medium-low and cook until the vegetables are very tender, 5 to 10 minutes more.

2. Serve garnished with coriander leaves.

MAKES 4 TO 6 SERVINGS

Steamed Greens

A dish of cooked greens is typical of a Nepalese meal. The original recipe for this dish calls for two bunches of broccoli rabe, but mustard greens are a fine substitute. If you want a more piquant dish, add sliced or whole green chilies to taste when you are heating the oil. But take care that you do the cooking in a venti-lated kitchen, or the chili fumes may cause tears and sniffles.

$^3/_4$ cup vegetable oil

1 teaspoon fenugreek seeds

2 bunches broccoli rabe or mustard
    greens, rinsed and trimmed

1 teaspoon minced garlic

1 teaspoon minced fresh ginger

1 teaspoon salt

1 teaspoon ground turmeric

Heat the vegetable oil in a large wok or saucepan over medium heat. Add the fenugreek seeds and cook, stirring, until fragrant, 2 to 3 minutes. Add the greens. Reduce the heat to medium-low, cover, and cook until the greens are tender, 10 to 15 minutes. Stir in the garlic, ginger, salt, and turmeric. Cover and cook for 5 minutes more. Serve hot.

MAKES 4 TO 6 SERVINGS

Golden Dragons—
China, Hong Kong, Macau,
and Tibet

Of all the millions of words about Chinese food, an ancient Chinese proverb describes it best: "For the people, food is heaven."

After all, Chinese cooking must be the emperor of the Oriental table, for its earliest cooks began forging a cuisine that has inspired all Asia, to say nothing of the rest of the world. There must be some reason, for example, why Chinese food has worked its way into the Western psyche and why every American shopping center has its very own "Golden Dragon," a restaurant where patrons can sit and dream their Oriental dreams.

Tiny Hong Kong and Macau, and remote Tibet, are, as everyone knows, under the thrall of that great Golden Dragon. But each also can take pride in its own pantry and special dishes that make them distinctive entities.

China and Hong Kong

If the early Chinese really did create the first epicurean soup, it's no wonder that the Chinese have turned cooking and eating into an art form. And the modern Chinese, in Hong Kong, the Mainland, and elsewhere, are natural heirs to the ancient tradition of soup making. Even at the simplest traditional home dinner at least one soup doubles as a nutritious course and the meal's main beverage. Indeed, the Fukienese in Eastern China apparently believe that if your host serves you only one soup during a meal, he does not consider you a friend.

And soups and stews suit perfectly the duality of Chinese cooking, since they provide a satiny counterpoint to the crunchier textures of stir-fried meats and vegetables. They also suit the frugal nature of the Chinese, because many soups and stews are good vehicles for tenderizing tougher ingredients and utilizing every edible food scrap.

The Chinese passion for these one-pot dishes is reflected in their language: Of the 75 or 80 different terms that describe cooking techniques, at least nine common expressions—from that for the simple act of simmering or boiling meat or whole poultry in water (*chu*), to boiling whole animals (*suan*), to a type of stewing (*men*), to the more complex technique of repeated boiling and cooling to thoroughly cook a food (*ch'uan*)—describe the various ways Chinese cooks boil and simmer foods to prepare soups. But these terms do not begin to explain their pleasure in making sweet soups—such as mashed almond soup, candy bird's nest soup, and candy white fungus soup with mandarin orange—that sweetly conclude a rich meal.

In fact, many traditional Chinese medicines come in the form of soups and infusions, so maybe the Chinese can claim to have discovered the restorative effects of tonics like chicken soup. In fact, the Chinese *do* believe that such exotica as shark's fin, green turtles, and bird's nests, when cooked in a chicken stock, can ensure a radiant complexion and might even go so far as to cure other ailments. Indeed, many traditional Chinese once believed—and perhaps still do—that a rich duck soup can reconcile the differences of an estranged couple.

At least five more expressions describe how Chinese prepare stews. Of these, *cha shao* and the similar technique *p'eng* involve a final step that might surprise the Western cook: The meat is spit-roasted after stewing and before serving— one might call it a "grilled stew."

Let the Chinese always find pleasure with their soups and stews. Everyone else benefits.

Macau

Just at the edge of Southern China, Macau reflects its hybrid heritage. Ruled by the Portuguese for several hundred years, Macau nonetheless seems intensely Chinese in its shopfronts and in its street talk. Macau also typifies that Asian clash between contemporary city and rural folk life. In fact, visitors to Macau may wonder where they are, for medieval Portuguese architecture and modern steel structures coexist with colorful Chinese temples.

Visitors also may wonder what country they are eating in. Noted Macau expert Harry Rolnick of Hong Kong tried to sort this out for me on a recent visit. He walked through Macau's twisting alleys to a market for special coffee beans. Then he sprinted down a hill and along the waterfront over the city's sidewalks—he was deciding, shall we lunch at the Bela Vista, the Lisboa, or the Pria Grande? As it turned out, we stopped short at a side entrance: the Estrelo do Mar restaurant, a longtime Macau lunch place that serves such Portuguese dishes as chickpea soup with vegetables, stewed lamb with potatoes, stewed rice with codfish, and stewed spaghetti—long, sticky noodles with a watery tomato sauce.

Over lunch he talked about the basic character of the local Macanese fare, which has become both Portuguese and Chinese. But the Portuguese still dominate, and the city and its two outlying islands of Taipa and Coloane offer a lusty menu of authentic Portuguese soups, stews, grilled foods, and wines.

Later, we strolled back toward the pier to get a return ferry to Hong Kong, stopping on the way at another of Rolnick's favorites, the Rest. Afonso III [sic] for a swig of heating brandy and a mug of pitch black coffee. Wiping his hands on a towel, the Portuguese owner greeted Rolnick, seated us, and launched into his favorite topic: food. China may be only a short swim across the waters, but in his company, the burgundies and garlicked lamb of Portugal felt right at home.

On a future visit, I intend to ask Rolnick to brunch with me at the Pousada de Coloane for a Portuguese buffet of fresh codfish and stews. In particular, I'll look for the Portuguese pork-and-sausage stew *cozido*, rendered, said Rolnick, in this Asian backwater with pork, Chinese cabbage, ginger, and coriander. And on the way back to the ferry, we can stand on a waterfront side street near an old Chinese temple and look across the water to mainland China.

Tibet

Tibet is so remote that it becomes a deliberate destination—a mountainous, frigid country of ancient gods and austere beauty with a cuisine that seems geared to warm the chilliest soul. Transplanted to America, Tibetan Tseten Wangchuk spoke of his native food, and in his description, one could almost hear the whistle of mountain winds and feel the bite of deep-freeze blizzards as he discussed roasted yak meat and rich soups and stews made with yak butter, yak cheese, and a barleylike grain called *tsampa*.

A weighty cross between Chinese and Indian cooking, Tibetan food has a stolid appeal for those who don't want to cut fat from their diets. Even Tibetan tea, Wangchuk says, is brewed from an herbal plant imported from India and stirred with milk, salt, and butter. It's really more like a soup, he says, but that liquid sounds as if it would start anyone's day with the best foot forward. "It's really important in high altitudes," he explained. And as an afterthought: "We need the fat to keep warm." This tea washes down a cereallike dish made with *tsampa* flour mixed with crumbled *chura* (dried cheese), sweetened with sugar, and moistened with tea and butter. It also serves as the beverage mainstay throughout the day, probably because it is hot and bracing, but more likely because chunks of warming yak butter float on the surface.

At midday, Tibetans head toward heartier fare when they sit down to a simple bread baked in ashes, plenty of good hefty stews of potatoes and radishes, and lots of curries and Bhutanese meat. These are accompanied by noodle soups and cheese soups, seasoned with salt and pepper and an abundance of dried red chilies, tempered, of course, with yak butter.

Tibetans also enjoy nibbling all day long, on various hearty snacks, but their thoughts probably do not stray far from their bracing, heating stews and yak butter.

Glossary

Years ago, when Westerners first started cooking Chinese meals, basic ingredients and cooking utensils were easy to come by. But now Westerners have discovered the joys of Southeast Asian, North Asian, and Indian dishes, and the hunt for ingredients becomes more complex. You may be lucky enough to have several broad-scope Asian markets in your locale, and many major supermarkets sell such basics as lemon grass and coconut milk, but chances are good you will still need to find a special grocer for Indian ingredients or a Japanese or Korean market at which to complete your shopping list.

Achiote: Also known as *achuete* or annatto, these reddish seeds impart a distinctive taste and reddish color to many Filipino dishes. Achiote is available at well-stocked Asian markets.

Asafoetida: A popular and distinctive Indian seasoning that imparts a curious musky aroma, asafoetida is the dried resin of a plant grown in the Middle East. Available as a granular powder and in lump form, it is sold at Indian markets.

Banana flowers or banana blossoms: These are the clusters of purplish heads growing from the ends of immature bananas. If you are using fresh banana blossoms, peel off the outer, protective leaf layer surrounding the blossoms, then slice the blossoms into ¼-inch-thick pieces and soak them for 15 minutes in salted cold water before use. Sometimes a well-stocked Asian market carries these fresh, but banana flowers come canned as well.

Basil, Thai: *See* Thai mint and basil

Bay leaf, Indonesian: The Indonesian bay, or *salam*, leaf is an aromatic leaf that grows on a tree native to Indonesia. Dried salam leaves are available at some Asian markets, particularly those that specialize in Southeast Asian foods. If you cannot find Indonesian bay leaves, substitute the Western bay leaf.

Bean paste: *See* Soybean paste

Black lentils: *See Dal*

Black rock salt: An Indian seasoning, and also known as black salt, this condiment is available

295

ground as a slightly reddish brown powder, or as a blackish lump; in either form, it has a sour taste. It is available at Indian markets.

Bitter gourd: This is an Asian vegetable that is classified as a melon, but it looks more like a misshapen cucumber. Its bumpy skin and slightly sour flesh should be green and firm to the touch. Bitter gourds are readily available fresh and are also sold canned at Asian markets.

Cabbage, preserved: Preserved, or pickled, cabbage is sometimes served as a side dish and is also used as a flavor and texture enhancer for some soups and stews. Depending on your market, you may find a number of different types, such as preserved Chinese cabbage, preserved mustard greens, and preserved bok choy. It is available in jars and may also be sold loose in large plastic bins. See also *Kimchi*.

Candlenuts: Once generally used in Indonesia as a substance for making candles (hence, the name), these rich nuts are intrinsic to many Indonesian dishes, but they are not readily available in the West. Macadamia nuts make a fine substitute and are readily available. According to one Indonesian, you should use three or four more macadamia nuts than the number of candlenuts called for; however, I tested the recipes using the the same number of macadamia nuts, and the results were fine. You may find candlenuts at some well-stocked Asian markets.

Cardamom: Westerners may know this spice for its elusive flavoring in pastries and breads, but Indians use its seeds and pods extensively in a range of dishes, from curries and soups to sweets and drinks. The seeds hold the flavor, but several Indian cooks have said that so long as you crack the pods open, pods and all can be stirred into savory dishes—the seeds will fall out during cooking and impart the wonderful flavor. Some recipes, however, specify cardamom seeds, and for these you must open the pods and shake out the tiny black seeds. Both green and black cardamom are available, but most recipes in this book call for green cardamom. This is readily available at Indian markets. Black cardamom is more difficult to find, but it would be available at Indian markets.

Chili leaves: Often used to add another level of flavoring to curries and other dishes in certain Southeast Asian countries, chili leaves are just that—the fresh leaves picked from chili plants. Unless you or a friend grow chilies, you will have a hard time finding these, as they are seldom available at Asian markets.

Chili pastes and sauces: Chili pastes, which are sometimes labeled sauces, are made primarily from ground or crushed fresh chilies, salt, oil, garlic, and sometimes vinegar. Chili sauces are made from similar ingredients, plus other ingredients to achieve the desired end result. As a general rule of thumb, explains my Malaysian food friend Harris Lokmanhakim, there is a big difference. "In a nutshell," he said, "The chili paste is usually referred to as a cooking ingredient and can be a thick 'spoon-it-out' consistency . . . Chili sauce, to me, typically refers to an after-cooking condiment that can be used as a dipping sauce or to add fire to any other dish."

A good example of a product that is labeled a paste but can be used both as a sauce and for cooking is the Indonesian chili paste, *sambal oelek*. It has the same color and consistency of a popular Vietnamese chili-based product (the chunky Tuong To Toi Viet-Nam brand), which is labeled a chili sauce.

Because each country has its own version, some cooks recommend you select a chili paste or sauce that comes from the same country as your recipe for the most authentic flavor. However, I often use the Vietnamese chili sauce, which is readily available, for cooking and the table. Pastes and sauces keep almost indefinitely if stored in the refrigerator in a tightly sealed container.

Chilies, ground: Made by grinding or pulverizing dried red chilies, chili powders vary according to country of origin. Many different types can be purchased, but the best powders come from home cooks who dry and grind their own chilies. The Indian red chili powder, or Kashmiri chili powder, is made from finely ground mildish red chilies and is the traditional red coloring used for tandoori dishes. The Korean red pepper powder can vary from mild to fiery. Malaysian, Thai, Burmese, and Singaporean red chili powders are generally hot. (For instructions on making your own, see Roasted Red Chili Powder, page 16, or substitute cayenne pepper or crushed red pepper flakes.)

Chinese dates: Unlike the familiar Western brown dates, Chinese dates—also known as jujubes— are small dried red fruits that apparently are not related to Western dates. Jujubes reputedly have some medicinal value and, hence, are a popular addition to soups and desserts. These are available packed in cellophane bags at most Asian markets. Dried jujubes need to be soaked in hot water for 20 minutes to soften them so you can remove the pits.

Chinese rice wine: A popular ingredient used either liberally or in moderation in many Chinese dishes, rice wine, such as Shaoshing yellow rice wine, adds a sweet, subtle flavor. This is readily available at any well-stocked Asian market and even in the specialty food section of some supermarkets.

Chrysanthemum leaves (crown daisy): Edible chrysanthemum leaves (crown daisy), known as *shungiku* or *kikuna*, have a beguiling citrusy aroma that enhances many meat and vegetable dishes. The edible leaves are *not* the same as those from garden chrysanthemums. The leaves are used fresh and are sold at most Japanese and Korean markets.

Coconut milk: Coconut milk actually refers to both the thick milk, or "cream," produced from the first pressing of coconut shreds and the thinner, more watery liquid—the thin milk—from the second and later pressings. Rich and oily, versatile coconut milk can be used as cream, sweetener, and thickener, and because of its oil content, it also may be used for pan-frying spices and pastes prior to cooking a curry or a soup. Coconut milk is available canned at many Asian markets and some supermarkets. Store any fresh or leftover milk in a tightly sealed container in the refrigerator for up to 2 days or in the freezer for up to 1 month. For more information on coconut milk and for instructions for making your own, see page 6.

Curry leaves: As with other Asian roots, leaves, and plants used for seasoning, curry leaves have their own distinctive taste and aroma, which seem both peppery and musky. Sometimes available fresh and also sold frozen or dried, the leaves are popular in Indian, Sri Lankan, and other Southeast Asian kitchens. Look for these at Indian or well-stocked Asian markets.

Dal: Dal refers to popular Indian legume dishes as well as the many types of lentils, peas, and beans—all of which are legumes—used in Indian, Chinese, and Southeast Asian cooking. Of the commonly used legumes, those that are called for in this book include black lentils (*urad dal*); whole green mung beans (*moong dal*); yellow split and hulled mung beans (also known as *moong dal*); yellow split peas (*chana dal*); yellow lentils (*toor dal*); and red lentils (*masoor dal*). They are readily available at Indian markets and some pan-Asian markets. If the Asian yellow split pea (*chana dal*) is not available, substitute the Western yellow split peas sold at supermarkets; do not, however, substitute the gray-brown lentil used in European cooking for the lentils called for in Asian recipes. For information on sorting, soaking, and cooking legumes, see the discussion on page 5.

Doenjang: *See* Soybean paste

Dried shrimp and shrimp powder: Southeast Asians love the salty, fishy bite that tiny dried shrimp give to their dishes. Made by sun- or air-drying tiny fresh shrimp, dried shrimp are used whole or chopped. If you find the flavor too strong, you may reduce the quantity called for or omit them altogether, although the resulting taste will lack a certain pungency. These shrimp are readily available in Asian markets and usually come wrapped in cellophane bags. Select shrimp that are pink; gray or white shrimp are old and may affect the flavor of the dish. They can also be pulverized into a tan powdery substance and then stirred into dishes for a subtle fishy flavor. You can make your own shrimp powder by dry-roasting dried shrimp and then pulverizing them in a food processor or blender. Dried shrimp and shrimp powder are available at most Asian markets.

Eggplant, Thai and Oriental: Most Asian markets stock two different varieties of eggplants from Thailand: the *makua yae,* which is slightly larger than a golf ball and generally white to pale green in color, and the pea eggplant, which vaguely resembles a cluster of green grapes on a stem. Both add flavor and texture to Thai dishes, particularly the curries. As for other eggplants, known generically in the West as Oriental eggplants, there are two varieties: the long, thin eggplant used throughout Asia and the short, thin eggplant favored by the Japanese. Some well-stocked specialty food stores carry Oriental eggplants; they are also available at Asian markets. Since you will most likely find just one type at your market, you may use either variety in the recipes.

Fermented bean curd: *See* Tofu

Fish cake, Japanese (*kamaboko*): This is more accurately called a fish paste, though it may be shaped into a cake, loaf, or roll. It requires no other preparation besides thawing (if frozen) and slicing. Look for this product in a Japanese or other Asian market.

Fish paste: As with many commonly used Asian seasonings, fish paste has many different local versions. For example, the Cambodians use one called *prahok* and the Lao use a comparable product called *padek*. This salty ingredient is usually made of the thick residue from the manufacture of fish sauce and may include chunks of fish. Fish paste is readily available at Asian markets and lasts almost indefinitely if stored in the refrigerator in a tightly sealed container.

Fish sauce: This fermented fish product is generally made by layering fish (usually anchovies) and salt in large jars or barrels and then siphoning off the liquid. The first pressing is a treasured flavoring ingredient; subsequent pressings yield a more diluted and less-prized sauce. An Asian market may provide a bewildering array of fish sauces, such as the Thai *nam pla* and the Vietnamese *nuoc mam*, but unless the type is specified, the sauces are interchangeable in a recipe. Several Asian cooks I know, regardless of their country of origin, prefer the Vietnamese Viet Huong (Three Crabs) brand. Fish sauce lasts almost indefinitely if stored in a tightly sealed container.

Five-spice powder: This aromatic Chinese seasoning powder is a blend of star anise seeds, cassia bark (or cinnamon), Szechuan peppercorns, cloves, and fennel seeds. It is readily available at both Asian markets and most supermarkets.

Galangal: This fragrant rhizome, with its citrusy-gingery taste, is an important seasoning for many Southeast Asian cooks. Fortunately, it is readily available frozen, and occasionally fresh, at Asian markets. If it is not available in either of these forms, you may find it as a powder labeled "*laos* powder" or as the dried and sliced rhizome wrapped in cellophane packets.

Garam masala: A popular and ever-present North Indian spice combination, this seasoning is used as a flavoring accent and usually contains coriander seeds, black peppercorns, cinnamon, cloves, cardamom, and nutmeg in varying combinations. Although a freshly ground garam masala is memorable (see the recipe on page 29), this mixture is also available commercially prepared at all Indian markets.

Ghee: This yellow butter product is essential to proper Indian cooking and is used for frying or seasoning. It is the end product, or solid butterfat, of the process of twice clarifying unsalted butter, and has the advantage over butter of withstanding high frying temperatures without burning. It is always available at Indian markets, but you can also make your own (see page 17). Some say it can be stored at room temperature, but refrigerating it prolongs its life. Although easy enough to make, you may substitute vegetable oil for ghee; however, the flavor will not be the same.

Ginger buds: These are the tender flowering tips of the ginger plant. In Malaysia, they are often eaten raw and shredded for salads or garnishes. Delectable and subtle, ginger buds are a treat if you can ever find them, but chances are you will need to omit them from your recipes.

Gingko nuts: Gingko nuts are the slightly bitter nuts from the maidenhair tree. These nuts are popular among Chinese, Japanese, and Koreans, who eat them as snacks or mixed in with other ingredients in more complicated dishes. The nuts are sold in cans at Japanese markets.

Gluten: A popular ingredient for vegetarian dishes, gluten is a natural protein derived from wheat. Because it is bland, it absorbs the flavors with which it is cooked. Fresh gluten is sold in my Asian market from a tub of water and resembles a plump, tan, misshapened frankfurter. Otherwise, you may find it in cans at Asian markets as part of another product—in this case, you would need to buy the product and remove and rinse the gluten.

Gram flour (besan): A flour made from pulverized dried chickpeas, gram flour, or besan, is used for making batters and dough and as a thickening agent. It is a popular ingredient in the Indian, and sometimes the Burmese, kitchen and is readily available in Indian and Middle Eastern markets. You can make your own by roasting dried chickpeas in a medium-hot skillet until they are aromatic and golden and then pulverizing them; or try substituting yellow split peas for the chickpeas. This can be stored in a tightly sealed container for up to three months.

Green papaya: Look for the elongated green papaya in your Asian market; the smaller Mexican or South American papayas are not suitable substitutes. If it is unavailable, use chayote instead.

Green peppercorns: Young green peppercorns, a favorite in the Thai kitchen, are not often available fresh in the West, but they are easy to locate water-packed in jars in Asian markets and in many supermarkets.

Harusame: *See* Noodles

Indonesian soy sauce: *See* Soy sauce

Jackfruit: This knobby, roundish fruit is used green in salads and curries; when ripe, the sweet fruit is used in dessert recipes or served on its own. Sometimes jackfruit is available fresh, but it is more commonly sold frozen at Asian markets. If you use fresh jackfruit, peel off the skin and discard the pits—some Asians roast the pits and eat them as a snack. Canned jackfruit comes packed in either a heavy sweet syrup or water. If you can find only the syrup-packed jackfruit, rinse it well to remove the sugar before using it in a curry dish.

Jaggery: *See* Sugar, Asian

Kaffir leaves and rind: Sometimes the juice of the knobby-skinned kaffir lime is used in cooking (although some Asians prefer to use the juice as a hair rinse), but the glossy leaves of this lime are a particular favorite in many Asian dishes and provide a subtle, but distinct, citrus flavor. The leaves are sometimes available fresh but can more often be found frozen or dried. Ardent Asian cooks, indeed many Asians, grow their own lime trees at home because the flavor of the leaves is so prized. Kaffir lime rind is also available frozen and imparts its own unique and rather heady citrus flavor. Only very occasionally are the fresh whole limes available at Asian markets in the West, and at that, they are very costly. The larger Western lime and its leaf are not a substitute for the kaffir lime and its leaf or rind.

Kewra: A relative of the screwpine or *pandan* family, *kewra* is an essence or extract often used in Indian and Sri Lankan cooking. Its slightly musky aroma provides a rather haunting flavor backdrop for various Indian dishes. Look for *kewra* water or essence at Indian markets.

Kimchi: *Kimchi* is a traditional Korean fermented pickle, usually made with napa cabbage and often heavily laced with hot chilies. Even in the humblest Korean home, a family meal calls for *kimchi*, preferably several kinds. "In the olden days," says the traditional Korean cook Bong S. Lee, "Koreans loved vegetables, and when they had a meat-based meal, not only did they serve vegetables, but they came up with the idea of spiciness (the chilies) to cleanse the palate of the meat taste." *Kimchi* is sold at Korean markets or specialty food stores in jars and may also be found loose in large plastic bins.

Kochujang: *See* Soybean paste

Kombu: *See* Seaweed

Konnyaku: *See* Noodles

Korean green chilies: These resemble Anaheim chilies, but the Korean variety is thicker and longer. Like their Western cousins, Korean green chilies are mild and easy on the tongue.

Lemon grass: An almost ubiquitous seasoning in many Southeast Asian dishes, this ingredient has a wonderful, fresh lemonlike flavor that seems to both intensify and complement many other flavors. The grass actually comes as clumps of tall stalks that look like leeks, but they are tough and require a sharp knife for cutting. Before using lemon grass, you must peel off the outer leaves and trim the ends. Smashing, or pounding, the plump root end before slicing it releases its full citrus flavor. One stalk yields about two to three tablespoons of sliced or chopped lemon grass, depending on the thickness and freshness of the stalk.

You can find dried lemon grass as shreds or a powder, but its flavor does not resemble that of the fresh. Fortunately, fresh and frozen lemon grass are almost always available at Asian markets and at some supermarkets. Lemon grass freezes well without losing its flavor and stores in the refrigerator for up to one week. The Western lemon bears no resemblance and is not a suitable substitute.

Lentils: *See Dal*

Longan: Also known as dragon's eye, longans are cherry-sized fruit that are delicate and plump. Rarely available fresh, they are readily available in cans at Asian markets.

Mango powder (*amchur* or *amchoor*): This product comes from grinding dried unripe mangoes to a fine powder and adds an astringent sourness to many Indian dishes. Because it loses its punch quickly, buy mango powder in small amounts and store it in the freezer.

Mint, Thai: *See* Thai mint and basil

Mirin: This sweet Japanese cooking wine imparts not only a sweet but also a slightly ricelike taste to food. Although mirin is readily available at most supermarkets, you can substitute sweet sherry or dry sherry sweetened with some granulated sugar.

Miso: *See* Soybean Paste

Mung beans: *See Dal*

Mushrooms: Dried Chinese mushrooms and dried Chinese black mushrooms are one and the same (and according to some experts, are the same as the Japanese shiitake) and are actually a mottled buff color. When you use dried mushrooms, soak them in hot water for 20 minutes to soften and remove the hard stems.

The mushrooms' soaking water can be strained and added to soups for extra flavor. Dried Chinese mushrooms are sold at Asian markets. They will keep almost indefinitely if stored in a tightly sealed container.

Straw mushrooms: These are readily available water-packed in cans and provide an earthy taste to whichever dish they are added. They should be drained and rinsed before use.

Shii mushrooms: Commonly known as shiitake mushrooms, these mushrooms from Japan are available both fresh and dried, but the dried mushrooms must be softened by soaking in hot water for 20 minutes before use.

Enoki mushrooms (or *enokitaki*): Also from Japan, these look like miniature cream-colored parasols. They are often available fresh, but they can also be found packed in cans. If you use the fresh mushrooms, which keep in the refrigerator if loosely wrapped in plastic for up to 3 days, rinse them in cold water before use.

Cloud ear mushrooms: These mushrooms are known by many other names, such as tree ear, rat's ear, wood ear, and Jew's ear. Their crunchy texture and delicate woodsy flavor make them a popular addition to many Asian dishes. Because they are dried, they must be soaked in hot water for 20 minutes and rinsed before use.

Mustard oil: Mustard oil is especially popular in Bengali cooking, but it is used in other Indian kitchens as well. Using pure mustard oil for cooking is costly, and now Indian markets sell a mustard oil mixed with a bland vegetable oil. Read the label on the bottle of pure mustard oil before purchasing: It may be marked "for external use only," and I don't know if that is safe for cooking and human consumption. To remove its raw taste, you must heat mustard oil until it just begins to smoke and then cool it before using for cooking.

Noodles: Asian noodles are justifiably famous for their extensive varieties, shapes, and uses, but looking at shelves of dried noodles and refrigerator cases of fresh noodles may bewilder many foreigners—many of the noodles look alike, and, indeed, some may be used interchangeably. When shopping for noodles, remember that you will need about twice the amount of fresh noodles as dried.

Asians have learned to make their noodles from a variety of basic ingredients, from wheat and buckwheat flours to rice flour, *agar-agar*, bean curd, mung-bean flour, and *ito-konnyaku*. Few things are more satisfying than a meal of noodle soup or noodles with a curry topping.

Generally, if dried noodles are used as accompaniments, you may cook, drain, rinse, and cool them ahead of time or while you are preparing the remainder of the meal. If the noodles are to be added to a soup or used in the cooked dish, you should cook or soak them while you are preparing the main dish so you can add them at the right time. In many cases, you may transfer them with tongs from their cooking or soaking water straight into the soup pot. Fresh noodles coated with oil should be rinsed in hot water before using. Otherwise, fresh noodles need no advance preparation.

Rice stick noodles and rice vermicelli: Both of these dried white noodles are extremely popular in many Asian countries and are made from rice flour and water. Rice stick noodles, or rice sticks (also labeled *Chantaboon* rice stick noodles or *banh pho* noodles), and rice vermicelli are almost the same—except that rice stick noodles are flatter, may be round, and can range in width from very narrow to $1/3$ inch

wide—and may be used interchangeably (as long as the vermicelli is not thread thin). One of my Thai friends soaks the noodles in warm water for about 10 minutes before use, but many cooks say the noodles need hot-water soaking for about 15 minutes. If you are adding the noodles to a soup, curry, or stew, simply transfer them to the simmering liquid, or drain the noodles if you plan to stir-fry them. To serve as an accompaniment, boil them until tender, then drain and rinse in cold water to remove the starch that causes them to stick together. Available in bundles and packages at most Asian markets, dried rice noodles last almost indefinitely.

Fresh rice noodles: Also known as "rice ribbon" noodles, fresh rice noodles are readily available at most Asian markets and have a wonderful, slippery, chewy texture. Ideally they should be used within a day of purchase; you can store unused noodles in the refrigerator, although they will become very hard. To use very fresh rice noodles, simply rinse them in hot water to remove the oil coating and to help separate them, and drop them into a hot soup, stew, or curry. If your noodles have been refrigerated, you will need to refresh and soften them: Rinse them in hot water; steam them for 3 to 4 minutes or boil them for 1 to 2 minutes, or until soft enough to separate; then add them to the hot liquid or drain and rinse in cold water before serving as an accompaniment. If overcooked, fresh rice noodles will lose their shape quickly, so watch them carefully when you are steaming or boiling them. Rice noodles are often sold in sheets, which you can slice to the desired width before use.

Bean thread noodles: Also known as "cellophane," "glass," or "transparent" noodles, these thin, clear strands are made from mung bean starch and water. (In Japan, *harusame*, which are also known as bean thread noodles, are actually made from potato starch and water, but the two kinds of bean thread noodles are interchangeable, since they are both intended to absorb flavors and provide texture.) Bean thread noodles are popular for soups, salads, and curries, and Malaysians and Singaporeans even use them in drinks and desserts. The noodles are so brittle and tough that they should be cut or trimmed after soaking. To soften them, soak them in hot water for 15 minutes; to keep them together, buy a brand of noodles that are tied or banded together and soak them that way. This helps keep them together for cutting. Softened noodles will be translucent and gelatinous. Once softened, bean threads are fragile and should be cooked only a short time or they will fall apart. If you are using them in a soup or stew, simply transfer the noodles from their soaking water; for stir-frying, however, they should be drained before use. These are readily available at most Asian markets.

Chinese egg and wheat noodles: Sold both fresh and dried at most Asian markets, these are better fresh, and they freeze well. You can substitute a Western spaghetti-type pasta if you cannot find this type of noodle. The fresh noodles cook quickly—just separate the strands as you drop them into plenty of boiling water, stir them once to keep them from sticking together, and when the water returns to a boil, cook until tender, about 3 minutes. Drain and rinse quickly with cold water to prevent them from sticking together.

Soba and somen: These Japanese noodles are commonly available at Asian markets, and at least somen are used widely by Southeast Asian cooks, who have told me that the noodles are a fine substitute for those from their native country. Some manufacturers package somen in paper-wrapped bundles; one bundle is usually enough for one person per meal. Soba are made from buckwheat flour; somen are made from wheat flour. Both cook easily: Slip the noodles into plenty of rapidly boiling water and add 1 cup cold water to the pot after the water returns to a boil. Cook them until tender, about 5 minutes, then drain. As with rice stick noodles, soba and somen should be rinsed in cold water after cooking to wash off the excess starch that causes them to stick together.

Konnyaku and ***shirataki:*** *Konnyaku* is a starchy calorie-free substance that comes from the devil's tongue plant and has a slippery, gelatinous texture and a bland taste. It is usually cut into pieces and added to soups and stews. Available in cans or bags at Japanese markets, *konnyaku* keeps in the refrigerator for about a week. You need to briefly boil it before use to remove the limestone odor.

The popular slippery Japanese noodles known as *shirataki* are shredded pieces from a block of *konnyaku*. Sold fresh at Japanese and Korean markets, these noodles store well in the refrigerator in a water-filled container for one to two weeks if you change the water daily. They should be briefly boiled to remove any limestone odor and then added directly to the recipe. If *shirataki* are not available, use rice vermicelli instead.

Udon: This wheat-based noodle is often available fresh at Japanese and Korean markets, but you will find it dried as well. When fresh, these noodles require only two to three minutes of boiling; if dried, cook them until tender, eight to ten minutes. Drain and rinse them in cold water to remove the starch and to prevent the noodles from sticking together.

Onions, Korean green: Known as *negi*, these resemble a cross between a leek and a scallion and are sold at Korean markets. Leeks are an acceptable substitute.

Palm sugar: *See* Sugar, Asian

Panch phooran: This special Bengali spice mixture contains equal amounts of the following: mustard seeds, fenugreek seeds, anise or fennel seeds, cumin seeds, and dill or caraway seeds. The seeds should be roasted separately and cooled before use (see page 11), then stirred together. *Panch phooran* is easy enough to make at home, but check your Indian market for its availability.

Pandan leaf: Also known as *pandanus* leaf or screwpine, the long, thin leaves of this plant provide an unusual fragrance and flavor for many Indonesian, Thai, Malaysian, and Singaporean dishes. The juice extracted from the leaves is often used for green coloring. *Pandan* leaves are sometimes available fresh, but are readily available frozen in Asian markets. If not available, vanilla extract makes an acceptable substitute.

Parsley, Japanese: Also known as mitsuba or trefoil, this relative of parsley is available at Japanese markets and may be used chopped or whole. Flat-leaf parsley is an adequate substitute.

Prahok: *See* Fish paste

Prawn crackers: *See* Shrimp crackers

Prawns: *See* Shrimp

Red chili powder: *See* Chilies, ground

Red lentils: *See Dal*

Red pepper powder, Korean: *See* Chilies, ground

Red rice vinegar: This has its own distinctive taste, adding a tart saltiness that enhances any recipe.

Rhizome (lesser galangal): Used in Cambodian, Thai, and Indonesian seafood dishes, rhizome looks like a cluster of fingerlike roots and tastes like a cross between ginger and galangal. In the West, this root seasoning is available frozen under the label "rhizome," but I could not find it fresh. There is no substitute.

Rice: Asian rice comes in seemingly infinite varieties, but practically speaking, the most commonly eaten types of rice are: in India, the basmati—a fragrant, long-grain rice with a distinctive aroma and taste; in Southeast Asia, the Thai jasmine rice—a fragrant, long-grain rice that retains a firm shape after cooking—and other standard long-grain rice; and in Korea and Japan, varieties of short-grain sweet rice that can be boiled or steamed according to the recipe and that, because the grains stick together, are ideal for eating with chopsticks. The "sticky," or glutinous or sweet, rice—a long-grain opaque and very starchy rice—needs to be cooked by soaking and steaming rather than boiling. This rice is eaten daily by the Laotians and enjoyed for its unique clumping characteristic. When steamed, the grains of rice cling together and shape easily into clumps or balls for eating: The Laotians clump the rice together and use it as a utensil to pick up bits of food. The Vietnamese and Thais, and sometimes the Chinese, use this rice in desserts. There is also a long-grained black sticky rice used in the Philippines and Indonesia. For more information on rice varieties and cooking techniques, see pages 2–5.

Rice cakes: Not at all shaped like a cake, these glutinous rice flour products come as long, slender, or thick cylinders or opaque ovals. When fresh, they are very soft; as the rice cakes age, they harden and need to be steamed or boiled to soften them again. Soft rice cakes make a delicious snack when dipped in honey, says Korean cook Hira Lee. These are sold at Korean markets and some well-stocked pan-Asian markets.

Rice vermicelli: *See* Noodles

Rock sugar: *See* Sugar, Asian

Sago: A starchy product made fom the sago palm, sago resembles tapioca pearls in shape and color. Sold in Asian markets, sago pearls cook more quickly with presoaking.

Sambal oelek: *See* Chili pastes

Sambar powder: This tart spice mixture is used in southern Indian kitchens. A *sambar* powder may be purchased at some Indian markets, but it is certainly easy to make at home and leaves a wonderful fragrance is your kitchen. (See the Note on page 225 for one cook's version.)

Seaweed: While seaweed is an important part of many Asians' diets, it is a very basic ingredient in many Japanese dishes. The three major Japanese seaweeds—*kombu*, nori, and *wakame*—as other seaweeds assuredly do—provide flavor, texture, and nutrition. The sea kelp *kombu* provides the basic flavor for Japanese stock, or *dashi* (see the recipes for Japanese First Stock and Japanese Second Stock on page 34). Available dried, it needs only a light wipe with a damp cloth; never wash *kombu*, as this would remove the white patches that hold all the flavor.

Nori is also available dried and is used in soups and other dishes as a condiment or seasoning. To bring out its full flavor, pass it over a gas flame or heat it in an oven briefly. Most Westerners would recognize nori as the seaweed wrapper on sushi.

Wakame is used as a vegetable in Japan and Korea and is often added to soups or stews. Soak dried *wakame* in warm water for 3 to 5 minutes to soften and trim off any tough spots before use.

Shichimi: A robust peppery Japanese seasoning powder made from seven different spices, shichimi is used to season a wide variety of foods. It is sold at Japanese markets.

Shirataki: *See* Noodles

Shrimp: Most Westerners use the word "shrimp" regardless of the size of these shellfish. But Asians generally use the word "prawn" when referring to shrimp that range in size from medium to jumbo and "shrimp" when referring to the tiny shrimp that are dried and used for flavoring.

Shrimp crackers: Shrimp crackers, prawn crackers, shrimp chips, or *krupuk* are Indonesian specialties usually made from shrimp and tapioca starch. They come as flattened discs, but when they are deep-fried, they puff up magically and can be used as garnishes and snacks. Shrimp crackers are available at Asian markets and some specialty food stores, and they are easy to prepare. Follow the package directions or heat 3 cups oil in a large wok or skillet, and cook several crackers at a time until puffed (they will cook in just seconds), then transfer to paper towels to drain.

Shrimp paste: You will find this paste made from dried, salted shrimp crushed with other ingredients in several different forms, so it is important to use the type specified in the recipe. Many cooks suggest frying or dry-roasting the dark brown, firm shrimp pastes from Malaysia (*belacan*) and Thailand (*kapi*) before using them (see page 10). The Chinese (*shajiang*) and Vietnamese (*mam tom*) pastes, which are sometimes labeled "shrimp sauce," are spoonable pink-gray mixtures. They are very pungent and fermented-tasting and may take some getting used to for the uninitiated, so add to suit your palate. There is also a potent, black-as-molasses paste from Malaysia called *petis,* which is made from shrimp heads. It is usually mixed with water before use to thin the paste.

Firm shrimp pastes keep almost indefinitely at room temperature when stored well wrapped or in a tightly sealed container. The saucelike pastes keep for up to 3 months if stored in the refrigerator.

Shrimp powder: *See* Dried shrimp and shrimp powder

Soba: *See* Noodles

Somen: *See* Noodles

Soy sauce: Among soy sauces, the thick, very dark, sweetish Indonesian soy sauce (*kecap manis*) is unique for its ability to add flavor depth, color, and sweetness to the recipe; it is also used as a condiment. It is sold at any Asian market and should not be used in place of the more common Chinese soy sauce, which is thinner, lighter in color, and saltier. The Chinese also produce a number of specialty soy sauces, including a dark, strong-tasting soy, a mushroom-flavored soy, and an oyster-flavored soy. Almost every type of soy sauce can be found in a well-stocked Asian market. The Japanese soy sauces are generally slightly lighter and less salty than their Chinese counterparts.

Soybean paste: Soybean paste, sometimes labeled soybean sauce, bean sauce, or bean paste, is made from fermented black or yellow soybeans and adds a strong, salty flavor to dishes; some countries also have a hot variety, which is made from chopped dried red chilies and mashed soybeans. Shopping for soybean pastes may be mystifying, for there are many different types, ranging from firm pastes to chunky, thick, saucelike liquids, and some are interchangeably labeled soybean pastes and sauces.

Soybean paste is an important seasoning in Singapore, Thailand, Malaysia, and many parts of China. Specific products from these countries that are called for in this book include Chinese yellow soybean paste *(mien see),* also sometimes labeled "yellow sauce" or "yellow bean sauce"; Chinese hot soybean paste (*lat chu jeung*); and Malaysian yellow soybean paste, called *taucheo* or *tau co*, which looks more like a sauce than a paste and may be labeled "yellow soybean paste" or "salted yellow soybeans."

Soybean paste also appears in Japan as miso and its variations and is one of the most important seasonings in the Japanese pantry; in Korea, it appears as the mild *doenjang* and the chili-spiked *kochujang*. Miso is available in various colors and flavors, but the most common are the red and white misos that are the foundation of miso soups. Miso requires some care in handling and must be thinned slightly with water before stirring it into a dish.

Soybean pastes are available at Asian markets, but you may need to search several sources to find a particular type of paste. After use, the paste should be stored in a tightly sealed container in the refrigerator, where it should keep almost indefinitely.

Split peas: *See Dal*

Sugar, Asian: Asians use a variety of sugars, which may be unfamiliar to Westerners, that have a distinct flavor and come in different forms and colors.

Jaggery: This is a dark, semirefined sugar used in Indian cooking. It has a pronounced flavor similar to caramel. If you cannot find this in an Indian market, use dark brown sugar or palm sugar instead.

Palm sugar: This sweet substance from the juice of either the *palmyra* palm or the sugar palm has different names and different forms depending on its country of origin. In Malaysia, palm sugar is known as *gula melaka* and comes in a solid dark-brown brick or cone that must be scraped or chopped apart before use. The Thai and Vietnamese versions may be semiliquid, having the consistency of a stiff peanut butter; firm, but not rock-hard; or hard and formed into circular discs or cylinders. To use the latter two types, simply break off chunks and use in whole pieces that eventually dissolve, or crush the pieces. If you cannot find palm sugar, substitute dark brown sugar, though the flavor is not the same.

Rock sugar: Also known as brown slab sugar, rock sugar comes as strips of two-toned layers compressed into rectangular slabs and is available wrapped in cellophane at Asian markets. Light brown granulated sugar makes a fine substitute.

Tamarind: When ripe, tamarind pods are a prized treat, for the interior flesh is delicious, sweetish, and unforgettable. Asian cooks have long understood that when this flesh is soaked in water to form a juice, the liquid seasoning adds a level of gentle sourness unmatched by the more acidic juices of lemons and limes. My Thai cooking teacher explained how to use tamarind pulp (a compressed block of tamarind flesh and seeds): Soak 2 tablespoons pulp in $1/2$ cup hot water for 30 minutes. After soaking, squeeze the juice from the pulp, then discard the pulp and seeds and use the thick brown liquid. Tamarind pulp is sold in packages at Asian markets. (Note: Before my teacher discards the pulp, she uses it to polish her brass, and it does a terrific job.) If you don't want to bother with making your own juice, use the concentrate available at Asian markets. Tamarind concentrate keeps in a tightly sealed container in the refrigerator for up to 3 months.

Tamarind leaves are often used for seasoning and are available in the freezer case of many Asian markets. If you cannot find tamarind in any form, substitute twice the amount of lemon juice for the amount of tamarind juice called for, although most Asian cooks would say there really is no substitute.

Taro root: With its dark, hairy skin that resists easy peeling, taro root is a starchy tuber that is popular throughout Asia and Latin America—hence most Asian and Latin American markets sell the tuber fresh. Look for it in large rootlike chunks. Trying to peel this with a paring knife can be daunting, so you may find a potato peeler a better choice.

Thai mint and basil: Ubiquitous seasonings in the Thai (and Vietnamese) kitchen and members of the mint family, these two herbs add a lively flavor to any dish. Thai mint has purple-black stems and deep green leaves. Thai basil, also known as sweet basil, comes in several varieties, but the most commonly used is the bai horapha, with its aromatic green leaves. Italian basil is not a substitute for the sweeter Thai variety. Both Thai mint and basil are now commonly available in Asian markets.

Tofu (bean curd): A popular food in many Asian countries and one many Westerners know well, tofu, or bean curd, is sold in many different forms and as many by-products—from the popular blocks to sheets, fried cubes, and a fermented bean curd "cheese." Special tofu products called for in this book include deep-fried tofu and the Japanese grilled or broiled tofu, or *yaki-dofu*, both of which are available prepared at Asian markets; tofu sheets; pressed tofu, blocks of tofu that have been weighted down to squeeze out excess liquid so that the tofu becomes very firm for easy shredding; and fermented, or preserved, bean curd, or "bean curd cheese," available either as a white or a dark red product sold in jars. The latter is favored for its strong, salty taste and may also be referred to as "salty" bean curd.

Turmeric: Turmeric is an essential seasoning agent in many curries and currylike dishes, imparting a distinctive golden color and a mildly astringent taste. Whole turmeric is not readily available fresh, but it can be found in the freezer case of some Asian markets. You may use ground turmeric as a satisfactory substitute, and most recipes in this book call for the ground form. Turmeric leaves are sometimes available frozen at Asian markets.

Udon: *See* Noodles

Vinegar, red rice: This has its own distinctive taste, adding a tart saltiness that enhances any recipe. It is available in Asian markets.

Wakame: *See* Seaweed

Yellow lentils: *See Dal*
Yellow split mung beans: *See Dal*
Yellow split peas: *See Dal*

Bibliography

Andersen, Juel. *Juel Andersen's Curry Primer*. Berkeley, CA: Creative Arts Communications, 1984.

Anderson, E.N. *The Food of China*. New Haven and London: Yale University Press, 1988.

Andoh, Elizabeth. *At Home With Japanese Cooking*. New York: Alfred A. Knopf, 1986.

Belleme, John and Jan. *Cooking with Japanese Foods*. Garden City, NY: Avery Publishing Group, 1993.

Brennan, Jennifer. *The Cuisines of Asia*. New York: St. Martin's Press, 1984.

The Cambodian Cookbook of H.R.H. Rasmi Sobhana. United States Information Service: Phnom-Penh.

Chang, K.C., editor. *Food in Chinese Culture, Anthropological and Historical Perspectives*. New Haven and London: Yale University Press, 1977.

China pictorial, eds. *The Secrets of the Master Chefs of China*. New York: Newton Abbot: David & Charles, 1983.

Cooking in Nepal, A Selection of International & Nepali Recipes. Kathmandu: University Press, Tribhuvan University.

Cost, Bruce. *Bruce Cost's Asian Ingredients, Buying and Cooking the Staple Foods of China, Japan and Southeast Asia.* New York: William Morrow and Company, 1988.

Cozinha Caseira, presented by The International Ladies Club of Macau

Cuisine in Kathmandu: a bilingual cookbook, American Women of Nepal and the United Nations' Women's Organization, Kathmandu, 1988.

Culinary Institute of America. *The New Professional Chef,* sixth edition. New York: Van Nostrand Reinhold, 1996.

Dan, Gong. *Food and Drink in China.* Beijing, China: New World Press, 1986.

Davidson, Alan. *Fish and Fish Dishes of Laos.* Vientiane, Laos: Imprimerie Nationale, 1975.

Davidson, Alan, and Davidson, Jennifer, eds. *Traditional Recipes of Laos.* London: Prospect Books, 1981.

de Berval, René. *Kingdom of Laos, The Land of the Million Elephants and of the White Parasol.* Saigon, Vietnam: France-Asie, 1959.

DeWitt, Dave, and Gerlach, Nancy. *The Whole Chile Pepper Book.* Boston: Little, Brown and Company, 1990.

Dorje, Renjing. *Food in Tibetan Life.* (Tibetan script by Venerable T.G. Dhongthon) London: Prospect Books, 1985.

Greeley, Alexandra. *Asian Grills.* New York: Doubleday, 1993.

Harlow, Jay. *Southeast Asian Cooking.* California Culinary Academy: San Francisco: Robert J. Dalezal, 1987.

Hyman, Gwenda L. *Cuisines of Southeast Asia.* New York: John Wiley & Sons, 1993.

Kalra, J. Inder Singh. *Prashad, Cooking with Indian Masters.* 4th Printing. New Delhi: Allied Publishers Limited, 1990.

Khaing, Mi Mi. *Cook and Entertain the Burmese Way.* Ann Arbor, MI: Karoma Publishing, 1978.

Lee, Karen, and Branyon, Alaxandra. *Chinese Cooking Secrets.* Garden City, NY: Doubleday & Co., 1983.

Lin, Florence. *Florence Lin's Cooking With Fire Pots.* New York: Hawthorne Books, 1979.

Lin, Hsiang Ju, and Lin, Tsuifeng. *Chinese Gastronomy.* New York: Hastings House, 1969.

Lo, Eileen Yin-Fei. *New Cantonese Cooking.* New York: Viking, The Penguin Group, 1988.

Lo, Kenneth. *Chinese Food.* Middlesex, England: Penguin Books, 1972.

Lo, Kenneth. *The Encyclopedia of Chinese Cooking.* New York: Galahad Books, 1992.

Lo, Kenneth. *Peking Cooking.* New York: Pantheon Books, 1971.

Loewen, Nancy. *Food in Korea.* Vero Beach, FL: Rourke Publications, 1991.

Miller, Gloria Bley. *The Thousand Recipe Chinese Cookbook.* New York: Simon & Schuster, 1984.

Millon, Marc, and Millon, Kim. *Flavours of Korea.* Great Britain: Andres Deutsch, 1991.

Nagel's Encyclopedia-Guide, China. English version by Anne L. Destenay. Geneva, Switzerland: Nagel Publishers, 1984.

Oon, Violet. *Violet Oon Cooks.* Singapore: Ultra Violet Pte Ltd., 1992.

Owen, Sri. *Indonesian Food and Cookery.* Jakarta, Indonesia: Indira, 1980.

Passmore, Jacki. *The Encyclopedia of Asian Food and Cooking.* New York: Hearst Books, 1991.

Parkes, Carl. *Southeast Asia Handbook,* second edition. Chico, CA: Moon Publications, 1994.

Perkins, David W., editor. *Hong Kong & China Gas Chinese Cookbook.* Hong Kong: Pat Printer Associates Limited, 1978.

Peiris, Doreen. *A Ceylon Cookery Book.* Second edition. Colombo, Ceylon: Lanka Trading Co.

Rai, Ranjit. *Curry, Curry, Curry, The Heart of Indian Cooking.* London: Penguin Books, 1990.

Richie, Donald. *A Taste of Japan.* Tokyo: Kodansha International, 1985.

Roth, Shirley Janiero. *Cooking the Filipino Way.* (Self published.) 1982.

Simoons, Fredrick J. *Food in China: A Cultural and Historical Inquiry.* Boca Raton, FL: CRC Press, 1991.

Sørensen, Felicia Wakwella. *The Exotic Tastes of Paradise, The Art of Sri Lankan Cooking*. Hong Kong: Lincoln Green Publishing, 1985.

Stewart, Katie. *The Joy of Eating. A Cook's Tour of History*. Owings Mills, MD: Stemmer House Publishers, 1977.

Stieglitz, Perry. *In a Little Kingdom*. Armonk, NY: M.E. Sharpe, Inc., 1990.

Stobart, Tom. *The Cook's Encyclopedia, Ingredients and Processes*. Edited by Millie Owen. New York, NY: Harper & Row, 1980.

Takahashi, Kuwako. *The Joy of Japanese Cooking*. Tokyo: Shufunotomo Co., 1992.

Tannahill, Reay. *Food in History*. New York: Stein and Day, 1973.

Tran, Paula. *Living and Cooking Vietnamese*. San Antonio, TX: Corona Publishing Company, 1990.

Tsuji, Shizuo. *Japanese Cooking, A Simple Art*. Tokyo: Kodansha International, 1980.

Von Bremzen, Anya, and Welchman, John. *Terrific Pacific Cookbook*. New York: Workman Publishing, 1995.

Willan, Ann. *La Varenne Pratique: The Complete Illustrated Guide to the Techniques, Ingredients & Tools of Classic Modern Cooking*. New York, NY: Crown Publishing Group, 1989.

Wong, Irene. *Great Asia Steambook*. Brisbane, CA: Taylor & Ng, 1977.

Yeo, Chris, and Jue, Joyce. *The Cooking of Singapore, Great Dishes from Asia's Culinary Crossroads*. Emeryville, CA: Harlow & Ratner, 1993.

Index